THE POLITICS OF
TELECOMMUNICATIONS

The Politics of Telecommunications

National Institutions, Convergence, and Change in Britain and France

MARK THATCHER

OXFORD
UNIVERSITY PRESS

OXFORD
UNIVERSITY PRESS

Great Clarendon Street, Oxford OX2 6DP

Oxford University Press is a department of the University of Oxford.
It furthers the University's objective of excellence in research, scholarship,
and education by publishing worldwide in

Oxford New York

Athens Auckland Bangkok Bogotá Buenos Aires Calcutta
Cape Town Chennai Dar es Salaam Delhi Florence Hong Kong Istanbul
Karachi Kuala Lumpur Madrid Melbourne Mexico City Mumbai
Nairobi Paris São Paulo Singapore Taipei Tokyo Toronto Warsaw

and associated companies in Berlin Ibadan

Oxford is a registered trade mark of Oxford University Press
in the UK and certain other countries

Published in the United States
by Oxford University Press Inc., New York

British Library Cataloguing in Publication Data

Data available

Library of Congress Cataloging in Publication Data

Thatcher, Mark.
    The politics of telecommunications: national institutions,
convergence, and change in Britain and France / Mark Thatcher.
    Includes bibliographical references.
    1. Telecommunication policy—Great Britain.   2. Telecommunication
policy—France.   I. Title.
HE8095. T48   1999 384'. 0941—dc21 99-15994

ISBN 0-19-828074-2

1 3 5 7 9 10 8 6 4 2

Typeset by Best-set Typesetter Ltd., Hong Kong
Printed in Great Britain
on acid-free paper by
Biddles Ltd
Guildford and King's Lynn

Preface

The present study represents the fruit of several years of research. From a starting point of wishing to analyse the importance of national institutions through cross-national comparison, I was drawn to telecommunications. Little did I know the complexities of the field, nor the time that I would spend in it.

Telecommunications offers a rich field for political scientists. It has become a remarkably important sector, vital to many if not most economic and social activities. Its expansion and diversification since the late 1960s have been rapid and accelerating. The economic and industrial stakes in the field are high, and correspondingly, policy-makers have devoted increasing attention to it.

Yet this is not primarily a study of telecommunications. It seeks to remain within political science, using the sector as a case study to address wider questions. In particular, it looks at the role of national institutions in the face of powerful transnational forces for change. The work therefore addresses questions of institutional stability and reform, and the impacts of institutions on policy making and economic outcomes. More generally, it seeks to demonstrate the value of cross-national historical methods in the study of politics.

Many individuals and institutions have contributed to the research and writing of the book. Considerable time was spent in the Département Économie et Management, École Nationale Supérieure des Télécommunications, Paris, which provided specialist expertise, whilst the Department of Government, London School of Economics has offered a stimulating home. A Leverhulme Trust research award and ESRC Fellowship were invaluable in providing financial support. The last touches were put whilst a Jean Monnet fellow at the Robert Schumarn Centre, European University. I also wish to thank the many interviewees who gave of their time and knowledge.

I am grateful to Professor Laurent Benzoni, whose practical and personal support made my research in France possible, also to Colin Scott at LSE, who offered many perceptive comments, and to Peter Hall for an insightful analysis of the questions posed. In Oxford, Nigel Bowles has given constant encouragement and counsel from the project's earliest days and Des King has provided critical attention and a host of valuable suggestions. I owe an incalculable debt of Vincent Wright, who throughout showed tremendous generosity and enthusiasm in his advice and assistance. Finally, my studies and research have been possible thanks to my parents, David and Nicole, whose understanding and support have been crucial throughout.

Contents

Abbreviations   ix

Introduction: Telecommunications in Britain and France, National
   Institutions, and Change   1

1. National Institutions, Differences, Stability, and Change   7

Part I. The British and French Telecommunications Sector in 1969 and External Pressures For Change

2. The Roots of History: Telecommunications in Britain and
   France before 1969   31

3. Technological and Economic Pressures for Change in
   Telecommunications from the 1960s to the 1990s   47

4. Pressures for Change from the International Regulatory
   Environment of Telecommunications from the 1960s to the 1990s   71

Part II. Institutions and Policy Making 1969–1979

5. The Institutional Framework of the Telecommunications Sector in
   Britain and France 1969–1979: Divergence, Reform, and Standstill   91

6. Policy Making in the 1970s: Constraints in Britain, Boldness in
   France   112

Part III. Institutions and Policy Making 1980–1997

7. The Institutional Framework of Telecommunications 1980–1997:
   National Change, Divergence, and Differences   143

8. The Impacts of Institutional Change and Divergence on Policy
   Making: The Network Operators in Britain and France
   during the 1980s   172

9. Competition in Network Operation 1990–1996: Differing
   National Paths away from Monopoly   205

10. Policy Making in a New Field of Telecommunications: Advanced
    Networks and Services and Customer Premises Equipment from
    the Late 1970s to the Mid-1990s   228

Part IV. Economic Outcomes in Telecommunications 1970–1997

11. Economic Outcomes in the Telecommunications Sector in
    Britain and France 1970–1997: Convergence Despite
    Institutional Divergence   263

Part V. Conclusions

12. National Institutions, Policy, and Change   305

Appendix I: Persons Interviewed   324

Appendix II: The Use and Interpretation of Statistics in Chapter 11   326

Appendix III: Conversion Rates Used in Chapter 11   329

Bibliography   331

Glossary of Terms   350

Index   353

Abbreviations

AEI	Associated Electrical Industry
ADC	access deficit contributions
AIPT	L'Association des ingénieurs des postes et télécommunications
AIT	Association des ingénieurs des télécommunications
ART	Autorité de regulation des télécommunications
AT&T	American Telephone and Telegraph Co.
ATM	asynchronous transfer mode
BABT	British Approvals Board for Telecommunications
BEUC	Bureau européen des consommateurs
BSA	bulk supply agreement
BT	British Telecom/British Telecommunications
BTS	British Telecommunications Systems
CE	Conseil d'État
CEGB	Central Electricity Generating Board
CEPT	Conference of European Postal and Telecommunications Administrations
CFDT	Confédération française démocratique du travail
CGC	Confédération des cadres
CGCT	Compagnie générale de constructions téléphoniques
CGE	Compagnie générale d'électricité
CGT	Confédération générale du travail
CNCL	Commission nationale de la communication et des libertés
CNES	Centre nationale des études spatiales
CNET	Centre nationale d'études des télécommunications
CNT	Caisse nationale des télécommunications
CPE	customer premises equipment
CSA	Conseil supérieur de l'audiovisuel
CSO	Central Statistical Office
DAI[I]	Direction des affaires industrielles [et internationales]
DATAR	Délégation de l'aménagement du territoire et l'action régionale
DBS	direct broadcasting by satellite
DG	Director General
DGP	Direction générale de la poste
DGPT	Direction générale des postes et télécommunications
DGT	Direction générale des télécommunications
DoI	Department of Industry
DRG	Direction de la réglementation générale
DRT	Directions régionales des télécommunications

DTI	Department of Trade and Industry
EC	European Community
ECJ	European Court of Justice
EDF	Electricité de France
EFL	external financing limit
EFTPOS	electronic funds transfer at point of sale
EPIC	Etablissement Public à caractère Industriel et Commercial
FCC	Federal Communications Commission
FT	France Télécom
GATS	General Agreement on Trade in Services
GATT	General Agreement on Tariffs and Trade
GEC	General Electric Company
GSM	Groupe Spécial Mobile-Global System for Mobiles
GTE	General Telephone and Electronics
INSEE	Institut nationale de la statistique et des études économiques
ISDN	integrated services digital network
ITAP	Information Technology Advisory Panel
ITT	International Telephone and Telegraph Company
ITU	International Telecommunications Union
LATA	local access and transport area
LMT	Le matériel téléphonique
MCI	Microwave Communications Inc.
MMC	Monopolies and Mergers Commission
OECD	Organization for Economic Co-operation and Development
Oftel	Office of Telecommunications
OSI	open systems interconnection
PABX	private automated branch exchange
PAD	packet assembler/disassembler
PAP	plan d'action prioritaire
PCF	Parti communiste français
PCM	pulse code modulation
PCN	personal communications network
PMG	Postmaster General
PO	Post Office
POEU	Post Office Engineering Union
POUNC	Post Office Users' National Council
PS	Parti socialiste
PSBR	public sector borrowing requirement
PSTN	public switched telephone network
PTE	[Ministère de] Postes, télécommunications, et de l'espace
PTO	public telecommunications operator
PTT	[Ministère de] postes, télégraphes, et téléphones
RBOC	regional Bell operating company

RPI	Retail Price Index
SFR	La Société française du radiotéléphone
SNA	systems network architecture
Socotel	La Société mixte pour le développement de la commutation dans la domaine des télécommunications
Sotélec	La Société mixte pour le développement de la technique des télécommunications par câbles
SPC	stored programme control
SPL	Self-Provision Licence
STC	Standard Telephones and Cables
TDF	Téléfusion de France
TMA	Telecommunications Managers Association
TSL	Telecommunications Services Licence
TUA	Telecommunications Users Association
UDF	Union pour la démocratie française
UPW	Union of Postal Workers
VADS	value added data services
VANS	value added network services
VSAT	Very Small Aperture Terminal
WTO	World Trade Organization

Introduction: Telecommunications in Britain and France, National Institutions, and Change

Telecommunications in Britain and France offer an excellent case in which to study the role of national institutions in countries' policy making and economic performance. Applying historical and cross-national comparison, the book examines the ability of nations to maintain dissimilar institutional arrangements in the face of powerful transnational forces for change. It then analyses the impacts of those national institutional arrangements on policy making and economic outcomes. It also discusses the conditions under which countries enjoy stable, different institutions and the limits to the consequences of cross-national institutional contrasts. A national institutionalist analytical framework is used to structure the study: it provides claims and hypotheses that are tested empirically; it allows the conclusions of the case study to be related to broader debates about institutions and to refine national institutionalist claims.

National institutions provide a framework within which a country's policies are made. Comparative studies frequently argue that long-standing institutional arrangements are a powerful independent factor in the determination of countries' policies and economic achievements. Institutions not only differ among states, but are also deeply rooted and resistant to change. Stable, dissimilar institutional features lead to persistently different patterns of policy formation and economic outcomes from one country to another. Even nations facing common international pressures and with similar geographical positions and factor endowments follow different paths of policy and economic performance due to their institutional frameworks.

If valid, such institutionalist contentions have significant implications for the study of countries' policies, pointing to the central place of states' organizational frameworks in any explanation of policy and economic performance and to the need for lengthy historical studies. They also raise wider issues such as the capacity of governments to alter policies and institutions and the role of the nation state faced with supra-national pressures. However, institutionalist analyses require critical scrutiny. Assertions of cross-national contrasts and of intra-national stability cannot be assumed to be true, but must be tested empirically. Moreover, to argue that 'national institutions are stable and matter' is only a first step in analysis: central issues such as what constitutes an 'institution', which institutions are important, what they matter for, how they exercise influence, and their impact relative to other factors, remain to be explored. Similarly, even if persistent institutional and policy features are found, the conditions for their continuation need to be considered, together with the circumstances under which change occurs.

To study the role and importance of national institutions, the present work begins by developing a theoretical model, or, more modestly, an analytical framework: 'national institutionalism'. It provides a set of arguments, hypotheses, and causal mechanisms concerning the features of national institutions and their influence on policy making that can then be applied to the empirical material. The framework covers both the role of national institutions in cross-national policy differences, and stability and change in institutions and policy making over time. At its core are arguments that nations maintain formal institutional arrangements that are dissimilar and give rise to contrasting policy patterns. These arrangements are stable and difficult to alter; even when reforms take place, they bear the imprint of past institutional histories and follow unique national paths of development. Similarly, policy change is marked by past and present institutional frameworks, and hence differs among countries. Institutions affect policy and economic performance through their influence over interests, strategies, the distribution of power among groups, state autonomy and the nature of markets. Hence causal linkages can be drawn between institutional features and policy and economic decisions. They explain why dissimilar national institutions give rise to differing long-term policy patterns and contrasting policy paths.

National institutionalism is then tested using a selected case study: telecommunications in Britain and France between 1969 and 1997. The sector, the two countries, and the time period were chosen for several reasons. Telecommunications is a strategic economic sector, whose supply has implications for a host of other economic, industrial and social fields. It has been seen as a core element of the state in Europe and a quintessential example of industrial policy in Britain and France; indeed, for most of the twentieth century, much of the sector in the two countries has been under public ownership. Yet, since the mid-1960s, telecommunications have been subject to increasingly powerful transnational pressures, arising both from technological and economic developments and from the international regulatory environment. Such pressures have been largely exogenous to Britain and France—national actors have had little control over them.

The case of telecommunications in Britain and France between 1969 and 1997 is therefore used as a form of 'critical case study' for national institutionalism. If the two countries were able to maintain dissimilar institutional arrangements in a sector marked by powerful external forces for change that were common to them, and those arrangements led to differing patterns of policy making and economic performance, then national institutionalist claims could also be expected to hold for other sectors, which are less marked by such forces.

The specific characteristics of the pattern of institutional development in Britain and France also offer rich opportunities to expose the influence of national sectoral arrangements and hence are utilized in the research design of the study. Before 1969, institutional arrangements in the sector were highly stable in both countries. Moreover, they shared many common features, as did policy. Insofar as change had occurred, it had led to institutional convergence between the two countries. Thus the late 1960s provide a point of considerable cross-national similarity from which to begin detailed analysis. However, thereafter, institutional divergence took place. Major reforms were introduced in Britain in 1969 and significant changes took place in France; hence 1969 provides an institutional baseline for the study. Then, in the 1970s, there were pressures for further institutional changes in both countries; however, they met strong resistance and little action was taken. Cross-national divergence increased in the 1980s, as comprehensive institutional reforms were introduced in Britain, whereas France experienced institutional continuity. In contrast, the 1990s saw a different cross-national pattern: the institutional framework was stable in Britain, whereas modifications were implemented in France in 1990 that reduced but did not eliminate many of the dissimilarities with Britain. Major institutional reforms in France were undertaken in 1996–7, which resulted in a considerable degree of convergence with Britain; they mark the end of the current study.

The particular institutional features of the telecommunications sector in Britain and France between 1969 and 1997, combined with the existence of powerful transnational pressures for change that were common to both countries, allows analysis of the two central parts of national institutionalism. The first consists of assertions that countries maintain differing organizational frameworks which are stable, with change being rare, difficult and following a country-specific path. The telecommunications sector in Britain and France offers examples of institutional reforms which were implemented and those that were not. Hence it is used to study the conditions under which institutional reforms were undertaken, the obstacles to change, the extent to which institutional evolution in the two countries differed and the reasons for cross-national contrasts in institutional arrangements and paths of reform.

The second central element concerns arguments that dissimilar national institutions lead to differing patterns of policy making and economic performance among countries. The application of the national institutionalist framework to the case study produces several hypotheses that are tested against detailed evidence to assess the impact of national sectoral institutions on policy-making processes and substantive decisions. Three 'evidential routes' are followed in this process. First, cross-national comparison is used. Given institutional divergence between Britain and France over the period 1969–90, followed by limited convergence, national institutionalism would suggest that policy formation and economic performance also became increasingly different until 1990, before experiencing a degree of convergence between 1990 and 1997. Institutional change within Britain and France offers a second source of evidence for the study. Institutional reforms in Britain during the 1980s and in France in 1990, would be expected to be followed by modifications in national policy making and economic results. Finally, the processes whereby specific institutional features led to patterns of policy making are traced, since national institutionalism claims that plausible links can be found between the two. Hence decision making in practice is compared with the roles and rules laid down by institutional arrangements, whilst the ways in which particular institutional characteristics permitted, encouraged, obstructed, or prevented policy choices are examined.

The study therefore provides a detailed evaluation of the role of national institutions in policy making in a vital sector, incorporating both transnational forces for change and institutional reform, using cross-national comparison and historical methods. Its findings offer considerable support for the importance of countries' institutional frameworks. At the same time, they point to the limits of institutionalist claims, notably concerning economic performance, and the need to develop more sophisticated arguments concerning change. The study therefore ends with a discussion of the strengths and limits of national institutionalism in explaining policy patterns, the incorporation of change and the factors that aid or restrict the influence of national institutions on policy making. It suggests modifications to national institutionalism concerning the phenomena that it seeks to explain and specification of the conditions for its propositions to hold.

The Remainder of the Book and its Main Arguments

The analytical framework, 'national institutionalism', is set out in Chapter 1, together with the ways in which it is to be tested in the present study. Thereafter, individual chapters deal with selected elements in the investigation of the role of institutions. Part One of the book analyses the position of the telecommunications sector in Britain and France in 1969 and the transnational/external pressures for change that existed from the mid-1960s until the mid-1990s and that were largely outside the control of British and French policy-makers. Chapter 2 briefly sets out the history of telecommunications in Britain and France, establishing the similarities in institutional arrangements and policy questions that existed in the two countries by 1969; it thus establishes that there was a common institutional starting point for the comparison, and indeed, that there existed many other long-standing similarities in telecommunications policy. The ways in which sweeping technological and economic developments altered the nature of the telecommunications sector are considered in Chapter 3. It is argued that in the twenty-eight years under consideration, these technological and economic developments were exogenous to Britain and France: policy-makers in the two countries could not greatly influence the technological and economic development of the sector, and resulting opportunities and pressures, but only whether and how to introduce new technology within their countries. Ideas and debates at the international level, especially in the United States, concerning telecommunications policy and regulation are then set out in Chapter 4. In addition, the development of European Community regulation is traced; whilst not entirely exogenous to British and French policy-makers, it was external and common to both countries.

Part Two examines institutions and policy making from 1969 until 1980. Chapter 5 shows that institutional reforms in the late 1960s, particularly in Britain in 1969, led to institutional divergence between the two countries. The process of reform is analysed, as are the failed attempts to introduce reforms during the 1970s in both countries. Policy making within the differing institutional frameworks during the 1970s is the subject of Chapter 6, which shows that differing patterns of policy making existed in Britain and France and relates these to contrasts to the institutional frameworks in the two countries.

Part Three covers the period from 1980 until 1997. Chapter 7 analyses institutional reforms in the 1980s and 1990s, notably those that took place in Britain in 1984 and in France in 1990 and 1996–7. It finds increasing institutional divergence until 1990, but thereafter a degree of convergence, notably due to the changes in France in 1996–7. Chapters 8, 9, and 10 look at policy making in network operation and advanced services and networks in the 1980s and 1990s. They find that patterns differed between Britain and France during the 1980s, but that dissimilarities narrowed after 1990, although remaining significant. Furthermore, the characteristics of policy formation altered in each country after institutional modification.

Claims that dissimilar institutions result in nations experiencing different economic performances are tested by analysis of 'economic outcomes' in telecommunications: Part Four (Chapter 11) sets out selected economic indicators pertaining to the fields of policy making considered in earlier chapters. Over the period 1970–97 the similarities between the two countries are seen to be much greater than the dissimilarities, with several indicators showing convergence instead of divergence.

The Conclusion summarizes the findings of the book. It relates the empirical findings of the case study to the claims made for national institutions and to national institutionalist analyses of policy making examined in this first chapter. It argues that several central tenets of 'national institutionalism' are supported by the evidence of the case of telecommunications in Britain and France between 1969 and 1997, notably by the existence of different institutional arrangements in the face of powerful and common technological and economic developments and the importance of these arrangements for patterns of policy making. However, the ability of policy-makers to alter institutions, the occurrence of innovation in the content of policy and the existence of similar economic outcomes despite dissimilar institutions suggest weaknesses in 'national institutionalism' and limits on the role of national institutions. Wider questions and implications of the findings of the study are then considered.

1

National Institutions, Differences, Stability, and Change

Do nations maintain different and stable institutional frameworks in the face of powerful transnational pressures for change? Do such national institutions lead to differing patterns of policy making and economic performance? How do a country's institutions influence policy formation? Insofar as institutions and policies alter, do they develop along differing national paths due to past institutional histories? These are the questions that the present study seeks to examine in a selected case, the telecommunications sector in Britain and France between 1969 and 1997.

The purpose of this first chapter is to set out an analytical 'national institutionalist' framework to answer these questions in a rigorous manner. It examines general institutionalist approaches to national policy making and then relates them to change. The analytical framework performs several functions. It provides a set of testable propositions and hypotheses concerning national institutions that are examined empirically in the present study. It aids in defining key terms. It assists in the selection of a form of 'critical case study' to test the role of national institutions.

'Institutionalisms' (new and old) abound in political science, economics and sociology; there is no single 'institutionalist' approach to public policy.[1] Disciplinary origins, assumptions and methodologies have been used to attempt to distinguish 'historical institutionalism', rational choice/'economic'

---

[1] For reviews, see: P. A. Hall and R. C. R. Taylor (1996), 'Political Science and the Three New Institutionalisms', *Political Studies*, 44(4), 936–57; K. Thelen, 'Historical Institutionalism in Comparative Politics', *The Annual Review of Political Science 1999* (Palo Alto: Annual Reviews, 1999); E. M. Immergut, 'The Theoretical Core of the New Institutionalism', *Politics and Society*, 25(1) (1998), 5–34; J. Kato, 'Review Article: Institutions and Rationality in Politics—Three Varieties of Neo-Institutionalists', *British Journal of Political Science*, 26(4) (1996), 553–82; T. A. Koelble, 'The New Institutionalism in Political Science and Sociology', *Comparative Politics*, 27(2) (1995), 231–43; A. Stone, 'Le "néo-institutionnalisme"', *Politix*, 20 (1992), 156–68; K. Thelen and S. Steinmo, 'Historical Institutionalism in comparative politics', in S. Steinmo, K. Thelen, and F. Longstreth (eds.), *Structuring Politics: Historical Institutionalism in Comparative Analysis* (Cambridge: Cambridge University Press, 1992); R. H. Bates, 'Contra Contractarianism: Some Reflections on the New Institutionalism', *Politics and Society*, 16(2–3) (1988), 387–401; W. R. Scott, 'The Adolescence of Institutional Theory', *Administrative Science Quarterly*, 32(4) (1987), 493–511.

institutionalism and 'sociological institutionalism'.[2] However, the purpose of the current study is to present an analytical framework to aid examination of the effects of national institutions on public policy rather than to develop a comprehensive categorization of institutionalisms. It therefore suffices to state that the analysis largely follows cross-national 'new' or 'historical' institutionalism within political science: its focus is on political institutions; it examines national institutions and policy over a sustained period of time; the behaviour of actors is examined from the empirical evidence available, avoiding strong assumptions of optimality and equilibrium. Selected general institutionalist approaches are used to derive and establish the analytical framework of the study.

The first section of the chapter analyses the key elements of static frameworks centred on national institutions and public policy; for shorthand, the approaches are labelled 'national institutionalism'. The second section turns to an examination of national institutions and change, setting out current discussions. Finally, in the light of the foregoing general arguments, the third section sets out the ways in which the relationships between national institutions and policy are to be analysed in the present study.

National Institutionalism

Cross-national institutionalist analyses of policy making and economic performance claim to find two important sets of regularities over considerable historical periods. First, there are very significant continuities: in a world of flux and strong pressures for change and in the face of economic developments and cycles, changes of government and mutations in the organizational resources of the state, persistent patterns exist in nations' policies and policy formation, lasting for decades and even longer.[3] Long-standing national conceptions of the role of the state exist.[4] Policy making is characterized by persistent 'logics', rules, and strategies, evidenced by enduring features in the processes of policy making, the direction of policy, the interests served by public decisions, and

---

[2] Hall and Taylor, 'Political Science and the Three New Institutionalisms'; P. J. Di Maggio and W. W. Powell, 'Introduction', in W. W. Powell and P. J. DiMaggio (eds.), *The New Institutionalism in Organizational Analysis* (Chicago and London: University of Chicago Press, 1991); N. Fligstein, 'Fields, Power, and Social Skill: A Critical Analysis of The New Institutionalisms', in M. Miller (ed.), *Power and Organization* (London: Sage, 1999).

[3] P. A. Hall, *Governing the Economy* (Cambridge: Polity Press, 1986), 263–6; E. M. Immergut, *Health Politics: Interests and, Institutions in Western Europe* (Cambridge: Cambridge University Press, 1992), 9; F. Dobbin, *Forging Industrial Policy: The United States, Britain, and France in the Railway Age* (Cambridge: Cambridge University Press, 1994).

[4] K. Dyson, *The State Tradition in Western Europe* (Oxford: Martin Robertson, 1980); K. Dyson, 'The Cultural, Ideological and Structural Context', in K. Dyson and S. Wilks (eds.), *Industrial Crisis* (Oxford: Martin Robertson, 1983).

the strategies pursued by actors.[5] Moreover, long-run traits are seen in nations' economic performance, for instance in terms of economic growth or income distribution.[6]

The existence of continuing, large-scale differences in policy making and economic achievements of nations is a second phenomenon revealed by cross-national studies. Contrasts are found across many fields including economic and industrial policy,[7] employment policy and the position of labour,[8] health policy,[9] and social policy.[10] Analysis of decision-making processes shows that the strategies, ideas, and self-defined interests of equivalent types of actors (such as interest groups, bureaucrats, and elected officials) differ from one country to another.[11] The participants in policy formation, their relationships and the distribution of power amongst them, are also dissimilar.[12] Consistent patterns of difference between countries are not fully explained by the features of groups: thus, for instance, even if groups have similar resources, their power over policy varies.[13] Hence institutionalists argue that the behaviour of participants in decision making cannot just be 'read off' the characteristics of those actors.[14]

Nations also make dissimilar substantive policy choices, even when faced by similar environments or challenges, such as technological and economic developments, revolutionary dissent or economic crisis.[15] Frequently they have

---

[5] Immergut, *Health Politics*, 3–4; Dobbin, *Forging industrial policy*; Hall, *Governing the Economy*. Cf. J. J. Richardson (ed.), *Policy Styles in Western Europe* (London: Allen and Unwin, 1982).

[6] Hall, *Governing the Economy*.

[7] See, for instance: Hall, *Governing the Economy*; Dyson, *The State Tradition in Western Europe*; Dobbin, *Forging industrial policy*; S. Steinmo, *Taxation and Democracy* (New Haven and London: Yale University Press, 1993).

[8] See e.g. D. S. King, *Actively Seeking Work* (Chicago and London: University of Chicago Press, 1995); V. C. Hattam, *Labor Visions and State Power: The Origins of Business Unionism in the United States* (Princeton: Princeton University Press, 1993); B. Rothstein 'Labor-Market Institutions and Working-Class Strength', in S. Steinno, K. Thelen, and F. Longsheth (eds.), *Structuring Politics: Historical Institutionalism in Comparative Analysis* (Cambridge: Cambridge University Press, 1992); P. Swenson, *Fair Shares: Unions, Pay and Politics in Sweden and West Germany* (London: Adamantine Press, 1989).

[9] Immergut, *Health Politics*.

[10] M. Weir, *Politics and Jobs: The Boundaries of Empolyment Policy in the United States* (Princeton: Princeton University Press, 1992); M. Weir, A. S. Orloff, and T. Skocpol, 'Introduction. Understanding American Social Politics', in their (eds.), *Understanding American Social Politics* (Princeton: Princeton University Press, 1988).

[11] Hall, *Governing the Economy*; Dobbin, *Forging industrial policy*.

[12] Immergut, *Health Politics*; Hall, *Health Politics*; Weir, *Politics and Jobs*; cf. K. A. Thelen, *Union of Parts* (Ithaca and London: Cornell University Press, 1991).

[13] Immergut, *Health Politics*.

[14] Dobbin, *Forging Industrial Policy*, 6; Hall, *Governing the Economy*; Hattam, *Labor Visions and State Power*.

[15] Hall, *Governing the Economy*; Immergut, *Health Politics*; T. Skocpol, *States and Social Revolutions* (Cambridge: Cambridge University Press, 1979); Dyson, 'The Cultural, Ideological and Structural Context'.

different conceptions of public policy problems and choices, whilst their aims and instruments also vary.[16]

Dissimilar policies lead to differences in outcomes between nations. These may concern the nature of the state—for instance, its financing and size,[17] the services it provides and the methods whereby these are provided.[18] They can also result in contrasting economic performances, seen in outcomes such as economic growth rates, export performance or the development and strength of different financial and industrial sectors.[19] Indeed, dissimilar institutions lead to several 'varieties of capitalism', as countries enjoy their own unique form of capitalism.[20]

How can national continuities and cross-national differences be explained? More generally, how can the features of countries' policy making be analysed? In response to these questions, scholars have turned to 'national institutions'—conceived as the structure or organizational framework within which a state's policy-makers take decisions. At the very least, a country's institutions provide the framework through which other factors—be they market, demographic or technological forces or conflicts between interests—must pass in order to influence public policy. However, institutions do not simply transmit such factors into the policy process: they 'translate' and strongly mediate them.[21] Thus, institutions are, in part at least, an exogenous factor, influencing behaviour and outcomes.[22] Institutionalist analyses share

[16] Immergut, *Health Politics*, 10; Weir, *Politics and Jobs*; Hall, *Governing the Economy*; Dobbin, *Forging Industrial Policy*.

[17] S. Steinmo and C. J. Tolbert, 'Do Institutions Really Matter?', *Comparative Political Studies*, 31(2) (1998), 165–87; S. Steinmo, *Taxation and Democracy*, (New Haven and London: Yale University Press, 1993); M. Levi, *Of Rule and Revenue* (Berkeley, Calif.: University of California Press, 1988).

[18] See e.g. Immergut, *Health Politics*, on health insurance, or on employment and work welfare policies, D. S. King (1992), 'The Establishment of work-welfare programmes in the United States and Britain: Politics, ideas and institutions', in Steinmo, Thelen, and Longstreth, *Structuring Politics*; King, *Actively Seeking Work*; D. S. King and B. Rothstein, 'Government Legitimacy and the Labour Market: A Comparative Analysis of Employment Exchanges', *Public Administration*, 72(2) (1994), 291–308, and also their 'Institutional Choices and Labour Market Policy: A British-Swedish Comparison', *Comparative Political Studies*, 26(2) (1993) 147–77.

[19] The literature, even in political science, is vast; for examples among 'historical institutionalists', see: Hall, *Governing the Economy*; J. Zysman, 'How Institutions Create Historically Rooted Trajectories of Growth', *Industrial and Corporate Change*, 3(1) (1994), 243–83; cf. J. Zysman, *Governments, Markets and Growth* (New York: Cornell University Press, 1983).

[20] See C. Crouch and W. Streek (eds.), *Political Economy of Modern Capitalism* (London: Sage, 1997), H. Kitschelt, G. Marks, P. Lange, and J. Stephens (eds.), *Change and Continuity in Contemporary Capitalism* (Cambridge: Cambridge University Press, 1999).

[21] Immergut, *Health Politics*, 5; Weir, *Politics and Jobs*, 16.

[22] J. March and J. Olsen, 'The New Institutionalism: Organizational Factors in Political Life', *American Political Science Review*, 78(2) (1984), 734–49, and, 'Institutional Perspectives on Political Institutions' *Governance*, 9(3) (1996), 247–64; Hall, *Governing the Economy*.

the proposition that 'institutions' are not merely a reflection of other forces nor 'neutral arenas within which political behaviour, driven by more fundamental factors, occurs'.[23]

Institutions have a degree of formal existence, and are equated with, or seen as based on, rules and procedures.[24] Thus, for instance, Peter Hall defines institutions as 'the formal rules, compliance procedures and standard operating procedures that structure the relationship between individuals in various units of the polity and economy'.[25] At times, informal rules and practices are included; thus, for instance, Ellen Immergut[26] uses institution' to cover *de jure* and *de facto* rules (the latter consisting of 'informal practices') that mediate conflicts and organize political systems as a whole,[27] whilst Colleen Dunlavy claims that 'institutions of any kind consist of rules, compliance procedures, and norms that order relations among individuals'.[28]

A wide range of national institutions exist that influence policy making. The framework directly surrounding elected decision-makers is of central importance, and in particular the structure of the state. Hence political institutions are analysed, either individually[29] or as a configuration of several institutions.[30] However, the range of institutions can be widened to include the structure of societal groups, firms, and markets and their relationship with the state.[31] Thus, for instance, Peter Hall argues that institutions exist not only within a country's constitution and formal political practices, but also in its society and the economy and therefore examines five 'organizational' variables: the organization of capital, labour, the State, the political system, and the position of each country within the international economy.[32]

National institutions are argued to be highly stable and resistant to change in institutionalist approaches. They are deeply rooted in a country's history,

[23] March and Olsen, 'The New Institutionalism', 734.

[24] Immergut, *Health Politics*; Hall, *Governing the Economy*; March and Olsen, 'Institutional Perspectives on Political Institutions', see also A. Cawson, P. Holmes, D. Webber, K. Morgan, and A. Stevens, *Hostile Brothers* (Oxford: Clarendon Press, 1990), who define markets as social institutions with rules enforced by the state.

[25] *Governing the Economy*, 19.   [26] Immergut, 1993, ch. 1, esp. 24–5.

[27] Immergut, *Health Politics*, 3, 24–6.

[28] C. A. Dunlavy, *Politics and Industrialization: Early Railroads in the United States and Prussia* (Princeton: Princeton University Press, 1993), 6.

[29] See e.g. R. K. Weaver and B. A. Rockman (eds.), *Do Institutions Matter?* (Washington, DC: Brookings, 1993), who look at presidential versus parliamentary systems.

[30] Cf. Immergut, *Health Politics*.

[31] Cawson *et al.*, *Hostile Brothers*; M. Atkinson and W. Coleman, 'Strong States and Weak States: Sectoral Policy Networks in Capitalist Economies', *British Journal of Political Science*, 19(1) (1989), 47–67. S. D. Krasner, *Defending the National Interest: Raw Materials, Investments and US Foreign Policy* (Princeton: Princeton University Press, 1978); cf. P. Evans, D. Rueschemeyer, and T. Skocpol (eds.), *Bringing the State Back In* (Cambridge: Cambridge University Press, 1985).

[32] *Governing the Economy*.

being the product of national crisis, long evolution and pre-existing institutions and distributions of power.[33] Institutions in one sphere are reproduced in another sphere of a nation's life.[34] Thus institutional frameworks are national in character, largely inherited and are not open to easy modification.

The institutions of countries also differ greatly. There are contrasts in political institutions—for instance, constitutional features such as electoral laws, the position of the executive and legislature, the distribution of powers between different levels of government.[35] Variations also exist in the structure and nature of the state: its policy instruments, organizational resources and the institutionalized relationships among different parts of the polity.[36] Market structures are not the same across nations, but range from state-supported monopolies to competitive markets; similarly, there are differences in the organization of labour and its relationship with capital from one country to another.[37]

National institutionalist analyses link the characteristics of institutions to the features of national policy making that they are seeking to explain (continuities and cross-national differences). Stable national institutions result in continuities of policy making in individual countries. Institutional differences between countries lead to dissimilarities in policy making and outcomes. Thus, for instance, institutions are used to explain national patterns and cross-national differences in economic performance,[38] patterns and strategies of industrial change,[39] the direction of the development of health systems,[40] tax income and welfare-state sizes,[41] labour relations,[42] and unionization rates.[43]

General claims for the importance of national institutions are supported by a number of specific causal mechanisms. Six interrelated channels whereby institutional 'structures' influence the behaviour of actors (individuals, organizations and groups) in policy making can be identified. First, national institu-

[33] Hall, *Governing the Economy*; Hall and Taylor, 'Political Science and the Three New Institutionalisms'; Weir, *Politics and Jobs*; Weir, Orloff, and Skocpol, 'Introduction'; Hattam, *Labor Visions and State Power*; Steinmo, *Taxation and Democracy*; Immergut, *Health Politics*; cf. C. Tilly (ed.), *The Formation of States in Western Europe* (Princeton: Princeton University Press, 1975).

[34] Dobbin, *Forging Industrial Policy*, 2–3.

[35] Immergut, *Health Politics*; Steinmo, *Taxation and Democracy*; Weaver and Rockman, *Do Institutions Matter?*; Weir, *Politics and Jobs*.

[36] Cf. 'State-centric' work and 'neo-corporatist' literature—P. Katzenstein (ed.), *Between Power and Plenty* (Madison: University of Wisconsin Press, 1978); M. Atkinson and W. Coleman, 'Corporatism and Industrial Policy', in A. Cawson (ed.), *Organized Interests and the State: Studies in Meso-Corporatism* (London: Sage, 1985).

[37] Cf. Cawson et al., *Hostile Brothers*; Atkinson and Coleman, 'Strong States and Weak States'; Kitschelt et al., *Change and Continuity in Contemporary Capitalism*.

[38] Hall, *Governing the Economy*.

[39] Dunlavy, *Politics and Industrialization*; Dobbin, *Forging Industrial Policy*.

[40] Immergut, *Health Politics*.   [41] Steinmo, *Taxation and Democracy*.

[42] Thelen, *Union of Parts*.

[43] B. Rothstein, 'Labor-Market Institutions and Working-Class Strength'.

tions affect the values, ideas, aims, and perceptions of actors, who are seen as 'flexible, malleable, culture-dependent and socially-constructed'.[44] Institution-alist approaches take 'an individual's or group's definition of self interest as problematical'.[45] Interests, preferences, and values are established in specific institutional contexts and are highly dependent on that context, rather than the functional position of actors.[46]

National institutions also affect the strategies of actors. Actors with similar aims and resources but facing dissimilar national institutions, choose different strategies and patterns of behaviour.[47] Moreover, national institutions may affect the nature of 'rationality', notably the 'logic of appropriateness' that actors apply in making choices.[48]

Institutional contexts affect the expression and organization of interests, con-stituting a third causal mechanism.[49] They are important for the establishment and structure of groups, and coalitions amongst groups.[50] Their roles arise from their importance in shaping ideas, interests and preferences of groups and hence the costs and benefits of collective action.[51]

The distribution of power between groups depends not only on the resources of groups, but also on their institutionally-determined opportunities for using those resources. A country's institutions offer a specific set of advan-tages and disadvantages for groups because 'institutional configurations are vul-nerable to political influence to different extents and at different points';[52] thus, for example, 'veto points' in the decision-making process vary from one country to another. The ease with which groups can press demands on policy-makers, their influence on the policy process and the courses of action that they adopt, are affected by national institutions, particularly the structure of the State.[53]

---

[44] March and Olsen, 'Institutional Perspectives on Political Institutions', 249.

[45] Steinmo, *Taxation and Democracy*, 7.

[46] Weir, *Politics and Jobs*, 24; March and Olsen, 'Institutional Perspectives on Political Institutions', 250; cf. G. Grendstad and P. Selle, 'Cultural Theory and the New Institutionalism', *Journal of Theoretical Politics*, 7(1) (1995), 5–27, esp. 20–3; Dobbin, *Forging Industrial Policy*, 220.

[47] Hall, *Governing the Economy*, 277; Steinmo, *Taxation and Democracy*, 7.

[48] March and Olsen, 'Institutional Perspectives on Political Institutions'; cf. J. G. March and J. P. Olsen, *Rediscovering Institutions: The Organizational Basis of Politics* (New York: The Free Press, 1989), March and Olsen, 'The New Institutionalism', and DiMaggio and Powell, 'Introduction'.

[49] Immergut, *Health Politics*; Weir, *Politics and Jobs*, 168–9, Dobbin, *Forging Industrial Policy*, 219; Hall, *Governing the Economy*.

[50] Katzenstein, *Between Power and Plenty*; Atkinson and Coleman 'Corporatism and Industrial Policy', and 'Strong States and Weak States'; cf. the wider neo-corporatist literature—P. Schmitter and G. Lembruch (eds.), *Trends toward Corporatist Intermediation* (Beverly Hills: Sage, 1979), and *Patterns of Corporatist Policy-Making* (Beverly Hills and London: Sage, 1982).

[51] Weir, *Politics and Jobs*, 15, 24; Hall, *Governing the Economy*; Immergut, *Health Politics*, 25–6.

[52] Immergut, *Health Politics*, 7, 9.

[53] Immergut, *Health Politics*; Hall, *Governing the Economy*, 19, 233; Weir, Orloff, and Skocpol, 'Introduction', 16.

A fifth channel for national institutions is through their influence on 'state autonomy'. Policy-makers can choose between different policies, shaping the policy agenda and modifying the constraints on them; using terms coined by 'state-centric' approaches, they enjoy 'autonomy' or 'relative autonomy' from society.[54] However, the extent of autonomy varies between nations: in particular, the instruments available to policy-makers will depend, in large measure, on the institutional framework of the state. In turn, choices depend on instruments, as 'governments are frequently prevented from adopting a particular policy in the absence of any means to implement it'.[55] In addition, the use made of autonomy will depend on the institutionally-framed preferences, ideas, and strategies of policy-makers.

A sixth channel relates especially to the impact of institutions on economic performance. The state is a central actor in markets, and hence public decisions influence economic outcomes. It plays a central role in structuring markets, not only in its direct role as purchaser and provider of services, but also through other means, such as regulation and legal frameworks governing contracts. The institutional framework of a market affects the economic behaviour of actors and hence outcomes.[56] In particular, the decisions of firms over matters such as production, investment, innovation, wages and profit targets are strongly conditioned by institutional factors.[57]

Thus, national institutions affect the interests, preferences, ideas, and values of actors, their strategies, the distribution of power among them, the resources and instruments of public bodies, and the interaction between actors in policy formation. They are central for the strength and character of pressures on policy-makers, as well as the distribution of power within a nation.

[54] P. M. Sachs, 'State Structure and the Aysmmetrical Society', *Comparative Politics*, 12 (1980), 349–74; T. Skocpol, 'Introduction', in Evans *et al.*, *Bringing the State Back In*; S. Krasner, 'Approaches to the State: Alternative Conceptions and Historical Dynamics', *Comparative Politics*, 16 (1984), 223–46; cf. E. Nordlinger, *On the Autonomy of the Democratic State* (Cambridge: Harvard University Press, 1981); for a powerful critique of 'state-centred' work, see G. Almond, 'The Return to the State', *American Political Science Review*, 82(3) (1988), 853–74 and replies, E. Nordlinger, T. Lowi, and S. Fabbrini, 'The Return to the State: Critiques', *American Political Science Review*, 82(3) (1988), 877–901.

[55] P. A. Hall, 'Policy Innovation and the Structure of the State: The Politics–Administration Nexus in France and Britain', *The Annals*, 466 (1983), 43–59, 24.

[56] Cf. work in 'new institutionalist economics', such as O. Williamson, *Markets and Hierarchies* (New York: The Free Press, 1975) and *The Economic Institutions of Capitalism* (New York: The Free Press, 1985), and D. C. North, *Institutions, Institutional Change and Economic Performance* (Cambridge: Cambridge University Press, 1990).

[57] For overviews, see: Zysman, 'How Institutions Create Historically Rooted Trajectories of Growth'; P. A. Hall, 'The Role of Interests, Institutions, and Ideas in the Comparative Political Economy of the Industrialized Nations', in M. I. Lichbach and A. S. Zuckerman (eds.), *Comparative Politics* (Cambridge: Cambridge University Press, 1997); D. Soskice, 'The Institutional Infrastructure for International Competitiveness: A Comparative Analysis of the UK and Germany', in A. B. Atkinson and R. Brunetta (eds.), *Economics for the New Europe* (Basingstoke: Macmillan, 1991).

Nevertheless, although national institutionalist explanations place a country's institutions at the centre of their explanations, they do not claim 'institutionalist determinism'.[58] Rather, institutions structure decisions: they offer the framework within which actors operate, shaping social action by providing 'incentives, opportunities and constraints'[59] and rules structuring behaviour.[60] Actors continue to make choices and to have margins of manoeuvre. 'Institutions constrain and refract politics but they are never the sole "cause" of outcomes'.[61] National institutions offer a framework through which non-institutional forces pass which leaves its imprint in terms of stable national patterns and persistent cross-national differences in policy making and economic performance. However, they also interact with other factors: 'domestic political institutions operate within . . . the broader social, economic and political setting within which they are embedded', and are in 'dynamic interaction' with the broader economic context, interests and values and ideas.[62] Hence, institutionalists 'should not shy away from the idea that institutions do not explain everything'.[63]

National Institutions and Change

At the heart of national institutionalist analysis is the claim that a country's institutions do not adjust rapidly to societal or other 'contextual' and environmental changes, but represent a set of independent variables that influence policy.64 Organizational frameworks are resistant to alteration because of both their deep historical roots and also the use of existing organizational models, so that when nations tackle new problems, the additional institutions created are based on, or copied from, existing ones.65

Stable national institutions give rise to enduring patterns of policy formation and economic performance: despite changes in the boundaries of public policy and the content of policy problems, institutional similarities lead to conceptions, logics, and strategies being replicated from existing domains to emerging fields of policy or new policy questions.[66] Since differences in countries' institutional frameworks are maintained, so are cross-national contrasts in policy.

[58] Dunlavy, *Politics and Industrialization*, 42; March and Olsen, 'Institutional Perspectives on Political Institutions', 252.

[59] Immergut, *Health Politics*, 32.

[60] March and Olsen, 'Institutional Perspectives on Political Institutions', 252; Dunlavy, *Politics and Industrialization*, 42.

[61] Thelen and Steinmo, 'Historical Institutionalism in Comparative Politics', 3.

[62] Steinmo, *Taxation and Democracy*, 12, 200–1; see also Weir, *Politics and Jobs*, 25, and Hattam, *Labor Visions and State Power*, 210.

[63] Skocpol, quoted in Steinmo, *Taxation and Democracy*, 12.

[64] March and Olsen, 'Institutional Perspectives on Political Institutions'; Hall, *Governing the Economy*.

[65] Dobbin, *Forging Industrial Policy*, 2–3.   [66] Ibid. 217, 229; Immergut, *Health Politics*, 3–4.

Nevertheless, national institutionalist analysis need not be entirely static: policy modifications are difficult but not impossible. Three types of change can be envisaged. First, policy alterations within a given set of national institutions is possible: since institutionalist determinism is rejected, there is scope for other factors to influence policy, and hence to modify it, within a given institutional framework. Second, national institutions themselves can be modified; institutionalist analysis claims that a country's institutions do not alter rapidly to contextual changes, not that they are eternal. Third, national institutions themselves may influence non-institutional pressures for change.

Change does not eliminate the importance of national institutions: on the contrary, dissimilar institutional frameworks may lead countries to respond differently even if faced by similar pressures for change. Whilst powerful socio-economic pressures for change may be strong, their impact can be ambiguous, indirect and mediated through other variables.[67] Just as non-institutional factors pass through institutions in the policy process, so too non-institutional forces for change are 'translated' by national organizational structures which leave their imprint on the nature, extent, speed and timing of change. The same causal mechanisms whereby national institutions influence policy in the static institutionalist analysis apply to policy change, including their importance for the values, aims, interests and strategies of actors in seeking modifications, the role of interest groups in the alteration of policy and institutions and the capacities and objectives of policy-makers in change.

In addition, however, national institutions are important for the starting point of reform. Policy modifications in a country are related to past circumstances, notably the institutional framework, which influence the actors involved in reform, their aims and ideas, and the distribution of resources and power amongst them. Moreover, policy formation and alteration are often processes, not one-off events, involving strategic manoeuvring, learning and constant adjustment of aims and modes of implementation.[68] 'Path dependency' may operate, whereby outcomes are not wholly determined by the original forces for changes, but are dependent on the path followed.[69] 'Policy feedback' offers one mechanism for path dependency: in the process of policy making, the effects of policy will in turn 'feed back' over time, for instance,

---

[67] R. Berins Collier and D. Collier, *Shaping the Political Arena* (Princeton: Princeton University Press, 1991), 730.

[68] Thelen, *Union of Parts*, 4; Weir, Orloff, and Skocpol, 'Introduction', term this the 'institutional–political process' perspective—16–17.

[69] P. Pierson, 'Not Just What but When: Issues of Timing and Sequence in Comparative Politics' (Boston: APSA conference paper, 1998), 'The Path to European Integration: A Historical Institutionalist Analysis', *Comparative Political Studies*, 29(2) (1996), 123–63, and 'When Effect Becomes Cause: Policy Feedback and Political Change', *World Politics*, 45 (1993), 595–628; March and Olsen, 'Institutional Perspectives on Political Institutions'; for an economic analysis, see North, *Institutions, Institutional Change and Economic Performance*.

altering State capacities and/or the identities, goals, and capabilities of social groups.[70] National organizational arrangements affect and mediate such feedback effects.[71] If the feedback involves self-reinforcing processes, it will result in larger, long-term cross-national contrasts. An alternative mechanism is for existing national institutions to affect the timing of changes, leading to differences in the interaction of factors, 'critical junctures', 'first mover' advantages or disadvantages and policy learning.[72] Thus institutions can result in countries following a different path of development, with lasting consequences for the trajectories of institutions, policies, and economic performance.

The various channels of institutional influence can be seen in analysis of the three types of change identified. Policy change within a stable institutional framework is possible if national institutions are sufficiently flexible to accommodate some innovation. Hence scope exists for non-institutional factors to lead to policy modification without necessitating institutional reform. Such factors may consist of 'broad changes' in the socio-economic or political context, or new ideas.[73] Exogenous factors can cause existing but previously latent institutions to become active and/or new actors to pursue new goals through existing institutions. They may also lead existing actors to alter their goals or strategies within a given institutional framework.[74] Moreover, actors (existing or new) may be able to alter the capacities of existing institutions.[75] These actors may include bureaucrats[76] or political parties that seek electoral success by offering new solutions to old problems.[77]

In accommodating policy modification, national institutions remain important. They affect the scope for change that is possible: within a given institutional framework, nations have differing capacities for policy innovation. Similarly, national institutions affect the form and nature of change. They present obstacles to certain types of policy modification, whilst permitting or

[70] T. Skocpol, *Protecting Soldiers and Mothers: The Political Origins of Social Policy in the United States* (Cambridge, Mass.: Harvard University Press, 1992), 58.

[71] Weir, Orloff, and Skocpol, 'Introduction'; Weir, *Politics and Jobs*; Pierson, 'When Effect Becomes Cause'.

[72] See e.g. Berins Collier and Collier, *Shaping the Political Arena*, or Skocpol, *Protecting Soldiers and Mothers*.

[73] Thelen and Steinmo, 'Historical Institutionalism in Comparative Politics', 16.

[74] Ibid. 16–17; P. A. Hall, 'Policy Paradigms, Social Learning and the State', *Comparative Politics*, 23 (1993), 275–96; Hattam, *Labor Visions and State Power*.

[75] Dobbin, *Forging Industrial Policy*, 228–9, argues that the administrative capacities of nations can be altered.

[76] For instance Heclo, *Modern Social Politics in Britain and Sweden* (New Haven: Yale University Press, 1974), or P. M. Sachs, 'State Structure and the Aysmmetrical Society', *Comparative Politics*, 12 (1980), 349–74.

[77] Hall, *Governing the Economy*, 273–6; but, see R. Rose, *Do Parties Make A Difference?* (London: Macmillan, 1984) and, 'Inheritance before Choice in Public Policy', *Journal of Theoretical Policy*, 1(2) (1990), 263–91 for contrary arguments.

easing the path for other forms that are congruent with the underlying organizational structure. Thus, for instance, whether new ideas are taken up, how they are transformed, and the nature of 'policy learning' will depend on a nation's existing institutions.[78] Due to institutional frameworks, responses to changing technological and economic developments will vary from one country to another, as will the choice of specific policy instruments.[79] Endogenous sources of change occur within institutional frameworks: policy feedbacks arise from previous policies, which were themselves conditioned by existing institutions, and take place within institutional configurations. Similarly, actors' strategic manoeuvring and modification of strategies and preferences take place within institutional structures that channel their development.[80] Thus nations, even if faced with similar external pressures, follow distinctive 'adjustment paths' thanks to their different organizational arrangements.[81]

Modification of national institutions provides a second route for policy change. Such modification may occur through a process of 'punctuated equilibrium': change is rare, but is rapid and substantial; highly stable institutional patterns endure in the intervening intervals.[82] An alternative view is that institutions change incrementally, evolving under piecemeal change as a result of specific battles or manoeuvring by actors.[83] A third view combines both types of institutional modification: the institutions of the State and society change incrementally, but are not open to dramatic change except at critical points in a nation's history, such as war or recession, when existing societal arrangements are called into question. In all three cases, national institutions change only with difficulty, with modification being rare and/or slow.[84]

However, when institutional change does take place, existing institutions affect its form. They influence the ideas, interests, resources, and strategies of actors engaged in reform. Institutional modification does not begin *de novo*, but involves adaption of, or reaction against, existing institutional arrangements. Thus, for instance, new institutions may be copied from old ones, leading to 'institutional isomorphism' and the operation of new structures can be affected

[78] Hall, *Governing the Economy*; Weir, *Politics and Jobs*; J. Goldstein and R. O. Keohane (eds.), *Ideas and Foreign Policy: Beliefs, Institutions and Political Change* (Cornell: Cornell University Press, 1993); J. L. Campbell, 'Institutional Analysis and the Role of Ideas in Political Economy', *Theory and Society*, 27(4) (1998), 377–409; D. S. King and S. Wood, 'The Political Economy of Neoliberalism: Britain and the United States in the 1980s', in Kitschelt *et al.*, *Continuity and Change in Contemporary Capitalism*.

[79] Dobbin, *Forging Industrial Policy*; Weir, *Politics and Jobs*; Steinmo, *Taxation and Democracy*.

[80] Weir, *Politics and Jobs*; Weir, Orloff, and Skocpol, 'Introduction', 16–17.

[81] P. A. Hall, 'The Political Economy of Europe in an Era of Interdependence' in Kitschelt *et al.*, *Continuity and Change in Contemporary Capitalism*.

[82] See Krasner, 'Approaches to the State'; cf. the discussion of 'discontinuities' in Berins Collier and Collier, *Shaping the Political Arena*, 11.

[83] Thelen and Steinmo, 'Historical Institutionalism in Comparative Politics'.

[84] Hall, *Governing the Economy*.

by previous ones.[85] Existing organizational arrangements may affect the lags in institutional responses to environmental pressures.[86] Timing can often be crucial to institutional paths: small differences at a early stage of development produce much larger contrasts later through self-reinforcing processes; institutions are created at 'critical junctures', so that even in a similar environment, cross-national institutional differences in the timing, sequence and simultaneity of events lead to dissimilar interactions of new organizational forms with non-institutional factors and hence country-specific institutional trajectories.[87] Finally, even if environmental pressures are powerful, there is no one unique matching institutional outcome or 'equilibrium';[88] thus nations can experience differing institutional adjustments to similar external forces for change.[89]

The foregoing discussion has assumed that non-institutional factors are exogenous. However, national institutions are argued not only to enjoy a high level of 'autonomy' from their environment, but also to influence that environment.[90] Thus a nation's institutional structures are both influenced by changes in society and themselves affect the development of social conflicts and of society. The strategies of the State affect society and the balance of intergroup relations—there is a dynamic relationship between State and society and the State has a degree of 'autonomy'. 'Organization does more than transmit the preferences of particular groups; it combines and ultimately alters them', and the State 'refracts' struggles between competing economic interests and 'acts as a distorting mirror to reproduce a highly imperfect reflection of these conflicts and one that imprints its own image on their resolution.'[91] An alternative impact of institutions is on ideas. The supply of ideas is not necessarily exogenous to institutions, and hence institutional practices and sites affect how problems are understood and the production of new ideas.[92] In the long-run, non-institutional factors and national institutions influence each other.

Dissimilar national institutions produce situations in which, even if faced with similar exogenous pressures for change, nations respond differently, as such pressures are translated in differing manners, responses vary and endogenous forces for policy and/or institutional modification within nations will be dissimilar. Moreover, countries will not adopt the same institutional

---

[85] March and Olsen, *Rediscovering Institutions*; Dobbin, *Forging Industrial Policy*; Weir, *Politics and Jobs*.

[86] Weir, *Politics and Jobs*.

[87] Pierson, 'Not Just What but When'; Thelen, 'Historical Institutionalism in Comparative Politics'; Berins-Collier and Collier, *Shaping the Political Arena*.

[88] March and Olsen, 'Institutional Perspectives on Political Institutions', 255–6.

[89] Hall, 'The Political Economy of Europe'.

[90] March and Olsen 'Institutional Perspectives on Political Institutions'; Weir, Orloff, and Skocpol, 'Introduction'; Weir, *Politics and Jobs*.

[91] Hall, *Governing the Economy*, 233.   [92] Weir, *Politics and Jobs*, 13, 21.

reforms, due to variations in institutional histories and the capacities to adapt and innovate of existing structures. Finally, nations are likely to face contrasting policy environments if their institutions affect non-institutional forces for change. Thus, nations experience differing policy paths or 'sequences of development', as 'institutions exercise an enduring effect on what is possible later, not so much by preventing change . . . as by sending change off in particular directions'.[93]

Examining the Role of National Institutions: Telecommunications in Britain and France 1969–1997

Testing the Claims of National Institutionalism

National institutionalism offers a set of clear claims, namely that stable, different national institutions lead to persistent and dissimilar patterns of policy making and economic performance and that, insofar as institutional and policy change occurs, it is rare, difficult and differs among countries. The model suggests several causal mechanisms for the operation of national institutions. It appears to offer a powerful, empirically applicable explanation for important phenomena (national continuities and persistent cross-national dissimilarities).

Claims for the role and significance of national institutions deserve critical scrutiny. There has been a lively debate over institutionalism in political science and sociology.[94] However, the purpose of the present study is not to evaluate the theoretical contribution of institutionalism, but rather to test empirically claims concerning the role and importance of national institutions derived from national institutionalist analyses. To that end, three lines of questioning are possible: the descriptive claims concerning the stability of national institutions and patterns of policy making, together with cross-national differences in institutions, policy, and economic outcomes, including paths of development; the causal role of national institutions; analytical issues concerning the definition and scope of national institutions.

National institutionalism rests on the assertion that the institutional frame-

---

[93] Weir, *Politics and Jobs*, 5, 166.

[94] For general discussions of the merits of institutionalism and its relationship to other models of public policy, see: Hall, *Governing the Economy*, chs. 1 and 10; March and Olsen, 'The New Institutionalism', *Rediscovering Institutions*, and 'Institutional Perspectives on Political Institutions'; Steinmo, *Taxation and Democracy*, ch. 1; J. Pontusson, 'From Comparative Public Policy to Political Economy: Putting Political Institutions in Their Place and Taking Interests Seriously', *Comparative Political Studies*, 28(1) (1995), 117–47; Koebel, 'The New Institutionalism'; cf. M. Blyth, ' "Any more Bright Ideas?" The Ideational Turn of Comparative Political Economy', *Comparative Politics*, 29(2) (1997), 229–50.

work of a country is durable and, once established, does not adjust quickly to other factors. Institutions are an independent/exogenous variable in that they affect non-institutional factors (which have to pass through them), but are not themselves affected by such factors. The extent of institutional stability must be tested empirically, to show that reform is difficult, and to analyse the circumstances under which change is possible. If modification of institutions is easy, then the clear distinction between 'policy' and 'institutions' disappears, as actors can alter national institutions for policy ends. Institutions cease to be a purely independent variable; instead, they become, at least in part, a dependent variable of other factors responsible for actors' ability and desires to modify the national institutional framework. Thus the causal and analytical priority accorded to institutions is undermined.

The existence of stable patterns of national policy formation requires empirical verification. Similarly, the existence of continuing cross-national differences in institutions and institutional trajectories must also be tested empirically and cannot be assumed: even if historically dissimilar, institutions may converge over time. If institutional arrangements differ, claims of persistent contrasts between countries in patterns of policy making and in economic performance, including paths of development, also call for validation. Moreover, the significance of cross-national differences in policy making and economic performance needs to be assessed, as contrasts may be small relative to similarities.

The causal claims made for national institutions are powerful and also well-supported, since causal mechanisms are put forward. Nevertheless, causal links between specific institutional features and patterns of national policy making need to be tested. The greatest challenge to causal claims arises from policy modification within a given set of institutions. Empirically, the causal importance of institutions is open to question, since non-institutional factors are seen to influence policy formation; however, this is not fatal, since claims of institutional determinism are not made. More serious are methodological problems, in that 'institutionalist' explanations may become unfalsifiable: policy modification without institutional change does not invalidate them. Therefore if policy change takes place without institutional modification, the ways in which institutions influence change must be shown for institutionalist claims to be upheld.

The definition and scope of 'national institutions' is crucial to national institutionalism. However, scholars offer varying uses of the term. In particular, at times, institutions are extended from formal structures and rules to informal rules, practices and norms.[95] Yet this usage blurs the distinction between 'institution' and patterns of behaviour in policy making, whereas the latter is to be

---

[95]   e.g. by Dobbin, *Forging Industrial Policy*, Immergut, *Health Politics*.

explained by the former.[96] Moreover, a wide range of institutions are used to explain behaviour: political institutions and the organization of the state, the structure of interest groups and their links with policy-makers or market structures. Thus testing the impact of institutions on policy making and economic performance requires an appropriate definition of institutions that separates them from the *explananda* and explicit choices as to which institutions are being studied.

A Critical Case Study to Test the Impact of National Institutions: Telecommunications in Britain and France 1969–1997

The telecommunications sector in Britain and France over the period 1969–97 is used as a form of 'critical case' for the influence of national institution on policy and economic performance in Western Europe. Critical case studies allow detailed historical research and are often necessary when there are 'many variables and few cases', a situation that exists especially for national-level variables such as institutions.[97] Telecommunications in Britain and France between 1969 and 1997 had characteristics that make them particularly appropriate to test claims for national institutions with respect to: the two countries chosen; the nature of the sector; the time period.

During the period studied, Britain and France had similar non-institutional structural features, including economic size, membership of the European Community (since 1972 for Britain) and geographical position. In both countries, the telecommunications sector was at the centre of industrial policy making. It became economically 'strategic': the supply of telecommunications services and equipment directly affected the supply of a host of other economic sectors, from tourism, finance, and computing to manufacturing.[98] Yet British and French policies and economic performances are frequently contrasted, especially their economic and industrial policies, with telecommunications

---

[96] A similar criticism can be made of Peter Hall's extension of 'institution' to include the 'relational character' of institutions in structuring the interactions of individuals—Hall, *Governing the Economy*, 19.

[97] For a discussion of the uses of case studies, notably in comparative politics, see e.g. H. Eckstein, 'Case Study and Theory in Political Theory', in F. Greenstein and N. W. Polsby (eds.), *Handbook of Political Science*, vii (Reading, Mass.: Adison-Wesley, 1975); D. E. Ashford (ed.), *Comparing Public Policies: New Concepts and Methods* (Beverly Hills, Calif.: Sage, 1978) and, 'Introduction: Of Cases and Contexts', in D. E. Ashford (ed.), *History and Context in Comparative Public Policy* (Pittsburgh and London: University of Pittsburgh Press, 1992); M. Dogan and D. Pelassy, *How to Compare Nations: Strategies in Comparative Politics* (Chatham, NJ: Chatham House, 2nd. edn., 1990); for comparison, see also A. Lijphart, 'Comparative Politics and the Comparative Method', *American Political Science Review*, 65 (1971), 682–93; H. Teune, 'A Logic of Comparative Policy Analysis', in Ashford (ed.), *Comparing Public Policies*; A. Prezeworski and H. Teune, *The Logic of Comparative Inquiry* (New York: Wiley, 1970).

[98] See ch. 3 for a discussion of the increasing use of telecommunications.

often being cited as an example.[99] The role of national institutions in contrasts is a recurrent theme of cross-national studies.[100]

From the mid-1960s onwards, the telecommunications sector in Britain and France were subject to very similar transnational/external pressures for change, notably technological and economic developments, but also ideas and, to a lesser extent, European Community regulation. The first two of these transnational factors were largely exogenous to the two countries in the period studied. These developments transformed the nature of the sector, challenging previous British and French institutional arrangements and patterns of policy and economic performance.

By 1969, the institutional frameworks for telecommunications in Britain and France had many common features, many of which were long-standing. The detailed study therefore begins in 1969, as it offers a similar institutional starting point for the two countries, together with many common policy features and a history of considerable institutional stability. After 1969, the institutions in the sector diverged: Britain comprehensively altered the framework of telecommunications in 1969, whilst France undertook limited changes in the late 1960s. During the 1970s, despite attempts at change, the key institutional features remained constant in the two countries, providing a period of institutional stability and cross-national difference. Divergence increased in the 1980s, as Britain undertook radical reforms in 1984, whilst institutional arrangements in France were largely unchanged; therefore the 1980s provide another period of institutional divergence, whilst also including organisational modification in one country. The increasing divergence between British and French telecommunications ended in the 1990s, with limited institutional reforms being introduced in France in 1990, followed by wider reforms in 1996–7. Hence the effects of institutional convergence can be analysed, together with those of alterations in France.

Thus the telecommunications sector in Britain and France between 1969 and 1997 offers an economically strategic sector subject to very powerful and largely exogenous transnational forces, but in which national institutions diverged, before experiencing a lessening of differences. Moreover, the case allows analysis over a considerable period of time of institutional reform and

---

[99] Cf. Hall, *Governing the Economy*; Dyson, 'The Cultural, Ideological and Structural Context'; V. A. Schmidt, *From State to Market? The Transformation of French Business and Government* (Cambridge: Cambridge University Press, 1996); Cawson *et al.*, *Hostile Brothers*; J. E. S. Hayward, *The State and the Market Economy* (Brighton: Wheatsheaf, 1986); A. Shonfield, *Modern Capitalism* (Oxford: Oxford University Press, 1969); Duch, R., *Privatizing the Economy: Telecommunications Policy in Comparative Perspective* (Ann Arbor: University of Michigan Press, 1991).

[100] Hall, *Governing the Economy*; Cawson *et al.*, *Hostile Brothers*; Zysman, *Governments, Markets and Growth*; P. Cerny, 'State Capitalism in France and Britain', in P. Cerny and M. Schain (eds.), *Socialism, the State and Public Policy in France* (New York and London: Methuen and Pinter, 1985), Schmidt, *From State to Market?*

its effects over a considerable period of time. The telecommunications sector is a form of 'critical case', in that if, despite such powerful transnational forces, the two countries were able to maintain dissimilar institutions that then led to differences in policy and outcomes, then national institutions can be expected to be important in other sectors in which transnational forces are less powerful.

Questions, Hypotheses, and Approach

In examining the role of national institutions, this book addresses three questions that match the central claims of national institutionalism concerning the features of institutions and their impacts. First, it looks at whether Britain and France maintained stable institutional arrangements in telecommunications and, insofar as changes were made, the circumstances under which they were introduced. Second, it examines whether and how institutional arrangements differed for the telecommunications sector in Britain and France, including the paths of institutional reform. Third, it asks whether national institutional arrangements influenced policy making and economic outcomes in the two countries, and if so, looks at how and why they affected policy; again, both static analysis and the patterns of policy development are considered.

The application of national institutionalist claims to the case of telecommunications in Britain and France between 1969 and 1997 provides certain hypotheses in answer to these questions, hypotheses that are tested and are used to structure the study. Institutionalist analyses would predict that institutional stability was strong; hence they suggest that the conditions under which institutions were modified would have had to be exceptional, with reform being slow and/or difficult. Moreover, the process and trajectory of reform should have been dissimilar in Britain and France. Hence the study looks at institutional arrangements, reforms, and attempts at reform, and compares the experience of the two countries.

If national institutionalist claims hold, divergent institutions after 1969 in Britain and France should have led to increasing contrasts in patterns of policy making and economic performance; conversely, institutional convergence after 1990 would be expected to have been followed by a lessening of differences. Furthermore, when institutional modification occurred, it should have resulted in changes in policy and economic outcomes in each country, either in static terms or in paths of development. Thus the study also examines patterns of policy making and economic performance in the two countries over a lengthy time period, paying particular attention both to the effects of cross-national divergence/convergence and to the impacts of institutional modifications within countries.

The study seeks three sources of evidence to answer its central questions and hence be able to compare its findings with those predicted by institutionalist analyses. First, cross-national comparison is used to establish whether national institutions, policy making and economic outcomes differed, as suggested by contentions for national institutions. Second, analysis over time allows examination of the stability of institutions and patterns of policy making and economic outcomes; moreover, it shows whether institutional change was followed by modification of policy formation and economic performance.

These two lines of enquiry can provide evidence that is consistent with institutionalist hypotheses or contrary to them. However, a third source of evidence arises from seeking causal linkages between specific national institutional characteristics and patterns of policy making. It requires detailed examination of the case study to see whether institutions influenced policy making in ways consistent with national institutional arguments. The study therefore considers whether actors created by institutional arrangements were important in policy making, how they used their institutional powers and positions, and whether institutionally created procedures and objectives were followed; this allows the role of institutions to be revealed, even if only as a transmission mechanism for other factors. In addition, it looks at whether institutions can be linked to the behaviour of policy-makers by examining how they encouraged, permitted, discouraged or prevented certain patterns of policy making; this is a stronger in terms of causation, as it indicates that institutions themselves influenced policy making.

Definitions of Key Terms and of the Scope of the Study

'Institutions' are defined as the formal (although not necessarily legal) rules governing decision making. They cover the formal structure of the sector but exclude behaviour. Thus 'institutions' as the potentially explanatory factor are separated from the features of 'policy' which constitute the potentially dependent variable or *explananda*; moreover, the concept is distinct from other uses of the term, notably those referring to patterns of behaviour, informal norms and cognitive templates.[101]

Certain national institutions are chosen for investigation. These consist of those relating to the telecommunications sector, such as ownership of suppliers, the establishment of sector-specific independent regulatory bodies and the formal powers of decision-makers. Thus the *explanans* of the study is explicitly defined.

In investigating the effects of institutions, the study examines 'policy making', which includes processes, instruments, objectives and substantive decisions, and, separately, 'economic outcomes'. Several reasons underlie the separation of the two: not all policy decisions are implemented: financial decisions are frequently made in nominal terms, whereas for economic

---

[101] See e.g. DiMaggio and Powell, 'Introduction'; March, and Olsen, *Rediscovering Institutions*.

performance, it is real values that are more telling; factors other than public policy may directly influence economic outcomes.

The Limits of the Study

The study concentrates on the impact of one factor, national institutions, on policy. Thus it does not seek to offer a complete explanation of the patterns of policy identified, a task that would require consideration of many factors. Hence, although other possible major influences on policy are set out (technological and economic developments, international regulation and ideas), and their effects on policy making can be seen in the discussion, they are not the focus of attention; instead, they are used to test the institutionalist argument that, despite a similar environment, national institutions affect policy.

The case study concerns one sector in two countries over a specified period, albeit a 'critical case' in an economically strategic industry. Certain national institutions have been selected for investigation, namely those relating to the telecommunications sector. Other general national institutions, such as electoral systems, the constitutional powers of the executive, legislature and judiciary or rules governing the representation of interests, are not examined.

A further limitation concerns the effects of national institutions on economic performance. Analysing the effects of institutions on the economic efficiency of nations, even if agreement could be reached on the definition of 'efficiency' and its measurement, would require knowledge of inputs and outputs. This is not possible in the present study, and is a task better suited to economists than political scientists. Instead, 'economic outcomes' are examined: these consist of quantitative indicators related to policy questions examined in the rest of the study. Furthermore, why certain economic outcomes were reached is not explained, and hence the links between national institutions, policies and economic outcomes are not considered: this would require econometric evidence and a market survey of suppliers, including private firms, looking at why they took certain decisions. Instead, economic outcomes are analysed solely to either falsify the contention that differing national institutions lead to dissimilar economic results, or to provide evidence that is consistent with that contention.

Conclusion: National Institutionalism as an Analytical Framework/Model

National institutionalism, as developed here, offers a set of empirically testable propositions. It incorporates an exogenous explanatory factor (national institutions) and *explananda* (the characteristics of national policy making and economic performance), together with causal mechanisms. It can be used for both static and dynamic analysis. Thus national institutionalism is a relatively well-developed analytical framework/model.

The framework raises deeper issues concerning the study of public policy. Important questions of structure and agency arise, notably over the extent to which national institutions constrain policy-makers and, conversely, the ability of the latter to modify the institutional framework within which they operate. Moreover, the selection of formal institutions for investigation in the study could lead to discussion of the role of law and formal organizational arrangements. National divergence and convergence can offer implications for the degree of internationalization or 'globalization'.

However, these broader themes are largely beyond the scope of the present study: before adding to the claims and scope of national institutionalism, it is important to apply it and test the fundamental arguments at its core. The task of the present study is therefore limited but essential, namely to use the case study to scrutinise empirically the role of national institutions in countries' public policy.

PART I

The British and French Telecommunications Sector in 1969 and External Pressures For Change

2

The Roots of History: Telecommunications in Britain and France before 1969

National institutionalist analyses suggest that the institutions and policies of countries have deep historical roots that constrain and influence paths of development. Study of telecommunications after 1969 therefore requires an understanding of the earlier history of the sector.

Examination of British and French telecommunications from the inception of the industry in the late nineteenth century until 1969 reveals three central features that are valuable for the later analysis. First, and most important for the design of the research, by the 1960s there were many similarities in telecommunications between the two countries. The institutional framework of the sector was strongly marked by common features, providing an equivalent institutional starting point for the two countries, an argument detailed in Chapter 4. In addition, the major actors in decision-making and several aspects of policy debates were similar. The features of telecommunications policy in Britain and France were often long-standing. Thus the choice of 1969 as a starting date for analysis of the period 1969–97 is not that of a fortuitous meeting of two divergent national trajectories. Rather, by the late 1960s, there was a combination of features that had existed for considerable periods of time and the emergence of newer similarities in the two countries. 1969 therefore provides a similar starting point for Britain and France, most clearly in terms of their institutional frameworks, but also, to a lesser extent, that of their policy histories.

The existence of well-established sectoral agendas and patterns of decision making that appeared linked to the institutional framework in the sector constitutes a second important theme of analysis. Decisions central to the sector, such as investment, growth and relations between publicly-owned network operators and privately-owned equipment manufacturers, were marked by the organization of the sector and long-standing mechanisms whereby institutions influenced policy are identifiable. Analysis of policy making over several decades is not only used to offer evidence for the importance of national institutions but also to indicate that policy changes after 1969 broke with persistent patterns of behaviour, thereby underlining their significance.

The third theme of the chapter is institutional reform. In both countries, the institutional framework of telecommunications enjoyed long periods of stability despite the existence of persistent problems in the sector and criticisms of policies and performance. Several discussions of proposed changes took place, especially in Britain, but reform was very difficult. It took place after other alternatives had failed and broad support for reforms had been garnered. Even then, modifications were often limited and implemented only under a constellation of favourable conditions, notably the presence of a strong and determined government. Hence there is support for institutionalist assertions that the organizational arrangements of nations are difficult to alter and do not respond rapidly and easily to socio-economic pressures, even if they result in considerable problems. Moreover, the length and persistence of institutional arrangements are essential in understanding the difficulties of attempts to modify institutions after 1969, the weight of the inherited historical legacy faced by policy-makers and the significance of the reforms that were introduced.

Britain

The Post Office and the Supply of Telephone Services

Far from being a period of economic liberalism, in telecommunications the period before 1914 saw the establishment of a public monopoly over telecommunications. The Post Office, a government department created in 1840 and headed by a minister, the Postmaster General, bought up private telegraph operators under the Telegraph Act of 1868.[1] The Telegraph Act 1869 gave the Post Office a monopoly over telegraph services. It defined 'telegraph' to mean 'any apparatus for transmitting messages and other communications by means of electric signals'.[2] When private telephone systems appeared after 1877, the Post Office asserted its monopoly over the new service, a position upheld in a High Court judgement of 1880.

The Post Office then licensed several suppliers and the period between 1880 and 1912 saw a mixture of public and private provision of telephone services and networks. The Post Office's network expanded through purchases, using options in licences granted to private companies and statutory powers. In particular, the Post Office bought the National Telephone Company's trunk network in 1896 and its remaining local networks in 1911. It thus took more than thirty years for the Post Office to transform its legal monopoly over telephone services into a *de facto* one.[3] A key constraint on Post Office expansion

---

[1] H. Robinson, *The British Post Office: A History* (Princeton: Princeton University Press, 1948), 406–9.

[2] D. Pitt, *The Telecommunications Function in the Post Office in the Post Office: A Case Study in Bureaucratic Adaption* (Hampshire: Saxon House, 1980), 27.

[3] The exception was Kingston upon Hull, where a municipal network remained.

was the Treasury: as a government department, the Post Office's spending and revenue formed part of the general budget and Estimates and were subject to general Treasury controls over the civil service. The Treasury frequently sided with 'restrictionists', sceptical of the need for increased public expenditure to expand the telephone service.[4]

On achieving a virtually complete monopoly over telephony in 1912, the Post Office faced inherited problems. Investment in the telephone service had been limited and in 1913 there were 1.6 telephone sets per 100 inhabitants in the UK compared with 9 per 100 in the United States.[5] Several different networks had to be integrated, whilst the emergence of new types of equipment offered both much greater reliability and also lower costs, but called for higher capital expenditure.[6] Yet the interwar period saw only modest Post Office investment. As a result, expansion of the network was far from rapid.[7] Modernization of the Post Office's network was also limited, as new technologies, particularly automated switching and new forms of cable, were introduced tardily. The United Kingdom had a lower telephone density than other countries: in 1938, there were 6.4 telephone sets per 100 population, compared with 15.1 in the United States.[8] Similarly, less use was made of the most modern equipment in the Post Office's network than elsewhere.[9]

The Post Office's institutional position as a government department was important in its problems, especially restrictions on its investment and growth.[10] The head of the Post Office was a minister, yet Postmasters General changed frequently and were rarely senior influential ministers. This was particularly important in struggles over public expenditure, as policy-makers, especially within the Treasury, held 'restrictionist' attitudes towards expansion. Policies of balanced budgets and public-spending reductions affected the Post Office whose expenditure formed part of the government's budget, and also meant that investment had to be financed from operating revenue rather than long-term borrowing, itself leading to high prices. Furthermore, as a central government department, the Post Office's budget fell within the annual

---

[4] See Pitt, *The Telecommunications Function in the Post Office*.

[5] B. Aurelle, *Les Télécommunications* (Paris: La Découverte, 1986), 33, derived from International Telecommunications Union figures.

[6] In particular, new mechanical 'semi-automated' exchanges could replace manually-operated exchanges, whilst in transmission, signals repeaters and multiplexing reduced signal attentuation and increased cable capacities—see J. H. Robertson, *The Story of the Telephone* (London: Isaac Pitman, 1947), 138 and Aurelle, *Les Télécommunications*, 42–3.

[7] For figures, see Viscount Wolmer, *Post Office Reform: Its Importance and Practicability* (London: Nicholson and Watson, 1932), 112–13.

[8] Aurelle, *Les Télécommunications*, 33; for a host of different indicators, including by revenue, see Wolmer, *Post Office Reform*, 116–29.

[9] In 1938, 55 per cent of exchanges were automated in the United Kingdom, as against 88 per cent in Germany (Aurelle, *Les Télécommunications*, 35).

[10] Pitt, *The Telecommunications Function in the Post Office*, 45–69.

Estimates, subject to Treasury control and parliamentary approval, making longer-term planning difficult. Any surplus revenue had to be repaid to the Treasury, and could not be put aside by the Post Office for future investment, a situation that lasted for most of the inter-war period, despite the nominal creation of a Post Office 'fund' in the mid-1930s.

The internal functioning of the Post Office was also marked by problems. There were frictions between the postal and telecommunications sides of the Post Office, with the former being larger and enjoying greater prestige and priority. The system of separate civil service classes led to administrative generalists holding a monopoly over the most senior posts. They had often held positions dealing with postal services, and lacked knowledge and ambitions concerning telephone services, whilst telephone engineers had few prospects of reaching the upper echelons of the Post Office.[11] Cumbersome civil service procedures applied to the telephone service and, locally, postal officials held powers over the development of the telephone.[12] In response, internal reforms were introduced in the 1930s: a Post Office Board was created, postal and telephone services were further separated and attempts were made to devolve power downwards, notably to new regions. Nevertheless, the Post Office remained a government department.

The period after 1945 saw attempts to end the problems of inadequate public funding, as demand for telephony rose rapidly and improved network equipment had become available, notably for exchanges (the new Crossbar exchange).[13] In the 1950s, investment plans offering stable growth were announced, together with greater freedom from Treasury control, and then plans for the replacement of remaining operator connections with automatic dialling for all trunk calls.[14] In the 1960s, attempts were made to increase investment, which had fallen in real terms between 1957 and 1961.[15] Under the 1961 Post Office Act, the Post Office was allowed to borrow up to £80m. per annum. In 1963, a White Paper promised a 'massive increase in capital investment' in order to increase the number of telephones, reduce waiting lists, and end manually-operated exchanges.[16] Ambitious targets

[11] Robertson, *The Story of the Telephone*, 92–3.

[12] Pitt, *The Telecommunications Function in the Post Office*, 56–61 and for reforms discussed and partially implemented in the 1930s, 70–101.

[13] See Pitt, *The Telecommunications Function in the Post Office*, 100–36; J. Hills, *Deregulating Telecoms: Competition and Control in the United States, Japan and Britain* (London: Pinter, 1986), 85–8, and *Information Technology and Industrial Policy* (London and Canberra: Croom Helm, 1984), 112–13; in particular, the Crossbar systems offered greater switching capacity and improved reliability.

[14] Pitt, *The Telecommunications Function in the Post Office*, 109–10; F. Bealey, *The Post Office Engineering Union* (London: Bachman and Turner, 1976), 263–4.

[15] See Pitt, *The Telecommunications Function in the Post Office*, 137–49; Bealey, *The Post Office Engineering Union*, 333–4 and 369–70.

[16] *The Inland Telephone Service in an Expanding Economy*, Cmnd. 2211 (London: HMSO, 1963).

for telecommunications were set in the National Plan of 1965: numbers of telephones and telephone traffic were to increase, producing an increase in telecommunications output of 10.9 per cent per annum in the period until 1970.

Considerable increases in the number of telephones did take place after 1945, especially in the 1960s: manual switching was virtually ended, notably in the trunk network, and improved transmission methods were introduced. Nevertheless, the high hopes expressed were not matched by reality. Long waiting lists existed throughout the 1950s and indeed the 1960s.[17] The network suffered from aged equipment offering low-quality service and high maintenance costs; in particular, modernization of switching was limited, as the Strowger switches used in the network became increasingly outdated. Prices were increased, notably for connections in the 1960s, in order to meet an 8 per cent rate of return of capital, repay an £800m. 'loan' to the Treasury and produce revenue for investment.[18] High prices restrained demand, but meant that for trunk services, tariffs greatly exceeded costs.[19]

Investment problems arose as the Post Office's capital expenditure was frequently restricted and modified to meet fiscal targets as part of 'stop-go' macroeconomic policies. Moreover, to restrict government borrowing, investment was mostly financed from current income, a position worsened by the suspension of the Post Office fund from 1939 until the late 1950s, so that Post Office surpluses continued to accrue to the Treasury.[20] During the 1950s, telecommunications engineers continued to complain of their low status and influence, although in the 1960s, a spirit of 'managerialism' was encouraged and at the highest levels of the Post Office, a limited separation of telecommunications and postal services occurred with separate Deputy Directors General.[21]

In the late 1960s, relative to many other industrialized countries, Britain still had a lower telephone density and a backward network with aged switches, resulting in low quality and few advanced services.[22] Obtaining a telephone line was subject to delays, sometimes lengthy ones; in 1970, 100,000 people were on the waiting list.

[17] For instance, in 1950, there was a waiting list of 552,000 and in 1960, the figure was 144,000—see M. Canes, *Telephones—Public or Private?* (London: IEA, 1966) 25, and Post Office, *British Telecommunications Statistics* (London: Post Office, annual).

[18] Bealey, *The Post Office Engineering Union*, 333.

[19] Perhaps by as much as 80 per cent—W. G. Shepherd, 'Alternatives for Public Expenditure', in R. E. Caves (ed.), *Britain's Economic Prospects* (Washington and London: Brookings Institute and Allen and Unwin, 1968), 401.

[20] The re-establishment of the fund was announced in 1955 but not implemented due to public expenditure restrictions.

[21] Pitt, *The Telecommunications Function in the Post Office*, 137–44 and 150–1.

[22] Shepherd, 'Alternatives for Public Expenditure', 399–403, and Canes, *Telephones—Public or Private?*

Relations between the Post Office and Equipment Manufacturers

The Post Office did not manufacture equipment for its networks but relied on private suppliers. Initially, most equipment was imported, but British-based manufacturers were rapidly established.[23] Their development was aided by a government decision in the early 1900s that Post Office orders should go to British manufacturers.[24]

The interwar years saw the formalization of relations between the Post Office and manufacturers, who became a tightly-knit, closed group. From 1923, the Post Office brought together its manufacturers of automatic switching equipment and agreed the allocation of orders amongst them, together with prices common to all its suppliers.[25] In 1928, the Bulk Contracts Committee was established with representatives of the Post Office and manufacturers. It decided policy, prices, the distribution of contracts, and technical specifications for exchanges. Similar arrangements were extended in 1936 to other forms of equipment.[26] At the same time, a policy of standardization of equipment was pursued. To this end, patent pooling amongst suppliers was introduced from the 1920s.[27] Technical developments were guided jointly by Post Office engineers and the equipment manufacturers, symbolized by both forming the British Telephone Technical Development Committee.[28] Exports were encouraged by Post Office orders and the development of British models.

Almost all Post Office orders went to British-based companies, notably General Electric Company (GEC), Standard Telephones and Cables (STC), Associated Electrical Industries (AEI), Automatic Telephone Engineering, and Ericsson Telephones.[29] By 1937, 98 per cent of Post Office equipment was manufactured in the UK, whilst exports of telephone apparatus and cables was worth over £3m.[30] Nevertheless, there were criticisms: costs of equipment and installation were argued to be considerably higher than in other countries[31] and it was claimed that 'the Ring' of manufacturers used their position within the patent pools to charge excessive prices.[32]

Criticisms increased after 1945, as the 'Ring' firms were accused of maintaining inflated prices, enjoying excessive profits, benefiting from Post Office funded research but not producing rapid technological advances, passing on lower costs engendered or achieving export success.[33] Difficulties were com-

---

[23] For details, see Robertson, *The Story of the Telephone*, 93–113.
[24] Ibid. 95.   [25] Ibid. 175–6 and 278.   [26] Ibid. 175.   [27] Ibid. 161–2 and 278.
[28] Ibid. 176.   [29] Hills, *Information Technology and Industrial Policy*, 124.
[30] Robertson, *The Story of the Telephone*, 277–8.
[31] Cf. Wolmer, *Post Office Reform*, 131–47.
[32] Questions and criticisms were raised in Parliament, notably by the Public Accounts Committee—cf. Robertson, *The Story of the Telephone*, 278–81.
[33] Pitt, *The Telecommunications Function in the Post Office*, 146–8; Hills, *Information Technology and Industrial Policy*, 124–8; Bealey, *The Post Office Engineering Union*, 372–3. For critiques, see

pounded by the failure of an attempt to develop a fully (digital) exchange in the mid-1950s undertaken by the Post Office in close collaboration with the manufacturers.[34] To make matters worse, in the mid-1960s, there were also problems of bottlenecks, especially in the supply of exchanges.

Blame for many of the problems was pinned on the cartel supply arrangements around the 'Ring' companies, cost-based pricing, and the bulk supply agreements. Therefore the various bulk-supply agreements covering different forms of equipment were ended; the last, for network exchanges, was terminated in 1968. Instead, competitive tendering was to be used for Post Office orders.

Institutional Reform

The performance of the Post Office was subject to attacks throughout the interwar period for inadequate levels of investment, unsatisfied demand, a 'restrictionist attitude' towards potential usage and internal inefficiencies. Critics pressed for institutional reforms. Modification of the Post Office's status as a government department was argued to be essential for a 'commercial' service such as telephony and to offer an escape from over-detailed bureaucratic Treasury control; a move to 'public corpoaration' status, as established for the Central Electricity Generating Board or BBC was generally mooted. New financial rules were also urged, notably to end the Treasury taking any Post Office financial surplus.

Critics were varied, but included individual MPs, the Liberal Party in the late 1920s (arguing for higher public spending), former ministers,[35] Post Office officials, and businessmen, especially Post Office suppliers, who in 1924 set up the Telephone Development Committee which argued for higher investment and reforms during the late 1920s and in the 1930s.[36] An important committee, the Bridgeman Committee of Inquiry, was established by the Postmaster General in 1932.[37]

Despite the considerable pressures for change, only limited institutional reforms were undertaken. The main modification was the creation of a financial regime specific to the Post Office after the 1932 Bridgeman Report; in

Shepherd, 'Alternatives for Public Expenditure', 403–5; Canes, Telephones—Public or Private?, 36–9; B. Maddox, Beyond Babel (London: Andre Deutsch, 1972), 218–24; Post Office Engineering Union, The Telephone Ring: It's Time to Investigate (London: POEU, 1962).

[34] The 'Highgate Wood disaster'—Hills, Information Technology and Industrial Policy, 130–5.

[35] Cf. Viscount Woolmer, former Assistant Postmaster General, notably in his book, Post Office Reform, and also Clement Attlee, Postmaster General in 1931; Pitt, The Telecommunications Function in the Post Office, 44–69; Bealey, The Post Office Engineering Union, 170–1 and 194–5; Robertson, The Story of the Telephone, 229–70.

[36] See Robertson, The Story of the Telephone, 192–9.

[37] Report of the Committee of Inquiry on the Post Office, Cmnd. 4149, 1932; for a discussion, see Pitt, The Telecommunications Function in the Post Office, 75–83.

particular, a fixed annual sum payable to the Treasury was set, so that any further surplus could be paid into a Post Office fund for future use. However, wider reforms met strong opposition. Trade unions representing postal workers feared any move that might weaken the postal side of the Post Office or remove it from the civil service, whilst the Treasury wished to keep controls over the Post Office. Ministers and the Bridgeman Committee report trod a middle path that was acceptable to opponents of reform, focusing on internal organizational reforms that were less contentious than the institutional position of the Post Office.[38]

After 1945, continued problems with the telephone service led to debate over greater separation of postal and telephone services within the Post Office and the weak position of telephone engineers. Few institutional changes were introduced in the 1950s: policy-makers emphasized non-institutional changes and the Post Office Engineering Union (POEU) concentrated on wage issues.[39] Nevertheless, as dissatisfaction with the telephone service continued in the late 1950s, Conservative politicians argued that the Post Office needed greater freedom from 'excessive' Treasury control and a regime appropriate to its position as a 'business'.[40] The POEU pressed for greater separation between postal and telecommunications services as well as greater autonomy and higher investment. In response, the Post Office Act 1961 was passed. It allowed the Post Office to borrow capital of £80m. per annum and revived the Post Office Trading Fund, outside Treasury control, so that annual surpluses could be used for future investment. The main financial requirement was that the Post Office should break even 'taking one year with another'. Treasury powers would be reduced, giving much greater freedom for operational decisions, whilst the annual appropriation accounts were replaced with a form of commercial accounts.

The 1961 Act made the Post Office a hybrid between a department and a public corporation. Yet more significant changes were rejected. Two possible reforms—a move to full public corporation status and the separation of telecommunications and postal services—were rejected: parliamentary control was held necessary to preserve the public's influence, whilst postal workers and the Labour Party opposed both changes. Moreover, a form of Treasury levy continued, as the Post Office was to repay £800m. on accrued liabilities over 25 years. In addition, the target rate of return on assets was fixed at 8 per cent whilst total investment levels remained within public expenditure totals and Treasury control. Overall, the 1961 Act was modest, and continuing

---

[38]   See Pitt, *The Telecommunications Function in the Post Office*, 71–99.

[39]   For instance, a report by the Estimates Committee in 1950 ('The Lunley report') argued for attitudinal and procedural changes, rather than organizational ones—Pitt, *The Telecommunications Function in the Post Office*, 112–14.

[40]   A view expressed in the Conservative Party's 1959 general election manifesto and by Ernest Marples, Postmaster General in 1957.

problems with telecommunications and a new atmosphere in the later 1960s led renewed pressures for institutional change, resulting in the Post Office Act 1969.[41]

France[42]

The PTT Ministry and the Supply of Telephone Services

From their earliest days, telecommunications services fell under a state monopoly: the law of 2 May 1837 stated that 'anyone who transmits, without authorization, signals from one place to another, either thanks to telegraph equipment or by any other means, will be punished'. In 1879, the government made it clear that the new telephone service fell within its monopoly. It created a Posts and Telegraph Ministry in 1879 in the form of a civil service 'administration' of post and telegraph services.[43] Although private operators were licensed for a short period, the licences were not renewed in 1889. The Post and Telegraph Ministry took over the private networks and telephony became a publicly-supplied monopoly service.

The development of the telephone service before the First World War was very slow. Thus, for instance, there were only 0.8 telephones per 100 inhabitants in 1913, less than one-tenth the level in the United States.[44] All switching was done manually until 1913. Levels of investment were very low, and indeed, zero in some years.[45]

The institutional framework played an important role in blocking expansion.[46] The general rules of the civil service applied to the supply of telephony. Both revenue and spending formed part of the annual budget, approved by Parliament. All receipts were paid to the Finance Ministry, which also controlled expenditure. In practice, between 1880 and 1914, the postal, telegraph, and telephone service made significant profits that were very useful for the general

---

[41] Discussed in Ch. 5.

[42] For studies, see: L.-J. Libois, *Genèse et croissance des télécommunications* (Paris: Masson and CNET-ENST, 1983), chs. 12–17; C. Bertho (ed.), *L'État et les télécommunications en France et à l'étranger 1837–1987* (Geneva: Droz, 1991), and *Télégraphes et téléphones: de Valmy au microprocesseur* (Paris: Livre de Poche, 1981); Aurelle, *Les Télécommunications*.

[43] It has generally been known as the PTT Ministry, but its formal name has varied: in 1925, it became the Ministère de Postes, Télégraphes, et Téléphones; in 1959, this became Postes et Télécommunications; in 1980, this was modified to Postes et Telecommunications et Télédiffusion; then in 1988, it became Postes, Télécommunications et de l'Espace; here, it is referred to under its abbreviated name, 'PTT Ministry'.

[44] Aurelle, *Les Télécommunications*, 33.

[45] Aurelle, *Les Télécommunications*, 27; Libois, *Genèse et croissance des télécommunications*, 71–2.

[46] P. Musso, 'Les Débats autour du vote de la loi de 1923', in Bertho, *L'État et les télécommunications*, 65–6; Aurelle, *Les Télécommunications*, 27–8.

budget; on the other hand, the Finance Ministry resisted higher capital spending which increased general budgetary totals. The PTT Ministry was usually attached to other ministries, such as Finance, and after the 1890s, Commerce and/or Industry, and its head was often merely a junior minister, unable to overcome the views of the powerful Finance Ministry.[47]

The PTT Ministry consisted of one *administration* which covered telegraph, telephone, and postal services. Postal services were much larger and better-established than telephone services, thereby enjoying priority within the PTT Ministry. In addition, many telephone network functions were undertaken by staff who also had postal responsibilities, especially in the countryside.[48] Finally, in the French administrative tradition, a specific higher education institution, the École supérieure de télégraphie, was made responsible for selecting and training *ingénieurs*, who then held senior positions; a Corps des ingénieurs des Postes et Télégraphes was created in 1902. However, numbers of ingénieurs were limited and the new *corps* was much less prestigious and powerful than the older *grands corps*.

After the First World War, the French network was still small, backward and incoherent, consisting of local networks that used different types of equipment and were poorly linked by an even more underdeveloped trunk network. In response, the government put forward in 1921 a 'catching up plan' (*plan de redressement*). It involved large-scale investment by the PTT Ministry over several years, particularly in the trunk network, and the development of networks in the countryside through local authority investment.[49] It led to expansion of the network and the introduction of newer automatic switching and transmission technologies. However, reductions in investment in the 1930s and the continued use of manual switching in the countryside limited expansion and modernization. In 1938, there were only 3.7 telephones per 100 inhabitants, whilst in 1939, 54 per cent of switches were still manually operated.[50] The telephone service continued to suffer from its lack of political weight and from being overshadowed by postal services.

The 1940s saw considerable internal reform of the PTT Ministry, giving its telecommunications side greater autonomy. In 1941, the Ministry was divided into several *directions*, including one for telecommunications. In 1946, the latter became La Direction générale des télécommunications (DGT), headed by a *directeur général*; only one official within the Ministry, the *secrétaire général*, stood above him. The DGT was responsible for running the telephone and telegraph

[47]   Libois, *Genèse et croissance des télécommunications*, 196.
[48]   For details of the internal organization of the PTT Ministry, see Libois, *Genèse et croissance des télécommunications*, 119–201 and 213–21.
[49]   Libois, *Genèse et croissance des télécommunications*, 75–8.
[50]   Aurelle, *Les Télécommunications*, 33 and 35, based on ITU figures.

networks. Moreover, at the local level, the regional telecommunications units were developed and their heads (*ingénieurs des télécommunications*) were given greater powers, notably over expenditure.[51] On the research side, the Centre nationale d'études des télécommunications (CNET) was created in 1944; it became a powerful instrument not only of research, but also of policy. Finally, the Corps des ingénieurs des télécommunications became an inter-ministerial corps in 1951, increasing its prestige and the range of posts open to its members.

Nevertheless, telecommunications were not essential to industrial development in post-war France, as seen in the planning process, which determined indicative levels of investment. They were not designated as a priority sector in the first 'Plan' of 1946, although the difficulties of the sector were recognised through the creation of a Telecommunications Modernization Commission and its official report in 1947.[52] In the second to fourth Plans (1954–65), only modest investment was allocated to telecommunications. The Commissariat du Plan believed that public opinion regarded telecommunications as less important than other sectors. Capital expenditure was financed from current revenue, requiring high tariffs, whilst PTT ministers and the telecommunications *ingénieurs* did not have the weight to achieve higher investment. Instead of domestically-financed investment, NATO was used as a source of funds for the telecommunications network. The weak position of telecommunications continued in the 1960s, especially as President de Gaulle personally disliked the telephone. Only in the fifth Plan (1966–70) was greater priority given to telecommunications investment, but even then, in large measure thanks to a supplement negotiated in the late 1960s by a determined and more influential PTT Minister, Yves Guéna, against a backdrop of increasing public discontent with the telephone network.

Hence the period between 1945 and the mid-1960s was one of only slow development for telecommunications in France. Growth in the number of telephones was sluggish, and in 1960 there were only 9.1 telephones per 100 population, compared with 39.5 in the United States.[53] Obtaining a telephone line involved long delays. Modernization took place, notably in transmission and the introduction of Crossbar exchanges,[54] but manual switching remained widespread, so that in 1961, 61 per cent of switches were automatic, whereas the percentage was 96 per cent in the United States. As demand rose, especially in the 1960s, so waiting lists grew. By the mid-1960s, telecommunications in France were backward relative to many other industrialized countries.

---

[51] Libois, *Genèse et croissance des télécommunications*, 214–16.
[52] Ibid. 252–4.   [53] Aurelle, *Les Télécommunications*, 33.
[54] See Libois, *Genèse et croissance des télécommunications*, 96–138.

Relations between Network Operation and Equipment Manufacturers

The manufacturing of equipment was undertaken by privately-owned companies. Although French-based firms were created in the late nineteenth century, they were mostly subsidiaries of foreign firms or manufactured under licence from foreign firms.[55]

After 1918, the position of foreign firms in France was strengthened.[56] ITT became the dominant supplier, as it bought several manufacturers and its switching equipment, produced by its French subsidiaries, was chosen for network modernization. The main rival in France to ITT was the Swedish firm Ericsson, through its subsidiary SFT-Ericsson. Attempts to expand by French firms, in particular, the Compagnie générale de l'électricité (CGE) group, largely failed. Nevertheless, the Posts and Telegraph Ministry used its orders to develop a manufacturing base in France and to prevent over-reliance on one supplier; thus in placing its orders for rotary switches in 1926 with LMT, a subsidiary of ITT, it insisted that LMT manufacture all equipment in France and share its patents with other suppliers.

Relations between the DGT and its suppliers were institutionalized after the Second World War. Mixed public–private companies comprising the DGT and its suppliers, were established: Sotélec (La Société mixte pour le développement de la technique des télécommunications par câbles) in 1946 for cables and Socotel (La Société mixte pour le développement de la commutation dans le domaine des télécommunications) in 1958 for switching equipment.[57] The division of market shares amongst suppliers and the setting of prices and share of certain patents were undertaken within Sotélec and Socotel. The CNET took a central role on the DGT side. It verified suppliers' costs, on which equipment prices paid by the DGT were based. It also moved to control the direction of research, especially in switching, and to link DGT orders to the structure of the subsector. It therefore became a key element in the public industrial strategy for the manufacturing subsector, a strategy that involved research, administered division of orders and the encouragement of powerful French manufacturers, with the hope of exports.

A series of attempts to strengthen French-owned manufacturers were made in the 1950s and 1960s.[58] In the mid-1950s, the DGT chose new, more sophisticated exchanges (Crossbar exchanges) that were designed by Ericsson and ITT and entirely manufactured by their French subsidiaries, SFT-Ericsson, and LMT and CGCT. Ericsson was obliged to share its patents with French firms, including CIT (formerly SIT), which had been taken over by the powerful French

---

[55] For a summary of the position of the manufacturing firms, see Aurelle, *Les Télécommunications*, 48–53.

[56] Ibid. 51–5.

[57] For histories, see H. Docquiert, *SOCOTEL: Expérience de coopération État-Industrie* (Paris: Socotel, 1987).   [58] See Aurelle, *Les Télécommunications*, 55–7.

conglomerate, CGE. Perhaps the most important element was that the CNET established teams to develop digital exchanges, working in co-operation with CIT.[59] The CNET's research into the switching technology of the future was an investment for future industrial policy.[60]

Institutional Reform

Discussion of modifications of the PTT Ministry's institutional position began before 1914, as the failure to invest held back development of the telephone. The main proposal was that the Ministry should have its own budget, a *budget annexe*, separate from the general one. Nevertheless, no reforms were implemented: it was argued that the legal doctrine of *service public* required one budget; the Finance Ministry opposed changes, especially as it enjoyed the large surpluses made by the postal and telephone services.

After 1914, pressures for reform grew, because of the failure to invest in the telephone network, changes in the climate of opinion as to the administrative and financial structures compatible with *service public* and, perhaps most important, losses made by the PTT Ministry after 1915, which represented costs for the general budget.[61] There was wide agreement in Parliament that the financial rules governing the PTT Ministry needed modification. On the organizational position of the Ministry, opinions were divided. One set of proposals envisaged increased autonomy for the post, telegraph, and telephone services through the establishment of a Post and Telegraph Office with its own legal personality, ability to issue bonds and other elements of financial independence; the separation of telephone services and even the licensing of private operators were mooted. It was argued that the postal and telecommunications services were industrial in character, and hence structures akin to those of a firm were needed. On the other hand, trade unionists on the left, pressed for 'nationalization', involving power for workers rather than control by 'the State'.

The reforms of the law of 30 June 1923 (forming part of the Finance Law) represented a middle path. A *budget annexe* was established for postal, telegraph, and telephone services in the PTT Ministry. The *budget annexe* was divided into two sections: operating income and expenditure; capital spending. It allowed the Ministry to keep surplus revenues and to create reserves for investment. Moreover, the law permitted the Finance Ministry to issue bonds repayable over up to thirty years, to raise funds for capital spending. In addition, a consultative council of senior officials, elected representatives of the personnel and

[59] Libois, *Genèse et croissance des télécommunications*, 158–66.
[60] See Ch. 6 for events in the 1970s.
[61] Musso, 'Les Débats autour du vote de la loi de 1923'.

representatives of interests (such as chambers of commerce and local authorities) was created to assist the Minister.

Whilst significant, the reforms maintained parliamentary control. The postal, telegraph, and telephone services continued to be supplied by the Ministry, and hence remained part of the civil service (*administration*). The *budget annexe* was appended to the general budget, required parliamentary approval, and followed all the procedures of the general budget. The Minister remained head of the services, responsible to Parliament for decisions. The consultative council played little role in decision making.[62]

Thereafter, until the 1960s, attention was focused on internal organizational developments rather than institutional reform. However, in the mid-1960s, criticisms of the state of the telephone network led to renewed discussion of the DGT's organization position. In particular, from 1967, Valéry Giscard d'Estaing called for the establishment of a form of public corporation (an établissement public de caractère industriel et commercial) for telecommunications, separated from postal services, with its own legal personality and financial autonomy, lying outside the civil service. His views represented the beginning of pressures for change that emerged at the very end of the 1960s and in the early 1970s.

Conclusion

By the 1960s, many features of telecommunications were similar in Britain and France in terms of institutional frameworks, the supply of telephone services, relations between the network operator and the equipment manufacturing subsector, and discussions of institutional reform. Moreover, many of the similarities were long-standing.

The institutional framework of telecommunications in Britain and France saw public monopolies over services based on law asserted from a very early stage in the development of telephony. After brief periods of private provision, telephone services were supplied by a government department—the Post Office in Britain and the DGT within the PTT Ministry in France. The departments also provided postal services in both countries. The telephone operators were part of the civil service and were headed by ministers (the Postmaster General and the PTT Minister). Many of the rules and procedures of the general civil services applied to them, including personnel structures, internal decision-making processes and parliamentary approval of their budgets. Nevertheless, during the course of the century, important exemptions were made; in particular, financial arrangements were introduced that allowed receipts to be channelled directly to expenditure and to permit limited

---

[62]   Libois, *Genèse et croissance des télécommunications*, 237.

borrowing, seen most clearly in the Post Office Trading Fund, the provisions of the Post Office Act 1961 and the *budget annexe* in France.

By the late 1960s, Britain and France were experiencing considerable difficulties in their telecommunications sectors, problems that had persisted over considerable periods of time. Although the telephone networks in the two countries had expanded, they remained considerably smaller than in other industrialized countries. Similarly, whilst their networks had been modernized, the latest technology was not being rapidly introduced (notably in switching). Although slower development was more evident in France than in Britain, both the Post Office and the DGT lagged behind operators in countries such as the United States and Germany. Investment levels were constrained and a high proportion of capital expenditure was financed from current revenue. Tariffs were often high; even so, demand frequently outstripped supply, leading to long waiting lists. Within the Post Office and PTT Ministry, the postal side enjoyed greater prestige and priority than the telephone service.

In the manufacturing subsector, the telephone operators and their suppliers formed a small, tightly-knit group. Their relations with each other were close and became institutionalized, through the Bulk Supply Agreements and joint research and development organizations in Britain, and Socotel and Sotélec in France. Equipment orders and prices were fixed administratively, patents were shared amongst manufacturers and new equipment was developed jointly by suppliers and the network operators. In both countries, there were industrial policy ambitions of creating a strong national subsector and encouraging exports. Nevertheless, these were far from being realized, as equipment manufacturers were criticized in Britain for their performance, whilst in France suppliers were mostly foreign owned and dependent on imported technology.

The difficulties faced by the Post Office and the DGT were linked to their institutional position. Financial constraints played a central role in backwardness: total investment levels were constrained, due to limits on public expenditure and borrowing, the use of the Post Office/DGT for broader macro-economic policy and opposition to higher spending by the Treasury in Britain and the Finance Ministry in France. High tariffs followed from excess demand and decisions to finance investment from current revenue rather than borrowing. The network operators were dependent on the political weight of the Postmaster General and PTT Minister, who generally were junior politicians, especially compared with financial ministers. In addition, the postal service dominated the Post Office and PTT Ministry, impeding, it was argued, the development of telephony. The application of civil service rules to provision of telephony also appeared to obstruct supply.

Institutional reforms were therefore the subject of debate on several occasions in each country. In both Britain and France, moving the Post Office and DGT out of government departments and hence the central civil service, by giving them institutional autonomy was discussed, together with the separation of telecommunications and postal services. Yet reforms were limited and slow. They mostly concerned the internal organization of the Post Office and PTT Ministry and financial rules relating to income and borrowing. Wider changes were blocked by opposition by postal workers and their unions, and also by the belief in the virtues of parliamentary control of the Post Office and DGT. Thus by the 1960s, persistent difficulties in telephony had not led to comprehensive institutional reform, and the basic structure of a monopoly civil service supplier of postal and telephone services established in the late nineteenth century remained intact.

3

Technological and Economic Pressures for Change in Telecommunications from the 1960s to the 1990s

Far-reaching and indeed remarkable transnational technological and economic developments transformed telecommunications from the 1960s onwards. The application of new technologies, especially microelectronic and computing, altered the telecommunications services and equipment that could be supplied, together with costs, investment, competition, demand and sectoral boundaries. The choices available to actors—whether as public policy-makers, suppliers, or users—were profoundly restructured. Indeed, the very participants in the sector evolved.

Technological and economic developments therefore offered powerful forces for change, in the form of pressures and opportunities. They challenged the traditional British and French telecommunications institutions and policies that existed in the 1960s. Moreover, such developments were transnational and largely outside the control of policy-makers and other actors in Britain and France; hence they were common and exogenous to both countries.

Consideration of technological and economic developments is essential for analysis of policy making in Britain and France, since there developments greatly altered the nature of the industry. However, this study uses such developments as part of its research design. Since they were common and exogenous, they provide a method of assessing the ability of nations to maintain stable and/or different sectoral institutions in the face of powerful forces for change and the effects of national institutions on policy in the face of powerful supranational forces.

After summarizing the technology of telecommunications in the 1960s, the chapter therefore briefly sets out the major technological and economic developments in three different areas of telecommunications and examines their policy implications. The treatment of the developments is schematic, since the purpose is not to explain how and why they took place but instead to draw out their implications for policy in Britain and France. Moreover, attention is selective, being concentrated on the developments most relevant for the policy issues that arose in Britain and France from the 1970s to the mid-1990s. The chapter then offers evidence that, at least over the period from the mid-1960s to the mid-1990s, technological developments were largely exogenous to policy-makers in Britain and France, and hence also common to them. Finally, it points to the ways in which the technological and economic developments challenged traditional telecommunications institutions and policies in Britain and France given the position at the end of the 1960s in the two countries (ch. 2), and underlines their major repercussions for policy.

Telecommunications in the 1960s

In the mid-1960s, the telecommunications industry had clearly-defined boundaries delimiting it from other sectors. Moreover, it contained three activities that constituted interrelated but distinct subsectors: network operation; the manufacture and supply of public switching and transmission equipment for the public switched telephone network (PSTN); the supply of customer premises equipment (CPE—also known as terminal equipment) and a very few advanced services.

Network operation dominated the telecommunications sector. Its core consisted of transmitting signals on the PSTN for voice telephony. It was structured around public switches/exchanges, which linked the caller with the person called: each subscriber was linked to a local exchange, which in turn was linked to a system of trunk (i.e. national) and international switches. The technology of the PSTN was well established in the mid-1960s. Signals were generally switched by electro-mechanical exchanges,[1] which had largely replaced manual switching.[2] Signals were switched and transmitted in 'analogue' form (i.e. speech or data is/are converted into a modulated continuous electrical current). Transmission was mostly over fixed links: in the local network linking subscribers to local switches, links generally consisted of multipair copper wire, which offered only a narrow 'bandwidth' (transmission capacity), although in trunk and international networks, coaxial copper cable with a larger bandwidth was used, and sometimes also microwave radio. Costs of transmission were strongly related to distance, so that if tariffs reflected costs, long-distance calls were much more costly than local calls.

Equipment for the PSTN—notably public switches and cable—accounted for the vast majority of equipment manufacturing. It had a long product life—for instance, the Strowger electro-mechanical exchange was invented in 1889 and Crossbar electro-mechanical systems began in 1916, but both were still being supplied in the 1960s. Equipment production required only limited research and development expenditure, as it involved evolution from previous designs.

In order to receive and transmit signals, and thus obtain services, customer

---

[1] See below for a description.
[2] Whereby operators plugged and unplugged links at the exchange to link the caller and the person called.

premises equipment is attached to telecommunications networks. In the 1960s, CPE was dominated by the supply of telephone sets and some private switches that connected private networks (for instance, within an office) to the PSTN for voice telephone. Few networks apart from the PSTN and few services other than voice telephony were available. Although newer forms of CPE services were emerging, such as simple fax machines and data terminals, together with simple specialised types of network created by separating some of the transmission capacity of the PSTN, these forms of CPE and networks were very limited, difficult to operate and unreliable. The major reason was that the PSTN was suitable for voice telephony, not for supporting other networks or services.

Thus telecommunications in the 1960s consisted of a slow-moving sector with identifiable boundaries, dominated by the supply of voice telephony and offering few other services. This position was to be transformed over the following decades, in large measure due to the impact of microelectronics and associated information industries.

Developments in MicroElectronics and Information Industries

From the 1960s onwards, microelectronics were revolutionized. Changes were largely based on remarkable increases in the capabilities of microchips, falling prices, and miniaturization. Thus, for instance, the cost of an integrated circuit fell by a factor of ten every five years in the 1970s, whilst its power rose from 700 bits per circuit in 1970 to 8,000 in 1980.[3] As a result, the cost of processing fell sharply—one estimate was that the cost of 1,700 operations (representing about one million instructions) fell from $0.47 in 1965 to $0.20 in 1975 to $0.07 in 1985.[4] Progress continued unabated in the 1980s and 1990s; for instance, a semiconductor chip in 1994 could store 16 megabits of memory; by 1997 the figure was 64 megabits.[5]

These developments in microelectronics then transformed other sectors, including telecommunications and information and communications as a whole. The most important change was the spread of digitalization: information is created, transmitted and stored in digital (i.e. binary 'on-off') form. On the supply side of telecommunications, the use of microelectronics and digitalization greatly altered the technology, costs, and quality of network operation, and the range of services and CPE supplied, with implications for investment and competition. On the demand side, the spread of computers increased demand for data transmission over the telecommunications network

[3] H. Pigeat and L. Virol, *Du Téléphone à la Télématique* (Paris: Commissariat du Plan, 1980).
[4] IBM estimates, cited in OECD, *The Telecommunications Industry* (Paris: OECD, 1988).
[5] *Financial Times* 3.10.97.

and aided the spread of services that used telecommunications networks into many other industries. Furthermore, sectoral boundaries were weakened: telecommunications, microelectronics, and computing, and then later in the 1980s also broadcasting and audiovisual entertainment services, moved closer together, based on a common core digital technology and the application of microelectronics.

The changes in microelectronics and their impact on telecommunications were so comprehensive and so rapid that it is accurate to speak of a revolution. The specific features of that revolution and the way in which it altered policy choices can be seen by looking at developments in each of the three subsectors of telecommunications of the 1960s: network operation, equipment manufacturing and CPE and 'advanced services and networks'. For each, the major technological and economic changes are set out briefly, before discussion of their policy implications.

Network Operation

Technological and Economic Developments

Network operation in the period from 1970s to the mid-1990s was reshaped by two factors: the digitalization of transmission and switching; the use of new means of transmission. On the demand side, operators had to face secular trends modifying the level and composition of demand.

The Digitalization of Transmission and Switching

Transmission of signals in digital form became commercially available in the mid/late-1960s. It could replace analogue transmission (i.e. use of a modulated electrical current). For the transmission of speech, a technique known as pulse code modulation (PCM) allowed the speech waveforms to be divided up into many pieces or 'strips', whose amplitude is measured and then signalled in binary form; at the receiving end these binary pulses are reconstituted into speech. Computers operate using binary signals, and digital transmission therefore allows messages to be sent from computers without conversion into analogue signals.

Transmission of digital signals offered a number of advantages over analogue transmission. These included lower loss of signal strength, less interference and better quality. The capacity of transmission media was increased thanks to higher speeds, lower resistance and the greater efficacy of digital multiplexing over frequency multiplexing of analogue signals.[6] Digital transmission

---

[6] Multiplexing allows a single transmission path such as a telephone line to be used to provide many transmission channels by interleaving streams of pulses from various sources; at the exchange or receiving end, the frequencies or streams of digits are 'unscrambled' and each

increased the capacity of physical networks; thus, for example, the British Post Office in the 1970s was testing high speed digital transmission over its *existing* trunk network to obtain 1,680 channels with a capacity of 120 million bits/s (bits per second) compared with 24 channels with a capacity of 1.5 million bits/s obtained at the time.[7] Moreover, it provided high quality transmission at much lower cost; thus, for example, in 1986 the cost of a 300 km-long circuit linking two fully digital 'time division' exchanges was estimated at FF25,580 for analogue transmission and FF3,070 for digital transmission per 'erlang' of transmission capacity.[8]

Microelectronics were also progressively introduced into switching. Public switching consists of two functions: 'switching'—i.e. connecting callers; 'control'—i.e. initiating and controlling necessary actions such as setting up and maintaining the connection during a communication, then closing it when the communication has ended, and identifying callers.[9] In electro-mechanical exchanges both functions were performed mechanically, with the movements of parts within the switch being determined by the electrical pulses sent when a caller dials.[10] An individual physical link between the caller and the person called was created and kept open for the duration of the communication.

During the late 1960s 'space division' or 'semi-electronic' exchanges were developed. In simple space division exchanges the control functions were performed by fixed electronic circuits and components; in more complex models, available in the mid–late 1970s, stored programme control (SPC) was applied, whereby computers implemented the control functions.

Space division exchanges offered many advantages over electro-mechanical systems. They were less fault prone (especially compared to Strowger electro-mechanical switches), easier to maintain,[11] more reliable in establishing correct

frequency/stream reconstituted; multiplexing signals provides greatly increased transmission capacity from the same transmission medium; frequency multiplexing became available in the late 1960s/early 1970s—see *The Times* 21.5.73 and *Financial Times* 27.4.81.

[7] *The Times* 13.12.74.

[8] D. Chatain and J. de la Chapelle, 'Le Réseau interurbain à l'aube de l'an 2000', *Revue Française des Télécommunications*, 63 (1987), 24–33.

[9] See J. Clark, I. McLoughlin, H. Rose, and R. King, *The Process of Technological Change* (Cambridge: Cambridge University Press, 1988), 17–20, and G. Dang Nguyen, 'Telecommunications: A Challenge to the Old Order', in M. Sharp (ed.), *Europe and the New Technologies* (London: Pinter, 1985).

[10] In 'Strowger' exchanges this is done by a 'step by step' process, whereby each digit dialled activates an 'arm' in the exchange which moves along a certain number of 'selectors' (according to the digit dialled) to create a physical contact; 'Crossbar' exchanges use a more complex 'matrix' system of horizontal and vertical reed relays which cross to make contact and hence create a physical link.

[11] For example the maintenance costs of the British TXE 4 space division exchange were one-quarter those of Strowger exchanges—D. Benson, 'Local Exchange Renewal Strategy: Formulating a Strategy', *Post Office Engineers' Journal*, 67(3) (1974), 130–5.

connections and smaller, saving valuable space in urban areas. Importantly, SPC provided great flexibility, as the software could be altered, for instance to change a subscriber's number (whereas in a Strowger exchange this necessitated an engineer physically disconnecting and relocating the wires) or to provide 'other services and networks'.[12]

Thus space division exchanges offered better quality, more sophisticated network facilities at lower operating costs. However, the signals switched remained analogue ones, as the switching function was still performed electro-mechanically—i.e. a separate physical path in the exchange was kept open for the duration of the communication by electrical contacts. Space division exchanges meant that if transmission were digitalized, signals had to be converted into analogue form for switching, and then reconverted into digital form for further transmission after being switched.

The next generation of public exchanges were fully digital switches, known as 'time division' switches. Signals were switched in digital form, as computers undertook both 'control' and 'switching' functions. Connections were no longer made by the physical cross-over of wires. Instead, a computer switched signals by calculating a path for a connection based on the assignment of particular time slots (hence 'time division' switching).

Time division switches offered major improvements over previous types of switches. They were more reliable, thanks to having fewer moving parts, automatic fault diagnosis, and signalling by their software. Moreover, modular design permitted parts of the exchange to be repaired or altered without affecting the functioning of other parts. As a result, less maintenance was required, with corresponding cost savings—one estimate is that whilst seven or eight people were required for maintaining 10,000 lines switched by Crossbar exchanges, only three were needed for a 10,000-line digital exchange.[13] Time division switches offered greater capacity, both in terms of operating at higher transmission speeds and in handling more lines. Connection times were much shorter and call quality improved.

Digitalization of switching resulted in sharply decreased switching costs. One estimate put the cost of one 'erlang' of switching capacity at FF38,000 (1986 French francs) for Crossbar equipment, but only FF6,700 for digital exchanges.[14] Furthermore, over the period 1970–97 costs decreased as digital

[12]   For further details see Clark et al., The Process of Technological Change, esp. 20–9, 45–7, and 192.

[13]   'Commutation: la filière numérique', (unsigned article) in Revue Française des Télécommunications, 42 (1982), 38–49.

[14]   Chatain and Lamy, 'Le Réseau interurbain'; another example is that the average purchase cost in the US of electro-mechanical exchanges installed 1980–5 was $600 per line, compared with $200 per line for digital switches—C. Antonelli, 'Le Dynamique des interrelations technologiques: le cas des technologies de l'information et de la communication', in D. Foray and C. Freeman (eds.), Technologie et richesses des nations (Paris: Economica, 1992); detailed figures from

exchanges were developed and improved. Thus, for instance, the OECD estimated that the cost-per-function in digital circuits between 1970 and 1980 had
fallen thanks to a remarkable doubling per annum in the functional complexity of digital integrated circuits, while their price remained constant; in contrast, reductions in the cost of analogue circuits had been only modest.[15] Rapid
progress in digital switches occurred during the 1970s and 1980s in terms of
processing power, physical size and number of lines handled.[16] In the 1990s,
new forms of digital switching were introduced or developed, often adapted
for data traffic, in particular asynchronous transfer mode (ATM) and Internet
protocols, which were designed for packet switching.[17]

Improved Transmission

The transmission of signals greatly improved from the 1960s onwards as existing means were better exploited and new methods were developed. The result
was a fall in costs, especially for long-distance transmission,[18] greater capacity
and improved quality.

The first satellite for public telecommunications, Intelsat 1, was launched
in 1965 by Intelsat.[19] A series of new generations of satellites followed, each
smaller, but with greater capacity and a longer lifetime, thanks to developments in use of weight, transmission, and miniaturization.[20] The costs of
satellite transmission fell sharply; thus, for instance, the charges levied by
Intelsat for leasing a circuit per annum in nominal terms alone decreased
from $35,000 in 1965 to $5,000 in 1985.[21] Furthermore, better transmission
technology meant that a greater volume of voice/data per circuit could be
sent by satellite. In addition, the performance of earth stations, from/to which
transmission to/from satellites is made, also improved, whilst their cost

legal proceedings in the United States support the cost advantages of digital switching—see
W. G. Bolter, J. W. McConnaughey, and F. Kelsey, *Telecommunications Policy for the 1990s and Beyond*
(New York: M.E. Sharp, 1990), esp. 166–8.

[15] OECD, *Telecommunications. Pressures and Policies for Change* (Paris: OECD, 1983), 53.

[16] For instance, the French MT25 installed in the mid-1980s had a capacity of 60,000 lines,
compared with 15,000 lines for the E10A installed in the early 1970s—PTT Ministry, *Les Télécommunications françaises* (Paris: PTT Ministry, 1982), 265.

[17] See e.g. *Financial Times* 28.7.98.

[18] One estimate was that the cost of long-distance transmission had halved every seven years
from the 1970s (H. Ungerer and N. Costello, *Telecommunications in Europe* (Brussels: Commission
of The European Communities, 1988).

[19] An international body composed of representatives of public telecommunications operators from around the world.

[20] See OECD, *Telecommunications. Pressures and Policies for Change*, and OECD, *Satellites and
Fibre Optics* (Paris: OECD, 1988); some idea of the improvement is given by the fact that Intelsat I offered 240 two-way telephone circuits, and had a design lifetime of one-and-a-half years,
whereas Intelsat Va, launched in 1985, had a capacity of 15,000 circuits, plus two television
channels, and a design lifetime of seven years.

[21] OECD, *Telecommunications. Pressures and Policies for Change*, and *Satellites and Fibre Optics*.

decreased.[22] By the 1980s, satellites could transmit to and from small dishes located directly on users' premises. In the mid-1990s, global mobile personal communications satellite networks, whereby satellite networks would be used for personal mobile communications, were being developed.[23]

Transmission by cable also enjoyed remarkable improvements in performance. The capacity of cable steadily increased thanks to digitalization and multiplexing. Moreover, copper coaxial cable that offered a larger bandwidth than traditional copper pair cable became cheaper and was improved; it was suitable for trunk and international networks. One example is that the transatlantic cable, TAT 5 (commissioned in 1970) carried 845 voice circuits, whilst a successor, TAT 7 (commissioned in 1983), carried 4,200 circuits.[24] Costs per circuit declined: for example, they fell from $12 for TAT 5 to $2.3 for TAT 7.[25]

The most important development in transmission was the use of optical fibre cables. Signals are converted into light pulses for transmission along the optical fibre by light-emitting diodes or lasers, and are then reconverted into speech or data at the receiving end. Transmission is in digital form, since the light is either 'off' or 'on'. Optical fibre offered many advantages over coaxial cable. It provided enormous capacity,[26] and hence could be used for 'broadband services' such as interactive television and future high definition television.[27] Signal attenuation fell and hence the minimum distance between costly signal 'repeaters' was higher than for coaxial cable.[28] Optical fibre provided better-quality transmission than other media, with a lower error rate, and immunity for signals from electrical interference. Moreover, it is resistant to corrosion, and requires less maintenance.

The 1980s saw the development of the production of optical fibre and associated equipment. Transmission capacity grew, thanks to multiplexing, better forms of optical fibre (notably monomode fibre) and advances in equipment, such as new light-emitting diodes and lasers.[29] In 1980, a fibre could offer trans-

---

[22] By 20–30 per cent per annum during the 1980s (OECD, *Satellites and Fibre Optics*).

[23] *Financial Times*, 13.11.97, 9.12.97.

[24] OECD, *Telecommunications. Pressures and Policies for Change* and *Satellites and Fibre Optics*.

[25] In 1984 US dollars, and assuming a twenty year life for the cable (OECD, *Satellites and Fibre Optics*, 33).

[26] Cables with a capacity of 565m. bits/s were installed in the mid-1980s and could offer 8,000 telephone circuits, compared to coaxial cable in the trunk network able to handle 2,000 telephone circuits—OECD, *Satellites and Fibre Optics*, and Ungerer and Costello, *Telecommunications in Europe*.

[27] See below.

[28] For optical fibre, the minimum distance was 10–15 km. in the early 1980s but this rose to over 30 km. in the mid-1980s and 100 km. by the late 1980s; in comparison, coaxial cable required a repeater every 2 km. (Ungerer and Costello, *Telecommunications in Europe* and *Financial Times* 27.4.81).

[29] *Financial Times* 5.3.86 and 20.9.88; see OECD, *Satellites and Fibre Optics*, and Ungerer and Costello, *Telecommunications in Europe*, for further details.

mission at 100m. bits per second; this had reached 1,000m. bits per second in 1985; by the late 1990s, a trans-Atlantic cable with a capacity of 30 billion bits per second of data was laid.[30] The price of optical fibre cable declined rapidly in the 1980s and 1990s: for example, in 1980 a fibre of 70m. bits/s capacity cost $11.8 per metre; by 1985 cable with a capacity of 900m. bits/s cost $0.35.[31] As a result of improvements, the cost of transmitting using optical fibre cables fell to a fraction of previous levels; thus, for example, the cost per voice path of transatlantic cable fell from 23,000 dollars in 1983 to below 2,000 dollars in 1995, while another estimate was that the basic cost of one minute of transmission on a transatlantic cable laid in 1996 was just over one (US) cent.[32]

Demand for Network Operation

Demand for network operation appears to have enjoyed a secular upward trend in industrialized countries in the 1970s and 1980s. Demand rose, both for connection to the PSTN and for usage by existing subscribers, due to demand for telephony being positively correlated with income and wealth and to increasing use of telecommunications by businesses. In addition, usage of telecommunications networks grew because of the development of 'advanced services'. One estimate put the growth of world demand at 10 per cent per annum between 1970 and 1976 compared with 2.5 per cent for electrical appliances and 5 per cent for cars.[33]

In addition, the composition of usage changed. The volume of communications by businesses, and especially large business users in sectors in information intensive sectors such as banking, financial services and tourism, appears to have risen sharply and to have increased as a proportion of total telecommunications income.[34] Furthermore, business users, especially multinationals, were often responsible for a high proportion of long distance communications, especially international ones, whose costs fell sharply from the 1970s onwards.

Policy Implications of Technological and Economic Developments in Network Operation

Investment and Borrowing

Whilst new technologies offered advantages for network operators, their introduction also required heavy investment. Previously, network operators could

---

[30] *Financial Times* 5.3.98.   [31] OECD, *Satellites and Fibre Optics*.
[32] *Financial Times* 27.8.97, quoting ITU figures; *The Economist, Telecommunications Survey*, 13.9.97, 25.
[33] L. Virol 'Du téléphone à la télématique', *Revue Française des Télécommunications*, 38 (1981), 40–51.
[34] E. Noam, 'Network Tipping and the Tragedy of the Common Network: A Theory for the Formation and Breakdown of Public Telecommunications Systems', *Communications et Stratégies*, 1 (1991), 43–72.

merely replace worn-out exchanges. Now Strowger and Crossbar electro-mechanical exchange could be written off as technologically and economically 'obsolete'.[35] Moreover, space division exchanges, generally installed in the 1970s, were rapidly overtaken by time division systems in terms of cost and technological advantages by the 1980s, and so were also obsolete, despite the recentness of their introduction. Furthermore, there were incentives for 'lumpy' investment: large orders for time division exchanges produced consid-erable economies of scale; it was disadvantageous to have part of the trunk network using analogue technology once a large part of the trunk transmis-sion network and other trunk switches were digitalized, because signals had to be converted into digital form and then reconverted into analogue form several times.

Large-scale investment needed to be financed. This could be achieved from retained profits, but increased capital expenditure would mean that a higher proportion of income would be used for long-term assets, and might also require large price increases. Other methods of raising capital became impor-tant, particularly borrowing, which could be repaid from savings offered by new technology.

Costs, Tariffs, and Competition

Lower unit costs from investment in new technologies offered the opportunity of lower prices, higher profits for the network operator or higher investment funds, or a combination of these. In addition, the new technologies altered the structure of costs. Traditionally, the cost of transmission had greatly varied with distance. Due to new technologies, the cost of long-distance transmission fell further than that of shorter distances: for satellite transmission, distance had almost no effect on cost, whilst distance was less important for transmis-sion using optical fibre cable than for copper and copper coaxial cable, espe-cially as the price of cable fell relative to equipment.[36] Thus cost became increasingly unrelated to distance.

The altered cost structure had implications for prices. Traditionally, many network operators had related tariffs to costs, so that long distance communi-cations cost more than local ones; in addition, there had often been cross-subsidization, with long-distance services being used to cross-subsidize other services, particularly local calls and access to the network (connection and rental charges). If the structure of tariffs failed to be modified as new technol-ogy was introduced, there would be increasing divergence between the cost and prices of services; specifically, long-distance tariffs might lie considerably above their costs. Divergence between costs and prices gives rise to incentives

---

[35] i.e. over the lifetime of the switches, and taking into account interest rates, digital switches offered higher real returns to capital.

[36] Cf. O. Stehmann, *Network Competition for European Telecommunications* (Oxford: Oxford University Press, 1995), 15, 18.

for competition in network operation, putting pressure on network operators to align prices with costs.

At the same time, technological change weakened the economic foundations of monopolies over network operation, as direct and indirect competition became easier. Although telecommunications networks had been regarded as a 'natural monopoly' (i.e. supplied most efficiently through only one network), during the 1970s and 1980s the cost of setting up new networks competing directly with the established network fell, because the costs of optical fibre, microwave equipment, and satellite capacity declined; in particular, establishing limited networks (as opposed to comprehensive ones serving the whole population over entire countries) became technologically and financially much easier. In the mid-1990s, one estimate was that a basic international voice-over-Internet network could be built for under $100m.; newer US operator such as Quest and Worldcom built networks with capacities equal to the existing largest operators, including AT&T, for one-tenth the aggregate investment; new entrants began establishing international optical fibre networks with local loops around big cities.[37] In the 1980s and especially from the early 1990s, the creation of high quality mobile communications and satellite networks became cheaper and easier. Moreover, rapid technological advances meant that a new network operator would enjoy an advantage over established operators by installing the latest equipment.

'Indirect competition' to network operators also became possible, through 'bypass' of the PSTN. A number of methods could be used to bypass the PSTN: voice telephony could be provided on networks designed for data, such as packet switched networks (for instance, offering telephony on the Internet); capacity could be resold to third parties on such networks or on lines leased for specialized purposes; 'call-back' services on international communications allowed callers to choose which country their call would originate from. 'Bypass' became easier thanks to advances in customer premises equipment, notably memorization by terminals, to allow retransmission of signals, and terminals usable for both data and telephony.

Network Operator Revenues and Profits

The growth of demand provided network operators with expanding markets, but also pressure to increase the supply of connections and network capacity. Moreover, the rapid expansion of long-distance traffic, especially international communications, where costs had fallen fastest, meant that for many operators large users accounted for a high proportion of revenue and especially of profits in the period; this was particularly the case if tariffs for long-distance communications were high, and above costs. Thus network operators were prone to

[37] *Financial Times* 14.1.98, 20.7.98, 28.7.98.

become financially dependent on a small number of users with considerable resources and high expenditure on telecommunications.

Network Equipment Manufacture and Supply

Technological and Economic Developments

Pressures for Concentration and Internationalization

Digitalization produced intense pressures for concentration and internationalization in public switching manufacture, due to higher fixed costs and shorter product lives. Such pressures also operated in cable supply, but to a lesser extent.[38]

The move from electro-mechanical switching to space and time division switching led to dramatic increases in fixed costs, both in absolute terms and as a proportion of total costs. The main reason was that R and D (research and development) costs increased, particularly for computer software. One estimate is that whereas an electro-mechanical switching system cost 15–20m. ECU (£23–30m.) in R and D in the early 1970s, in the 1980s a digital system cost 1000m. ECU (£1,515m.);[39] other estimates put the development costs of a digital switch at $500m.–$1b.[40] and £500–£1b.[41] In addition, further expenditure to update the software of digital exchanges was needed, put as high as $100m.–$200m. per annum.[42] Moreover, high R and D spending did not end with digital switches: in the late 1980s new research was being undertaken on optical switching.

At the same time, rapid innovation reduced the commercial life of switches. Electro-mechanical systems had a product life of twenty to thirty years.[43] Space division exchanges were intended to have a product life of twenty years, and time division exchange systems of ten years.[44] Thus the period over which fixed costs could be recovered fell, together with the time between large-scale investment efforts to develop new systems.

---

[38] J. Müller, *The Benefits of Completing the Internal Market for Telecommunications Equipment, Services, in the Community (Research on the 'Cost of Non-Europe', Basic Findings)*, x (Brussels: Commission of the European Communities, 1988).

[39] Ungerer and Costello, *Telecommunications in Europe*, 113.

[40] OECD, *The Telecommunications Industry*, 72.

[41] Monopolies and Mergers Commission, *The General Electric Company PLC and the Plessey Company PLC—A Report on the Proposed Merger* (London: HMSO, 1986).

[42] *Financial Times* 4.12.85, and J. Hausman, 'Réglementation et incitations aux alliances dans les télécommunications', in L. Benzoni and J. Hausman (eds.), *Concurrence, Innovation, Réglementation dans les Télécommunications* (Paris: CNET/ENST, 1991).

[43] Ungerer and Costello, *Telecommunications in Europe*.

[44] Ibid. and OECD, *Telecommunications. Pressures and Policies for Change*.

Policy Implications

In most European countries, network operators traditionally favoured one or two national suppliers (such as GEC and Plessey in Britain or Siemens in Germany), who developed equipment according to national standards and derived most of their orders from their domestic market. Higher costs and shorter product lives created strong pressure for concentration of suppliers, as very large economies of scale existed,[45] whilst the share of world markets needed for financial viability rose. One estimate was that a firm needed 8 per cent of the world market for a digital switch to be viable, and that 16 per cent would be required for the next generation of switches.[46] The effects of higher R and D costs are illustrated by figures indicating that in the early 1980s sixteen major digital systems with total R and D costs of $6b. were competing for a world market put at $12b.[47] The cost pressures were particularly acute in Western Europe where no single national market accounted for more than 6 per cent of the world market by the 1980s.[48]

Manufacturers based in small/medium sized markets, such as in Western Europe, therefore found it increasingly difficult to rely solely on their domestic markets—they had to find overseas orders. Yet the world industry was dominated by a few firms: in 1985 twelve firms accounted for 98.5 per cent of world sales of public switching equipment.[49] Fierce competition existed amongst these firms in international markets, especially for digital switches.[50] Few national markets were open to foreign firms.[51] Moreover, with high fixed costs and economies of scale, and captive national markets, marginal cost pricing for exports was profitable. It appears that by the mid-1980s prices for digital switches were falling considerably in real terms.[52] Thus there were powerful factors for cross-national co-operation or mergers and takeovers.

[45] For instance, Oftel suggested that the incremental cost per line of a digital switch over one million lines was only just over half that of the first one million lines-Oftel, *BT's Procurement of Digital Exchanges* (London: Oftel, 1985).

[46] OECD, *The Telecommunications Industry*, 73.

[47] OECD, *Telecommunications. Pressures and Policies for Change*.

[48] Commission of the European Communities, *Towards a Dynamic European Economy—Green Paper on the Development of the Common Market for Telecommunications Services and Equipment* (Brussels: Commission of the European Communities, 1987).

[49] Derived from, Monopolies and Mergers Commission, *The General Electric Company PLC and the Plessey Company PLC—a report on the proposed merger*.

[50] See OECD, *The Telecommunications Industry*, for a list of firms and their time division switches and dates of development.

[51] In the early 1980s, 70–80 per cent of world markets were estimated to be dominated by established producers, and offering little prospect of entry by other suppliers (OECD, *Telecommunications. Pressures and Policies for Change*).

[52] One estimate was a fall of 20 per cent per annum—*Financial Times* 4.12.85; other figures are that in the US, digital switch prices per line fell from $230 in 1983 to $144 in 1988—Hausman 'Réglementation et incitations aux alliances'.

'Other Services and Networks' and Customer Premises Equipment

The Development of 'Other Services and Networks' and CPE

From the mid-1960s onwards, numerous new 'advanced services and networks' and types of CPE became available, driven by the 'marriage' of micro-electronics and computing with telecommunications. The services supplied on telecommunications networks and accompanying CPE became highly diverse, differing in terms of technical complexity, functions and potential users. The costs of services and CPE fell, whilst their reliability improved. As a result, from being a stable sector largely based on a single service (telephony) with simple telephone equipment, telecommunications was transformed into a rapidly-changing, heterogeneous, multi-service field, with a wide range of CPE. It became closely linked to other information and communications industries. The pace of change became particularly rapid in the 1980s and 1990s.

The sheer variety of 'other services and networks' and CPE defies classification and comprehensive description. Nevertheless, five groups of services illustrate the main developments, together with CPE.

'Enhanced Basic Services'

Thanks to the introduction of micro-electronics into public switches, network operators were able to offer enhanced telephony services, such as itemized billing, premium rate services (higher cost services on special numbers) such as 'chatlines' and recorded information, and freephone services.

VANS/VADS

These services are derived by attaching various types of CPE to the network, which is used to transmit signals. Many of these have been classified as VANS value-added network services (VANS) or value-added data services (VADS), as their features add 'value' to the basic transmission of signals. The concept of VANS suffers from many defects,[53] but nevertheless has been widely used in policy debates and regulatory arrangements. In the 1960s, VANS/VADS were limited, expensive, and unreliable; by the 1980s, they were more numerous, diverse, and reliable, and many were affordable even for individuals.

One example is fax services: in the 1960s it took ten minutes to fax an A4 sheet, quality was poor and terminals were difficult to operate, often requiring specialist staff; by the early 1980s, fax machines could transmit a page of A4 in

---

[53] Particularly its assumption that the telecommunications network is primarily adapted for voice telephony, which became less appropriate in the 1980s with digitalization; see OECD, *Telecommunications Network-Based Services* (Paris: OECD, 1989), esp. ch. 3, and R. Mansell, 'Telecommunications network-based services', *Telecommunications Policy*, 12(3) (1988), 243–56.

12–20 seconds and offered higher resolution;[54] by the 1990s, a range of high-speed fax machines existed and faxes could even be received as files by personal computers. E-mail services offer another example: although possible since the 1970s, they developed in the 1980s and especially the 1990s. Finally, database services allow consultation of computer databases, with data being transmitted via a telecommunications network. 'Videotex systems' involve such information being displayed on the screen of a terminal. Interactive database/videotex services allow the user to communicate with the database and enable a vast range of services to be provided, based on the user requesting information from the computer database, receiving it and then sending messages back to the database, which acts on the instructions sent. Such services range from relatively simple reservation services (such as for travel tickets) and banking services (for instance, cash withdrawal or transfer of funds) to sophisticated modern share and commodity dealing systems, whereby traders receive information on screens and buy/sell shares or commodities by sending messages to the database.

Specialized Networks

The telecommunications network can be used to support specialized networks other than the PSTN. 'Leased lines' involve the network operator setting aside capacity and then leasing it for the exclusive use of the lessee. The latter can choose to configure them, notably through private automated branch exchanges (PABX) to create forms of private network for services ranging from voice telephony to sophisticated VANS. Specialized public networks for data transmission and for large bandwidth services (i.e. those demanding high transmission capacity) can be also created on the telecommunications network. In the late 1960s/early 1970s, packet switched networks were developed, in which data were broken up into 'packets' containing a number of 'bits' by a packet assembler/disassembler (PAD). They were ideal for data transmission as they were digital, offered high transmission speeds, and made efficient use of capacity by multiplexing and breaking up data into separate packets, each of which is sent separately and reassembled on reception. Thus they became the basis for the Internet in the 1980s and 1990s. Moreover, using digital switching and transmission, an integrated services digital network (ISDN) can be provided—i.e. end-to-end digital transmission suitable for simultaneously transmitting voice, data, and images.

Mobile Communications

Mobile communications systems had been available since the 1950s, but suffered from very limited capacity and no automatic 'handover' facility

---

[54] Grosvenor Press International, *Developing World Communications* (Hong Kong: Grosvenor Press, 1988), and M. O'Brien, 'Will the Fax Boom go Bust?', *Telephony*, 25.9.89, 41–46.

(important for car phones), when crossing from a zone served by one transmitter to another zone served by another transmitter. During the 1980s, analogue cellular systems were introduced, whereby areas were divided into small 'cells', each covered by a low-power transmitter and radio base station. The base stations were linked together (usually by leased lines) and connected to a computer-controlled exchange. Low-power transmitters and small cells allowed the same frequencies to be reused in different cells for different calls without risk of interference. As a result, cellular radio systems offered automatic handover and can accommodate a much greater number of subscribers than traditional systems.[55]

During the late 1980s other types of mobile telephony were developed. 'Telepoint' or 'CT2' systems allowed subscribers to call (but not be called), provided they were close to a base station. There was no automatic handover, and so the system was unsuitable for car phones. Digital systems were also created for operation in the 1990s, offering greater capacity, better quality and greater suitability for data transmission. Moreover, paging networks for sending messages were improved: originally transmission of a radio signal only produced a 'bleep' on the pager, but, by the 1980s, communication of short messages or numbers became possible. Finally, satellite networks became more commercially affordable from the late 1980s, thanks to cheaper satellites and the ability to receive communications on small dishes. By the late 1980s and 1990s, mobile and satellite systems could also communicate data, and hence could support mobile fax, e-mail, and other advanced services.

Visual Services and Networks

The 1980s saw the 'convergence' of telecommunications and broadcasting technology. Images can be transmitted on a telecommunications network; until the 1990s, coaxial cable was needed for high quality television, but by the mid-1990s, relatively good television could even be sent on the twin-pair copper wires that have often been used in domestic homes. Moreover, the wider bandwidth of coaxial and especially of optical fibre cable, and techniques reducing the bandwidth needed for transmission, allowed interactive visual services such as videoconferencing, to develop from the 1980s onwards. At the same time, developments in cable television networks aided their capacity to be configured and switched, so that they could also transmit telecommunications services.

Satellite transmission of television also improved. In the 1970s and early 1980s, signals could be sent from a low/medium power satellite to a large reception 'dish', and then distributed to individual homes via a cable network.

---

[55] See: P. Peston, 'Cellular Radio—The Revolution Rolls On', in Grosvenor Press, *Developing World Communications*; *Financial Times* 1.10.82 and 6.5.86; B. Ghillebaert, 'Le Système cellulaire de télécommunication avec les mobiles', *Annals des Télécommunications*, 42(7–8) (1987), 44–9.

However, by the late 1980s advances in satellite transmission and reception permitted direct broadcasting by satellite (DBS) to small, cheaper dishes which can be mounted on individual homes. Finally, the development of digital television in the mid-1990s has offered the prospect of a common technology across telecommunications and television.

Customer Premises Equipment

New services became possible thanks to improved or new forms of CPE, ranging from handsets, videotex terminals, fax machines, and mobile terminals to larger equipment such as videoconferencing equipment, PABXs, and earth stations and antennae for satellite services. Almost all types of equipment were subject to major change and innovation. New functions were added to equipment thanks to 'intelligence' derived from the use of microchips. Moreover, office equipment became linked to telecommunications, so that terminals could be connected to other terminals, either via the PSTN (using a modem to convert signals into or from analogue ones for transmission) or via a switched private network, formed of leased lines and a PABX. As a result, 'distributed processing systems' were possible, whereby terminals could both be used independently in different locations, and can also communicate with a central computer and/or other terminals, thanks to transmission of data via telecommunications systems.

Rapid innovation and the use of increasingly cheap micro-electronics resulted in lower costs and world prices. Prices of CPE rose significantly slower than those of manufactured goods in the 1970s in most OECD countries[56] and this trend appears to have accelerated, in the 1980s and 1990s.[57]

Policy Implications of Developments in 'Advanced Services and Networks' and CPE

Competition and Regulation and the Relationship of 'Advanced Services and Networks' with Network Operation

The development of 'advanced services and networks' resulted in a complex set of relations with network operation. If services are transmitted over the PSTN, the quality and transmission speed of the PSTN affect their supply. Many of the new services produce digital signals or are much more efficient in digital form; these include fax, e-mail, videotex services, data transmission, and videoconferencing. Thus the digitalization of the PSTN became important, since analogue transmission required a modem to transform digital signals into analogue ones for transmission, and then at the receiving end to reconvert signals

---

[56] See OECD, *Telecommunications. Pressures and Policies for Change*, 26.

[57] Ungerer and Costello, *Telecommunications in Europe*; for the prices of specific products, see Grosvenor Press, *Developing World Communications*.

into digital form; this process limited transmission speeds and reduced quality. The calibre of specialized networks was also affected by the modernization of the PSTN, as such networks were often built by separating network capacity. Services created demand for network capacity, either on the PSTN or because network capacity was used to support other networks (for instance packet switched networks or leased lines).

At the same time, network operators frequently found that their monopolies over services were threatened. The supply of most 'advanced services and networks' and of CPE was not generally regarded as a natural monopoly, as often it did not require heavy investment, and the services and equipment were highly heterogeneous, frequently subject to dynamic efficiency gains thanks to rapid innovation and afforded only limited economies of scale.[58] Monopoly provision of services such as fax or data transmission, became difficult to enforce, as the attachment of CPE to networks could not be prevented. Moreover, alternative networks to the PSTN carried the danger of bypass for the network operator—i.e. leased lines or packet switched networks could be used not only for transmission of other services, but also for voice telephony.

Competition in new services and CPE had implications for regulation, especially in relation to network operators. Charges for transmission on the network became central for the financial viability of new services, either directly, if a service was carried over the PSTN, or indirectly, by influencing the costs of alternatives to the PSTN such as packet switched networks and leased lines. Moreover, when rival networks (mobile networks or private networks) were built, their operators often wished to connect them to the PSTN; hence terms for interconnection with the network, notably prices and standards, influenced their commercial viability. Similarly, for CPE, standards and terms for connection to the network were important. Yet vertically-integrated network operators, who wished to supply CPE and 'advanced services and networks' (which were growing rapidly by the 1980s) were both infrastructure supplier and competitor with other suppliers. Vertical integration thus posed issues of 'fair competition'.

Competition, Standards, and Compatibility

Competition in the supply of 'advanced services' and CPE also had implications for the setting of norms and standards. Interconnection of services required compatibility, both in terms of CPE and software. Compatibility requires either standardized norms or norms sufficiently close to allow conversion systems to provide interconnection. The adoption of norms and

---

[58] G. Locksley, *The EEC Telecommunications Industry: Competition, Concentration and Competitiveness* (Brussels: Commission of the European Communities, 1982), 105; J. Vickers and G. Yarrow, *Privatization: An Economic Analysis* (Cambridge, Mass.: MIT, 1988).

proprietary standards are important for the operation of markets for 'advanced services' and CPE.

For users, compatibility influences the economic benefits of adopting a technology or buying a service. Most services are subject to 'network effects', notably 'network externalities', whereby the value of a network or service depends on who else is connected to it; important examples include videotex, fax, and e-mail. Hence greater compatibility increases the value of a technology or service for users. On the other hand, incompatibility may result in a user being 'locked' into a particular product. The user may face high 'sunk costs' of existing hardware and/or software, including training and expertise: changing to another product would involve costs in writing-off these investments or in converting hardware or software which would exceed the gains offered by the new product.[59]

For suppliers, compatibility influences the size of potential markets: incompatibility reduces their size, whilst compatibility increases it. If interconnection is difficult, expensive conversion systems may have to be developed, reducing the size of profitable markets. Incompatibility may result in a particular norm/standard becoming the *de facto* general standard, even though competing standards and technologies may be more efficient, due to increasing returns arising from network externalities, increasing returns to adoption or users' sunk costs.[60] Certain firms may have invested heavily in developing technologies and products based on certain norms, and so the adoption of particular standards will affect their commercial success. Norms affect the vertical integration of suppliers, especially of service providers and equipment manufacturers: if a manufacturer's hardware and its particular and specific norms become widespread, that manufacturer may be advantaged in supplying services (i.e. software), being able to tailor them to the hardware, whilst competitors' services are either incompatible with the hardware or perform less well with it.[61] Furthermore, if users are 'locked' into a supplier's products, the latter has market power over them, which it can exploit to earn 'super-normal profits'.

The Weakened Sectoral Boundaries of Telecommunications

The development of new services and CPE saw a weakening of boundaries between telecommunications and other sectors. In services, the division

---

[59] See P. A. David, 'Clio and the Economics of QWERTY', *Economic History*, 75(2) (1985), 332–7.

[60] See W. B. Arthur, 'Competing Technologies, Increasing Returns and Lock-in by Historical Events', *The Economic Journal*, 99 (1989), 116–31, and David, 'Clio and the Economics of QWERTY'.

[61] See W. Adams and J. W. Brock, 'Integrated Monopoly and Market Power: System Selling, Compatibility Standards, and Market Control', *The Quarterly Review of Economics and Business*, 22(4) (1983), 29–42.

between telecommunications, computing/micro-electronics and broadcasting sectors was eroded: telecommunications services were developed thanks to micro-electronics, whilst telecommunications networks were used for the transmission of data in computer, micro-electronics and broadcasting networks. Similarly, in CPE, the boundaries between telecommunications, communications, electronics/computing and office equipment were weakened as CPE became increasingly based on micro-electronics, whilst office equipment and computers were linked through telecommunications networks.

The blurring of boundaries posed a threat to the closed world of telecommunications supply dominated by network operators. It provided opportunities and pressures for computing/microelectronics and broadcasting firms to participate in telecommunications services. On the one hand, such companies could supply services using telecommunications networks. On the other hand, they were dependent on the telecommunications network to supply high quality advanced services, which offered growth and profits. Similarly, in CPE supply, firms from other sectors, notably computing and office equipment, were able to enter the market, supplying equipment with a mixture of telecommunications and other functions. Network operators were both suppliers of crucial infrastructure for such firms, but also potential rivals.

Telecommunications as a Strategic Service: Applications of 'Other Services' and CPE

Demand for CPE and associated advanced services grew rapidly, particularly by businesses.[62] It was highly diverse, in terms of types of application, customer, and sectors. Many sectors used and became reliant on advanced services—finance and banking, tourism, travel, retailing, and even manufacturing with stock control and computer-aided design and manufacture. E-mail, data transmission, and other services have become everyday tools in business life. Computers spread, together with 'distributed processing' and 'remote access' whereby terminals in one location communicate with each other and with central computers via telecommunications networks. Stock exchanges, foreign exchanges, and other trading markets in the world introduced videotex systems. Banks established electronic payments systems for transactions both between themselves and with their customers. Retailers and banks in the 1980s implemented electronic payments systems at checkouts (EFTPOS), and linked these to computer programmes for autonomic ordering, stock, and sales analysis.

The widespread application of advanced services and networks and accompanying CPE meant that the effects of the price, quality, and availability of services became important for sectors other than telecommunications, and indeed for the economy as a whole. The economic implications of telecommunica-

---

[62]   OECD, *Telecommunications. Pressures and Policies for Change*, 68.

tions grew beyond those suggested by figures for the size of the industry. Indeed, telecommunications became economically 'strategic': the operation and development of a host of other sectors were dependent on information and communications, including telecommunications services and networks.

Technological and Economic Developments: Exogenous and Common for Britain and France

The technological and economic developments in the supply of telecommunications services and equipment were largely exogenous to policy-makers in Britain and France: they had little influence on the development of the new technologies. Both countries therefore faced similar technological and economic developments which their policy-makers were unable to greatly affect. Three factors were highly important in this lack of influence.

First, the microelectronics, switching, and transmission equipment incorporating the new technologies was internationally tradable and traded; hence the new technology was available to users and suppliers. Yet both countries were small/medium-sized markets and suppliers of equipment; they lacked 'market power' over the world supply, demand and prices of products. Thus, for instance, in the crucial field of micro-electronics, Europe as a whole only accounted for 17.3 per cent of world semi-conductor production in 1982, with France producing only 6 per cent and Britain even less.[63] Total gross investment by network operators (as a percentage of OECD totals) was 8.1 per cent for Britain in 1970 and 4.3 per cent for France, compared with 43.6 per cent for the US and 15.4 per cent for Japan; the figures for 1980 were 6.3 per cent for Britain, 7.4 per cent for France, and 41.1 per cent for the US and 13.5 per cent for Japan.[64] Similarly, in equipment purchases and supply, both countries were small/medium-sized: one estimate was that in 1985 Britain accounted for 5.4 per cent of the major world markets and France for 4.3 per cent, with the figures for 1989 being 5.8 per cent and 4.0 per cent respectively,[65] whilst another estimate was that France's share of world production in 1986 was 5 per cent in switching systems, 4 per cent for transmission equipment, 4 per cent for terminals, and 3 per cent for cable.[66]

Second, the scientific knowledge for technological development had been established well before the 1970s, and was publicly available; the clearest example was digitalization, which was based on research undertaken in the

---

[63] Compared with 47.6 per cent for the US and 29.6 per cent for Japan—Locksley, *The EEC Telecommunications Industry*, 211, based on Dataquest figures.

[64] Source: International Telecommunications Union, *Annual Statistics* (Geneva: ITU, annual) with calculations using purchasing power parities supplied by the OECD.

[65] OMYSC, *Telecommunications Statistics* (Paris: ENST, 2nd. edn., 1989).

[66] B. Aurelle, *Les Télécommunications* (Paris: La Découverte, 1986).

1940s. The developments of the 1970s and 1980s largely represented the commercial application of that knowledge. The path of technological development towards the application of micro-electronics resulting in a move towards digital technology and a range of services based on computing and producing digital signals was clearly signalled.[67] Many questions thus concerned the timing and form of the introduction of new technology.

A third factor is that although domestic demand in Britain and France was the result of the decisions of domestic actors, this demand[68] was also subject to secular forces common to industrialized nations. In particular, shifts towards greater use of information and communication, raising the demand for telecommunications and increasing the importance of its supply for a variety of sectors, took place in all Western economies. Activity in service sectors, many of which use telecommunications networks to transmit information grew rapidly. Telecommunications became widely used by firms, and developed into an important tool for gaining competitive advantage in certain information-intensive sectors, such as finance, tourism or retailing. As a result, there was pressure for widespread adoption of telecommunications technology, especially in internationally exposed fields, such as foreign exchange and share trading.

Conclusion

Until the 1960s, telecommunications had formed a distinct sector that used well-established technology that was centred on one service, voice telephony. Thereafter, powerful technological and economic forces, based on developments in micro-electronics and largely exogenous to policy-makers in Britain and France, transformed the industry. The new features of telecommunications offered a comprehensive set of opportunities and challenges to the features of the sector in Britain and France that existed in the 1960s. In particular, they challenged institutions and policies concerning investment and borrowing by network operators, their tariff structures, the monopolies of the Post Office and DGT, the regulation of competition and the structure of relations between the network operators and their equipment suppliers.

In network operation, the digitalization of transmission and switching and

[67]   The clearest example was in public switching, in which telecommunications research establishments in most countries were working on developing time division switches in the 1950s and 1960s; for a particularly lucid view of the future development of telecommunications, accurately foreshadowing future events, see J. Martin, *Future Developments in Telecommunications* (Eaglewood Cliffs: Prentice Hall International, 1971); see also E. Cohen, *Le Colbertisme 'high tech'* (Paris: Hachette, 1992), 65–6.

[68]   i.e. the demand curve, not the actual level of demand which will also have been influenced by the domestic price and availability of services and equipment.

the use of new means of transmission promised lower costs, better quality, greater capacity, and a network suitable for the transmission of many 'other services'. However, the introduction of new technologies required large-scale investment, at much higher levels than previously undertaken by the Post Office and DGT. Increased capital spending offered greatly reduced costs, especially for long-distance communications, but would have to be financed, a development conflicting with traditions of strict limits on spending by the two network operators. Moreover, the issue of borrowing by publicly-owned suppliers arose: given the scale of expenditure needed to introduce new technologies rapidly, and the speed of returns in terms of costs and new services, there were good reasons to finance higher capital expenditure through borrowing rather than current revenue. Again, a move towards large-scale borrowing conflicted with traditional restraints on Post Office and DGT borrowing and with controls over the public sector exercised by the Treasury and the Ministère des Finances.

Technological developments altered cost structures; in particular, distance became less important. In turn, previous tariff arrangements were challenged. If the Post Office's and DGT's tariff structures remained unchanged, there existed the prospect of widening divergence between costs and prices, particularly for long-distance communications as their costs fell rapidly, that would give rise to incentives for competition, which itself undermined the ability of policy-makers to set tariffs.

Indeed, technological and economic developments also threatened the monopolies of the Post Office and DGT. In network operation, competition became easier, both indirect competition (notably through 'bypass') and direct competition from the creation of new networks, both fixed networks and then mobile ones. In the supply of the new advanced services and CPE there were powerful forces for competition to be allowed: such services were not natural monopolies; the diversity in their features, applications, and types of user made supply by one network operator difficult to justify; the blurring of sectoral boundaries created incentives and pressures for new suppliers in previously distinct industries (notably office equipment, electronics and computing, and broadcasting) to enter markets for advanced services and CPE. In addition, the increasing breadth of applications of telecommunications services meant that telecommunications became economically strategic, its supply affecting actors across the economy. It became increasingly important for nations to ensure an adequate supply of telecommunications, or run the risk of other sectors being damaged.

Yet competition raised many institutional and policy questions. The setting of standards was important for consumers and for the development of competition. Ensuring that competition would be 'fair and effective' involved issues of how to regulate suppliers, especially vertically-integrated network operators with market power. In addition, whereas most policy making in Britain and

France had traditionally been undertaken by a limited group of actors (dominated by the Post Office/DGT, civil servants in other government departments such as the Treasury/finance ministry, manufacturers, and elected politicians), competition involved new and more numerous actors. In addition, as a result of the blurring of sectoral boundaries and the wide usage of telecommunications services, a broader range of actors developed interests in telecommunications, both as suppliers and as users. These actors were directly affected by telecommunications policy and, if competition were permitted, could act both in the supply and demand for telecommunications and as participants in the policy process.

In the network equipment manufacturing subsector, the move from electro-mechanical to time division switches saw powerful pressures for concentration and internationalization. These pressures were particularly acute for manufacturers reliant on orders from one small/medium-sized country, such as GEC, Plessey, and CIT-Alcatel. Moreover, they threatened the traditional structure of relationships whereby the Post Office and the DGT worked closely with several national or nationally-based suppliers.

The technological and economic developments were common and exogenous to policy-makers in Britain and France. They offered powerful forces for change and represented challenges for the traditional institutional arrangements and patterns of policy in the two countries. However, they were not the only ones: the international environment of regulation provided another set of factors that called into question the British and French models of policy making that existed in the 1960s.

4

Pressures for Change from the International Regulatory Environment of Telecommunications from the 1960s to the 1990s

Telecommunications policy formation in Britain and France took place within an international regulatory environment—ideas and policies developed in other countries and by supra-national bodies. That environment provided a further set of forces for change for British and French policy-makers, in addition to technological and economic pressures. It could influence national institutions and policy making through several channels, notably by its effects on market structures, the strategies of firms, the competencies of international organizations, supra-national rules, new ideas, and policy-learning or emulation.

Developments in the international regulatory environment were common and external to Britain and France; several were also exogenous, as policy-makers in the two countries exercised little control over them. Moreover, certain international regulatory changes challenged the traditional institutional frameworks and policies that existed in Britain and France in the 1960s.

The evolution of the international regulatory environment is therefore used as another element in establishing the study of telecommunications in Britain and France between 1969 and 1997 as a critical case to test national institutionalist claims. Developments in the environment that offered pressures or opportunities for change for British and French policy-makers are set out together with their repercussions for policy in the two countries. Hence later chapters can analyse whether, in the face of these international regulatory pressures for change, Britain and France maintained stable and different national institutions and the impact of such institutions on policy making and economic performance.

Three sources of pressures for change for British and French policy arising from the international regulatory environment are examined in the period from the late 1960s to 1996: regulatory reforms in the United States; changes in international agreements and organizations; the development of European Community (EC) regulation. All three factors became much stronger in the 1980s and especially in the 1990s and represented significant challenges to the traditional telecommunications institutions and policies of Britain and France that existed in the late 1960s. Each is described only briefly, since the purpose is not to explain how and why the international environment altered but rather to establish the external pressures common to the two countries.

Pressures for Change from the United States

Regulatory Reform in American Telecommunications

For most of the twentieth century, the organizational structure of American telecommunications differed significantly from that seen in Britain, France and other European countries. A vertically-integrated supplier, American Telephone and Telegraph Company (AT&T), with its twenty-two local operating companies, held a virtual monopoly over the entire telecommunications sector, including international, inter-state and intra-state communications, together with customer premises equipment. Unlike public telecommunications operators in Western Europe, AT&T was privately owned, its monopoly was not statutory and its vertical integration extended to the manufacture of equipment (through ownership of Western Electric). Moreover, there was a specialized independent regulator, the Federal Communications Commission (FCC), which coexisted with regulation at the state level. Regulation of AT&T was extensive, notably with regard to tariffs.

Major regulatory reforms in the United States began in the late 1950s onwards and took place at an increasing pace in the 1970s, 1980s, and 1990s.[1] They led to the widespread introduction of competition, the break up of AT&T and attempts at comprehensive structural changes in the 1980s and 1990s.

Competition spread earliest in the supply of customer premises equipment.[2] AT&T restrictions on the attachment of 'foreign' (i.e. non-AT&T) CPE were undermined by judicial and FCC decisions in the 1950s and 1960s,[3] and in 1975, the FCC decided to accept direct connection of 'foreign' CPE. During the

---

[1]   For overviews until the 1980s, see J. Hills, *Deregulating Telecoms. Competition and Control in the United States, Japan and Britain* (London: Pinter, 1986), 50–77, and R. W. Crandall, *After the Breakup: U.S. Telecommunications in a More Competitive Era* (Washington: Brookings, 1991), 16–42; for more detailed analyses, see R. B. Horwitz, *The Irony of Regulatory Reform: The Deregulation of American Telecommunications* (New York and Oxford: Oxford University Press, 1989), and G. W. Brock, *The Telecommunications Industry: The Dynamics of Market Structure* (Cambridge, Mass. and London: Harvard University Press, 1981); for debates about ideas and interests, see M. Derthick and P. Quirk, *The Politics of Regulation* (Washington, DC: Brookings, 1985), Peltzman, S., 'The Economic Theory of Regulation After A Decade of Deregulation', *Brookings Papers on Economic Activity* (Microeconomics), 1989, 1–41.

[2]   See Brock, *The Telecommunications Industry*, 234–53.

[3]   The 'Hush-a-Phone' case (1956) and the 'Carterfone decision' (1968).

1970s, competition developed in the CPE market and in 1983, regulation of AT&T's tariffs for CPE was ended.[4]

AT&T's monopoly over the expanding market for advanced or 'enhanced' services, combining telecommunications and computing, was also gradually ended. In 1956, a Consent Decree[5] confined AT&T to supplying common carrier services and Western Electric to equipment for those services; hence AT&T was excluded from advanced services, notably those involving data communications. The FCC then issued new rules in 1971 (following its Computer I inquiry): services which were wholly or primarily for data processing were unregulated, so that the FCC only regulated services which were wholly or mainly for communications; AT&T continued to be excluded from supplying data processing services. Later in the 1970s, resale restrictions imposed by AT&T on firms that leased capacity on its network to provide value-added services were ruled unlawful by the FCC.[6] Finally, in the 1980 Computer II decision, the FCC ruled that only basic transmission, defined as 'a common carrier offering of transmission capacity for the movement of information' would continue to be regulated; other services were classified as 'enhanced services', and their prices were not regulated. AT&T was allowed to supply 'enhanced services', although it (and other common carriers) had to do so via fully separate subsidiaries.

AT&T's monopoly over private networks and domestic satellite communications also came under increasing attack from the late 1950s. In 1959, the FCC decided that private microwave networks could be established using frequencies above 890MC.[7] Then in 1969, the FCC approved an application by Microwave Communications Inc. (MCI) to offer a public microwave service between two cities. When hundreds of other applications to offer trunk-line private networks followed, the FCC decided to change policy to favour the principle of competition in 'specialized services'.[8] Moreover, restrictions on resale of capacity and cost sharing were progressively challenged and removed. Attempts by AT&T to prevent competition were prohibited in FCC rulings and in court cases in the 1970s; in particular, AT&T was obliged to offer interconnection to MCI subscribers, allowing them use AT&T's local network to access MCI's private network and was forced to lower its interconnection tariffs for MCI.[9] In addition, competition spread to domestic satellite communications

---

[4] By the Computer II decision of 1980—G. W. Brock, *Telecommunications Policy for the Information Age: From Monopoly to Competition* (Cambridge, Mass.: Harvard University Press, 1994), 93–8.

[5] Settling anti-trust suit begun against the company in 1949 by the Department of Justice.

[6] Brock, *The Telecommunications Industry*, 270–1.

[7] Allocation of Frequencies above 890MC, 27FCC 359 (1959).

[8] Its 'Specialized Common Carrier' decision of 1971.

[9] See Brock, *Telecommunications Policy for the Information Age*, 107–9 and 131–45.

networks: the FCC's 'open sky' decision of 1972 permitted AT&T's competitors to establish satellite networks for television distribution, private line services, and any new services created.[10]

The most far-reaching change came in network operation. The Department of Justice began an anti-trust suit against AT&T in 1974. Repeated attempts by AT&T to fend off the suit, including obtaining legislation recognizing its monopoly, all failed. Moreover, the academic climate of opinion had become increasingly hostile to monopolies, especially in telecommunications; ideas of 'natural monopoly' were challenged by concepts of 'contestable markets',[11] the virtues of competition and the dangers of regulatory capture.[12] Fearing an unfavourable court ruling, AT&T accepted that it would be broken up in 1984, an agreement that formed the basis of the Modified Final Judgement issued by Judge Harold Greene in the case itself. AT&T retained its trunk ('long line') and international networks, together with its CPE business, but was divested of its local operating companies which became seven separate regional Bell operating companies (RBOCs, also known as 'Baby Bells'). The US was divided into 161 local access and transport areas (LATAs); the RBOCs were allowed to offer services within the LATAs, but not inter-LATA services or 'information services'. Competition was allowed in all services other than communications within LATAs, where state commissions could allow continued monopolies by RBOCs.

After the 1984 break up, competition developed in inter-LATA communications, together with international services, from operators such as MCI, Sprint, and GTE, and from resellers; AT&T's share of the market fell substantially.[13] However, the structural separation introduced in the Modified Final Judgement of 1984 was gradually weakened by FCC rules[14] and court decisions after 1984. Requirements that common carriers establish separate subsidiaries for enhanced services were ended and restrictions on the RBOCs supplying enhanced and 'information services' were largely removed.[15] AT&T was also allowed to enter mobile communications in the 1990s (via its purchase of MaCaw Cellular Communications). The RBOCs' monopoly over intra-LATA services under the Modified Final Judgement was not confirmed by legislation

[10] See Brock, The Telecommunications Industry, 256–66.
[11] W. J. Baumol, J. Panzar, and R. D. Willig, Contestable Markets and the Theory of Industry Structure (New York: Harcourt Brace Jovanovich, 1982).
[12] G. J. Stigler, 'The Theory of Economic Regulation', Bell Journal of Economics and Management Science, 2(1) (1971), 1–21; S. Peltzman, 'Towards a More General Theory of Regulation', Journal of Law and Economics, 14 (1976), 109–48; cf. G. Kolko, The Triumph of Conservatism: A Reinterpretation of American History 1900–1916 (New York: Free Press, 1977).
[13] See Crandall, After the Breakup, and R. W. Crandall and L. Waverman, Talk is Cheap: The Promise of Regulatory Reform in North American Telecommunications (Washington: Brookings, 1995) for details.
[14] Notably in the Computer III inquiry of 1985 and subsequent rules of 1986.
[15] For a discussion, see Brock, Telecommunications Policy, 217–42.

and a considerable number of states allowed intra-LATA competition.[16] Moreover, the RBOCs' local monopoly was weakened in the late 1980s and 1990s by competitive access providers who offered local access private lines and switched circuits, and gained interconnection rights with the RBOCs' local networks.[17]

The erosion of the 1984 structural boundaries was recognized and accelerated by the 1996 Telecommunications Act.[18] The RBOCs' monopoly over local markets was ended. A long list of requirements was imposed on them to enable competition to operate and be 'fair'; the most important included offering interconnection throughout the local network at fair and non-discriminatory terms. In turn, when a local market was deemed to have become 'competitive', the remaining restrictions on the RBOCs were to be lifted, allowing them to become vertically integrated firms, including in the supply of long-distance communications. The 1996 Act marked a further diminution of the RBOCs' monopolies and offered the prospect of competition throughout the telecommunications sector.

Repercussions of American Regulatory Reforms for Britain and France

Regulatory reforms in the United States were undertaken with almost no reference to policy-makers or events in other countries. However, they had major repercussions for telecommunications policy in Western European countries: they provided an example of change and a source of ideas; they contributed to modifying the competitive dynamic of telecommunications; they were followed by direct pressure by American firms and policy-makers for regulatory reform in other countries.[19]

Changes in American telecommunications offered a powerful example of reform. Supporters of liberalization could point to the operation of competition 'disproving' theories of natural monopoly in telecommunications. Moreover, the American experience seemed to indicate that once competition began, it was difficult to stop or confine it, especially with technological advances that blurred boundary lines between telecommunications and computing and

---

[16] Crandall and Waverman, Talk is Cheap, 46–8.

[17] See Brock, Telecommunications Policy, 243–56.

[18] For details, see P. W. Huber, M. K. Kellog, and J. Thorne, The Telecommunications Act of 1996 (New York: Little Brown, 1996); for a critical overview, see R. Klinger, The New Information Industry: Regulatory Challenges and the First Amendment (Washington: Brookings, 1997).

[19] Cf. S. K. Vogel, Freer Markets, More Rules: Regulatory Reform in Advanced Industrial Countries (Ithica and London: Cornell University Press, 1996), 35–8; Hills, Deregulating Telecoms; K. Dyson and P. Humphreys, 'Introduction: Politics, Markets and Communications Policies' in Dyson and Humphreys (eds.), The Political Economy of Communications: International and European Dimensions (London and New York: Routledge, 1990).

between advanced services and basic transmission. Yet ending monopolies in the United States did not lead to the demise of AT&T or to the break down of the network. Indeed, supporters could point to gains such as lower prices and rapid innovation and growth for CPE, private networks, advanced services, and long-distance services, with consequent advantages for users (especially businesses) and general competitiveness. Moreover, if competition was believed to be inevitable, European countries and suppliers had reasons to follow the United States in order to limit any 'first mover' advantages for American firms. On the other hand, AT&T's fate provided managements of public telecommunications operators (PTOs) in other countries with the fear that they could follow suit in being broken up and losing their monopolies; hence it underlined their need to prepare to face a changing regulatory environment. In addition, opponents of competition could argue that it led to tariff rebalancing which damaged small residential users.

Regulatory reform in the United States also altered the competitive dynamic of world telecommunications, notably because of the size of the American market, which was the largest market for telecommunications services and equipment in the world and was several times the size of national markets in Western Europe.[20] On the one hand, the end of AT&T's monopolies over CPE, services and networks appeared to offer opportunities for foreign suppliers, including European ones, to enter the American market.[21] On the other hand, competition in their domestic market created powerful incentives for AT&T and the RBOCs to expand abroad. After 1984 AT&T did indeed pursue a strategy of international expansion, as did the RBOCs in the 1990s.[22] American firms were often large (even the RBOCs had revenues similar to British Telecom and France Télécom), had lengthy experience of telecommunications markets and as private companies were able to form alliances with European companies or establish subsidiaries in Europe. National public telecommunications operators such as British Telecom and the DGT/France Télécom thus faced rivals who were internationalizing, creating competitive pressures to follow suit, especially as the number of potential partners was limited and large business users were believed to demand global services. In the 1980s, a small number of international links were formed, especially in equipment supply, but the 1990s witnessed a series of international alliances and joint ventures between PTOs. The most important in the early/mid-1990s were Concert, Global One, Unisource and World Partners; they involved European PTOs including BT (in Concert) and France Télécom (in Global One) linked to other European and non-

[20] See Ch. 11 for figures.
[21] E. M. Noam, 'International Telecommunications in Transition', in R. W. Crandall and K. Flamm (eds.), *Changing the Rules: Technological Change, International Competition and regulation in Telecommunications* (Washington: Brookings, 1989), 287–90.
[22] Ibid. 281 and A. Mouline, 'Les Stratégies internationales des opérateurs de télécommunications', *Communications & Stratégies*, 21 (1996), 77–93.

European PTOs, including powerful US operators such as AT&T, MCI, and Sprint.[23] In turn, international alliances created further dynamic pressures for national policies and institutions; in particular, they broke with the tradition of nationally-separated PTOs in Britain and France, they involved co-operation with other PTOs who might require organisational compatibility and they often required the agreement of regulatory authorities outside the two countries (notably in the US and EC).

Direct lobbying of European policy-makers by American actors (public and private) offered a third mechanism linking regulatory events in the United States to policy in Britain and France. American companies, including AT&T, IBM, and PanAmSat, pressed European policy-makers for greater freedom to supply services and equipment. American policy-makers, including those in the Federal government and Congress, also lobbied for regulatory change, attacked restrictions on competition as 'unfair trade barriers' and used the need for reciprocity in market access to argue for liberalization of European telecommunications.

International Organizations

The Changing Role of International Organizations

Until the 1980s, the role of international organizations in the regulation of telecommunications was limited.[24] Rules for standards and revenue-sharing for international communications were decided within the International Telecommunications Union (ITU), established in 1865; satellites were covered by Intelsat, created in 1964. Both organizations protected the monopolies of national PTOs over international communications. They lacked powers to impose decisions on members and operated slowly, acting by consensus. In effect, they acted as coordinating organizations that brought together PTOs on matters that required international co-operation.

From the 1980s, the international regulation of telecommunications faced increasingly strong pressures for reform, led by American policy-makers and firms.[25] An early indication came in satellite policy. Intelsat had been established

---

[23] See D. Elixmann and H. Hermann, 'Strategic Alliances in the Telecommunications Service Sector: Challenges for Corporate Strategy', *Communications & Stratégies*, 24 (1996), 57–88.

[24] For a history, see J. G. Savage, *The Politics of International Telecommunications Regulation* (Boulder and London: Westview, 1989).

[25] See: Hills, 'Deregulating Telecoms', esp. 156–82; J.-L. Renaud, 'The Role of the International Telecommunications Union: Conflict, Resolution and the Industrialized Countries' and M. Komiya, 'Intelsat and the Debate about Satellite Competition' in Dyson and Humphreys, *The Political Economy of Communications*; K. B. Stanley, 'International Settlements in a Changing Global Telecom Market', in W. H. Melody (ed.), *Telecom Reform: Principles, Policies and Regulatory Practices* (Lyngby: Technical University of Denmark, 1997).

as a non-profit making international consortium that owned and operated satellites for international communications; it leased capacity, both to PTOs from member countries and to other organizations, but it had to offer the same tariffs for all routes. In 1984–5, President Reagan and the FCC authorized the launch of private satellite systems. They criticized Intelsat's 'monopoly'[26] and argued that competition should be allowed because of its benefits to American firms and users. Thus profit-making private suppliers, able to vary tariffs by route, could develop.

Pressure for change spread to the ITU. In the late 1980s, the United States, supported by Britain, sought to exclude advanced international services and networks from ITU regulations (which cover matters such as standards and tariff principles); they were only partially successful in this.[27] Tariff and access arrangements for international services came under attack in the 1990s. Traditionally, monopoly PTOs had agreed a fixed price (the 'accounting rate') to be paid by the PTO from which an international call originated to the PTO in the receiving country on whose network the call was terminated to prevent tariffs from being undercut. The system was protected by restrictions on resale of international capacity. However, it encouraged rates to be set above cost and by the 1990s, PTOs in certain countries with many originating calls, notably the United States, were making very large payments to other PTOs which were receiving calls.[28] In the mid-1990s, proposals for reform were being seriously discussed, including altering or removing resale restrictions, reforming the accounting rate system and allowing access to foreign markets so that a PTO in one country could terminate calls in other countries.[29]

Perhaps the most significant alteration in international regulation was the inclusion of telecommunications in free trade arrangements. During the 1980s, the United States pressed for services, including telecommunications, to be covered by the GATT (General Agreement for Tariffs and Trade). This occurred in the 1990s, when telecommunications services were classified as 'traded services' and were included in the Uruguay Round and then in the WTO negotiations that ended in the General Agreement on Trade in Services (GATS) concluded in 1997. The general principles of GATS apply to telecommunications, together with specific measures in an Annex on

---

[26] Despite the existence of regional satellite systems such as Eutelsat in Europe—see Hills, *Deregulating Telecoms*, 168–9.
[27] See Renaud, 'The Role of the International Telecommunications Union', 42–9.
[28] Over the decade 1985–94, the 'net settlement' paid by American public telecommunications operators totalled $26.9 billion—see Stanley, 'International Settlements'.
[29] See R. Mansell, 'Network Governance: Designing New regimes', in R. Mansell and R. Silverstone (eds.), *Communication by Design: The Politics of Information and Communication Technologies* (Oxford: Oxford University Press, 1996).

Telecommunications; in addition, countries were able to choose to add further commitments in schedules appended to the agreement.[30] Progressive liberalization was to be introduced, through successive 'rounds' of multilateral negotiations, but in any case, WTO members had to provide rights of access to domestic networks. Regulatory decisions had to be non-discriminatory, transparent and 'impartial' with respect to all market participants. A Reference Paper, adopted by most countries which took part in negotiations on basic telecommunications services, added much greater detail concerning matters such as interconnection and abuse of dominant position. The GATS signalled that the WTO could achieve considerable legal powers over national regulators.

International Regulation and Pressures for Change in British and French Telecommunications

The Post Office/British Telecom and the DGT/France Télécom earned large profits from international services and networks in the period 1969–97, funds which were then available to cross-subsidize losses made on other services.[31] Developments in international regulation such as permission for private satellites systems, new access and interconnection regimes and an end to accounting rates, all threatened to undermine their ability to set prices above costs and to earn lucrative profits from international services. They aided the entry of new operators who could build specialized international networks and bypass national PTOs. Greater competition in international services increased the pressures on existing PTOs to establish global networks that would fulfil the needs of multinational companies, the source of very large revenues.

International regulation also indicated that that the ability of policy-makers to maintain national monopolies was being undermined. At first, this only concerned international services. However, the WTO agreement widened international regulation of telecommunications to domestic telecommunications services and networks as the scope of traded services was extended and offered the prospect of domestic monopolies being ended by international regulation. Moreover, the WTO was given the power to make decisions that are binding on member states. Whilst international organizations had had limited impacts on national regulation by the 1990s, they offered a direction for change and hence could influence expectations of the future path of telecommunications regulation.

---

[30] L. Tuthill, 'The GATS and New Rules for Regulators', *Telecommunications Policy*, 21(9–10) (1997), 783–98.   [31] For indicative figures, see Ch. 11.

The European Community

The Development of EC Regulation of Telecommunications[32]

The EC played little role in telecommunications policy until the 1980s.[33] Telecommunications were regarded as a matter for member states, no attempt was made to apply EC competition law to PTO monopolies and the sector was excluded from the 1976 directive on the opening of public procurement supply contracts.[34] However, from the early 1980s, steps were taken to establish an EC presence in information and communications. The EC pursued a two-pronged approach:[35] the establishment of research and development programmes in information and communications;[36] the creation of an EC regulatory framework for telecommunications. The second emerged as of much greater importance for national telecommunications policy.

At first, the EC appeared to represent only a source of influential advice for member states, and, moreover, one pressing for rather limited change. In the early 1980s, it passed non-binding calls for greater competition in CPE and advanced services.[37] Modest steps were taken in the mid-1980s, including the first European Court of Justice case against a telecommunications monopoly[38] and the establishment of a new Commission Directorate General for Telecommunications, Information Industries, and Innovation (now known as DG XIII) in 1986. However, in 1987, the Commission issued a Green Paper which argued that EC action was needed to ensure a common market in telecommunica-

---

[32] References are to the European Community (EC), as action has mostly been taken under the EC 'pillar' of the European Union.

[33] W. Sandholtz, *High-Tech Europe* (Berkeley, Los Angeles, and Oxford: University of California Press, 1992), 92–9; V. Schneider and R. Werle, 'International Regime or Corporate Actor? The European Community in Telecommunications Policy', in Dyson and Humphreys, *The Political Economy of Telecommunications*; H. Ungerer and N. Costello, *Telecommunications in Europe* (Brussels: Commission of the European Communities, 1988), 129.

[34] Council, *Council Directive of 21 December 1976 coordinating procedures for the award of public supply contracts* (77/62/EEC, OJ L 13/1, 15.1.77).

[35] M. Thatcher, 'The Development of European Regulatory Frameworks: The Expansion of European Community Policy Making in Telecommunications', in E. Stavridis, E. Mosialos, R. Morgan, and H. Machin (eds.), *New Challenges for the European Union* (Aldershot: Dartmouth, 1997).

[36] See J. Peterson and M. Sharp, *Technology Policy in the European Union for overall research policy* (Basingstoke: Macmillan, 1998).

[37] See Commission, *Recommendations on Telecommunications* (COM(80)422 Final, 1 September 1980) and Commission, *Communication from the Commission to the Council on telecommunications*, (COM(84) 277, 18 May 1984), agreed by the Council, December 1984; cf. Sandholtz, *High-Tech Europe*, 226–8 and Ungerer and Costello, *Telecommunications in Europe*, 135–6.

[38] Over telex-forwarding services—*Italy v Commission*, Case 41/83 (1985), 2 *Common Market Law Review*, 368; for a discussion, see R. Schulte-Braucks, 'European Telecommunications Law in the Light of the British Telecom Judgement', *Common Market Law Review*, 23 (1986), 39–59.

tions.[39] EC measures would not only adapt the regulatory framework to technological and economic changes that made competition in the supply of advanced services and CPE advantageous and/or inevitable, and allow European firms to enjoy economies of scale, but were also needed to satisfy the legal provisions of the Treaty of Rome.[40] The Green Paper therefore suggested substantial changes in the EC's regulatory role. EC law should end PTO monopolies over CPE and advanced services and networks. Moreover, EC rules should ensure that competition was 'fair and effective'. However, it did not suggest revolutionary modifications: public ownership of PTOs was not questioned;[41] member states could maintain PTO monopolies over the infrastructure and over 'reserved services', namely voice telephony and telex services, which accounted for 85 per cent of the telecommunications services market; the 'public service' tasks (such as universal service) of PTOs were recognized and promised protection.

The Council of Ministers accepted the Commission's approach (in June 1988) and the Commission turned to implementing its proposals. Two sets of measures were taken. The first were 'liberalization' directives that permitted competition and prohibited member states from maintaining monopolies ('special and exclusive rights') over the supply of equipment and advanced services. The 1988 Terminals Directive[42] required member states to permit competition in all types of CPE by the end of 1990. It was followed by the 1990 Services Directive[43] which ended the right of member states to maintain special and exclusive rights over advanced services and networks, such as value-added network services and data transmission services, together with simple resale of leased line capacity.[44] Again, a timetable was issued, which extended to the end of 1992. In the field of public procurement, a Council Directive in 1990 banned monopoly telecommunications operators from

---

[39] Commission, *Towards a Dynamic European Economy—Green Paper on the development of the common market for telecommunications services and equipment*, (COM(87) 290, 30 June 1987).

[40] Notably Article 30 (prohibitions on quantitative restrictions on trade within the EC or measures having equivalent effect, including non-tariff barriers), Article 37 (commercial monopolies that prevent non-discrimination or removal of quantitative barriers), Article 85 (agreements restricting competition), Article 86 (banning abuse of a dominant position) and Article 90 (applying Treaty provisions to public undertakings and those enterprises to which member states grant 'special and exclusive rights').

[41] Article 222 of the Treaty of Rome prevents the EC from determining ownership in member states.

[42] Commission, *Commission Directive of 16 May 1988 on competition in the markets in telecommunications terminal equipment* (88/301/EEC OJ L 131/73, 27.5.88).

[43] Commission, *Commission Directive of 28 June 1990 on competition in the markets for telecommunications services* (90/388/EEC, OJ L192/10, 24.7.90).

[44] i.e. transmission capacity can be rented from a PTO (often at a fixed sum for a 'leased line') and then resold.

discriminating in favour of their national champions and against other EC companies.[45]

EC liberalization did not mean 'deregulation'. On the contrary, EC legislation contained a second set of measures governing the operation and regulation of competition in member states. Decisions by national authorities had to be undertaken in conformity with general EC law, including principles such as non-discrimination, proportionality and transparency. Member states had to ensure that regulation and supply were legally separated: PTOs could not continue to be regulators. EC legislation then set other, specific rules for services and equipment, many of which were designed to ensure that competition was 'fair' and effective and to prevent member states and/or their PTOs from inhibiting the development of real competition.[46] Suppliers and users of CPE and advanced services were given the right of access/connection to the infrastructure. Harmonized conditions for access to the infrastructure were established, dealing with matters such as tariff principles, supply and usage conditions and technical interfaces. Moreover, although member states could license suppliers, they could only require compliance with EC-determined conditions, notably 'essential requirements' of safety, protection of network integrity, and interoperability. The process of establishing EC-recognized standards and norms was begun, whilst for public procurement, rules governing tenders were laid down to ensure that contracts were awarded 'fairly'.

In the Council of Ministers, member states accepted the principle of the EC developing a legislative framework regulating the supply of equipment and advanced services.[47] However, telecommunications legislation saw a major innovation, both for EC regulation of the sector and for EC policy in general: the use of Article 90(3) by the Commission to pass directives. Article 90(1) forbids member states from introducing or maintaining any measures contrary to the Treaty of Rome with respect to 'public undertakings' and those enterprises to which member states grant 'special and exclusive rights'; it specifically mentions Articles 7 and 85–94. Under Article 90(3), the Commission ensures the application of the Article and if necessary, can issue appropriate directives and decisions on its own.

---

[45] Council, *Council Directive of 17 September1990 on procurement procedures of entities operating in the water, energy, transport and telecommunications sectors* (90/531/EEC, OJ L 297/1, 21.10.90).

[46] For services, the most important provisions were contained in the Open Network Provision (ONP) Directive—Council, *Council Directive of 28 June 1990 on the establishment of the internal market for telecommunications services through the implementation of open network provision* (90/387/EEC OJ L 192/1, 24.07.90), a framework directive which was followed by directives dealing with specific services; for a discussion, see W. Sauter, 'The System of Open Network Provision Legislation and the Future of European Telecommunications Regulation' in C. Scott and O. Audéoud (eds.), *The Future of EC Telecommunications Law* (Cologne: Bundesanzeiger, 1996).

[47] For an overview of the process, see Thatcher, 'The Development of European Regulatory Frameworks'.

Article 90 had never been used to end monopolies granted by member states or for establishing general competition policy.[48] However, the Commission (led by the Directorate General for competition, DG IV) decided to issue the 1988 Terminals Directive under Article 90(3). This meant that approval by the Council of Ministers and the European Parliament was not needed. The use of Article 90 was strongly opposed by some member states, including France,[49] despite the wide agreement in the Council of Ministers over the content of the Terminals Directive and they launched a legal challenge. In an important ruling, the European Court of Justice (ECJ) largely upheld the Commission's position. [50] It ruled that the Commission did have the right to issue the directive under Article 90(3). Moreover, it held that regulatory measures which could, directly or indirectly, harm trade amongst member states were illegal, being incompatible with Article 30 of the Treaty of Rome, and hence held that 'exclusive rights' over the supply of CPE were unlawful. A second challenge to the Commission's use of Article 90(3) (to issue the Services Directive) also largely failed, as the ECJ again upheld the Commission.[51]

The 1990s saw the extension of the EC's role in telecommunications. The legal basis for its approach was strengthened by the 1993 Treaty on European Union (the Maastricht Treaty) whose Article 129 presented the objective of a 'system of open and competitive markets' and by the 1994 Bangemann Report's call for further EC action to extend fair and effective competition, including to infrastructure provision and 'the Information Society' in Europe.[52] Following the rulings of the ECJ, the Commission used Article 90(3) to issue other liberalization directives ending the right of member states to maintain 'special and exclusive rights'. Thus the right to compete was extended to the supply of satellite services and equipment under the 1994 Satellite Directive,[53] whilst for mobile communications, maximization of competition (at least a duopoly) was

[48] See C. Scott, 'Changing Patterns of European Community Utilities Law: An Institutional Hypothesis', in J. Shaw and G. More (eds.), *New Legal Dynamics of European Integration* (Oxford: Oxford University Press, 1996).

[49] Britain, despite its image of 'Euro-scepticism', supported the Commission's move.

[50] Case C-202/88 French Republic, supported by Italy, Belgium, Germany, and Greece, v. Commission of the European Communities [1990] ECR I-2223.

[51] Joined cases C-271, C281 and C289/90, Spain, Belgium, and Italy v. Commission [1992] ECR I-5833.

[52] High-Level Group [chairman, M. Bangemann], *Europe and the Information Society: Recommendations to the European Council* (Brussels: Commission, 1994); the report was the product of a high-level group, largely of industrialists, chaired by Commissioner Martin Bangemann; for an overview, see C. Scott, 'Current Issues in EC Telecommunications Law', in C. Scott and O. Audéod, *The Future of EC Telecommunications Law* (Cologne: Bondesanzeiger, 1996).

[53] Commission, *Commission Directive of 13 October 1994 amending Directive 88/301/EEC and Directive 90/388/EEC in particular with regard to satellite communications* (94/46/EC, OJ L 268/15, 19.10.94).

required under the 1996 Mobile Communications Directive.[54] In June 1993, the Council of Ministers accepted Commission proposals for new measures extending competition to the core of telecommunications (notably voice telephony and possibly the infrastructure) and creating further rules for regulating its operation. Hence competition was extended to network operation, the heart of the telecommunications sector. The Voice Telephony Directive of 1995 ended the ability of most member states to maintain 'special and exclusive rights' for voice telephony from January 1998.[55] Directives were passed allowing use of cable television networks for the supply of non-reserved services from 1996 and competition in infrastructure provision from January 1998.[56] Thus by 1998, competition was permitted throughout the telecommunications sector in most member states by EC law.

The extension of competition was accompanied by 're-regulatory' measures, as the EC's regulatory framework became increasingly detailed and comprehensive. Thus, for instance, the Voice Telephony Directive contained many rules governing competition and supply, such as rights of access to the infrastructure, appeals against PTO decisions to national regulatory authorities, the basis of tariffs, quality of service and the publication of information. In 1997 directives establishing EC rules for matters central to competition were passed, notably concerning universal service, network access/interconnection and tariffs, licensing, and the behaviour of national regulatory authorities.[57] Furthermore, the mid-1990s saw the Commission (and especially DG IV, the competition Directorate General) become involved in regulating international alliances and agreements between PTOs, deciding on their compatibility with

[54]   Commission, *Commission Directive of 16 January 1996 amending Directive 90/388/EEC with regard to mobile and personal communications* (96/2/EC, OJ L 20/59, 26.01.96).

[55]   Council, *Council Directive of 13 December 1995 on the application of open network provision (ONP) to voice telephony* (95/62/EC, OJ L 321/6, 30.12.95); it contained temporary derogations for countries with less developed or very small networks.

[56]   Commission, *Commission Directive 95/51 of 18 October 1995 amending Directive 90/388/EEC with regard to the abolition of the restrictions on the use of cable television networks for the provision of already liberalized telecommunications services* (95/51/EC, OJ, L 256/49, 26.10.95), Commission, *Commission Directive 96/19/EC of 28 February 1996 amending Directive 90/388/EEC regarding the implementation of full competition in telecommunications markets* (96/19/EC, OJ L 74/13, 22.03.96); temporary derogations were available to certain member states with small or underdeveloped infrastructures.

[57]   For licensing, see European Parliament and Council, *Directive 97/13/EC of the European Parliament and of the Council of 10 April 1997 on a common framework for general authorizations and individual licences in the field of telecommunications services* (OJ L 117/15, 07.05.97); for universal service and interconnection, see European Parliament and Council, *Directive 97/33/EC of the European Parliament and of the Council on interconnection in telecommunications with regard to ensuring universal service and interoperability through application of the principles of open network provision (ONP)* (OJ L 199/32, 29.10.97); European Parliament and Council, *Directive 97/51/EC of the European Parliament and of the Council amending Council directives 90/387/EEC and 92/44/EEC for the purpose of adaptation to a competitive environment* (OJ L 295/23, 29.10.97).

EC competition law.[58] By 1997 there were few aspects of the regulation of telecommunications competition that had not seen the development or application of EC law and a comprehensive EC regulatory framework was rapidly being put into place.

EC Regulation and Pressures for Change in Member States

From its very limited steps in the mid-1980s, the EC had, by 1997, established its presence in most important areas of telecommunications regulation traditionally decided at the national level. It had passed legislation ending the right of member states to maintain monopolies in all areas of the sector. It had established rules for the operation of competition and the pursuit of wider policy objectives.

EC regulation was a common external factor for Britain and France, but was not a wholly exogenous factor for them, because policy-makers from both countries participated in EC decision-making. Nevertheless, they had to share decision-making with other countries and with other EC institutions. In particular, the Commission developed its own approaches to telecommunications regulation,[59] and by using Article 90(3), it was able to pass legislation to liberalize markets without approval by the Council of Ministers and European Parliament. The European Court of Justice was important in upholding the Commission's approach and in having the legal power to impose its rulings on member states.

Analysis of the growth of EC regulation has focused on the roles of member states, the Commission and interest groups, or the processes of development and the use of legal instruments.[60] Debate has often centred on the extent to which EC policy was imposed on member states, whether it has reduced 'state autonomy' and its effects in creating a 'multi-level game'. However, the current study is not concerned with how and why EC regulation grew but rather with stable and differing national institutions and policy making in the face of common international or supranational forces for change, including the development of EC policy. Without entering into debates about the expansion of

---

[58] In particular, it examined the agreement between France Télécom and Deutsche Telekom, insisting on certain changes, and that between MCI and BT.

[59] Cf. Schneider and Werle, 'International Regime or Corporate Actor?'.

[60] Cf. C. Scott, 'Changing Patterns of European Community Utilities Law and Policy: An Institutional Hypothesis', in J. Shaw and G. More (eds.), New Legal Dynamics of European Union (Oxford: Oxford University Press, 1996); M. Thatcher, 'Regulatory Reform and Internationalization in Telecommunications', in J. E. S. Hayward (ed.), Industrial Enterprise and European Integration (Oxford: Oxford University Press, 1995); S. Schmidt, 'Sterile Debate and Dubious Generalisation: European Integration Theory Tested by Telecommunications and Electricity', Journal of Public Policy, 16(3), 233–71, and 'Commission Activism: Subsuming Telecommunications and Electricity under European Competition Law', Journal of European Public Policy, 5(1), 169–84; Sandholtz, High-Tech Europe.

EC regulation, three sets of implications for British and French institutions and policy making, can be underlined, in terms of paradigms, institutional frameworks and levels of decision-making, and competitive dynamics.

EC regulation offered a European paradigm of regulation that differed from the traditional framework of policy in Britain and France. That paradigm centred on ending monopolies and measures, both substantive and procedural, to ensure that competition was 'fair' and effective. It sought to create a single European market with European rules governing its operation, instead of nationally determined policy and separate national markets.

The legal powers of EC member states to act unilaterally at the national level were limited by EC legislation. Key institutional and regulatory decisions were made at the EC level (regardless of whether they were imposed on national government and other actors or voluntarily accepted by them) and in forms that were legally binding on member states. EC regulation outlawed traditional institutional arrangements and policies in Britain and France, notably by prohibiting member states from maintaining monopoly supply and by its re-regulatory measures aimed at ensuring 'fair' regulation, including the separation of regulation and supply and the application of principles such as transparency, non-discrimination, and proportionality.

Finally, EC regulation altered the competitive dynamic in Western Europe. It removed the ability of national governments to keep domestic markets closed to other European operators and gave entrants rights such as interconnection and cost-based tariffs. European rules for fair and effective competition prevented legal monopolies for national PTOs, but also created opportunities for PTOs to expand into the markets of other EC member states. For PTOs, the competitive dynamic pointed to pressure on domestic markets from new entrants, but opportunities for expansion abroad, both directly or through alliances with other operators.

Conclusion

Telecommunications policy-makers in Britain and France faced increasing pressures for change from the international regulatory environment, forces that greatly intensified from the mid-1980s onwards. Those pressures arose from the impacts of regulatory reforms in the United States, changes in international organizations and the development of the EC's regulatory framework. The pressures were common to both countries. They were also largely exogenous to them—regulatory reforms in the United States took place with little consideration of policy in Britain and France, whilst the two countries were only two voices among several within international organizations, whereas the United States was very powerful. EC regulation was less exogenous in that Britain and France were influential members of the EC, but even so, the Commission supported by the European Court of Justice established and used its powers to impose decisions on member states.

International regulatory developments provided several forms of forces that conflicted with the traditional institutions and policies that had existed in Britain and France in the late 1960s, notably new ideas and paradigms, supra-national decisions demanding compliance and influences on market structures and competitive dynamics. In all of these, the central pressures concerned the extension of competition. Changes in the United States, international organizations, and the EC all resulted in national monopolies based on legal protection of domestic PTOs coming under increasing attack. With competition came issues of regulation to ensure that competition was 'fair and effective'. Thus the ending of national monopolies did not mark the end of public policy but rather a new agenda, based around questions such as market access, licensing, interconnection, cost-based tariffs, the organizational basis of regulation, and the decision-making procedures of regulatory bodies. New entrants (potential and actual), foreign governments (especially that of the US), international organizations, and the EC all had interests in the regulation of competition.

International regulatory pressures for ending national monopolies also held implications for market structures, competitive dynamics, and relationships among market actors. National PTOs lost their assured national markets and became exposed to other suppliers. Hence they became vulnerable to attack, especially if tariffs did not match costs or if governments placed burdens on them. At the same time, the spread of competition allowed PTOs to expand abroad and to move away from being merely national monopoly suppliers. Internationalisation offered the prospect of offsetting losses of domestic market shares.

Developments in the international regulatory environment offered challenges to the traditional institutions and policies of Britain and France. They stood in sharp contrast to national monopoly PTOs which had few foreign activities, engaged in large-scale cross-subsidization, were frequently used as instruments of government industrial, social, and economic policy, and were set in close and well-established relations with national champion equipment manufacturers. Moreover, the impact of developments in the international environment was increased by their congruence with several of the pressures arising from technological and economic developments described in the previous chapter. The issue to be examined is whether Britain and France maintained differing institutional frameworks and patterns of policy making in the face of these common pressures for change.

PART II

Institutions and Policy Making 1969–1979

5

The Institutional Framework of the Telecommunications Sector in Britain and France 1969–1979: Divergence, Reform, and Standstill

The late 1960s offer a useful starting point for a comparative analysis of the stability, dissimilarities and impacts of institutions in British and French telecommunications. On the one hand, by 1969, the institutional frameworks—defined as the formal organization of the sector, notably the bodies established in the sector and their formal powers governing decision making—in the two countries shared many common elements.[1] Moreover, several key institutional features were long-standing, having been established for decades.[2] On the other hand, there was dissatisfaction with existing arrangements in the two countries and they faced similar issues concerning institutional reform. Furthermore, the 1960s and 1970s saw increasing international pressures for change, arising from technological and economic developments and, to a lesser degree, from the international regulatory environment in the form of new ideas and reforms in the United States.

The present chapter therefore analyses two sets of issues concerning the institutional framework of telecommunications between the late 1960s and the end of the 1970s. First, it looks at institutional reform, and in particular, whether Britain and France maintained their long-standing institutional frameworks in the face of domestic and international pressures for change, the processes of change, and the conditions for institutional modification. A second area of investigation centres on cross-national comparison and looks at whether, from a position of relative institutional similarity, but facing common external pressures for change, the two countries followed similar or different institutional paths, and the reasons for any differences. Both these sets of issues are central to national institutionalist claims that countries maintain stable and different national institutional arrangements and/or follow dissimilar institutional paths. The chapter also performs an essential function for later analysis of the impacts of national institutions by identifying major institutional features and cross-national differences; examination of the policy process during

---

[1] For the definition of 'institutions', see Ch. 1.   [2] See Ch. 2.

the 1970s in Chapter 6 can therefore study how policy making in practice related to those formal institutional arrangements and consider whether they aid in explaining national patterns and cross-national differences.

1969 is an important date for a comparison of telecommunications as it saw major institutional reforms in Britain, and more limited ones in France, which ended several of the similarities between the two countries and hence resulted in divergence in the organization of the sector between the two countries. The chapter begins by analysing the process of reform that led to the Post Office Act 1969. It then examines the central aspects of the institutional arrangements that existed after 1969, before turning to attempts to introduce further reforms during the 1970s and the reasons for their failure. Analysis of the French case begins with the institutional arrangements that existed in 1969 and continued throughout the 1970s; equivalent characteristics to those in Britain are studied in order to allow comparison between the two countries. Pressures for institutional reform and the considerable obstacles to change that allowed only limited alteration to be made are then analysed. The concluding section directly compares the major institutional features of telecommunications in Britain and France and relates the findings to national institutionalist claims. It underlines that the key institutional features of the sector were similar by 1969 and that dissatisfaction with the organization of the sector existed in both countries, leading to attempts at reform. Nevertheless, the two countries followed dissimilar paths of institutional modification from 1969, resulting in institutional divergence. Hence the chapter also analyses the processes of institutional change, and considers the conditions under which reform was possible, together with the obstacles to its implementation, in order to explain the contrasting institutional evolutions seen in the two countries.

Britain

Pressures for Change in the Institutional Framework in the 1960s[3]

The 1960s saw increasing pressures for change in several of the long-standing institutional features of telecommunications (described in Chapter 2). One was the Post Office's (PO) position as a government department, headed by a minister, the Postmaster General (PMG) and forming part of the civil service. Another was the existence of postal and telecommunications services within the same organization. The third, although much less important, was the extent of the PO's legal monopoly.

[3] For a short history, see J. Hills, *Deregulating Telecoms: Competition and Control in the United States, Japan and Britain* (London: Pinter, 1986), ch. 3, and *Information Technology and Industrial Policy* (London: Croom Helm, 1984), ch. 4; for a detailed history see D. Pitt, *The Telecommunications Function in the British Post Office* (Hampshire: Saxon House, 1980).

The 1960s saw renewed dissatisfaction with constraints on PO capital spending, excess demand, lack of long-term policies, as PO spending became caught up in 'stop-go' policies, and government intervention over PO pay. The PO was reproached for taking a restrictive attitude towards demand and civil service structures and attitudes were criticized as unsuitable for an organization supplying telecommunications services.[4] The Post Office Act 1961 was designed to deal with some of these problems through reforms such as the creation of a PO 'trading fund' into which PO surpluses could be paid for use in future years, permitting PO borrowing (up to £80 m. per annum) and the introduction of commercial accounts instead of appropriation ones. However, PO difficulties continued after 1961, and hence momentum grew for broader institutional reforms to offer the PO greater independence (particularly from Treasury control), to allow it to move away from civil service procedures, and to encourage it to adopt more commercial and 'market-minded' methods of operation and management.

The Post Office telephone engineers' union, the POEU, altered its policy to favour both a move towards public corporation status and separation of telephone and postal services following the PO's continuing financial difficulties and the application of a government 'pay pause' in 1961.[5] It lobbied the government, especially the newly-elected Labour government of 1964, in which Anthony Wedgewood Benn was Postmaster General. Increasing momentum built up for institutional reform. Wedgewood Benn commissioned a report by the management consultants, McKinseys; in 1965, an Economic Development Committee was established to look at Post Office matters, whilst in 1966, the Select Committee on Nationalized Industries began a major inquiry into the PO, producing a large report in 1967.[6] All three called for major institutional reform.

The Labour Government then published a White Paper, *Reorganization of the Post Office*,[7] and then the Post Office Bill in 1968. There was broad agreement, both between the political parties and amongst other groups (including the trade unions), that the Post Office should cease to be part of the civil service and become a public corporation in order to enjoy greater freedom and be transformed into a more dynamic organization, better able to respond to demand. Instead, debate centred on how far institutional reform should be taken. The (unpublished) McKinsey report recommended separation of telecommunications and postal services, a position supported by most Conservatives and the POEU. However, the Union of Postal Workers (UPW), a large trade union with well-established links to the Labour Party, strongly

---

[4] See Pitt, *The Telecommunications Function in the British Post Office*, ch. 6 for details.

[5] Ibid. 142–4.

[6] Ibid., esp. 148–53; House of Commons, Select Committee on Nationalized. Industries, *The Post Office*, HC 340–1 (London: HMSO, 1967).

[7] Postmaster General, Cmnd. 3233 (London: HMSO, 1967).

opposed separation, fearing that postal services would suffer in contrast to the expanding telecommunications business. The Conservatives wished to limit the PO's monopoly to network operation in order to allow greater competition in the supply of CPE and the small range of 'advanced services' then available and were also concerned to prevent the PO being permitted to expand its manufacturing operations, in competition with the private manufacturers; the latter shared such views, arguing that the PO's monopoly damaged CPE manufacturing and exports by restricting demand and insisting on slow, expensive and unnecessary approvals.[8] There was also brief discussion of some form of 'privatization' by the injection of private capital into the PO, raised by a Conservative backbencher, Kenneth Baker.[9] However, these more far-reaching ideas were rejected and the Post Office became a public corporation under the Post Office Act of 1969.

Institutional Arrangements 1969–81

The Post Office Act 1969 (referred to hereafter as 'the 1969 Act') provided many elements of the institutional framework for telecommunications in Britain in the 1970s. The Act ended the PO's position as part of the civil service, transforming it into a public corporation. The Act created the Minister for Post and Telecommunications ('the Minister'), replacing the PMG; his Ministry[10] was the PO's 'sponsoring ministry' in Whitehall.

Under the 1969 Act, powers were largely confined to the Minister, the Treasury, and the PO. Other possible participants, such as users and Parliament, were given almost no role. The Act's guiding principle was the separation of spheres of responsibilities and functions between the Minister and the Treasury, on the one hand, and the PO on the other, with each enjoying considerable institutional autonomy within its respective sphere. Decisions concerning the day-to-day operation of the telecommunications network and provision of telecommunications services lay almost exclusively with the PO. The Minister was responsible for general policy and oversight of the PO, and, with the Treasury, for overall financial matters. Only in financial matters was this separation of roles muddied by public expenditure rules concerning public corporations in general, which lay outside the scope of the 1969 Act.

The Post Office

The PO was established as a public corporation consisting of a chairman and six to twelve full or part-time members (known as the Post Office Board). It

---

[8] Hills, *Information Technology and Industrial Policy*, 117–18; *The Times* 9.4.69.

[9] *The Times* 23.1.69 and 24.1.69.

[10] Or the ministry of which it was part, if absorbed by another department, notably the Department of Trade and Industry, or the Department of Industry; all persons are referred to as 'him', following the wording of legislation.

gained its own legal existence and identity, and its staff were no longer civil servants. The Act did not provide any further details concerning the PO's organization; the PO was free to decide its internal structure and matters such as
staffing and salaries.

The Act gave the PO a wide monopoly over all forms of transmission of electric signals, including sound, visual images, and data, used in public telecommunications systems—i.e. transmission of signals by electrical means for
business purposes for use by a third party (§24.1). In addition, the PO's monopoly effectively covered customer premises equipment, as the PO determined
what apparatus could be connected to its network. Only 'private systems'[11] fell
outside the scope of the PO's monopoly, whilst broadcasting by wireless telegraphy and cable television enjoyed distinct treatment, in that the Minister could
issue licences under the 1949 Wireless Telegraphy Act. The PO could issue
licences to other bodies for services within its monopoly, but only with the
agreement of the Minister. Infringement of the Post Office's monopoly was a
criminal offence, punishable by fines and imprisonment (§24.2–4).

The PO was given responsibility for running the telecommunications
network, and a correspondingly wide set of powers. It was permitted to provide
postal, telecommunications, and data processing services in the UK and abroad
(§7) and could do whatever it believed necessary to provide the aforementioned
services (§7.2). Particular examples were given, which included the power to
expand into equipment manufacture and repair, to subcontract activities and
to take stakes in private sector firms. The PO's non-capital spending and its revenues did not require approval by the Minister, and it was free to decide its
procedures for expenditure. Under §28.1–2 of the Act, it was empowered to
determine charges and terms and conditions for its services; no mention at all
was made of the Minister in §28. The PO could borrow from the Minister and
other persons, including those overseas, but only up to a limit of £2.8b. Its
budget, including capital investment, was not laid before Parliament.

Although duties were imposed on the PO, they were mostly phrased in very
wide terms. Thus, for instance, the PO's general duty was laid down by §9.1 of
the Act: 'It shall be the duty of the PO . . . to exercise its powers as to meet the
social, industrial and commercial needs of the British Islands in regard to
matters that are subserved by those powers and in particular to provide
throughout those Islands (save in so far as the provision thereof is in its opinion
impracticable or not reasonably practicable) such services for the conveyance
of letters and such telephone services as satisfy all reasonable demands for
these.'

Although the section contained some element of duty to provide a 'universal service', its force was vitiated by the requirement of 'reasonable practica-

---

[11] Defined as transmission within a single set of premises occupied by the person running the
system, or transmission for domestic purposes or within a business.

bility' and the judge thereof being the PO. Section 9.2 offered more specific indications of the PO's duties and aims than §9.1. Its provisions were oriented towards technical and economic developments and efficiency, as it required the PO to 'have regard to . . . the desirability of improving and developing its operating systems, to developments in the field of communications; and to efficiency and economy'. Nevertheless, very wide scope for discretion remained, especially as the Act excluded legal effects or liability arising from the general duties imposed under section 9 (see §9.4). The most tightly-worded general duty was financial: the PO to at least break even over the years, including making provision for depreciation (§31).

The Powers of the Minister and the Treasury

Decisions concerning non-financial regulation and general policy were made almost exclusively by the Minister. He appointed the Chairman of the PO, and the other Board members. In contrast, he could only dismiss a member of the PO Board under specified circumstances, the most important for policy being if the member was 'unable or unfit' to discharge his functions.[12] He could demand information from the PO, and could issue 'directions of a general character' to the PO as to the exercise of its powers if it 'appeared requisite to him . . . in the national interest' or to remedy defects in the PO's general plans or arrangements (§11.1–2). Nevertheless the directions were general, and their legal scope was in doubt.[13] Only in exceptional circumstances could he issue 'directions' (which were not qualified as being 'general') to the PO over the running of the network; such circumstances included national security, matters relating to international agreements and organizations, or if the Post Office was 'showing undue preference to, or exercising undue discrimination against any person or persons of any class' in providing services within its monopoly (§11).

In financial matters, current expenditure and revenue were, under the Act, left to the PO, but capital expenditure by the PO was to take place in accordance with an overall plan agreed with the Minister, under §11.8. Moreover, PO borrowing required approval by both the Treasury and the Minister. The Minister, with the approval of the Treasury, could give the PO directions concerning its general reserve.

The Act placed few specific constraints on the Minister: almost no duties were imposed on him, nor were guidelines for the exercise of his powers laid down. The main institutional constraints on the Minister lay outside the

---

[12] Schedule 1, §5.1.
[13] For instance, the Attorney-General suggested in 1949 that they could not be used as instruments of macro-economic policy—see N. Chester, *The Nationalisation of British Industry* (London: HMSO, 1970), 984–5.

Act, notably Ministerial responsibility and answerability to Parliament for the exercise of his statutory powers, and the possibility of judicial review of his actions; however, the latter was very difficult to use, especially over 'policy issues' in the 1960s and 1970s, whilst parliamentary mechanisms for control were limited.[14]

Users

The legal position of users was weak. Although the PO was a public corporation and subscribers therefore had contracts with it, such contracts could exclude PO liability. Moreover, the 1969 Act prevented PO liability in tort for failure or delay in providing telecommunications services (§29). Furthermore, failure by the PO to perform its general duties imposed under §9, did not give users any legal rights.

Institutional provision for the voice of users was made under the 1969 Act through the establishment of the Post Office Users' National Council, (POUNC), together with country user Councils for Scotland, Wales, and Northern Ireland. The POUNC's duty was to consider representations made to it and any other matters which it believed should be considered. However, POUNC members were appointed by the Minister. Moreover, the POUNC had no powers: the PO was under a duty to refer proposals to it and to consult with it before putting into effect 'major proposals', but POUNC approval was not necessary and no legal action could be founded on the PO's failure to consult the POUNC (§15.4). Furthermore, the Minister decided whether a proposal was 'major'.

Parliament

The 1969 Act contained almost no specific provisions for a role for Parliament. As a public corporation the PO had no direct responsibility to Parliament. The Minister answered Parliamentary questions, but these only had to be accepted on subjects relating to his powers or to 'matters of sufficient public importance';[15] thus ministers had wide discretion to reject questions as falling within the responsibilities of the Post Office, but outside their powers.[16] As a nationalized industry, the Post Office fell within the remit of the Public Accounts Committee, but one of its main sources of information, the Comptroller and Auditor General, did not have access to the records of public corporations, but

---

[14] For Parliament, see below and T. Prosser, *Nationalised Industries and Public Control* (Oxford: Basil Blackwell, 1986), ch. 10.

[15] See S. de Smith and R. Brazier, *Constitutional and Administrative Law* (Harmondsworth: Penguin, 7th edn., 1994), 240, and W. Wade and C. Forsyth, *Administrative Law* (Oxford: Clarendon Press, 6th edn., 1992), 175.

[16] For public corporations in general, see Prosser, *Nationalised Industries and Public Control*, 27–8.

only to those of government departments which have given voted moneys to corporations.[17] The most effective method of detailed monitoring for Parliament was through its select committees, notably the committee on the nationalised industries which existed between 1956 and 1979 and which could undertake investigations, hold hearings and publish reports.

Financial Arrangements outside the 1969 Post Office Act

Despite being a public corporation, with its own legal existence and powers to determine its charges and current expenditure, the PO's finances were linked to general public expenditure, due to British government accounting conventions. Until 1977 all capital expenditure by nationalized industries was counted as part of the 'planning total' definition of public expenditure, together with any operating deficit.[18] Thus an increase in PO investment raised total public expenditure, whilst a reduction in the latter could be achieved by a cut in the capital spending of the nationalized industries. In 1977 these rules were modified. A system of external financing limits (EFLs) was introduced: only the change in the net external borrowing of the nationalized industries over the financial year counted as part of public expenditure.[19] EFLs applied to all external borrowing, regardless of whether raised from the government or capital markets. Thus to meet an EFL, a nationalized industry could increase revenue, reduce costs, sell stock, reduce working capital or reduce capital spending. Investment covered by internally-generated funds did not count towards the EFL. In contrast, investment financed by borrowing counted towards the EFL and hence raised general public expenditure.

These accounting rules had two important features for the PO and Government. Firstly, the PO's finances and the general budget were intertwined. This was particularly significant if targets for total public expenditure or the PSBR existed. Secondly, no distinction was made between current and capital expenditure: both counted equally towards total public spending before 1977 and then the EFL after 1977.

Manufacturing

In 1969 the PO's major suppliers were privately-owned manufacturers. Under the 1969 Act, the PO needed to 'consult' the Minister if it wished to significantly expand its manufacturing operations; moreover its general duties included meeting 'the social, industrial and commercial needs' of Britain. Nevertheless, the Minister did not possess powers over the PO's relations with its suppliers, other than his general powers over the PO's investment programme. Outside the Act, institutional arrangements for co-operation between the PO

[17]   Ibid. 204.
[18]   A. Likierman, *Public Expenditure* (Harmondsworth: Penguin, 1988).
[19]   See J. Redwood and J. Hatch, *Controlling Public Expenditure* (Oxford: Basil Blackwell, 1982).

and its suppliers were limited. Although joint committees of the PO and British switching manufacturers existed for matters such digital switching (the Joint Electronic Research Committee) and definitions and specifications (the Advisory Committee on Telecommunications Systems Definitions), the formal bulk supply agreements that set prices, the division of PO orders and patent sharing arrangements had been ended by 1969.

Institutional Change in the 1970s

Major institutional changes were not introduced in the 1970s. Nevertheless, there were strong pressures for reform. There was significant dissatisfaction with the performance of the Post Office with respect to waiting lists, sharp price rises (especially in 1974-5), government intervention in PO decisions, the unpredictability of financial planning for investment and required rates of return set for the PO. There was serious disquiet over the manufacturing subsector: disputes took place between the PO and its suppliers and serious criticisms were expressed of the supply and export performance of British equipment manufacturers.[20] The equipment manufacturers argued that private firms should be able to compete on equal terms with the PO and that the need for PO approval of new equipment damaged exports by PO insistence on unsuitable and over-complex specifications.[21] Users, especially large businesses and computer companies, also claimed that the PO's CPE monopoly resulted in inadequate supply of equipment such as modems and PABXs and lengthy applications to approve non-standard equipment.[22]

During the passage of the 1969 Act, the Conservatives had suggested a wider reshaping of the institutional framework, notably the separation of postal and telecommunications services and the creation of greater opportunities for competition by a restrictive definition of the PO's monopoly (so that CPE and some advanced computer service might lie outside it) and placing the power to licence suppliers other than the Post Office in the hands of the Minister.[23] The Conservative Government of 1970-4 looked briefly at ideas of partial or total privatization, but rejected them due to fear of union opposition and to the belief that privatization would merely result in a private monopoly replacing a public one.[24] The PO's monopoly over network operation was considered to be a 'natural monopoly', with competition being impossible or resulting in inefficiencies.[25] In office, the Conservatives did not even alter the PO's control over CPE, accepting the PO's argument that competition or a loosening of its

---

[20] For details, see ch. 6.   [21] STC submission to Carter Committee, *The Times* 26.7.76.
[22] Evidence of Computing Services Association to the Carter Committee—*The Times* 2.7.76; statement by Telecommunications Managers Division, *The Times* 25.11.77.
[23] *The Times* 7.2.69, Hills, *Information Technology and Industrial Policy*, 117–18.
[24] Interview, Minister.   [25] Interviews, PO staff, department officials and Minister.

powers would lead to CPE being connected that would damage the network.[26] They relied heavily on the views and advice of the Post Office,[27] and their attention was concentrated on arguments about equipment manufacturing and Post Office orders rather than institutional reform.

The Labour governments of 1974–9 did introduce some limited reforms, but failed to implement others that enjoyed wide support. The main change was to include trade union representatives on the Post Office Board.[28] The Labour Party election manifestos of 1974 promised to extend worker participation in industrial decision making. The new Secretary of State for Industry, Tony Benn, asked the PO and unions to present their views on industrial democracy. The PO Board was generally opposed to change, especially the Chairman, Sir William Ryland,[29] whereas the unions were in favour of having representatives on the top bodies of the PO. Thereafter, in the process of change, 'the government played a central role throughout',[30] including inviting submissions, initiating negotiations, resolving some of the disagreements in negotiations, and passing the necessary legislation. After lengthy negotiations, in July 1977, an Act was passed so that the new Board, as of January 1978, consisted of an equal number of management and union representatives, plus a smaller number of independent members. Despite the manifesto commitment and the influence of the trade unions with the Labour governments, the result was modest in the face of the determined opposition: the new Board was established as a two-year experiment and worker participation was confined to the national Board, not the entire PO and in practice, little changed.[31] The experiment was not renewed in 1980.

Pressures did build up for more far-reaching institutional reforms. In the 1974–5 period, widespread criticism of the PO was voiced by POUNC, MPs, and trade unions, especially over very large price rises introduced to stem PO losses. In response, the Government set up a public inquiry, chaired by Sir Charles Carter, to look at the workings and structure of the PO. Submissions to the Committee revealed strong support for separation of telecommunications and postal services, notably from the PO Board, POUNC, the CBI, and the POEU. Only the UPW opposed it, fearing the effects of the loss of the profitable telecommunications side of the PO on postal services.[32]

The Committee's report argued that major flaws existed in institutional arrangements.[33] The postal and telecommunications businesses were very dif-

---

[26] Interview, Minister.   [27] Interview, Minister.
[28] For a detailed history and analysis, see E. Batstone, A. Ferner, and M. Terry, *Unions on the Board: An Experiment in Industrial Democracy* (Oxford: Blackwell, 1983).
[29] *The Times* 26.3.76.   [30] Batstone *et al.*, *Unions on the Board*, 41.
[31] Ibid.   [32] *The Times* 21.2.77.
[33] Carter Committee, *Report of the Post Office Review Committee*, Cmnd. 6850 (London: HMSO, 1978).

ferent, particularly in their use of capital, and decision making in the PO was too centralized at Board level.[34] The report strongly criticized the framework governing relations between the government and PO and the use made of policy instruments. It argued that the government lacked the capacity to conduct policy analysis, to evaluate the trade-offs between standards of service, investment, operating costs, and prices, and hence play its part in stimulating PO efficiency.[35] There was a lack of mutual trust and understanding between the Department of Industry (DoI) and the PO, a confusion of their respective roles and a failure to provide a framework for setting long-term aims and strategy.[36] Ministerial intervention had been of the wrong kind, concerned with subsidiary and short-term matters, not central long-term policy.[37] The POUNC was too weak and had been unsuccessful in safeguarding consumer interests.

The Committee's report therefore recommended major reforms. The PO should be divided into two corporations covering the postal and telecommunications businesses. A new advisory Council on PO and Telecommunications Affairs, whose members would be independent of the two corporations and would include a POUNC representative, should be established. It would be able properly to scrutinize the PO's operating plans and long-term capital programme and strategy and would have the resources to give strong and well-informed advice to the government. Nevertheless, the Secretary of State would take decisions, aided by a new power of giving the corporations specific directions. Having been impressed by a visit to the United States, the Committee argued that competition in CPE should be considered, beginning with an experiment in one type of CPE.

The Government responded to the Carter Committee report with a White Paper.[38] It rejected most of the Committee's proposals for a new framework for relations with the Post Office, claiming that the proposed Council on Post Office and Telecommunications Affairs would merely add a new layer in decision making and would detract from the role and responsibility of the Board. Instead, the White Paper's main proposals were new powers for the Minister to issue specific Directions and to approve the PO's long-term plans. Despite the widespread view of the benefits of change, the Government feared trade union opposition, especially to separating the two businesses by the UPW.[39] Most importantly, it had other priorities, and it lacked parliamentary time and a majority for major legislation and the desire to begin the long process of reform. Thus no bill was drawn up before the 1979 general election.

---

[34] Ibid. chs. 1 and 9.   [35] Ibid. 39.   [36] Ibid. ch. 8.   [37] Ibid. 59.
[38] Department of Industry, *The Post Office*, Cmnd. 7,292 (London: HMSO, 1978).
[39] Interviews, officials.

France

The Institutional Framework of Telecommunications in France in 1969

Telecommunications services in France were supplied by a government ministry, the PTT Ministry,[40] which was also responsible for postal services. The PTT Ministry was divided into various *directions générales*, including after 1946, the Direction Générale des Télécommunications (DGT), headed by a civil servant (*fonctionnaire*) the Directeur général des télécommunications. Telecommunications services were provided by the DGT, whilst postal services were supplied by another *direction* within the PTT Ministry, the Direction Générale de la Poste (DGP), known as La Poste. A unit within the PTT Ministry, the DGT was an *administration*, i.e. it formed part of the central government civil service; its institutional situation was frequently referred to as its '*statut*'. Most of the elements of the institutional framework for telecommunications arose from the DGT's position as part of the *administration*, although certain provisions specific to the PTT Ministry were established as exceptions to the general rules of the civil service.

The DGT's Position as an *Administration*

Institutionally, the PTT Ministry combined the roles of network operator, policy maker, and regulator. The DGT had no autonomous legal existence: it was a part of the PTT Ministry and formally it merely implemented the decisions of the Minister. Many decisions were in legal form, frequently in regulations and decrees (*règlements* and *décrets*) issued by the government; the legal rules governing telecommunications were codified in the PTT Code.

The PTT Ministry had a wide-ranging monopoly over the transmission of electro-magnetic signals of all kinds, dating from a law of 1837 (although the Minister could license other suppliers). This was incorporated in the PTT Code, as Article L33: 'no telecommunications installation can be established or used for transmission of signals except by the Minister of Posts and Telecommunications or with his authorisation. The provisions of this article are applicable to the emission and reception of radio-electric signals of all kinds.'

The wide range of the provisions was reinforced by the definition of signals given in Article 32 of the Code: 'all transmission, emission or reception of signs, signals, written messages, images, sounds or information of all kinds, by wire, radio-electrical, optical or other electro-magnetic systems'. The DGT did not have a monopoly over the supply of CPE, but all equipment had to be licensed (*agréé*) by the PTT Ministry.

[40] *Ministère des Postes, Télégraphes, et Télécommunications*; for a detailed history of the Ministry see L.-J. Libois, *Genèse et croissance des télécommunications* (Paris: Masson, 1983), and C. Bertho, *Télégraphes et téléphones: de Valmy au microprocesseur* (Paris: Livre de Poche, 1981).

Almost no specific duties over providing telecommunications services were imposed on the PTT Minister by legislation but their supply formed part of the *service public*. In an important judicial case in 1968, (the *arrêt Ursot*), the legal position of the services supplied by the PTT Ministry was clarified by the Tribunal des Conflits: the Tribunal ruled that PTT services were 'public administrative services' of the State, as opposed to 'public industrial and commercial services'. This classification meant that the principles of administrative and public law applied to the supply of PTT services, notably: equality of citizens and users, and, as a consequence, provision of services under the same terms and conditions throughout France; permanence/non-interruption of service; provision of service for the 'general good'.[41]

Within the framework of administrative law, the PTT Minister decided which services were supplied, the conditions under which they were provided, the PTT Ministry's internal organization, and DGT appointments. Many of the rules of the general civil service (*administration*) applied to the DGT as part of the PTT Ministry. Thus the internal procedures for expenditure of the general *administration* had to be followed, such as book-keeping practices and legal regulations on delegation of the power to spend credits given to the Ministry;[42] financial operations were open to scrutiny by the Cour des comptes, in its judicial capacity of verifying the budgetary and financial regularity of all expenditure and receipts. Permanent DGT employees were civil servants. They were covered by the *statut général de la fonction publique*, and hence were recruited by competitions (*concours*), and enjoyed security of employment and centrally-determined pay and conditions. In 1951, a decree gave the DGT's elite Corps des ingénieurs des télécommunications (CIT), exclusive rights to posts of *cadres ingénieurs*, the most senior posts in the DGT.[43]

Certain exceptions were made to the general rules of government ministries for financial matters. The PTT Ministry had its own budget, a *budget annexe*, separated from the general budget, created by the 1923 *loi des Finances*. The *budget annexe* meant that PTT expenditure, receipts and borrowing were not included in the general budget's totals and that PTT receipts could be directly channelled to PTT spending without having to pass through the *Trésor*. The DGT was able to produce accounts similar to those of a public company, as the *budget annexe* was divided into a profit and loss account and a capital account. Moreover, the PTT Ministry could borrow by issuing bonds under the 1926 *loi des Finances*.[44]

[41] J. Chevallier, 'La Mutation des postes et télécommunications', *Actualité Juridique—Droit Administratif*, Oct. 1990, 667–87.
[42] J. P. Lukawaszewicz, 'Service public administratif ou entreprise commerciale', *Actualité Juridique—Droit Publique*, Feb. 1975, 52–71, 58.
[43] See Libois, *Genèse et croissance des télécommunications*.
[44] J. Lintingre, *Droit des télécommunications et de la communication audiovisuelle* (Paris: ENST, 1990).

Nevertheless, many elements of the general Budget continued to apply to the *budget annexe*. It formed part of the *loi des Finances*. It was prepared by the Finance Ministry, voted annually by Parliament and followed the timetable of the general Budget. It was in the form of budgetary authorizations covering both expenditure and receipts, similar to the form of the general Budget. More generally, it did not alter the process of setting DGT tariffs, which were fixed by the interministerial council (Conseil interministériel), acting on proposals put forward jointly by the PTT and Finance Ministers, and both of whose agreement was required for any tariff changes.[45] Furthermore, telecommunications was covered by the general national planning process (from the Second Plan of 1954–7 onwards); the volume of investments over several years formed part of decisions about which sectors were given priority and a division of forecast total resources available, formally undertaken through the Commissariat du Plan.[46]

The main method whereby the rules of the *administration* could be avoided was by the PTT Ministry setting up subsidiaries as private limited companies in which the State, via the *Trésor*, held all or some of the shares. Such subsidiaries were outside the *administration* and operated under private law. Hence their position differed from that of the DGT in a number of important respects: they could make commercially-binding contracts with customers; as legal persons they could own shares and engage in joint ventures; their operations lay outside the *loi des Finances* and Parliamentary financial control; employees were not civil servants.[47] Subsidiaries offered the PTT Ministry greater flexibility than activities undertaken within the DGT, whilst also maintaining public control.

Parliament

Parliament's role in policy making was potentially significant: the PTT Minister was answerable to it; the PTT *budget annexe* formed part of the annual general budget and had to be passed by Parliament. Yet the general weakness of the French Parliament limited the scope for its intervention: its sphere of competence were severely limited under the Constitution, (notably Article 37), and outside these the Government could issue *règlements* and *décrets* under its *pouvoir réglementaire*; many constitutional provisions limited the ability of Parliament to obstruct and alter Government legislation, especially the budget; it had few powers to control ministers.[48]

[45] Lukawaszewicz, 'Service public administratif ou entreprise commerciale', 58.

[46] Libois, *Genèse et croissance des télécommunications*, ch. 17.

[47] G. Bonnetblanc, *Les Télécommunications françaises. Quelle statut pour quelle entreprise?* (Paris: La Documentation Française, 1985), 213–27.

[48] See V. Wright, *The Government and Politics of France* (London: Unwin Hyman, 3rd. edn., 1989), 132–56.

Users

The position of users in relations with the DGT was extremely weak following the classification of DGT services as 'public administrative services of the State', in the Ursot case. The Tribunal des Conflits in Ursot and the Conseil d'État in the Bourgeois case[49] held that a subscriber had only an 'administrative contract' with the PTT Ministry. Therefore, he could not sue in private law: his relationship with the DGT was governed by administrative law, and in particular, the PTT Code. Article L37 of the Code excluded State liability for losses resulting from private transmission on the telecommunications network. Thus subscribers could not sue the PTT Ministry over failures in the supply of services. The situation was slightly altered when State responsibility for *faute lourde* (the equivalence of gross negligence) was accepted by the Conseil d'État in 1976 but this was difficult to prove.[50] Moreover, whilst the Minister was head of the PTT Ministry, there was no public organization specifically to represent users and defend their interests.

Manufacturing

Specific institutional arrangements existed for co-operation between the DGT and its privately-owned equipment suppliers: the firms and the PTT Ministry formed two joint public-private companies, Socotel for switching equipment and Sotélec for cable equipment.[51] These companies were set up to develop products and engineering and to encourage co-operation between the PTT and the manufacturers, including patent sharing agreements. They were also used to determine shares of DGT orders and prices paid by the DGT for equipment, using the many exceptions to the general principle of open formal written tenders for public orders.[52] At the same time, Article 54 of the 1963 *loi des Finances* allowed public bodies to demand information on costs and technical matters from suppliers in public markets in which competition was not possible; this power was available to the PTT Ministry after 1963.[53] Hence the DGT or CNET could verify that prices were based on costs.

Pressures for Institutional Change from the Late 1960s: Limited Modifications and Obstacles to Large-Scale Reforms

During the 1950s and 1960s the telephone network in France suffered from excess demand and outdated equipment and it fell well behind other European

[49] CE section 29 Juin 1979, *Mme Vve Bourgeois*.
[50] See Bonnetblanc, *Les Télécommunications*, 77, and Libois, *Genèse et croissance des télécommunications*, 186–7.
[51] B. Aurelle, *Les Télécommunications* (Paris: Le Découverte, 1986).
[52] See Bonnetblanc, *Les Télécommunications*, 172–85.
[53] Bonnetblanc, *Les Télécommunications*, 172–3, and B. Touret, 'Le Financement privé des télécommunications', *Actualité Juridique—Droit Administratif*, June 1974, 284–97, 285.

countries. The situation was described as *la crise du téléphone* and led to calls by politicians, industrialists, and the CIT for institutional reform of the DGT's finances and *statut*.[54]

Only limited investment was being undertaken in the 1960s. This was partly due to methods of raising capital. DGT investment had mostly been financed by internally-generated funds rather than borrowing, despite the fact that such expenditure was for long-term assets producing income and profits.[55] The DGT's position within the PTT Ministry also appeared to help hinder development of telephone services, which enjoyed lower priority than postal services. Discussions centred around two related, but nevertheless distinct issues. The first was the separation of telecommunications and postal services into two organizations; this arose from concerns that the two branches had very different operating requirements, (in particular, the DGT was a capital intensive business and La Poste was labour intensive), the use of the DGT to cross-subsidize postal services and fears that the postal side of the PTT Ministry was obstructing the development of the DGT. Second, there was the question of the *statut*—the DGT's position as an *administration*. It was argued that the DGT needed more autonomy, notably from the Finance Ministry, and that civil service rules were unsuitable to the industrial and commercial nature of the supply of telecommunications services, especially an annual Budget for telecommunications programmes that were spread over several years and the application of employment categories used in the general civil service.[56]

Major financial changes were undertaken in the late 1960s to create instruments to provide access for the DGT to private capital outside the *budget annexe*. In 1967 the Caisse Nationale des Télécommunications (CNT) was created as a 'public administrative body' under the control of the PTT Minister but with 'legal personality and financial autonomy'.[57] The CNT's purpose was to borrow on foreign capital markets by issuing bonds in order to finance telecommunications investments. In 1971 it was also permitted to issue bonds in France. More controversially, in 1969 the PTT Minister, Yves Guéna, persuaded President de Gaulle to create the power to establish *sociétés de financement du téléphone*; the power was included in the December 1969 amending *loi des Finances* under his successor, Robert Galley.[58] The *sociétés de financement* were to be limited companies, with a share capital which could be owned by private bodies and enjoyed fiscal privileges.[59] Their function was to provide capital for

---

[54] See e.g. the views expressed by the Association des ingénieurs des postes et télécommunications (AIPT), representing the CIT—*Le Monde* 12.10.72 and 10.10.74.

[55] Libois, *Genèse et croissance des télécommunications*, 255–6.

[56] See Libois, *Genèse et croissance des télécommunications*, 255–6; arguments used by the AIPT, *Le Monde* 12.10.72.

[57] *Décret* of 3 Oct. 1967 quoted in Libois, *Genèse et croissance des télécommunications*, 256.

[58] Interview, PTT Minister.

[59] For the detailed legal arrangements see Touret, 'Le Financement privé des télécommunications', and Bonnetblanc, *Les Télécommunications*, 152–71.

telecommunications equipment on the basis of leasing arrangements (*crédit-bail*): they raised money either from their own share capital or by issuing bonds; they signed contracts with the PTT Ministry to provide those sums for the purchase of equipment which was then leased to the PTT Ministry at an annual 'rent'; the contract stipulated that at the end of the lease the Ministry could buy the equipment at a certain price.

The *sociétés de financement* thus provided a method of allowing the PTT Ministry to borrow private capital indirectly. Their main advantage was that the DGT paid only an annual 'rent' for equipment, allowing it to repay the capital cost over several years from the extra revenue and profits earned by the expansion of the network made possible by the new equipment. At the same time, there was no transfer of control over the telecommunications network to the *sociétés de financement*. The PTT and Finance Ministries had to approve both the establishment and articles of association of each *société*. Furthermore, the contracts stipulated that the PTT Ministry was responsible for placing the equipment orders and for operating the equipment. The *sociétés de financement* lay outside the *loi des Finances* and did not need parliamentary approval. Thus PTT borrowing was 'debudgetized', although PTT capital expenditure still fell within the national planning process.

The power to create the *sociétés* was vigorously opposed by the Finance Ministry.[60] It was also attacked by the unions, the Socialists, and the Communist Party, who saw the use of private capital as heralding the beginning of a privatization of the DGT and argued that the 'rents' offered high profits to private companies, which could have been earned for the public sector.[61] Nevertheless, the reform was passed: de Gaulle and especially Pompidou supported Guéna and Galley; the Right had a large majority in Parliament; there was the prospect of higher orders for equipment manufacturers in France; users, including companies, were pressing for action; the bonds sold by the *sociétés* provided a profitable investment opportunity, including, at times, for the general public.

In contrast to financial arrangements, reform of the DGT's position in the PTT Ministry proved much more difficult. In the 1969 presidential elections, Georges Pompidou took up an idea first proposed by Valéry Giscard d'Estaing in 1967 that the DGT should become a *compagnie nationale du téléphone*, or an *entreprise nationale* (a status akin to a public corporation in Britain) following the example of Eléctricité de France (EDF); it would have its own legal personality, management autonomy, and the legal capacity to borrow in its own name, separated from postal services.[62] Between 1969 and 1971 there was much public discussion of the idea.[63] In 1971, a working party set up by the Prime Minister examined a proposal that an *Office national des PTT* be created; it

---

[60] Interview, senior DGT/CNET official.   [61] *Le Monde* 27.9.69.
[62] *L'Express* 26.5.69.
[63] See *Le Monde* 15.7.69, *Le Figaro* 22.6.70 and *Le Nouveau Journal* 6.2.71.

differed from the earlier proposals in that postal and telecommunications services would not be separated.[64] Nevertheless, no reforms were implemented.
One reason was fierce opposition from the trade unions; postal workers in particular feared the consequences of PTT autonomy and/or separation from
telecommunications for their unprofitable services.[65] Another was that reforms
of the PTT's Ministry's internal organization were undertaken, as well as the
creation of the *sociétés de financement du téléphone*.[66] The changes separated the
operation of the postal and telecommunications sides of the PTT Ministry,
increased the autonomy of the DGT and provided new methods of raising
investment capital. Only a minor institutional modification was made: a Conseil
supérieur des Postes et Télécommunications, was set up in 1972, with the PTT
Minister, senior civil servants, and representatives of PTT staff and users, but
it was a purely advisory body.[67]

Discussions continued in the mid-1970s and circumstances appeared
favourable to institutional reform. In 1973–4, the PTT Minister, Hubert
Germain, ordered a detailed report, which proposed that change be implemented in two phases: the complete separation of the budgets, organizational
structures, and personnel of the DGT and La Poste; then alteration of the
statut, with a special *statut* within the civil service for PTT personnel.[68] It
appears that the report was accepted by President Pompidou, but the latter died
before any action could be taken.

Institutional reform seemed likely with the election of Giscard d'Estaing as
President: he had been publicly in favour of reform since 1967, and during the
1974 presidential campaign had suggested that the DGT should have a separate
budget, and that Parliament would have to 'pronounce' on suitable institutional
structures for the DGT. Furthermore, he argued that such a structure should
draw a clear distinction between the powers of *tutelle* (regulation and policy),
and the running of the network, and should be appropriate for an industrial
and commercial undertaking.[69] The wide support for change was underlined
by a Parliamentary report in 1974 which had been set up to look at the *crise
du téléphone*. It recommended that the DGT become an Établissement public à
Caractère commercial (EPIC), close to a public corporation in Britain), with its
own legal personality and financial autonomy and that it should be managed
according to the rules and methods used by industrial and commercial companies.[70] In addition, the AIPT continued to call for the separation of postal and
telecommunications services and a new *statut* for the DGT.[71]

[64]   Libois, *Genèse et croissance des télécommunications*, 241–2.
[65]   Interviews, senior DGT/CNET officials; *l'Express* 28.9.69.   [66]   See Ch. 6.
[67]   Lukaszewicz, 'Service public administratif ou entreprise commerciale', 55.
[68]   Libois, *Genèse et croissance des télécommunications*, 242.
[69]   *Le Monde* 8.5.74 and 10.5.74.
[70]   *La Vie Française* 6.6.74 and *Le Monde* 22.6.74.   [71]   *Le Monde* 10.10.74.

After the 1974 presidential election, both Gérard Théry (Directeur Général des Télécommunications 1974–81) and President Giscard d'Estaing wanted to alter the DGT's institutional position.[72] Nevertheless, this was not attempted during 1974–81. The main factor was fear of union opposition. A long postal strike took place from October to December 1974, provoked in large part by fears of a change in the DGT's *statut* and a separation of postal and telecommunications services.[73] It cost the PTT Minister, Pierre Lelong, his post, and almost caused Chirac's downfall as Prime Minister. The strike marked the end of attempts at comprehensive reform of the DGT's *statut*.[74] Moreover, in the late 1970s, whilst the issue of institutional reform was discussed occasionally, there was little belief in the need for action. The main reason was the DGT's success, especially its rapid growth and ability to meet demand. Despite its position as an *administration*, the DGT appeared to be able to provide excellent services and behave as if it were a commercial enterprise.[75] The DGT's record of modernisation and innovation in the 1970s,[76] appeared to answer the earlier critics of its *statut*.

Conclusion: Increasing Divergence of Institutional Arrangements in Britain and France and Institutional Change

In 1969, institutional arrangements for the telecommunications sector in Britain and France had many similar features. The network operators, the Post Office and the DGT, were part of the civil service/*administration*, as units linked with postal services within government departments. They had no institutional autonomy—formally, they merely carried out ministerial decisions. Both were monopolies; few duties specific to telecommunications were defined; administrative law and procedures applied to most decisions and users had few rights. Although the budgets of the network operators required Parliamentary approval, exceptions to the general rules governing the civil service/*administration* were made for financial matters in both countries; in particular, budgetary rules were modified, so that PO and DGT income could be channelled directly to expenditure, accounts presented in commercial form, and, in France, the DGT's accounts separated from those of the general budget by having a *budget annexe*.[77]

Between 1969 and 1979 institutional arrangements diverged between the two countries due to reforms in each country. Differences grew in the position of

---

[72] Interview, senior DGT official.
[73] Cohen, E., *Le Colbertisme 'high tech'* (Paris: Hachette, 1992), 55 and interview, senior DGT official.
[74] Interview, senior DGT official.   [75] Interview, senior DGT/PTT Ministry official.
[76] See Chs. 6, 10, and 11.   [77] For further details, see also Ch. 2.

the network operators, financial rules, and relationships between PTOs and equipment manufacturers. In Britain, the Post Office Act 1969 gave the PO a formal legal existence. The roles and spheres of the PO and ministers were separated and defined: the PO was given wide powers to run the network; the Minister was made responsible for general policy and regulation and, together with the Treasury, for overall financial matters. The PO and ministers each enjoyed considerable autonomy in their own respective fields. The 1969 Act greatly reduced Parliament's functions specific to telecommunications and the PO's budget did not require parliamentary approval. Moreover, institutionalized relationships for the supply of equipment to the PO were ended. In contrast, the DGT in France remained an *administration* as part of the PTT Ministry, whilst formal arrangements to promote co-operation between the DGT and its equipment suppliers continued. However, financial reforms in France gave the DGT increased access to capital and created borrowing instruments that lay outside the budgetary process. In Britain, although the PO became a public corporation, public sector accounting rules meant that its spending continued to count towards total public expenditure, no distinction was drawn between capital and current expenditure and extra-budgetary means of borrowing were not created for the PO.

Paradoxically, increasing dissimilarities occurred at a period when transnational forces for change were strengthening (notably technological and economic developments and the international regulatory environment). Moreover, they took place after a period in which certain institutional features had been similar in the two countries, and or had become similar, leading to a degree of institutional convergence by 1969. Furthermore, in both countries, there was domestic dissatisfaction with the performance, organisational position, autonomy and investment levels of the network operators and debate about institutional changes. The divergence indicates that national institutions can differ and their evolution can follow dissimilar paths, even if there are common powerful external pressures; these findings support national institutionalist claims. However, it also indicates the importance of institutional change, which was responsible for the growth in national differences.

Institutional reforms were introduced in both Britain and France during the late 1960s. However, they were infrequent in the period from the 1960s to 1979, conforming to a pattern of punctuated change. They often followed long periods of discussion, especially for major changes that achieved considerable consensus, such as the Post Office Act 1969. Moreover, institutional modifications were limited in the 1960s and 1970s, even when a comprehensive reconsideration of sectoral arrangements was undertaken. Thus, for example, the Post Office Act 1969 did not end the PO's wide-ranging monopoly, it left the duties of the Minister unspecified, it imposed few requirements on the PO and it created only a weak body to represent consumers. More radical ideas, such as extending competition or separating postal and telecommunications services, failed to be implemented. In France, even limited attempts to alter the DGT's *statut* were quickly terminated.

Institutional change was rarely easy, as an analysis of both the reforms implemented and those that were not, indicates. General dissatisfaction, extensive discussion, and wide support were not always sufficient for reform, because determined opposition, even by a small group, often prevented it. Thus, for example, in Britain, considerable support for modifications of the PO's position in the mid–late 1970s was not translated into action; in France, despite a strong desire for change by powerful elements within the political executive and the DGT from the late 1960s until the mid-1970s, reforms were stalled. In particular, trade unions in both countries, especially those representing postal workers, were able to mount effective resistance to ideas that they opposed, whilst finance ministries were also reluctant to see changes that might threaten their control over network operators. For institutional alteration to take place in the 1960s and 1970s, the active participation and leadership of governments were essential, which in turned required governments to have the strength to act (for instance, in terms of parliamentary majorities) and to give priority to overcoming resistance, both by unions and by other actors such as finance ministries. Moreover, if the performance of existing institutions improved, or if other issues in telecommunications obtained attention, pressures for institutional reform subsided.

Thus the experience of British and French telecommunications in the 1960s and 1970s supports national institutionalist arguments that countries' organizational arrangements have deep roots and do not respond immediately and in the same way to pressures for change. Moreover, a combination of strong political leadership and continuing major discontent with performance were needed for institutional change to take place. Furthermore, existence of divergent institutions after 1969 leads to the question of whether they resulted in growing contrasts in policy making and economic performance.

6

Policy Making in the 1970s: Constraints in Britain, Boldness in France

The period between 1969 and the end of the 1970s offers a good first test for the impact of national institutions in telecommunications. On the one hand, institutional arrangements in British and French telecommunications differed in several important respects following reforms in each country during the late 1960s, and were also stable throughout the 1970s. On the other hand, transnational forces for change grew, notably due to technological and economic developments, but also arising from new ideas and regulatory reforms in the United States. These external factors tended to challenge traditional institutional arrangements by weakening monopolies, increasing demand for telecommunications, offering new opportunities and pressures for investment in new technology and modifying cost structures.

The chapter therefore analyses the impact of the differing institutional frameworks on policy making in Britain and France, given the powerful external pressures common to the two countries. It does so in two ways. First, it looks for linkages between the major features of institutional frameworks and patterns of policy making (processes of decision making, strategies, and major areas of substantive policy). Thus it considers whether policy in practice followed the institutional arrangements, the use of institutional powers and instruments, and the ways in which institutional characteristics encouraged, discouraged, permitted, or prevented policy choices; these elements are brought together in the concluding part of the chapter. In analysing cross-national differences, it focuses on those features that differed between the two countries (the position of the network operator, the powers of the government/political executive, financial rules, and structures covering the relationship between the network operator and its equipment suppliers). Second, also in the concluding section, it compares the patterns of policy formation seen in the two countries, in order to assess the differences between them and to consider whether the cross-national institutional dissimilarities contributed to the policy contrasts identified.

Britain

The Processes of Decision Making and Overall Policy

Policy making in network operation was dominated by the Post Office (PO) and the government throughout the period. The PO played a central role: it was the monopoly network operator, the main purchaser for British equipment manufacturers, and almost the sole source of technical expertise. Within the government, two departments were directly involved in telecommunications policy making: the Department of Posts and Telecommunications, which formed a separate Ministry between 1969 and 1974 but thereafter formed part of the Department of Industry (the Ministry responsible is referred to as 'the Department', and the relevant Minister as 'the Minister', whilst the Department of Industry is referred to as the DoI);[1] the Treasury, which played a major role in financial matters, notably investment and borrowing.

Policy making was largely a closed process between the PO and the government, and other actors were confined to minor roles in policy making. Trade union leaders had little contact with civil servants, and saw the Minister only occasionally, even during the Labour Governments of 1974–9; the experiment between 1977 and 1979 with union representatives on the Post Office Board had little impact on the position of unions,[2] whose direct role was confined to protesting against PO investment cuts and to acting as an important obstacle to institutional change. The Post Office Users National Council was largely unimportant, being consulted on price rises, but having little influence on final decisions.[3] Parliament played only a very minor role in telecommunications policy making, as did user groups such as the Telecommunications Users Association (TUA) and the Telecommunications Managers Association (TMA).[4] The partial exception to the closed pattern of decision making came in questions involving equipment manufacturing, in which the Post Office's largest suppliers—GEC, Plessey, and STC—were additional major participants.

Relations between the PO and the Department were close: there was 'continuous dialogue' and consultation between them on most important matters.[5] The Minister almost never exercised his powers of issuing Directions or general Directions to the PO, although they remained in the background as 'weapons

---

[1] The post of Telecommunications Minister was held by John Stonehouse (1969–70), and then by the Conservative Ministers, Christopher Chataway (1970–2) and Sir John Eden (1972–4), neither of whom were in the Cabinet; the Secretaries of State at the DoI were Tony Benn (1974–5) and Eric Varley (1975–9) under the Labour Government of 1974–9, and then, after the Conservatives' election victory of 1979, Sir Keith Joseph (1979–81).
[2] E. Batstone, A. Ferner, and M. Terry, *Unions on the Board: An Experiment in Industrial Democracy* (Oxford: Blackwell, 1983), interview, DoI official.
[3] Interviews, Minister and PO managers.   [4] Interviews, PO.
[5] Quote, senior PO manager; also interviews, PO and DoI officials.

of last resort' if relations between the PO and Department broke down.[6] The Minister saw the PO Chairman regularly (every few weeks), as well as senior PO staff, whilst civil servants in the Department established a web of regular contacts with PO employees.[7]

The PO and the government did not develop a joint overall strategy for the telecommunications sector. Rather, decision making involved a separation of roles between them, as each pursued its own objectives in its spheres of influence. The government dealt with general policy and particularly PO finances. The PO acted to secure specific goals linked to its direct interests as network operator, such as modernization of the network and profitability.

Thus the PO made most decisions concerning the running of the network, including the implementation of expansion, modernization, and its internal organization. The government rarely acted or took the initiative at a detailed level, and the PO enjoyed considerable autonomy in its sphere. A major factor in the government's limited role was the lack of technical knowledge of the civil servants in the Department: frequently the PO was 'educating' the Department, which lacked the capacity to formulate its own plans and at best could modify PO plans if it wished.[8]

Instead, the government's role was mostly at a general level and/or indirect. Much of its activity was concentrated in the financial field, notably capital investment and borrowing.[9] Within the government, the role of the Treasury was crucial in these financial matters. The Treasury generally did not deal directly with the PO, but wielded its influence through the Department, which acted as the PO's spokesman in negotiations with the Treasury on financial matters.[10] The Treasury's decisions and scrutiny of PO financial matters were based on aggregate figures: it was primarily concerned with the overall effects of PO financial decisions on general economic policy and the fiscal position of the government.[11]

The separation of roles between the PO and the government and its effects were seen most clearly in policy over switching suppliers. Both the PO and the Department wanted change in the structure of the subsector. Nevertheless, they failed to co-ordinate their actions. The PO was largely left autonomous in placing its orders and in relations with the suppliers; it pursued its narrowly-defined aims concerning equipment for its network, and lacked wider industrial policy goals. The Department, for its part, failed to formulate and implement a coherent plan for the subsector; it rarely took the initiative itself, taking refuge in commissioning reports, and was only brought in when disputes arose between the PO and its suppliers, acting as 'umpire'. The Department lacked suitable policy instruments to act, and in particular, was not able

[6] Interviews, Minister, PO and DoI.   [7] Interviews, PO.
[8] Quote PO manager; also interviews, DoI and PO.   [9] Interviews, Minister and PO.
[10] Interviews, Minister and PO.   [11] Interviews, DoI and PO.

to use the PO's orders to lead any restructuring. As a DoI Permanent Secretary put it, ' from an early stage, the Department was anxious to reduce the number of suppliers', but it lacked 'suitable artillery', which itself then contributed to a lack of political will.[12] The result was that neither the PO nor the Department was able to lead restructuring.

Expansion and Modernization of the Network

During the 1970s, it was clear that demand for telecommunications was growing rapidly.[13] In periods of economic upturn, waiting lists lengthened, with the problem reaching very significant proportions by the end of the 1970s.[14] The response was expansion of the network. Growth was largely planned and decided upon by the PO.[15] The government did not formulate any overarching plan for the network, nor did it issue targets for new subscribers or quality of service, and the choice of priorities was largely left to the PO. Instead, its role was indirect, influencing expansion through decisions on overall PO investment levels and target rates of return, which affected prices and demand.[16]

Policy over network modernization was also led by the PO, which based its decisions on criteria of demand and profitability.[17] The government's role was limited to approval of the PO's overall plans. Thus, in 1970–1, the PO decided to digitalize the transmission and switching of signals in the trunk network after a report by an internal PO group, the Trunk Task Force (TTF) showing the large cost advantages of digitalization and recommending that the PO should accelerate the replacement of electro-mechanical exchanges with space and time division ones.[18] The report was presented to the Department, 'for information'; this was necessary, since government approval was required for the ensuing investment programme under the 1969 Post Office Act.[19] After the PO set out the economic model of cost savings, the Department accepted the digitalization plan in 1972/3.[20]

Modernization of switching and transmission was then implemented. Its pace was left largely to the PO, after the overall plan had been accepted by the Department. In particular, the PO took a strategic decision over the type of switch to be introduced, with consequences for the modernization and quality of the network and for the manufacturing subsector. The British time division public switch, System X was far from ready, and the sole time division

[12] Interview, DoI.
[13] Figures of 8–10 per cent p.a. growth for usage were commonly quoted *The Times* 24.3.70, 8.10.70, 7.4.71, 22.10.71.
[14] Waiting lists rose from 108,000 in 1970 to 218,000 in 1972, falling to only 47,000 by 1976, before rising again in the late 1970s, and reaching 500,000 by 1980—*The Times* 22.4.70, 11.5.72, 29.7.76, and 15.10.80.
[15] Interviews, PO.   [16] See below for discussion of both of these.
[17] Interviews, PO.   [18] Interview, PO.   [19] Interview, PO.
[20] Interviews, PO staff.

exchange available was the French E10, which was small and suitable only for rural exchanges. The PO therefore decided to begin buying the intermediate technology which was not fully digital, namely space division exchanges, until the fully-digital System X became available. The government played almost no part in these decisions; only later, when there were implications for the division of PO orders amongst suppliers, was it drawn in.

The Allocation of PO Orders and Relations with its Equipment Suppliers

Equipment supply policy was overwhelmingly concerned with public switching equipment. Throughout the 1970s, there was considerable dissatisfaction both in the Department and the PO with the three largest switch producers—the British firms GEC and Plessey, and STC, a subsidiary of the American firm ITT.[21] Supply of equipment was marked by long delays, sometimes constraining PO expansion.[22] There were concerns that the PO was being overcharged.[23] Exports fell during the 1970s and Britain's share of world trade declined, from 25 per cent in 1963 to 10.5 per cent in 1970 to 5.9 per cent in 1975.[24] Perhaps most important of all, there were problems with Britain's time division exchange, 'System X', which was crucial to modernization of the PO's network. Nevertheless, there was little co-operation between the PO and the Department in the allocation of PO orders, nor were there co-ordinated attempts to use the allocation of PO orders to restructure the manufacturing subsector. Instead, PO efforts to modify its relations with its suppliers were largely blocked.

The opportunity to alter the allocation of PO orders appeared to open after 1969. Previously, the supply of public switches was covered by a bulk supply agreement (BSA), which laid down the division of orders between the various 'approved PO suppliers'; in 1969, they consisted of AEI/GEC (40 per cent), Plessey (40 per cent) and STC (20 per cent). Prices were fixed on a 'cost-plus' basis. The system of BSAs was severely criticized in the 1960s, and after its formal end in 1968 for public switches, the system was progressively abandoned between 1969 and 1972. In its place, the PO instituted a system of competitive tendering. Moreover, the advent of a new generation of equipment in the late 1960s and 1970s, namely space division exchanges replacing electro-mechanical ones, made competition in supply easier. Each supplier produced electro-mechanical exchanges to slightly different specifications and achieving compatibility between electro-mechanical exchanges was far from straightforward;

[21] Interviews, DoI and PO.   [22] The Times 7.12.70; interviews, PO.
[23] Interview, DoI official; report by the Comptroller and Auditor General 1969, The Times 11.9.69.
[24] National Economic Development Council working party on telecommunications equipment report—see The Times 22.3.78.

hence it was difficult to introduce a new supplier with a different type of exchange and extension orders tended to go to the original supplier of the switch, resulting in limited changes in market shares.[25] The purchase of space division exchanges thus offered an opportunity for the PO to alter supply arrangements; furthermore, their use of software made it easier to create extensions and linkages with exchanges manufactured by other suppliers.

The PO sought to exploit these opportunities by introducing new suppliers and modifying the rigid division of orders among the 'Big Three' manufacturers in Britain (GEC, Plessey, and STC). However, it met with little success. When competitive tendering began, Pye, a British subsidiary of the Dutch firm Philips, announced that it wished to become a switching supplier to the PO, with the encouragement of the latter, especially its Chairman, William Ryland.[26] Given the vast expense of developing a new switch, Pye attempted to enter the supply of an existing switch, STC's space division exchange, the TXE4. In principle, this should have been possible: the PO's contracts with the Big Three stated that patents had to be shared with all 'approved suppliers'. Yet, despite the PO formally approving Pye as a supplier, the strong support of Ryland, and talks with the Permanent Secretary at the DoI, Pye was unable to obtain a licence from STC, whose position was supported by GEC and Plessey.[27] Later, in 1975/6, Pye again tried to enter switching supply, by becoming a partner in the development of System X. As in 1973–4, the Big Three were able to repulse the attempt. In both cases, the PO did not form a co-ordinated strategy with the government to overcome resistance. It found itself unable to exert sufficient pressure on the Big Three: it was reluctant to destroy good working relations with them; there were legal problems over patents; most importantly, it wished to maximize progress over System X, which was hindered by disputes over Pye.[28]

The PO also considered buying exchanges from a foreign manufacturer. An initial foray rapidly revealed the difficulties of such a move. The PO ordered two international exchanges from the Swedish firm LM Ericsson in 1972 and 1975: Plessey was the only British supplier of these specialized exchanges, and did not have sufficient capacity to meet PO demand. Ericsson performed the contracts very successfully and the PO believed that it operated more professionally than the Big Three.[29] However, the purchase of Ericsson international exchanges was fiercely opposed by the Big Three—their chairmen (including the influential Arnold Weinstock of GEC) lobbied ministers and the Prime Minister—and by the trade unions.[30] Ultimately, the government supported the PO, but in 1972 told it not to repeat the experience;[31] in 1975,

[25] Interview, PO/BT.   [26] Interview, PO/BT.
[27] Interview, PO/BT; The Times 1.1.74.   [28] Interviews, PO/BT.
[29] The Times 17.1.75; interview, PO.   [30] Interviews, PO/BT; The Times 17.1.75.
[31] Interview, PO.

the government again upheld the PO, but by then Ericsson had formed a joint venture with a British firm, Thorn, and a large share of the £30m. contract was to be spent at the newly-built Scunthorpe factory. Given its experience, the PO did not turn to foreign suppliers for inland exchanges. Not only did it have a 'buy British' policy, and took seriously the clause in the 1969 Post Office Act (§9.1) that it should exercise its powers to meet the social, industrial, and commercial needs of Britain,[32] but also the Ericsson episode had seen major conflict for small-scale contracts for very specialized equipment. The extent of the opposition led the PO to conclude that buying foreign equipment was 'politically impossible'.[33]

Even altering the allocation orders among the PO's existing suppliers was beyond the reach of policy-makers, given the lack of co-ordination between the government and the PO. If one supplier appeared to be gaining a competitive advantage, the other two protested and sought government help. For its part, the PO believed that the 'political constraints' meant that it could not allow any of the three suppliers to fail; on the other hand, it was unable to restructure the subsector on its own initiative.[34] No attempt was made to link decisions over the distribution of orders to wider industrial policy purposes, such as reshaping the manufacturing subsector.

The clearest example of the effects of the absence of close co-operation between the PO and the department arose in 1971–2 when STC offered the PO a large space division exchange, the TXE4, which would then be developed as a more sophisticated exchange, the TXE4A. The other two suppliers, GEC and Plessey, bitterly opposed the TXE4, since they had not developed it and would lose market share to STC. Instead, they proposed an advanced version of the Crossbar electro-mechanical exchange.[35] GEC and Plessey lobbied hard at all levels, including the Minister, the Department, the Department of Trade and Industry, and even the Prime Minister.[36] The PO wanted the TXE4 on grounds of efficiency and quality, and produced figures indicating its advantages. The Department regarded the question as a 'technical' one which should not be decided on 'political' grounds, and also did not have the resources to challenge PO plans nor to examine alternatives, even if it had wished to.[37] Hence the Department largely favoured the PO's position.[38]

The result of the manoeuvrings was a compromise over the allocation of orders: the PO was to order £100m. of TXE4s, and £350m. of Crossbar equipment between 1973 and 1980; GEC and Plessey were able to manufacture TXE4s, under licence from STC. Moreover, the PO was able to increase TXE4 orders by 20 per cent in 1974,[39] and to cease ordering Crossbar equipment later

---

[32] Interviews, PO/BT.   [33] Interview, PO.   [34] Interviews, PO and Minister.
[35] Interviews, BT/PO; *The Times* 25.2.72.   [36] Interview, Minister.
[37] Interviews, Minister and PO/BT.   [38] Interviews, PO/BT.
[39] *The Times* 29.11.74.

in the 1970s, when it proved to be unsatisfactory.[40] In terms of the pattern of supply however, the outcome was little change: the PO's main concern was to be able to buy the TXE4 and the Department did not seek to take the initiative and co-operate with the PO to use the distribution of orders to alter the configuration of the equipment manufacturing subsector.

Developing New Equipment: System X

PO policy of buying 'British' equipment left its modernization strategy very dependent on its suppliers, especially in the digitalization of switching. 'System X' was the British time division exchange. It was developed jointly by the PO and the Big Three, with all parties involved in determining its specifications, and the PO funding research and managing the project. Competition would only operate during the production phase, when all three firms would manufacture System X exchanges.

System X had major problems throughout the 1970s; many of the criticisms of the project were forcefully articulated in the 1977 Carter Committee report.[41] There were long delays in setting specifications and contract terms, large cost overruns and complaints that the specifications were over-complex and unnecessarily rigid. The suppliers suffered from insufficient capacity and investment, especially in computer software engineering. During most of the 1970s, little attention was given to exports. The Big Three derived the bulk of their orders from the PO, and were 'remote from the market'.[42]

These problems were attributed, notably by the Carter committee, to two major causes. First, the PO lacked the necessary expertise and experience to manage the project. However, the PO was determined to control the evolution of System X, as it was paying for its development and was unhappy with the performance of the Big Three.[43] Second, and perhaps more importantly, System X involved three competing manufacturers. They were 'not a natural team',[44] and their relations with one another were marked by rivalry, suspicion, and personality clashes.[45]

The need for rationalization in System X was appreciated from an early stage: due to enormous fixed costs, the number of firms in the project was too great and an internal PO report in 1974 found that all PO orders could be met by

[40] A. Cawson, P. Holmres, D. Webber, K. Morgan, and A. Stevens, *Hostile Brothers* (Oxford: Clarendon Press, 1990), 119.
[41] Ch. 12 of the Carter Committee report, *Report of the Post Office Review Committee*, Cmnd. 6850 (London: HMSO, 1978); see also Cawson *et al.*, *Hostile Brothers*, 106–20, and also the National Enterprise Board report on System X, unpublished, 1978, cited in ibid. 111.
[42] Quote, PO manager.   [43] Cawson *et al.*, *Hostile Brothers*, 109.
[44] Carter Committee, *Report*, 102.
[45] Particularly between the GEC chairman, Arnold Weinstock, and the Plessey chairman, Sir John Clark.

two firms operating on four sites.[46] The PO had long wished to reduce the number of firms involved in System X, especially as three firms hindered exports, which were important in expanding the potential market for System X and thereby spreading fixed costs. However, rationalization required the strong support and involvement of the government, which were not forthcoming. In the early 1970s, an attempt was made by the DoI to persuade STC to merge with one of the two other suppliers; STC refused.[47] A more sustained endeavour was made in 1978-9. The Government commissioned a report by the National Enterprise Board focusing on System X. The report recommended that the number of suppliers be reduced to two, and that Plessey and STC should merge.[48] Despite talks involving the DoI and PO, neither firm accepted a merger. Then, in 1979, the PO tried to exclude STC from the project; STC appealed to the DoI, which failed to support the PO and hence no change took place.[49]

Even exports saw only limited progress: the PO was primarily concerned with fulfilment of its orders and the DoI played little role in encouraging sales abroad. In 1979, after a NEDO (National Economic Development Office) sector working party report pointed to the decline in Britain's share of world trade in telecommunications equipment and called for the establishment of a new joint PO–supplier export company and for a clear and detailed strategy for exporting. Only then, with the force of considerable governmental pressure, was British Telecommunications Systems (BTS) set up, as an international marketing company to sell System X.[50]

Thus in 1980, the PO remained tied to three competing suppliers, locked into 'quasi-vertical' relationships with its suppliers, whereby it was both purchaser and partner in developing switches, with only one type of time division switch planned.[51] The suppliers, for their part, were almost entirely dependent on PO orders for recouping the costs of System X.

Staffing and the Internal Organization of the PO

The government generally respected the PO's institutional autonomy and rarely intervened in the PO's decisions concerning its internal organization. Within the PO, telecommunications policy was largely determined by the Board and an informal Telecommunications Board. Following its change of status, the PO was able to separate its telecommunications and postal branches, to attempt to operate more as a 'commercial organization', and to decentralize decision making.[52] The government played some part in wage rises,

[46] Interviews, PO/BT.   [47] Cawson et al., Hostile Brothers, 111.   [48] Ibid.
[49] Ibid.   [50] Interview, PO/BT; Cawson et al., Hostile Brothers.
[51] Cf. G. Dang Nguyen, 'Telecommunications: A Challenge to the Old Order', in M. Sharp, (ed.), Europe and the New Technologies (London: Pinter, 1985).
[52] See D. Pitt, The Telecommunications Function in the Post Office: A Case Study in Bureaucratic Adaption (Hampshire: Saxon House, 1980).

but generally through incomes policies which applied to the entire public sector.[53]

Ministers did not use their powers of appointment and dismissal to attempt to control the PO or for wider policy purposes. Board members were internal staff or, if external to the PO, were not chosen on policy grounds.[54] Only once was a PO Board member removed: in November 1970, the Minister, Christopher Chataway, dismissed the PO Chairman, Lord Hall, but this was on grounds of personal unfitness, not because of disagreement over policy.[55] Hall was replaced by William Ryland, a PO telecommunications 'insider'. Although Tony Benn appears to have considered appointing another chairman in 1974, after representations, he reappointed Ryland,[56] who was in turn succeeded by an industrialist, Sir William Barlow, in 1977.

PO Profitability and Tariffs

Decisions over prices and rates of return were taken by the government and the PO respectively. On the one hand, the PO decided price changes. It informally cleared all major price rises with the Department, but generally obtained the price rises it had proposed, sometimes with some delay and after argument.[57] The POUNC was consulted both informally before price changes and then formally after their announcement (as laid down by the 1969 Post Office Act), but was fairly unimportant, securing at best only minor adjustments in proposed rises.[58] On the other hand, in most years in the 1970s, the government set the PO a 'target rate of return' on its assets. Although there was some measure of negotiation and consultation, in large measure the target was imposed by the Department on the PO; within Whitehall, it was decided by the Treasury.[59]

The target rate of return was frequently the crucial influence for other decisions, notably over prices, depreciation provisions and the level of investment. This was especially so after 1977, when the system of External Financing Limits was introduced: the EFL only limited borrowing, and hence higher investment had to be financed from internal profits.[60] Moreover, when the PO overshot its target rate of return, it was vulnerable to criticism and action by the Price Commission.[61] The target therefore provided an important indirect method of control for the government: if it wished to maintain a high level of investment financed from internally generated funds it set

---

[53] Interviews, Minister, DoI official and PO.   [54] Interviews, DoI official and PO.
[55] Interviews, Minister and PO/BT.   [56] *The Times* 3.12.74.
[57] Interviews, PO/BT, Minister and DoI official.
[58] Interview, Minister; *The Times* 9.5.70 and 27.11.75.
[59] Interviews, DoI official, Minister and PO/BT.
[60] Interview PO/BT.
[61] e.g. in 1977 the Price Commission investigated PO profits and ordered a repayment of £100m 'excess profits'.

a high rate of return;[62] if it desired lower price rises, it set a lower rate of return.

Prices were generally set to generate 'sufficient' profits, which in practice, meant both avoiding losses, and meeting the target rate of return in order to finance investment.[63] This approach was sometimes temporarily overridden by general prices policies (notably between 1971 and 1974), but when price constraints ended, charges rose to prevent losses and to meet the target rate of return. These principles of tariff-setting were accepted not only by the government and the PO, but also by less important bodies; thus in 1975–6 the trade unions opposed the PO being loss-making and receiving subsidies from the government, whilst the POUNC accepted large-scale prices increases was justified by the need to make sufficient profits for investment.[64]

The relationship between target rates of returns, profits and prices can be seen over the course of the 1970s. In 1970 the Minister, John Stonehouse, increased the target rate of return from 8.5 per cent to 10 per cent to cover higher investment. Price increases followed to meet the new target.[65] However, in 1972 the PO accepted the CBI's 5 per cent price increase ceiling, and the statutory price controls that followed; no target rate of return was set for 1973–5. With rapid inflation, the PO slipped into loss and large deficits appeared.[66] Profitability was regarded as essential and the PO Board (supported by the trade unions) protested; the government accepted that prices should rise, if necessary very steeply, in order to restore profitability.[67] The PO therefore sought and obtained permission from the Price Commission for price rises in 1973, 1974, and 1975, which were passed on the grounds that the PO should not be loss-making.[68] The importance of avoiding losses was most clearly illustrated in 1975: a large increase was introduced in April 1975, but it appeared insufficient to avoid a telecommunications deficit; thus prices were again sharply increased a second time in October 1975. In total, the nominal rise for several services was up to 100 per cent in one year.

After the massive price rises of 1975, unexpectedly high profits were generated, above the new target rate.[69] In response, between 1976 and 1979 prices were kept generally stable in nominal terms (and hence fell in real terms) or

[62]   e.g. this was Stonehouse's justification for raising the target from 8.5 to 10 per cent in 1970—
The Times 24.3.70.
[63]   Interview, PO/BT.   [64]   *The Times* 17.6.75, 29.7.76, and 23.8.75.
[65]   *The Times* 24.3.70, 4.4.70, and 22.4.70.
[66]   In 1972–3, £9.7m, (1 per cent of total income), 1973–74 £61.4m, (5.3 per cent of income) and in 1974–5 a loss of £194.5m, (14.0 per cent of income).
[67]   Post Office, *Post Office Report and Accounts*, Chairman's Statement, 1973–4 and 1974–5; *The Times* 17.6.75; interviews, PO/BT.
[68]   *The Times* 28.3.73, 15.9.73, 18.4.74, 17.7.74, 4.1.75, 22.2.75, and 23.8.75.
[69]   The target was set at 6 per cent per annum in real terms; out-turns were 6.9 in 1976–7, 6.1 per cent 1977–8 and 6.9 per cent 1978–9—Post Office/British Telecom, *British Telecommunications Statistics* (London: Post Office/BT, annual).

were reduced, whilst in 1977 'excessive' profits above the Price Code limits led to an enforced price reduction (by the Price Commission), which the PO implemented via a one-off £7 rebate to subscribers. In the late 1970s, the situation altered again. Although a government White Paper in 1978[70] laid down a target of a 5 per cent per annum decline in the real cost of telecommunications services between 1977–8 and 1982–3, pricing policies since 1976 meant that the PO was no longer meeting its target rate of return, and so major tariff increases were announced in September 1979 to take effect in 1979–80.[71]

Price changes were not evenly spread across all services in the 1970s. During the early–mid-1970s, there was some limited movement towards prices which were closer to costs: in particular, connection and peak rate local call charges rose in real terms, whilst trunk and international call prices fell. However, the PO believed that sweeping rebalancing of prices, especially increases hitting residential subscribers hardest, was politically unacceptable.[72] In the mid-1970s, price rises were concentrated on services used more by businesses than by residential subscribers—for instance, peak rate local calls rose sharply between 1974 and 1978, as did trunk calls, whilst connection and rental charges decreased in real terms. The distribution of price rises was used by the PO to justify higher tariffs, since increases for business subscribers were more politically acceptable than those for residential subscribers.[73]

Investment and Borrowing

Policy over investment and borrowing reflected the PO's position as a public corporation and public sector accounting rules. The government, and in particular the Treasury, saw the PO as an instrument of macro-economic management. It used its powers under the 1969 Post Office Act and over the Post Office as a public corporation to influence total PO investment and its financing to fulfil its budgetary and macro-economic objectives, especially those concerning the PSBR and the exchange rate.[74] Negotiations between the Department and Treasury, and with the PO, generally dealt only with global totals, not the distribution of investment.[75] Moreover, investment was not linked to wider industrial policy for the equipment manufacturing subsector.

In 1969 the PO was mid-way through a £2b. investment programme covering the period 1968–73. In the face of growing demand, evidenced by lengthening waiting lists and congestion, the Government approved a new £2.7b. programme by the PO from 1970 for the following five years.[76] In

[70] Department of Industry, *The Post Office*, Cmnd. 7292 (London: HMSO, 1978).
[71] *Financial Times* 18.9.79.   [72] Interviews, PO/BT.   [73] Interview, PO.
[74] Interview, DoI official.   [75] Interviews, PO/BT.
[76] Post Office, *Report and Accounts 1969–70*.

March 1970 the Minister, John Stonehouse, announced that the rate of internal financing would rise from 34 per cent to 52 per cent, thereby reducing government borrowing.[77] In 1972, another large investment programme of £4b. for the following five years, was announced by the new Conservative Minister, Christopher Chataway, with a concomitant increase in the PO's borrowing limit.[78]

Worsening macro-economic conditions and prices policies saw a reversal of earlier policies in the mid-1970s. In December 1973, the government reduced PO expenditure by £150m. for the financial year 1974–5 as part of the crisis measures announced by the Chancellor of the Exchequer to control public expenditure. The telecommunications side of the PO suffered most of the decrease (£140m.) and, within its spending, capital investment bore the brunt of the cuts, being reduced by 20 per cent.[79] This decrease was imposed on the PO by the government, and was bitterly criticized by the former.[80] Moreover, as PO prices were controlled and profits fell, a much lower share of investment was financed by internally generated funds: the proportion fell to under 40 per cent for the years 1972–5. At the same time, the Treasury encouraged the PO to borrow in foreign currencies in order create a capital inflow which aided the balance of payments and supported the pound; unfortunately, the PO suffered losses when the pound fell.[81]

Further large reductions in PO telecommunications investment were made in 1975 and 1976. These were decided by the PO voluntarily and on its own initiative because demand was lower than estimated in the plans formulated in the early 1970s.[82] Strong pressure on the government to intervene arose: senior executives from the Big Three equipment manufacturers lobbied the Department, as did trade union leaders.[83] The decline in PO orders was claimed to result in thousands of job losses, concentrated in areas of high unemployment, frequently in Labour Party seats.[84] In 1976 the Minister, Eric Varley, saw the PO Chairman to discuss the matter, but the government did not seek to alter the PO's decision.[85] The government's sole action was to set up the 1975 McKinsey inquiry on equipment ordering procedures and commission a report in 1977 by an economist, Michael Posner. Both reports supported the PO and argued that it should not be obliged to order equipment that it did not immediately require merely to assist the manufacturers; they argued that PO orders

---

[77] A target largely achieved—see Post Office/British Telecom, *British Telecommunications Statistics*.
[78] *The Times* 3.11.72.   [79] *The Times* 19.12.73 and 6.2.74.
[80] see Ryland's comments, *The Times* 6.2.74, and *The Times* 11.10.74; interviews, PO/BT.
[81] *The Times* 18.7.74 and 20.5.76.
[82] Interviews, PO/BT; *The Times* 12.9.75, 9.11.76, and 11.3.77.
[83] *The Times* 12.9.75, 3.10.75, 16.1.76, and 10.11.76.
[84] *The Times* 16.11.76, 12.8.75, 11.9.75, and 20.9.75.
[85] *The Times* 16.1.76, 30.11.76, and 11.3.77.

should be based on its requirements and on criteria of its profitability, not uti-lized as part of any wider industrial policy.[86] Thus investment remained driven by the PO's financial requirements.

The late 1970s saw changes in the levels and composition of investment and borrowing. Capital spending stabilized or rose slightly in real terms. As profits rose, the investment programme was entirely financed by internally generated funds, the figures being 92 per cent in 1975–6, 109 per cent in 1976–7, 114 per cent in 1977–8, and 106 per cent in 1978–9.[87] This was highly advantageous to the government, as PO investment did not increase public expenditure and the Public Sector Borrowing Requirement. Moreover, as a macro-economic policy objective became capping the rise in the foreign exchange value of the pound, the government reversed its earlier policy and limited foreign currency bor-rowing by nationalized industries after 1977.[88]

France[89]

The Processes of Decision-Making and Overall Policy

Policy-making in France lay largely in the hands of senior DGT officials and members of the political executive. The latter consisted of the President and Élysée staff, and certain government ministers, notably the PTT and Finance Ministers, and, more sporadically, the Prime Minister and the Industry Minister. In strategic decisions over the restructuring of the equipment supply, large private manufacturers were also significant participants.

Other actors occupied only minor roles. The Délégation de l'aménagement du territoire et de l'action régionale (DATAR) looked at the territorial implica-tions of telecommunications policy,[90] whilst the Commissariat du Plan enjoyed some importance before 1974, especially in matters concerning investment,[91] but was of almost no importance after 1974, merely formalizing decisions made elsewhere.[92] The trade unions were not important participants in decision making, except as a powerful brake on institutional reform. Users and Parlia-ment were not closely and directly involved in policy making.

---

[86] *The Times* 3.6.77.

[87] Post Office/British Telecom, *British Telecommunication Statistics*.

[88] *The Times* 30.3.77.

[89] For histories of telecommunications in France see L.-J. Libois, *Genèse et croissance des télé-communications* (Paris: Masson, 1983), E. Cohen, *Le Colbertisme 'high tech'* (Paris: Hachette, 1992), 33–47, C. Bertho, *télégraphes et Télécommunications: de Valmy au microprocesseur* (Paris: Livre de Poche, 1981) and B. Aurelle, *Les Télécommunications* (Paris: La Découverte, 1986).

[90] Interview, Direction des Affaires Industrielles/Direction des Affaires Industrielles et Inter-nationales (DAI/DAII).

[91] Interview, DGT and Libois, *Genèse et croissance des télécommunications*.

[92] Interviews, DGT, DAI/DAII.

The Presidency was at the centre of policy decisions, especially strategic ones. PTT Ministers changed frequently,[93] and their power appears to have fluctuated, but they took an active part in matters concerning network operation, such as growth, modernization, and prices.[94] The Finance Minister and his Ministry were involved in all financial decisions. Although the DGT was an *administration*, its senior personnel gained power and influence, especially Gérard Théry (Directeur général des télécommunications 1974–81), and Jean-Pierre Souviron (head of the DAI in the DGT 1974–8). Many decisions were taken in informal negotiations between the DGT and the Élysée.[95] This situation is frequently described as the DGT enjoying great 'autonomy'.[96] However, the DGT's position depended on close relations and similarity of aims between its senior personnel and the Élysée. Moreover, 'autonomy' did not mean that the DGT enjoyed its own separate sphere of competence; on the contrary, the political executive was closely involved in most major decisions, including senior DGT appointments, staffing, the internal organization of the PTT Ministry/DGT, expansion, modernization, and the setting of tariffs.

Policy-makers in France linked measures in different areas: senior appointments and changes in the DGT's organization were part of manoeuvres and strategies concerning wider industrial policy and the role of the DGT, and decisions were presented and elaborated in terms not merely of 'technical' choices, but also as part of wider industrial and economic aims. Often a *grand projet* strategy was adopted, whereby public bodies established a comprehensive plan involving co-operation among public and private actors designed to create a world lead for France.[97] Thus the aims of expanding and modernizing the network were linked to provision of a suitable infrastructure for economic growth and to national modernization. Choices of new equipment for network modernization saw the co-ordinated application of several policy instruments—close co-operation between the publicly-owned DGT and privately-owned manufacturers, public funds for research and development, and large public orders for French firms—in pursuit of a French world lead in digital switching, restructuring the equipment manufacturing subsector and altering DGT relations with its suppliers. In the *grands projets* of expansion, modernization, and equipment manufacturing restructuring, the Presidency co-operated closely with the DGT in order to achieve their common aims.

---

[93] The Ministers were: Yves Guéna 1967–9; Robert Galley 1969–72; Hubert Germain 1972–4; Pierre Lelong 1974–5; Aymar Achille-Fould 1975–6; Norbert Ségard 1976–80.

[94] Interviews, DGT and DAI/DAII.   [95] Interviews, DAI/DAII and DGT.

[96] See e.g., Cawson *et al.*, *Hostile Brothers*, ch. 6 and P. Humphreys, 'France: A Case Study of "Telematics" in K. Dyson, and P. Humphreys, (eds.), *The Political Economy of Telecommunications* (London: Routledge, 1990) who suggests that the DGT began to acquire the attributes of a 'state within the state'.

[97] See Cohen, *Le Colbertisme 'high tech'*, 96–100 and 108–12.

The Expansion of the Telephone Network

In the 1960s the French telephone network was one of the smallest in the industrialized world; waiting lists were lengthening and congestion worsening.[98] Concern with the underdevelopment of the telecommunications system grew and was an issue in the 1969 presidential election campaign;[99] the difficulties of making a simple telephone call even led to a popular comedy sketch entitled 'Le 22 à Asnières'. In response, policies of vigorous expansion of the telephone network were pursued after 1969. They involved political support, notably from the President, and use of financial instruments, particularly new methods of borrowing to finance increased investment.

After the election of Georges Pompidou as President in 1969, more attention and resources were given to telecommunications. Development of the telephone network formed part of Pompidou's 'industrial imperatives' and general policies of encouraging industrialization, especially by providing a modern infrastructure for business.[100] Moreover, waiting lists were lengthening, congestion was deteriorating, and there were increasing complaints from businesses.[101] Targets for rapid growth in the telephone network were set. As part of the VIth Plan (1971–6), an objective of attaining a telephone density comparable to France's neighbours by 1980 was laid down. The objective of 9.5m. lines by the end of 1977 was set, followed by 1m. lines per annum thereafter.[102] Under the pressure of increasing demand, the growth targets were again raised in the 'programme de Provins' announced by the Prime Minister, Pierre Messmer, in 1973, which set an objective of 12m. lines by the end of 1978.[103] The support of Pompidou and the Élysée was vital, particularly for the increase of 1973, which involved negotiations between Galley (the PTT Minister), the Finance Ministry, and the Élysée.[104]

The most rapid period of growth of the telephone network, however, came

---

[98] Twelfth in terms of number of main lines per 100 inhabitants out of thirteen industrialized countries in 1970—DGT/France Télécom, *Statistique Annuelle* (Paris: DGT/France Télécom, annual); in 1961 the waiting list was 119,000, by 1969 it had reached 377,000—*Le Monde*, 3.8.70, and *La Vie Française* 24.5.72; for the deterioration in call quality, see ibid., and also *Le Monde* 30.5.73, with problems being particularly severe in Paris; see A. Le Diberder, *La Modernisation des reseaux de télécommunications* (Paris: Economica, 1983), 54–60 for a discussion.

[99] See e.g. the series of articles entitled, 'La Crise du téléphone' in *Le Monde* 10.7.69–13/14.7.69, and an influential book written by a group of DGT officials, *Le Téléphone pour tous?*, published under the pseudonym J. F. Rugès (Paris: Seuil, 1970); Bertho, *Télégraphes et télécommunications*, 471–4.

[100] Interviews, DGT.   [101] Bertho, *Télégraphes et télécommunications*, 471–6.

[102] Libois, *Genèse et croissance des télécommunications*, 259–61.

[103] Interview, DGT; *Les Echos* 16.5.73; Libois, *Genèse et croissance des télécommunications*, 260–1.

[104] Interview, DGT; Bertho, *Télégraphes et télécommunications*, 476–7; M. Palmer and J. Tunstall, *Liberating Communications* (Oxford: Basil Blackwell, 1990), 140.

in the period from 1975 to 1980. Valéry Giscard d'Estaing had been elected President in 1974 on a platform of modernizing French society. Initially, he had thought of a sweeping project to 'computerize' France, but, Gérard Théry (newly promoted to Directeur général des télécommunications) was able to persuade him that computerization required a developed telecommunications system.[105] Thereafter Giscard d'Estaing made telecommunications 'his concern' and his personal support for the DGT was 'the decisive factor' in the DGT's battle with the Finance Ministry to be allowed to increase its spending.[106] The DGT's position was aided by the political influence of Théry and Souviron and their access to the Élysée. Decisions were made in the context of political pressure provoked by the further growth of waiting lists: despite the increased priority given to the telephone network, by 1975, there were no fewer than 1.2m. requests for a line on the waiting list.[107] There had been media and Parliamentary criticism and questions in the 1974 presidential election campaign.[108]

In 1975 discussions took place between the DGT (notably Théry and Souviron), Matignon, the Finance Ministry, and the Élysée concerning the telephone network, culminating in a *conseil interministériel* at the Élysée on 22 April 1975. It was decided that telecommunications would become a, if not *the*, major economic priority for public spending. This decision was incorporated into the VIIth Plan (1976–80), which included a 'catching up' plan (the *Plan de rattrapage du téléphone*), whereby France would have 20m. main lines by 1980 in order to catch up with its neighbours in terms of telephone density. Correspondingly, the DGT was allowed a massive investment programme, financed from a variety of sources.

The results of the *Plan de rattrapage* were remarkable: between 1974 and 1980, the number of main lines grew from 5.5m. to 15.6m., 29.7 per 100 inhabitants. In 1980 the waiting list was 805,000, the average waiting time for connection was 4.1 months, and call congestion had fallen.[109]

The Internal Organization and Staffing of the DGT/PTT Ministry

The DGT was an administrative unit (a *direction générale*) within the PTT Ministry and its staff, including the Directeur général des telecommunications, were civil servants. Several major modifications were undertaken of the organization of the PTT Ministry, the DGT within it and senior personnel during the late 1960s and 1970s. They formed part of wider strategies to alter the balance of power within the PTT Ministry and to modify industrial policy.

In the late 1960s, the DGT (led by PTT Ministers Yves Guéna and Robert

---

[105] Interviews, DAI/DAII and DGT.   [106] Interviews, DAI/DAII and DGT.
[107] *Les Echos* 22.5.75.   [108] *La Vie Française* 6.6.74 and *Le Figaro* 21.6.74.
[109] DGT/France Télécom, *Statistique Annuelle*.

Galley successively) and the Corps des ingénieurs des télécommunications, engaged in 'a violent struggle to win autonomy' from the postal side of the PTT Ministry.[110] Although the DGT gained autonomy and its own powers, in the late 1960s La Poste retained important powers over telecommunications services at the central and local levels.[111] At central level, in 1968 the DGT obtained its own units, separated from their counterparts in postal services, for equipment and orders, commercial matters, planning and personnel; the post of Secrétaire général des PTT, the official responsible for the entire postal and telecommunications services, was abolished in 1971.[112] At the local level, decrees in 1971–2 formally placed responsibility for all telecommunications matters under the sole authority of the DGT's local unit, the Directions regionales des télécommunications (DRT).[113] In addition, from 1970, the draft *Budget Annexe* of the PTT was divided into separate parts for telecommunications and postal services, allowing their very different financial situations to be more visible.

After Giscard d'Estaing's election as President in 1974, there were further changes. Since 1945, the DGT's research centre, the CNET, had been highly influential: it provided senior members of the DGT, notably the Directeur général des télécommunications;[114] it was at the centre of industrial policy, relations with suppliers and the development of new technology and equipment. However, in 1974, President Giscard d'Estaing removed Libois and appointed a relative outsider to the CNET establishment, Gérard Théry, as Directeur général des télécommunications. In turn, Théry obtained support from Giscard d'Estaing for organizational changes within the DGT.[115] In October 1974 a new and powerful body, the DAI, was created within the DGT.[116] It was given powers and responsibility for industrial policy and for relations with the DGT's equipment suppliers. The CNET was stripped of its industrial policy functions and made subordinate to the DAI and its Director was demoted.[117] Théry brought in members of other *corps*, particularly in posts dealing with general policy. The DGT was allowed derogations to the rules of an *administration* in the mid-1970s, including subcontracting work and recruiting staff on short-term contracts and applying new management techniques.

The reforms of 1974 had several aims. First, Théry wanted to introduce fresh

---

[110]   Quote, DGT official, interviews, PTT Minister and DGT.

[111]   See Libois, *Genèse et croissance des télécommunications*, 213–40.

[112]   Ibid. 239.   [113]   Ibid. 216.

[114]   e.g. both Pierre Marzin (Directeur général des télécommunications 1967–71), and Jean-Louis Libois (Directeur général des télécommunications 1971–4) were former heads of the CNET.

[115]   Interviews, DGT and DAI/DAII; for details of reforms see J.-P. Lukaszewicz, 'Service public administratif ou entreprise commerciale', *Actualité Juridique–Droit Administratif*, Feb. 1975, 52–72 and *Le Monde* 18.10.74.

[116]   In 1976, international matters were added and it became the DAII.

[117]   Libois, *Genèse et croissance des télécommunications*, 240.

blood into the DGT and to increase the DGT's political influence and connections.[118] He chose as the first head of the DAI Jean-Pierre Souviron, an *ingénieur des mines* who had no previous experience of telecommunications, but enjoyed a wide network of contacts, including within the Élysée.[119] Second, Théry wanted to break the CNET's power, and concentrate responsibility for general policy within one body.[120] This was related to a third aim: modifying relations between the DGT and its suppliers. The CNET had developed close links with CIT-Alcatel, and favoured the use of DGT orders to establish CIT as the sole 'national champion'.[121] Théry and Souviron wished to break with this approach by introducing competition into equipment supply, especially public switching. Removing industrial policy from the CNET was a first step in this process. A fourth aim was to allow the DGT to operate almost as if it were a company, with Théry as its chief executive;[122] internal reforms were a substitute for modification of the DGT's *statut*, which was blocked by trade union opposition.

Modernization of the Network, the Allocation of DGT Orders and Industrial Restructuring[123]

Modernization of the network was used as part of a *grand projet* strategy involving an overall industrial policy for telecommunications. In the 1970s, the allocation of DGT orders to modernize the network was linked to the structure of the equipment manufacturing subsector, relations between the DGT and its privately-owned suppliers and support for new technology. Public switching provided the best example of the *grand projet* approach, including possible variants: between 1969 and 1974, the CNET's policy of a single national champion, Alcatel; after 1974, Théry's and Souviron's strategy of two competing national champions.

In 1969, the French network was one of the least modern in industrialized countries, with no less than 22 per cent of connections being switched manually.[124] DGT orders for public switches were divided according to set quotas, decided within Socotel, the joint DGT–manufacturers company.[125] The majority of DGT orders went to subsidiaries of foreign firms, namely LMT and

---

[118] Interviews, DGT and DAI/DAII.

[119] See Palmer and Tunstall, *Liberating Communications*, 141.

[120] Interviews, DGT and DAI/DAII.

[121] Interview, DGT; P. Griset, 'Le Développement du téléphone depuis les années 1950', *Vingtième Siècle/Revue d'Histoire*, 24 (1989), 41–53; Cohen, *Le Colbertisme 'high tech'*, 57–9; Cawson *et al.*, *Hostile Brothers.*

[122] Interview, DGT; see Cawson *et al.*, *Hostile Brothers*, 123.

[123] For a history of public switching in France, see Libois, *Genèse et croissance des télécommunications*, 158–73, and Griset, 'Le Développement du téléphone'.

[124] Ibid.

[125] Le Diberder, *La Modernisation des reseaux de télécommunications*, 44–5; for a history of Socotel, see H. Docquiert, *SOCOTEL: Expérience de coopération État–Industrie* (Paris: Socotel, 1987).

CGCT, subsidiaries of the American firm ITT, and SFT-Ericsson, a subsidiary of the Swedish firm LM Ericsson.[126] There was no French indigenous technology in electro-mechanical switches: all firms, including the main French supplier, CIT-Alcatel, a subsidiary of the Compagnie générale des eaux (CGE) produced exchanges under licences from foreign companies (ITT and Ericsson).[127] Little scope for competition existed and exports were negligible.

The CNET was the dominant actor in the DGT/State side of the relations with the manufacturers. It performed several roles, including: undertaking and leading research into new types of equipment, notably digital switches; influencing the distribution of DGT orders between firms; drawing up and implementing industrial policy for the subsector; distributing funds for research contracts; checking the prices and costs of the equipment suppliers to prevent excessive profits from their contracts with the DGT, since prices were calculated on a cost-plus basis.[128]

The CNET's policy was to end the predominance of foreign firms by nurturing one 'national champion', CGE's subsidiary CIT-Alcatel, which would supply time division switches.[129] Modernization of the network was linked to the pace of development of Alcatel's time division switches. One part of its industrial policy in the 1970s was to provide large DGT orders for French manufacturers of equipment. The other part was research collaboration with selected suppliers. The CNET actively co-operated with CIT to develop a world lead in digital switching. In the 1960s, the CNET set up a special team led by Libois to research into time division switching.[130] At an advanced stage of the work, and in the face of the considerable scepticism of CIT, the CNET transferred its knowledge, patents and team of engineers to CIT, in order for the latter to move to the production phase of the operation.

CIT-Alcatel began to manufacture commercially the world's first operational time division switch, the E10, a small exchange suitable for 10,000–20,000 lines in 1970. As it was developed, researchers worked on larger versions, notably the E-12. Time division exchanges were seen as the switching system of the future and already in 1971 the PTT Minister, Robert Galley, announced that by 1975 10 per cent of DGT orders would be for time division exchanges, reaching 50 per cent by 1985.[131] Large-scale DGT orders would not only create a modern French network, but also allow CIT-Alcatel to develop a world lead in time division switches.[132]

The E10 was a small exchange, suitable only for rural areas. The DGT's

[126] The quotas in 1968 were: LMT—28 per cent; CGCT—14.5 per cent; SFT-Ericsson—18 per cent; CIT—29 per cent; AOIP—10.5 per cent (Le Diberder, *La Modernisation des reseaux de télécommunications*, 46).

[127] Aurelle, *Les Télécommunications*, 56.

[128] See Le Diberder, *La Modernisation des reseaux de télécommunications*, 44.

[129] Cohen, *Le Colbertisme 'high tech'*, 86–92, and Griset, 'Le Développement du téléphone'.

[130] Griset, 'Le Développement du téléphone', 43–5.   [131] *L'Express* 28.6.71.

[132] Interview, DGT; Griset, 'Le Développement du téléphone'; Cawson *et al.*, *Hostile Brothers*; Cohen, *Le Colbertisme 'high tech'*, 49–112.

strategy was to move directly from electro-mechanical switches to time division switches, omitting the intermediate technology of space division exchanges. It thus used the E10 for small exchanges and continued to order the electro-mechanical Crossbar exchanges for larger exchanges in urban areas, waiting until a large time division switch was available from CIT-Alcatel. Moreover, the single national champion policy meant the CNET permitted and indeed encouraged CIT-Alcatel to become the main French public switching manufacturer. In 1969 CGE and Thomson, a potential French supplier, signed a five-year agreement not to compete in certain activities; heavy electrical engineering, including public switching, was left to CGE.[133]

The CNET's blueprint was open to criticism. The prices charged by DGT suppliers were alleged to be excessive, far above those of suppliers in other countries.[134] Furthermore, CGE used its position to siphon off profits from CIT-Alcatel for the main group, and hence underinvested in telecommunications research and production.[135] Exports were not regarded as important by the manufacturers who could earn large profits from contracts with the DGT. It was not clear when larger time division exchanges would become available.[136]

In 1974, Théry and Souviron decided to alter the DGT's strategy. Having broken the power of the CNET by transferring its industrial policy functions to the newly-created DAI, they pursued a new strategy of using the allocation of DGT orders to pursue three objectives: ending the single 'national champion' approach of the CNET and replacing it with competition in supply to the DGT; altering the structure of the subsector to reduce foreign ownership, resulting in two 'national champions'; increasing the importance of exports.[137] The approach adopted by Théry and Souviron was strongly opposed by the CNET and supporters of a close relationship between the DGT and the 'national champion', CIT-Alcatel.[138]

The first step was taken in 1975–6. Théry and Souviron decided to order space division exchanges, even though this was clearly an intermediate technology. One major factor was the desire to restructure the manufacturing subsector, in order to increase the DGT's scope for choice over suppliers, lower prices and break up the quota system used for DGT orders.[139] The instrument to achieve these aims was an international tender (consultation) to supply DGT space division exchanges, launched in 1975. The competition replaced the quota

[133]   Aurelle, Les Télécommunications, 58; Le Monde 12.7.69.
[134]   See H. Jannès, Le Dossier secret du téléphone (Paris: Flammarion, 1970) and Rugès, Le Téléphone pour tous.
[135]   Cawson et al., Hostile Brothers.   [136]   Interviews, DGT.
[137]   Interview, DAI/DAII; Griset, 'Le Développement du téléphone', 48.
[138]   Cohen, Le Colbertisme 'high tech', 56–61; Griset, 'Le Développement du téléphone'; Bertho, télégraphes et Télécommunications, 482–3.
[139]   Interviews, DGT and DAI/DAII.

system of the past. Foreign firms were permitted to submit offers, but only in association with a French firm. Moreover, in order to encourage competition, two types of space division exchange were to be ordered, contrary to the view of many in the DGT (especially the CNET) that only one further system should be introduced, in order to minimize the increased complexity of running the network.[140]

Decisions as to the choice of suppliers and type of switch were made at the highest political level, with the active involvement of Théry, Souviron, Ségard (PTT Minister), Matignon, and the Élysée, including Giscard d'Estaing personally; final decisions were taken at a Conseil interministériel on 13 May 1976.[141] Three systems were selected from the six tenders received: Ericsson's AXE offered by SFT-Ericsson; the D10 offered by SLE Citeral[142] and the Japanese firm NEC; ITT's Metaconta switch, which was proposed by its subsidiaries CGCT and LMT.[143]

A complex set of negotiations then ensued between Théry and Souviron, and ITT and Ericsson. Using the prospect of orders for the two firms' systems, with subsequent effects on world-wide sales, but the threat of choosing the D10, the DGT was able to 'persuade' Ericsson to sell SFT-Ericsson to the French firm Thomson; similarly, it induced ITT to sell its public switching and transmission equipment subsidiaries LMT and LTT to Thomson. In return, the DGT ordered Ericsson's AXE system and CGCT's Metaconta system, both of which would be produced by Thomson under licence from Ericsson and ITT, who thereby received both payments for selling their subsidiaries and royalties from the licences. Moreover, ITT's remaining subsidiary, CGCT, was also to produce the Metaconta.

The outcome of the 1975 *consultation* was that most of the switching manufacturing industry was 'frenchified'. Whereas before 1976 a majority of DGT orders had gone to subsidiaries of foreign firms, now only CGCT, with 16 per cent of public switching orders, remained in overseas hands. Furthermore, the 'national champion', CIT, was faced by a powerful French rival, namely Thomson; the DGT had a choice between two French firms, albeit offering different technologies.

The next step in the DGT's new strategy was the introduction of competition into the supply of time division exchanges. By 1977, it appeared that large time division exchanges would be available sooner than previously believed; in particular, CIT-Alcatel's E12 trunk exchange was nearing completion. In 1977, Théry announced that the DGT would accelerate the introduction of time

---

[140] Interviews, DGT.

[141] Interviews, DGT and DAI/DAII; for a detailed account of the manoeuvres, see *Le Point* 10.5.76, and *Les Echos* 14.5.76. See also Cawson *et al.*, *Hostile Brothers*; Le Diberder, *La Modernisation des reseaux de télécommunications*, 93–8; Griset, 'Le Développement du téléphone'.

[142] A joint subsidiary between CIT, which held two thirds of the capital, and Ericsson, which held one third.   [143] Aurelle, *Les Télécommunications*, 57–9.

division exchanges, and largely end orders of space division switches.[144] Hitherto, CIT had enjoyed a monopoly, via the E10, over what was clearly the technology of the future. However, in order to maintain competition, Thomson was 'invited' to develop its own time division exchanges.[145] When it bought the transmission company LMT from ITT, it fortuitously found plans for a time division exchange.[146] During the late 1970s, the DGT gave Thomson financial aid for research, in order for it to develop a time division switch series known as the MT, which would rival CIT-Alcatel's exchanges.

Policy towards the supply of transmission equipment closely followed that concerning public switches. Thomson re-entered supply, with ITT selling LTT to it. By 1976, most DGT orders went to French firms, with only TRT, a subsidiary of the Dutch company Philips, left as a major foreign supplier.[147] Competitive tendering was introduced and hence the role of Sotélec was much reduced after the arrival of Théry and Souviron in 1974.[148]

Exports of equipment were strongly encouraged by the DGT and the political executive: they improved the balance of payments and were also designed to offset anticipated future declines in DGT orders in the 1980s, as the DGT's modernization programme was completed. The DGT and PTT Minister laid down a target that 30 per cent of the subsector's turnover should be derived from exports by 1980, threatened to alter DGT orders according to export success or failure and insisted that CGE and Thomson co-operate in exporting. Moreover, the government gave considerable financial aid for exports so that the suppliers were able to offer lower prices to overseas customers than to the DGT.[149]

Thus by 1980, the structure of public switching manufacturing had greatly altered. The bulk of DGT orders in both public switching and transmission equipment went to French firms.[150] Moreover, the DGT had a choice between two large French firms, CIT-Alcatel and Thomson, offering switches based on French technology, and competing fiercely with each other, instead of the previous cost-based quota system.

[144] Libois, *Genèse et croissance des télécommunications*, 170–3; Cohen, *Le Colbertisme 'high tech'*, 63–5.
[145] Interview DAI/DAII; Cawson *et al.*, *Hostile Brothers*, 138–9
[146] Cawson *et al.*, *Hostile Brothers*, 138.
[147] See Le Diberder, *La Modernisation des reseaux de télécommunications*, 98–100, and Aurelle, *Les Télécommunications*, 59–63.
[148] Interview DAI/DAII.
[149] Cawson *et al.*, *Hostile Brothers*, 139–40; *Financial Times* 17.5.79; *Les Echos* 3.6.76 and 3.11.76.
[150] The shares of DGT public switching orders in 1979 were: Thomson—40 per cent; CIT-Alcatel—32 per cent; CGCT—16 per cent; AOIP—11 per cent; in transmission, the only major non-French supplier was TRT, a subsidiary of Philips; see Le Diberder, *La Modernization des reseaux de télécommunications*, 98–100, and Aurelle, *Les Télécommunications*, 59–63.

Profits and Tariffs

Profitability did not play a major role in policy making in France during the 1970s: profit targets were not set, and pricing decisions were not greatly influenced by concerns about profits. DGT profitability as a proportion of total income was very high in 1970, then declined somewhat, but remained at a fairly stable and high level, mostly around 25 per cent of total income, throughout the 1970s.[151] Moreover, high profits were not essential to finance investment: the DGT was able to borrow to raise capital.

In contrast, the PTT and Finance Ministries, and sometimes also the Élysée, played active parts in setting tariffs, mostly acting to keep them down to pursue objectives other than DGT revenue, including expansion, pressure for greater investment, regional development and control of inflation.[152] The DGT and PTT Ministry's strategy was to maintain a high level of demand as part of the general policy of expansion and to keep up the pressure on the Finance Ministry to allow greater investment.[153] Telecommunications were also increasingly perceived as an important cost for companies, whose price should therefore not be increased; the regional development agency, the DATAR pressed for long distance tariffs to be held down.[154] Furthermore, in the late 1970s they became a more important element in the calculation of the price index, and so the Finance Ministry opposed tariff increases in order to keep down inflation.[155] The personal interventions of the President and the Élysée also played a role: Giscard d'Estaing was involved in the reduction of connection charges in 1978 and in 1979 'asked' the PTT Ministry to freeze the cost of the unit for 1980.[156]

Thus, despite excess demand, tariffs in nominal terms remained unchanged between 1966 and 1973, resulting in a sharp fall in real terms. Then, in 1973, some increases were implemented, notably in rental charges and usage charges, with the extra revenues being used to fund higher investment.[157] However, further increases in tariffs thereafter were modest. When a large rise in connection charges was attempted in 1974–5 (from FF500 to FF1,100), it was highly unpopular and it was rapidly scaled down.[158] Local calls produced little revenue, were loss-making, and took up much investment and capacity; nevertheless, rebalancing, involving higher charges, was rejected, in part because of fear of political opposition.[159] Thus local calls remained charged at one unit per call, regardless of duration.

---

[151] See Ch. 11   [152] Interviews, DGT and DAI/DAII.
[153] Interviews, DGT and DAI/DAII.   [154] Interview, DGT.
[155] Interviews, DGT and DAI/DAII.   [156] Le Monde 21.1.78 and 23–24.12.79.
[157] Le Monde 30.6.73 and Les Echos 23.8.73.
[158] Les Echos 23.10.74 and Le Monde 6.10.75.
[159] Interviews, DGT; Tribune Socialiste 5.3.70, Le Quotidien de Paris 13.9.72; Le Point 7.1.80.

Investment and Borrowing

DGT investment had been very low in the 1950s and 1960s, as it was given little priority in the *Plans* and was mostly financed by internally-generated funds.[160] In the 1970s, it increased dramatically thanks to the active support of the political executive and the use of new instruments for borrowing. Already, in 1968 the PTT Minister, Yves Guéna, obtained an increase in DGT investment above the levels in the Vth Plan (1966–70); this occurred after de Gaulle's personal support overcame resistance by the Finance Ministry.[161] Then, in the VIth Plan (1971–5) telecommunications were allocated a significantly larger volume of investment funds, notably when the totals were revised upwards in 1972/73 as part of the 'Programme de Provins' announced by the Prime Minister, Pierre Messmer, in 1973. The Élysée and the Finance and PTT Ministers, were particularly closely involved in the decisions to allocate greater funds to DGT investment.[162] Pompidou and his industrial affairs adviser, Bernard Esambert, intervened personally in the battle between the PTT Ministry/DGT and the Finance Ministry over limits for permitted DGT investment.[163]

The most dramatic increases in DGT investment came between 1975 and 1980. In 1975, FF1.7b. were allocated to the DGT as part of the 'growth Plan' *(Plan de relance)* designed to offset the effects of the 1974 oil crisis.[164] Moreover, President Giscard d'Estaing personally decided that telecommunications were to be the major priority of the VIIth Plan (1976–80). Discussions concerning investment were held between the Élysée, Matignon, the Finance Ministry, and other important parts of the administration, including the DATAR. The President's support was vital in overcoming resistance by the Finance Ministry to higher DGT expenditure.[165] Furthermore, *Plans d'action prioritaires* (PAPs) were launched to increase public investment over the period 1975–80, and thanks to the higher political priority given to the DGT over 50 per cent of the funds devoted to the PAPs (FF104b. out of a total FF200b. for the period 1976–80) were allocated to the DGT.[166] As a result of these decisions, DGT capital spending rose dramatically in the mid/late 1970s (in nominal terms, from FF14.5b. in 1975 to 25.5b. in 1980).[167]

Higher investment was largely financed by the new instruments for borrowing created in the late 1960s, namely the CNT and *sociétés de financement du téléphone* (using powers laid down in 1969). The unions, the Socialists, and the

---

[160] Libois, *Genèse et croissance des télécommunications*, 247–63.
[161] Interview, PTT Minister.   [162] Interviews, DGT and PTT Minister.
[163] Interview, DGT.
[164] Libois, *Genèse et croissance des télécommunications*, 260; *Les Echos* 25.4.75.
[165] Interviews, DGT.
[166] *Les Echos* 25.5.77 and Cawson *et al.*, *Hostile Brothers*; however, the money was only lent to the DGT, not given to it as suggested by Cawson *et al.*
[167] *Les Echos* 19.11.75 and *Le Monde* 21–2.10.79.

Communist Party strongly opposed the creation of *sociétés de financement du téléphone*, seeing them as leading to privatization of the DGT and offering high profits to private companies at the DGT's expense. Nevertheless, with strong support from Pompidou, much use of the *sociétés de financement du téléphone* was made in the early 1970s. In total, five were created, generally by private companies such as large banks.[168] They issued several types of bonds, including those designed for the general public. In addition, the CNT was allowed to borrow in France after 1971. DGT borrowing via the CNT and *sociétés de financement du téléphone* rose from 19 per cent in 1970 to more than 40 per cent of DGT investment for most of the 1970s, enabling the massive investment programme to be financed.[169]

Conclusion

Patterns of policy making in Britain and France differed during the 1970s despite the existence of similar external forces for change. The roles played by dissimilar national institutions factors in the contrasts between the two countries can be seen by comparing policy-making processes, the ways in which actors used their institutional powers and positions, and the means whereby institutions encouraged, discouraged, permitted, or prevented policy choices.

In both Britain and France, policy making largely followed the processes and division of roles laid down under the institutional framework. The main participants in decisions concerning the operation of the network in the two countries were the monopoly network operator and the political executive, with other actors being much less important, a position that corresponded to the distribution of institutional powers. In Britain, a fairly clear division of roles existed that reflected the 1969 Post Office Act. On the one hand, the government dealt with general policy (notably by approving PO modernization plans) and, more importantly, determined the PO's overall financial position, including its target rate of return, total investment and borrowing. On the other hand, the PO dealt with running the network, including matters such as its internal organization, staffing, and growth, and it was the main body initiating tariff changes. It held primary responsibility for relations with suppliers and the division of its orders between them. Although the Minister was consulted and given much information over matters lying within the PO's sphere of action, and the PO was obliged to explain and justify its decisions, the Department generally accepted the PO's choices. Even in relations between the PO and

---

[168] Finextel (1969), Codétel, Agritel (1972), Créditel (1972), and Francetel (1975); for details, see *Le Monde* 19.12.74 and 20–1.6.76, and Libois, *Genèse et croissance des télécommunications*, 156–7.

[169] For full figures, see Le Diberder, *La Modernisation des reseaux de télécommunications*, 79.

equipment manufacturers, the government's role was limited to that of 'umpire' when disputes arose, and it generally accepted the PO's view. In contrast, in France, the DGT did not enjoy its own sphere of action. Instead, the political executive was involved in most major types of decision, including senior DGT appointments and staffing, the internal organization of the PTT Ministry/DGT, prices, investment, growth, and modernization. In equipment supply, policy was made within specific institutional arrangements governing relations between the DGT and manufacturers (notably Socotel and Sotélec), but the political executive was able to utilize its powers over the DGT's orders and internal reorganization to lead a restructuring of the subsector. Policy largely depended on the desires of the political executive, especially of the presidency; insofar as the DGT enjoyed 'autonomy', this was dependent on relations between its senior staff and the political executive, and on the latter supporting DGT decisions. Policy-making processes were thus true to the DGT's institutional position as an *administration*.

The policies pursued in the two countries also differed. In Britain, the PO's strategies in growth, modernization, and prices related to delimited goals offering it direct advantages, such as greater efficiency, lower costs, better quality of service, and avoidance of losses. The PO's plans were limited in scope and ambition. The government did not formulate comprehensive proposals for the sector and neither it nor the PO linked decisions in network operation to a blueprint for the equipment-manufacturing subsector or to broader objectives. Avoidance of losses and meeting financial targets were priorities, even if large price rises or cuts in orders for suppliers were required. In France, the DGT and the political executive formulated much more comprehensive plans than in Britain, sometimes taking a *grand projet* approach. Thus decisions over matters from growth, modernization, tariffs, investment, and borrowing were made in relation to broader policy concerns such as development of the DGT's network, the general needs of the economy, and industrial policy towards the equipment-manufacturing subsector. Profits were not the central focus of policy; instead, large-scale borrowing was used to finance investment, making considerable use of new financial instruments created in the late 1960s and early 1970s.

The differing institutional frameworks contributed to the distinctive patterns of policy making in each country and to the contrasts found between the two countries. In Britain, the institutional division between the PO and the government and the autonomy of each in its sphere, encouraged both parties to formulate plans independently of the other. The PO used its position as a public corporation with an organizational identity and powers, to establish and implement its own plans concerning growth, modernization, internal organization and staffing, and often prices. This situation allowed and encouraged the PO to pursue its aims as the network operator, rather than to formulate broader schemes for the sector. Its financial approach also respected the 1969 Post Office

Act, which had specifically set the PO the objective of breaking even. For its part, under the institutional framework after 1969, the government had the policy instruments and an incentive to act to control the PO's overall financial position, particularly to pursue the needs of the general budget, rather than to make plans concerning the running of the network, which lay within the PO's sphere. In particular, it had powers to approve the PO's overall investment plans, and to set target rates of return and borrowing limits (via External Financing Limits) for the PO. Moreover, the accounting rules of the public sector meant that the finances of the Government and those of the PO were linked: before 1977 the PO's investment, and any operating deficit contributed to overall public expenditure; after 1977 its net borrowing counted as part of public spending. Furthermore, there were no financial instruments for the PO to borrow outside the general budget. However, outside the financial realm, the Minister lacked the institutional powers and the technical knowledge to scrutinise or challenge PO decisions, even if he had wished to.

In France, as an *administration*, the DGT lacked institutional autonomy and was dependent on the political executive's support to implement its plans. Hence it had incentives to co-operate closely with the latter to fulfil its objectives, such as expansion and increased investment. The political executive had wide powers over the DGT and hence could use the DGT to implement ambitious plans for expansion and modernization, to alter the DGT's internal organization and staffing, and to determine prices, investment, and borrowing. Unlike Britain, the political executive was able to link DGT decisions to wider aims than those sought by the PO, such as the modernization of industrial infrastructure or industrial restructuring, seen most clearly in the *grands projets*. The pursuit of ambitious and expensive plans was assisted by the ability of the DGT to use the specific policy instruments to raise capital created in the late 1960s and early 1970s, namely the *sociétés de financement* and the CNT. In addition, the DGT's *Budget Annexe* allowed the DGT's financial position to be separated from that of the general budget, so that higher DGT investment did not raise the main government deficit, unlike the position in Britain.

Perhaps the clearest evidence of the impact of institutional arrangements on policy and their importance in explaining the contrasts identified between Britain and France can be found in the equipment-manufacturing subsector. The major policy instrument in both countries was the distribution of the network operators' orders. However, in Britain, the PO's orders were largely determined in bilateral relations between the PO and its suppliers. The government played only a limited direct role as an 'umpire' and although it saw the need for restructuring and concentration, and wished it to occur, it lacked suitable policy instruments. The PO and the government did not co-ordinate their actions, and so PO orders did not form part of a wider industrial strategy for the subsector. In contrast, in France, the CNET was able to utilize DGT orders and research funds to build up CIT-Alcatel as the sole 'national champion' before 1974. Thereafter, the political executive applied its powers over DGT orders, staffing, and internal distribution of functions to restructure the equipment-manufacturing subsector, creating two French 'national champions', and to modify relations between the DGT and its suppliers. It acted, in close co-operation with senior DGT staff whom it had appointed, to wield DGT orders as effective policy instruments for wider industrial policy goals, whereas its British counterparts were unable to do so.

The experience of the 1970s therefore offers strong evidence to support the argument that differing national institutions give rise to dissimilar patterns of policy making. Policy-making processes followed those laid down in each set of formal institutions. Differing national institutional arrangements, including the policy instruments available and the institutional positions of the actors, permitted, encouraged or discouraged courses of action, contributing to the distinct patterns of policy formation in the two countries. Despite common powerful international pressures, Britain and France experienced distinctive patterns of policy making, influenced by their differing institutional frameworks.

PART III

Institutions and Policy Making 1980–1997

7

The Institutional Framework of Telecommunications 1980–1997: National Change, Divergence, and Differences

The 1980s and 1990s saw Britain and France facing increasingly strong external pressures for change (technological and economic developments, European legislation and international regulation). In contrast to the 1970s, comprehensive institutional change in Britain took place in the 1980s and significant reforms in France during the 1990s. Yet, institutional reforms in Britain led to increasing divergence between the two countries during the 1980s. The French reforms of 1990 reduced differences somewhat, but it was only after further reforms in 1996–7 that significant convergence occurred and, even so, important institutional contrasts with Britain remained.

Divergence and dissimilarities between the institutional framework in Britain and France in the 1980s and 1990s arose from the path of reform followed by each country. Institutional reform is thus the central focus of the present chapter, which therefore performs two functions. First, it addresses national institutionalist claims that nations have differing but stable institutional frameworks, and that when institutional change occurs, countries follow different paths. The process of institutional change is analysed, to consider how and why institutional contrasts developed in the two countries despite common pressures for change. The differing experiences of Britain and France offer valuable material for a discussion of the conditions under which reforms are implemented. Second, the substantive changes in the institutional frameworks are detailed. Hence the extent of reforms and the differences between the two countries are set out. The following chapters can therefore consider whether institutional reforms led to changes in national patterns of policy formation and hence also resulted in divergence between the two countries in policy making and economic performance. The chapter follows the definition of institutions set out in the first chapter by analysing the organization of the sector, namely the bodies given a public role in the sector, examining their formal position, powers and the rules governing the use of their powers.

Britain

Institutional Change 1980–1984

On being elected in 1979, the Conservatives did not have a radical strategy for institutional change. In Opposition, they had merely promised to split posts and telecommunications and to end the Post Office's (PO) monopoly over customer premises equipment. Nevertheless, comprehensive institutional change took place concentrated in a short space of time, between 1980 and 1984, beginning with limited reforms in 1981, followed by comprehensive changes in 1984.

The Creation of BT and the Sale of Cable and Wireless 1981

In September 1979 Sir Keith Joseph, Secretary of State, at the Department of Industry (DoI, referred to as 'the Department'),[1] announced that the PO would be split into two public corporations, the PO and British Telecommunications (BT), the latter being responsible for telecommunications. There was widespread support for the move: the PO Board had been consulted and was in favour, as was the Post Office Engineering Union; only the Union of Postal Workers was strongly opposed.[2] Joseph also announced that the experiment with worker directors would be ended; the PO chairman had pressed hard for this, and the unions were not enthusiastic concerning the results of the experiment.[3]

The creation of BT was implemented by the 1981 British Telecommunications Act. The Act applied most of the institutional arrangements of the 1969 Act to BT, including the PO's monopoly over network operation, powers and duties to break even and provide services. Similarly, the Minister retained powers over appointment of the BT Board, the issue of Directions and overall plans, borrowing and capital spending.

Nevertheless, certain significant changes were made, which strengthened the Minister. Under section 15 of the Act, BT's monopoly could be broken by a licence to supply services issued by either the Secretary of State 'after consultation with' BT, or by BT with the agreement of the Secretary of State; moreover, the Secretary of State could direct BT to issue licences. This contrasted with the 1969 Act, in which only the PO issued licences, with the agreement of the Secretary of State. Section 16 allowed standards for equipment connected to BT's network to be set by the Secretary of State, or by a person appointed by him. Thus the Secretary of State could end BT's effective monopoly over CPE by setting standards for it.

New financial powers were also introduced. The Secretary of State could,

---

[1] A post he held until 1981; after 1983, the DoI became the DTI—Department of Trade and Industry.

[2] *Financial Times* 13.9.79.   [3] Ibid.

with the approval of the Treasury, determine BT's financial objectives, which BT would be obliged to implement. Under §79, the Treasury was empowered to sell shares in the then publicly-owned Cable and Wireless corporation, which supplied telecommunications services in overseas markets; this was undertaken later in 1981.

Privatization of BT and the New Regulatory Regime of the 1984 Telecommunications Act

No mention of the privatization of telecommunications in Britain had been made in the Conservatives' 1979 general election manifesto. Nevertheless, in July 1982, Patrick Jenkin (Secretary of State at the Department of Industry, 1981–3) published a White Paper setting out the Government's intention to sell shares in BT and to create an independent regulatory body for telecommunications.[4]

Various reasons lay behind the Government's decision to privatize BT.[5] The DoI was frustrated over the effects of BT's capital investment counting towards its external financing limit and therefore the public sector borrowing requirement (PSBR); in particular, since the mid-1970s, PSBR targets had led to conflict with the PO/BT, and Sir George Jefferson (BT Chairman 1981–8) made vociferous complaints that EFLs failed to distinguish between capital and current expenditure and were constraining the highly profitable modernization of BT's network.[6] The DoI had been grappling with methods of allowing BT to borrow for capital schemes outside the PSBR, but the Treasury had blocked all proposals. Instead, the latter favoured privatization because the proceeds of the sale were counted as 'negative expenditure' and therefore reduced the PSBR. Privatization was also linked to introducing greater competition, as BT's position appeared to conflict with liberalization: a public corporation competing with private companies, subject to investment and price controls, but also enjoying a monopoly in many fields was argued to be incompatible with 'fair competition'.[7] Moreover, privatization allowed the Conservatives to claim that they were 'rolling back the State', in contrast with the 'pro-nationalization' Labour Party. Finally, the US experience of privatized utilities under strong

---

[4] Department of Industry, *The Future of Telecommunications in Britain*, Cmnd. 8610, (London: HMSO, 1982).

[5] See A. Cawson, P. Holmes, D. Webber, K. Morgan, and A. Stevens, *Hostile Brothers* (Oxford: Clarendon Press, 1990), 95–7; J. Hills, *Deregulating Telecoms: Competition and Control in the United States, Japan and Britain* (London: Pinter, 1986), 122–30; J. Moon, J. J. Richardson, and P. Smart, 'The Privatization of British Telecom: A Case Study of the Extended Process of legislation', *European Journal of Political Research*, 14 (1986), 339–55 for analyses of the privatization.

[6] Interview, DoI Minister.

[7] This point was discussed at length in the Beesley Report, *Liberalisation of the Use of British Telecommunications Network* (London: HMSO, 1981), which suggested that BT be freed from price and investment controls in order to be able to compete fairly.

regulation appears to have offered an attractive example to many politicians, including Jenkin.[8]

The process of privatization indicated the extent and limits of the Government's ability to alter the organization of the sector.[9] The overall policy was conceived and decided on by ministers, particularly Patrick Jenkin, with little consultation or advice from the traditional 'policy community' that had existed in the sector, such as BT, the equipment manufacturers, and DoI civil servants.[10] Even potential beneficiaries such as large business users and their representatives, including the TMA, did not press for the sale of BT.[11]

Privatization needed to be passed in the face of parliamentary and extra-parliamentary resistance. The Opposition parties were against the change and the trade unions set up the BT Union Committee (BTUC) to organize lobbying and industrial action.[12] The equipment manufacturers were also hostile to privatization, especially Lord Weinstock (chairman of GEC, BT's largest supplier), fearing loss of orders to imports, and the power of a private domestic monopsonist (BT) over them. Within the Conservative Party, there were concerns that BT would merely be a private monopoly, that it would abuse its power and that it would withdraw from desirable but 'uneconomic' activities such as services in rural areas.

The form of privatization was influenced by the need to garner sufficient acceptance for the reforms to overcome opposition.[13] The support of BT's top management appeared vital to its implementation.[14] The main issue was the break up of BT, perhaps into regional companies or separate companies for long-distance transmission and local services, similar to the 1982 break-up of AT&T in the US. The splitting of BT was strongly supported by the Prime Minister[15] and some Conservative backbenchers.[16] The BT Board's main concern was to avoid such a policy, and in informal consultations it threatened to oppose privatization if it were linked with break-up.[17] In addition, dividing up BT might

[8] Moon et al., 'The Privatization of British Telecom', 341–3; interview, DoI Minister; Financial Times 23.1.82.

[9] For more detailed accounts, see: J. Kay, 'The Privatization of BT', in D. Steel and D. Heald (eds), Privatising Public Enterprises (London: RIPA, 1984); K. Newman, The Selling of BT (London: Holt Rinehart and Winston, 1986).

[10] Moon et al., 'The Privatization of British Telecom'; interview, DoI Minister.

[11] Cawson et al., Hostile Brothers, 93.

[12] See Moon et al., 'The Privatization of British Telecom', 345–9.

[13] N. Lawson, The View from No.11 (London: Corgi edn., 1993), 222–3.

[14] Ibid., 222; interviews, DoI Minister and PO/BT.

[15] Interviews, DoI Minister and DoI/Oftel; cf. M. Thatcher, The Downing Street Years (London: Harper Collins, 1993), 680.

[16] The most prominent was Richard Shepherd.

[17] Lawson, The View from No.11, 222; interviews, BT and DoI Minister.

have reduced sale proceeds, and would have greatly delayed privatization, as little accounting information was available within BT.[18]

A sale also required sufficient demand for the shares, especially as it was the largest ever flotation at that time. The government[19] sounded out City institutions on the conditions for a successful offer; the main one was predictable regulation by a body independent of the government.[20] The other main factors were BT's licence (see ch. 9), which was negotiated whilst the privatization Bills were going through Parliament, and the share price.

The need to pass an Act gave Parliament a rare opportunity to play a significant direct role in policy making in the sector.[21] The first Telecommunications Bill was passed by the House of Commons under a parliamentary guillotine, in the face of opposition by the Labour Party and the Alliance. A few amendments were made, notably to protect rural areas, to strengthen the powers of the newly-established Director General of Telecommunications (DG) to deal with anti-competitive practices such as undue preference or discrimination and to oblige network operators to publish their terms and conditions.

Patrick Jenkin had announced that the sale of BT shares would take place only after the following election. Due to the June 1983 election, the Bill fell. After the Conservatives' sweeping victory, and their manifesto commitment to privatizing BT, a new Bill was introduced in June 1983, with a small number of modifications. Having passed the Commons, it was considered in the Lords. Here it was attacked not just by Opposition peers, but by Lord Weinstock, who claimed that BT would be an uncontrolled private monopoly, and said the Bill was a 'pig's ear' which should be called 'Hello Folly'.[22] No fewer than three hundred amendments were made, some of which were accepted. The most important modifications were: the licences for BT, Mercury, and other public telecommunications operators were made subject to parliamentary debate and approval, although not amendment; BT was required to define its businesses and not to cross-subsidize its manufacturing operations; the Act specified duties to enable UK equipment suppliers to compete effectively overseas; unfair discrimination against subscribers in rural areas was banned; greater protection was given to vulnerable users, such as the disabled and elderly.[23] The Bill received Royal Assent in April 1984. Industrial action against privatization failed, notably due to court rulings against the POEU.[24]

---

[18] Interviews, DoI Minister and DTI official.

[19] Using its advisers, notably Sir Jeffrey Sterling, special adviser to Jenkin.

[20] Interviews, DoI Minister and Oftel.

[21] For details of the preparation and passing of the 1984 Telecommunications Act, see Moon, et al., 'The Privatization of British Telecom'.

[22] *Financial Times* 17.1.84 and 30.3.84.

[23] *Financial Times* 3.4.84 and Moon et al., 'The Privatization of British Telecom'.

[24] Moon et al., 'The Privatization of British Telecom', 348.

Institutional Arrangements under the 1984 Telecommunications Act

The 1984 Telecommunications Act (referred to below as 'the Act') represented radical institutional change, involving the privatization of BT, the ending of its statutory monopoly, a new licensing regime, and the creation of a new, institutionally-separate regulator for telecommunications. The framework set out the functions, powers and duties of the actors in telecommunications, but only in broad terms, allowing significant scope for interpretation and considerable discretion in policy making. The two key actors in public policy making were the newly-created DG and the Secretary of State for Trade and Industry. A relatively clear division of functions and powers was laid down in the Act, with the DG being concerned with the behaviour of licensees and the Secretary of State having a broader, less direct role, notably through licensing. Each enjoyed considerable autonomy in his sphere of activity, especially the Secretary of State.

The Privatization of BT

The Act transformed BT into a private limited company and allowed for the sale of shares by the government. It made few specific provisions for government powers over BT; instead, BT's duties were to be codified in its licence. In November 1984, 50.2 per cent of BT shares were sold. Large numbers of private investors bought shares, taking advantage of special schemes and reductions for subscribers and BT employees.[25] The issue was heavily oversubscribed, and the share price rose considerably above the sale price.

The Ending of BT's Monopoly and the Licensing of Suppliers

The Act abolished BT's monopoly over telecommunications systems.[26] Instead, a system of licences was instituted to run a telecommunications system and maintain equipment, whilst all equipment connected to telecommunications systems had to be approved. The only exceptions were 'private systems' and broadcasting systems licensed under the 1949 Wireless Telegraphy Act.[27]

Certain systems could be designated by the Secretary of State as 'public telecommunications systems', and hence the licensee was a public telecommunications operator. A PTO licence had to contain one or more conditions specified under §8, including requirements that the operator had to provide certain services, connect with other systems, avoid undue preference or discrimination in providing services and publish charges.[28] PTOs were empowered to install equipment on public and private land. The most notable examples of

---

[25] For details of the sale, see Newman, *The Selling of BT*.   [26] Sections 2 and 4.
[27] Licences for cable television transmission were allocated by the Cable Television Authority between 1984 and 1990, under the 1984 Cable and Broadcasting Act.
[28] See also the Telecommunications Code, appended to the Act.

PTOs were BT and its competitors such as Mercury, and the cellular operators, Vodafone and Cellnet.

The Act contained a few procedural rules for the issue of licences (for instance, over publication of notices), but almost no substantive criteria. In particular, it gave no right to a licence and did not define those networks or services which would be open to competition. Instead, the Secretary of State was left to decide the extent and terms of competition in granting licences.

The Director General of Telecommunications

The Act created the office of Director General of Telecommunications, appointed by the Secretary of State for a term of five years. The DG was funded by monies voted by Parliament.[29] He chose his staff, subject to Treasury approval over numbers and pay. His main functions and powers related to enforcing and modifying licenses and to providing information; he could issue licences for a public telecommunications system, or approve contractors or equipment, only with the authorisation of the Secretary of State.

The DG was responsible for the enforcement of licences, by issuing provisional and then final orders to the licensee (§16–§18). A final order by the DG could only be challenged in court, and the Secretary of State played no part in licence enforcement. The DG was to investigate all non-frivolous representations to him.

Licence modification was more complex. The DG could alter licences with the licensee's consent (§12), subject to a power by the Secretary of State to block the change. However, the DG could also modify licences without the licensee's consent through a reference to the Monopolies and Mergers Commission (MMC), under §§13–15. He could refer any matters relating to the supply of services or CPE by a licensee to the MMC to investigate whether they 'operate or may be expected to operate against the public interest', and whether the adverse effects could be remedied or prevented by licence modifications (§13.1). If the MMC report was favourable to the DG's reference, the DG was to alter the licence. He was free to 'make such modifications of the conditions of the licence as appear to him requisite for the purpose of remedying or preventing the adverse effects specified in the report' (§15.1) and only had to 'have regard to' the changes specified in the MMC report. Thus the DG enjoyed considerable discretion over making references to the MMC and then, if a favourable MMC report was forthcoming, also to alter a licence; the main potential constraint on the DG was judicial review.

The DG was to keep a public register of all licences and approvals granted. It was his duty to collect information concerning commercial activities in telecommunications. (§47). He was empowered to demand documents and

---

[29] See §1 and schedule 1.

information 'for any relevant purpose' (§53). He could then publish information and advice, although he had to consider whether publication prejudiced the interests of individuals or firms concerned. He was to provide information, advice and assistance to the Secretary of State and the Office of Fair Trading as requested by them (§47.4), and an annual report to the Secretary of State that was laid before Parliament.

In exercising his powers, the DG had two primary duties (§3.1): to ensure that 'all reasonable demands' for telecommunications were satisfied throughout the UK, except if not reasonably practicable';[30] to ensure that suppliers could finance the provision of such services. Thus the DG was given a duty to ensure both some form of 'universal service'.

Section 3.2 then added a further set of duties guiding the DG's actions. These included:

- 'to promote the interests of consumers, purchasers and other users in the United Kingdom (including, in particular, those who are disabled or of pensionable age) in respect of the prices charged for, and the quality and variety of, telecommunications services provided and telecommunication apparatus supplied';
- to maintain and promote effective competition;
- to promote efficiency and economy by suppliers;
- to promote research, development and use of new techniques;
- to encourage major users of telecommunications services to establish places of business in the United Kingdom and the provision of international transit services;
- to enable suppliers to compete effectively.

The DG's duties were very general and liable to conflict, both with one another. They thus provided the DG with scope for choice and discretion. In addition, the same duties were placed on the Secretary of State.

General Competition Law; the Courts

General competition law applied to telecommunications: the Director General of Fair Trading (DGFT) was empowered to ask the DG to exercise his powers under the 1973 Fair Trading Act against courses of conduct detrimental to the interests of the consumer. Moreover, the DGFT's powers to refer monopoly situations to the MMC and to deal with anti-competitive practices could be exercised concurrently with the DG.

The courts were given few powers specific to telecommunications; the main exceptions concerned orders issued by the DG to enforce licences, for which licensees had rights to challenge orders. Otherwise, the main role that the courts could play was via judicial review.

---

[30] Specific examples were also given, such as emergency services and services in rural areas.

The Secretary of State (for Industry/for Trade and Industry)

The Secretary of State had strategic powers over the telecommunications sector. He controlled the issue of licences. Under §7 he could either issue licences for running a telecommunications system himself, after 'consultation' with the DG, or by giving consent to licences issued by the DG, or a general authorization to the DG. Moreover, he designated systems as public telecommunications ones and hence their licensees as PTOs. He also approved contractors and CPE (§20 and §22), but for CPE, he could delegate his power to another body (§25). The Secretary of State could block licence changes agreed between the DG and licensee, but only in similar exceptional circumstances could he prevent the DG from imposing licence modifications after a favourable MMC report. He also appointed the DG.

However, the Secretary of State's powers over the DG's day-to-day activities were limited. He could issue 'general directions' to the DG as to the order of priority and the considerations to which he should have particular regard in reviewing telecommunications and commercial activities. He could intervene to prevent publication of material or enforcement or modification of licences under exceptional circumstances, generally national security or relations with foreign countries. He could only remove the DG because of 'incapacity or misbehaviour'.

The Act laid down the same general duties for the exercise of the Secretary of State's powers as for the DG. The wide discretion thereby afforded was increased by the lack of detailed rules over the exercise of the Secretary's powers, notably in appointing the DG and over licensing.

Parliament

Parliament's specific powers over policy making under the Act were limited. Any designation of a system as a public telecommunications system by the Secretary of State was by Order, which was laid before each House of Parliament and only came into force 28 days thereafter. Thus each House could prevent the issue of a PTO licence through revoking an order by voting a resolution, but could not amend licences. In addition, the funding of the DG and his staff was by monies voted by Parliament.

Users

The interests of users were expressly mentioned in the general duties of the DG and Secretary of State. The latter was also empowered to recognize bodies representing the interests of consumers, and to fund such bodies (§27). Moreover, he was to set up advisory bodies for each country within the UK (§54), whilst the DG was obliged to set up an advisory body for matters affecting small businesses and one for the disabled and those over pensionable age, and could establish other advisory bodies as he wished and appoint their members.

However, consumer bodies were given no powers- their role was purely advisory.

Institutional Reform 1984–1997

Conservative Governments, facing continuing fiscal pressures, proceeded to sell the remaining publicly-owned shares in BT in 1990 and 1993. Almost no controversy was generated by the sales and by the 1992 general election, the Labour Party was not even seeking to renationalize BT. In 1997, the Government announced the ending of its 'golden share' in BT that could be used to prevent takeovers: it wished to aid BT to obtain regulatory approval in the United States for its proposed takeover of the American operator MCI, and believed that the share was either unusable in practice or that it could apply other institutional instruments to prevent an unwelcome takeover.[31]

Despite criticisms of utilities regulation in the mid-1990s and discussion of reform to deal with increased convergence between telecommunications and broadcasting,[32] in the 1990s the only major institutional change in the sector was the Competition and Service (Utilities) Act 1992, which empowered the Director General for Telecommunications (and the DGs for other utilities) to set performance standards and ensure compensation for inadequate service. More fundamental reforms, such as creating an Office of Communications to regulate telecommunications and broadcasting or replacing individual DGs with a Board, were not introduced.

France

During the 1980s, few changes were made to the institutional framework in France, resulting in increasing divergence with sectoral institutions in Britain. Even after significant but not comprehensive reforms were undertaken in 1990, the two systems remained very different. Only with the changes of 1996–7 did more substantial convergence occur. Institutional alteration in France was slower, took place later and was more gradual than in Britain. The forces for institutional modification took a long time to gather and faced strong and effective opposition, especially by trade unions. Periods of reform were closely linked to the character and position of the political executive.

The Left 1981–1986

With the success of the *grands projets* of the 1970s fresh in the minds of policy-makers and the public, discussion of the DGT's organizational position (its

---

[31]   Interview, DTI.
[32]   Cf. R. Collins and C. Murroni, *New Media, New Policies: Media and Communications Strategies for the Future* (Cambridge, Mass.: Blackwell, 1996).

statut) and monopoly grew only gradually in the mid-1980s. An official report in 1984 by Jacques Chevallier into La Poste envisaged a separation of the postal and telecommunications sides of the PTT Ministry, with each becoming an *établissement public administratif* or a form of public corporation, with legal personality and statutory autonomy.[33] There were voices within the DGT suggesting that the end of the DGT's monopoly was inevitable (notably under the pressure of international 'deregulation') and perhaps even desirable, and that the DGT's *statut* should correspondingly be altered.[34] The Association des ingénieurs des télécommunications (AIT[35]) argued that the DGT and La Poste should each become an autonomous *'société nationale'*, subject to clear rules and that regulation, the supply of services and industrial policy should be institutionally separated.[36]

Nevertheless, the Socialists and Louis Mexandeau (PTT Minister 1981–6) gave little consideration to institutional change for the DGT between 1981 and 1986. On coming into office, Mexandeau affirmed the importance of the unity of the postal and telecommunications sides of the PTT.[37] Although he recognized that the DGT should be run as an enterprise, he believed that alteration of its *statut* was unnecessary. Sufficient flexibility existed within the existing framework, notably by use of subsidiaries and internal reorganization.[38] Moreover, under Mexandeau, the AIT was not influential, and its proposals were not implemented.[39]

Thus the DGT's organisational position was left largely untouched between 1981 and 1986; even the 1984 law on 'public service and telecommunications' merely transposed judicial decisions on *service public* into legislative requirements.[40] Instead, institutional reform focused on the nationalization of the DGT's three main equipment suppliers in 1981–2—Alcatel (part of the CGE group), Thomson, and CGCT; nationalization had been part of the Socialist Party's programme in the 1981 elections. Nevertheless, the firms remained separate entities, and continued to have their own profit and loss accounts. Between 1981 and 1986, institutional reform was more concerned with broadcasting than telecommunications.[41]

---

[33] *Le Monde* 9.6.84; J. Chevallier, *L'Avenir de la Poste* (Paris: La Documentation Française, 1984).
[34] *La Vie Française* 4–10.11.85 and *Libération* 29.11.85.
[35] Successor to the AIPT.
[36] *Des structures nouvelles pour les télécommunications?* (Paris: AIT, 1985).
[37] *L'Unité* 5.2.82.
[38] Interview, member of PTT Minister's *cabinet* and comments by Jean-Claude Hirel, Mexandeau's *directeur de cabinet*, *Le Monde* 15.6.85.
[39] Interview, member of PTT Minister's *cabinet*.
[40] It confirmed the right to a telephone line, the principle of 'neutrality' of the operator concerning the content of messages and the liability of the DGT for *'faute lourde'* (gross negligence).
[41] See M. Palmer and J. Tunstall, *Liberating Communications* (Oxford: Blackwell, 1990).

The Right 1986–1988

Support for telecommunications reform developed in the mid-1980s as part of the fashion for 'economic liberalism,' among part of the Right. The 1985 'liberal convention' called for the DGT to become a *société publique* (public enterprise), whose subsidiaries might be privatized.[42] The programme of the Right for the 1986 legislative elections was ambiguous, promising, on the one hand, to allow competition in international and inter-firm links and in new services and to transform the DGT into an *entreprise à statut public*, but, on the other hand, to permit competition only for VANS.[43]

On coming into office, the Right did introduce limited reform. The Left's nationalizations were partially reversed with the privatization of CGE and the sale in 1987 of CGCT to a consortium led by Matra and Ericsson.[44] Moreover, the 1986 *loi Léotard* on freedom of communications was passed. Although it was mainly concerned with broadcasting, it established an independent regulatory body, the Commission nationale de la communication et des libertés (CNCL) which was given a limited role in telecommunications, including authorizing private networks (i.e. those not open to third parties), licensing non-interactive cable networks, and allocating radio frequencies.

Attempts to alter the DGT's *statut* or its basic monopoly revealed the constraints on institutional change. Gérard Longuet (PTT Minister 1986–8) and the Right wished to extend competition whilst also protecting the *service public* and ensuring that the DGT could compete effectively.[45] Longuet believed that widespread competition needed to be accompanied by other changes: the financial rules applicable to the DGT had to be clarified, especially with respect to government-imposed levies (*prélèvements*); DGT prices had to move closer to costs; most important of all, the DGT's *statut* had to be reformed, so that it compete fairly and enjoy the operating freedom of a public firm, acting under private law and with a certain autonomy from Ministers.[46]

Alteration of the DGT's financial position and tariffs faced opposition inside and outside the government,[47] but the most important obstacle to Longuet's plans was trade union opposition to any alteration of the *statut*. The unions, principally the CGT, the CFDT, and Force Ouvrière, feared that DGT staff would lose civil service status which offered advantages such as protection against dismissal, a national pay structure and an important role for unions in decisions affecting employees. They opposed a separation of the postal and telecommunications sides of the PTT Ministry, claiming that it would reduce

---

[42] *Le Monde* 8.10.85.   [43] See *Le Monde* 16–17.3.86.

[44] See ch. 9 for details, as the sale was related to the distribution of DGT orders.

[45] *Le Quotidien de Paris* 21.5.86.

[46] See his comments, *Tribune de l'Économie* 21.5.86 and *Le Quotidien de Paris* 8.7.87, and G. Longuet, *Télécoms. La conquête de nouveaux espaces* (Paris: Dunod, 1988) esp. 67–90.

[47] See ch. 9.

career opportunities and increase the vulnerability of the unprofitable postal side. They were also against greater competition, seeing it as a threat to *service public*.[48] Prime Minister Chirac, a candidate in the 1988 presidential elections and with vivid memories of the 1974 strike (which almost caused his fall as Prime Minister), was not prepared to risk a confrontation with the unions; he blocked any serious attempt at modifying the *statut*.[49]

Thus, although in 1986, a second law to complement the *loi Léotard* had been promised, Longuet was only able to publish a consultative document in August 1987.[50] It proposed the extension of competition, but insisted that 'basic services' (network operation, packet switching, leased lines and telex services) would require a licence from the CNCL and PTT Minister. Moreover, public service obligations would be defined, the CNCL would obtain regulatory powers to ensure interconnection and fair competition and the DGT would become a wholly publicly-owned 'public telecommunications company' by 1992. Even the existence of the document was met with a strike organized by the unions and no action was taken to implement its suggestions.

The Left 1988–1993

After the return of the Parti Socialiste to office, the new PTT Minister, Paul Quilès, appeared to reject reform of the *statut*.[51] Nevertheless, in December 1988 he announced a 'major debate' on the future of the PTT and *service public*. This formed part of the process of 'modernizing the public service' put forward by the Prime Minister, Michel Rocard.[52] It was also justified by new EEC telecommunications legislation requiring the separation of regulation and supply and limiting national legal monopolies.[53] Large users were also increasingly demanding flexibility and international services, especially for data transmission, causing worries about the need to adapt France Télécom's institutional position.[54] Moreover, it followed a long postal strike which had caused much bad feeling, both inside La Poste and among its large business customers.[55]

The 'debate' was led by Hubert Prévot, a friend of Rocard and a former prominent trade unionist. Following a more than 2,000 national debates and hearings, Prévot published his final report in August 1989.[56] Its main recommendations were that France Télécom and La Poste should become two

---

[48] *Le Monde* 20.5.87; see the Prévot report—H. Prévot, *Rapport de synthèse* (Paris: PTE Ministry, 1989), 133–6.
[49] Interview, *mission à la réglementation*; *Le Quotidien de Paris* 23.6.87.
[50] *Texte de travail pour un avant projet de loi*; for a full text, see Longuet, *Télécoms*, Annexe 21.
[51] *Le Monde* 20.7.88.
[52] Interviews, DGT/France Télécom and Prévot Commission.
[53] Interview, DGT/France Télécom.   [54] Interview, Prévot Commission.
[55] Interview, Prévot Commission.   [56] Prévot, *Rapport de synthèse*.

bodies with their own legal personalities and real operating autonomy; nevertheless, their personnel would be able to remain civil servants. Regulation and supply should be separated, with the PTT Minister being responsible for the former and clear rules for competition being established.

The Prévot report paid great attention to the concerns of staff and was favourably received. The need for reform was strongly supported by Matignon (under Rocard), which provided vital political impetus, and by Quilès, who became persuaded that change was essential and that the PTT Minister would be judged as a regulator rather than as a supplier.[57] The Élysée was more reticent—its main concern was to avoid industrial unrest—but Quilès saw Mitterrand personally to discuss the matter and obtain his agreement.[58] Within France Télécom, the *ingénieurs des télécommunications* and senior management pressed hard for change, in order to allow France Télécom to adapt to a more competitive environment and obtain greater autonomy. The trade unions were divided: whilst Force Ouvrière and the CGT were hostile, the CFDT was open to its conclusions.[59]

The Prévot report was largely implemented in two pieces of legislation which formed a comprehensive framework for the telecommunications sector, the *loi du 2 juillet 1990 relative à l'organisation du service public de la Poste et des Télécommunications* and the *loi du 29 décembre sur la réglementation des Télécommunications*, together with two decrees of 12 and 29 December 1990 on France Télécom's *statut* and *cahier des charges* (licence conditions).[60] The legislation was passed despite the opposition of the Right and the Parti Communiste Français (PCF). More importantly, it did not provoke industrial unrest. The main reasons were not only that change was introduced by a government of the Left, but also that there had been extensive consultation and that the reforms represented a compromise between desires for autonomy, clearly expressed by the AIT, and pressure by the unions for a continuation of a strong public role and protection for employees.

On 1 January 1991 France Télécom ceased being an *administration* and became an *exploitant public* (a form of public corporation), separated from La Poste. It was to enjoy operating and financial autonomy, including its own budget, the ending the *budget annexe* (reducing Parliament's role and the procedures of the general *administration*). Furthermore, from 1994, it was taxed as a firm. At the head of France Télécom was a Board, with twenty-one members (seven representing the State, seven chosen on grounds of their expertise, and seven elected by the personnel) and a Chairman.

---

[57]   Interviews, PTT Ministry/DRG/DGPT and Prévot Commission.
[58]   Interviews, PTT Ministry/DRG/DGPT and Prévot Commission.
[59]   Interview, Prévot Commission.
[60]   For summaries of the legislation, see A. Bensoussan and I. Pottier, 'Réglementation et concurrence', *Communications et Stratégies*, 2 (1991), 154–71 and M. Gensollen, 'Les Réformes institutionelles et Réglementaires des télécommunications en 1990', *Communications et Stratégies*, 3 (1991), 17–34.

France Télécom retained its monopoly over the public telecommunications network infrastructure (PSTN and leased lines), and also over 'reserved services', namely voice telephony, telex and public call boxes. It operated under a licence, whose conditions sought to protect *service public*. Thus, for instance, France Télécom was to maintain national coverage of networks, equality of treatment between users in access to services and tariffs, and participation in regional development.

The government retained many powers over telecommunications: no independent regulator was established and regulation of the sector was carried out by *Directions* within the PTE/PTT Ministry (notably by the DRG direction de la réglementation generale, dealing with matters such as licensing, and the direction du service public, which scrutinized France Télécom's activities, which merged into one unit in 1993, the direction générale des postes et télécommunications-DGPT). The PTT Minister kept a *tutelle* (formal responsibility) for France Télécom and La Poste and chose seven members of France Télécom's Board. He also laid down the licence conditions imposed on France Télécom. The chairman was nominated by the President and Prime Minister, subject to the Board's approval. A non-legally binding pluriannual *contrat de plan* between the PTT Minister, the Minister of Economics and Finance, the Minister for the Budget, and France Télécom fixed objectives for France Télécom, including tariffs, employment, investment, and indebtedness. Many services required a licence issued by the Minister, who therefore determined the licence conditions; for certain network services (*service supports*), such as packet switched networks, a licence could be refused if it was considered to conflict with France Télécom achieving its public service obligations.

France Télécom personnel could continue to be civil servants, governed by the terms of the *fonction publique* and arrangements were to be made to enable staff to move between France Télécom and La Poste. However, it became a little easier to hire staff on a contractual basis, rather than as civil servants through the system of administrative competitions (*concours*).

The Right 1993–1997: The Difficult Path to Comprehensive Reform

The reforms of 1990 were rapidly followed by pressures for further institutional changes when the Right returned to government in 1993. Already, in opposition, it had discussed privatisation of France Télécom, and in April 1993, Gérard Longuet, who became Industry, PTT, and Commerce Minister, ordered a report on the future of telecommunications in France by his former *directeur de cabinet*, Marc Dandelot.[61] Its institutional recommendations comprised

---

[61] Interview, *mission à la réglementation*; M. Dandelot, *Le Secteur des télécommunications en France: Rapport au Ministre de l'Industrie, des Postes et Télécommunications et du Commerce Extérieur* (Paris: PTT Ministry, July 1993).

reform of the framework governing competition and transforming France Télécom's into a limited company with the sale of a minority stake. The government accepted these conclusions, beginning a process of reform that lasted four years.[62]

Modification of the regulation of competition involved ending the remaining elements of France Télécom's monopoly over voice telephony and the infrastructure, altering the rules governing the operation of competition, and creating a new regulatory body. The reforms generated remarkably little disagreement. The extension of competition was justified or accepted as outside the control of French policy-makers by reference to the requirements of EC legislation, technological and economic developments, and the international pressures to maximise competitiveness and innovation.[63]

Although a few voices were raised against the principle of greater competition,[64] critics focused on the rules governing competition to protect *service public* and the position of France Télécom.[65] The trade unions argued that universal service was a national matter and should rest solely with France Télécom. Moreover, there was concern that interconnection charges with France Télécom's network had to be sufficiently high to cover its costs and that universal service should include advanced networks such as ISDN.[66] Perhaps most importantly, ensuring that services within 'universal service' would be affordable and at the same price throughout France required the continuation of cross-subsidization. In response to these points, PTT Ministers offered reassurances that the new regulatory framework would reconcile competition and *service public*. In particular, France Télécom was given responsibility for universal service and funding mechanisms were established to cover its costs.[67]

The main argument for an independent regulatory authority was that the government, as majority shareholder and investor in France Télécom,

[62] Cf. B. Quelin, 'L'Avenir de la réglementation du secteur des télécommunications', *Revue d'Économie Industrielle*, 76, (1996), 125–40.

[63] See, for instance: DGPT, *Quelle réglementation pour les Télécommunications françaises?* (Paris: DGPT, 1994) (report by Bruno Lasserre); Dandelot, *Le Secteur des télécommunications en France*, 38–39; interview, France Télécom; J. Chevallier, 'La Nouvelle Réforme des télécommunications: ruptures et continuités', *Revue Française de Droit Administratif*, 12(5) (1996), 909–51, especially 910–15; *Les Echos* 4.4.96; *Le Monde*, 6.7.93, 6.6.96; interview, *mission à la réglementation*.

[64] H. Prévot, 'Les Télécoms entre le libéralisme débridé et la coopération intergouvernmenatale', *Le Monde* 12.6.93; criticisms by the CGT, *Le Monde* 7.3.96.

[65] *Libération* 23.2.95; *Le Monde* 19.3.96.   [66] *Le Monde* 19.3.96.

[67] See, for instance, F. Fillon, (PTT Minister 1995–7), 'Cette réforme concile service public et concurrence', *Le Figaro* 2.10.95 and 'Réussir la révolution des télécommunications', *Le Monde* 7.5.96; for interconnection charges and financing the universal service fund, the government ordered a detailed economic report—P. Champseur, *Rapport du groupe d'expertise sur la loi de réglementation* (Paris: DGPT, March 1996).

could not also be the regulator of competition; in addition, EC requirements that regulation and supply be institutionally separate justified new arrangements.[68] Whilst there was some opposition to a body independent of the government, from the Left and some sections of the old Gaullist Right,[69] the need for an impartial regulator was supported by economic 'liberals' in the UDF, the main employers' organization (the CNPF) and influential experts and civil servants, notably the head of the DRG/DGPT (Bruno Lasserre); moreover, Oftel provided a powerful example of the merits of a regulator institutionally separated from the government.[70] The DGPT organized an influential *consultation*, including public hearings, that indicated support for an independent regulator, especially from telecommunications specialists.[71] Finally, parliamentary critics won an important concession during the Bill's passage through the National Assembly, namely the addition of two members to the new regulatory body who would be nominated by the heads of the two houses of Parliament.[72]

It was transformation of France Télécom into a limited company and the sale of a minority stake that provoked the greatest controversy. France Télécom's senior management pressed hard for change; they enjoyed strong support from ministers (notably the PTT Ministers and Alain Juppé, Prime Minister 1995–7) and parliamentarians interested in telecommunications.[73] It was argued that France Télécom needed greater commercial autonomy and freedom from political control in order to adapt to the new competitive environment of telecommunications. It was facing new competitors within France, due to liberalization.[74] However, its senior management felt handicapped by decisions by its political masters. In particular, there was resentment at its use

---

[68] DGPT, *Quelle réglementation pour les télécommunications françaises?* 55; interview with Fillon, *Le Monde* 18.12.95; B. Lasserre, 'L'Autorité de régulation des télécommunications (ART)', *Actualité Juridique–Droit Administratif*, 3 (1997), 224–8, 224–6; interviews, *mission à la réglementation* and France Télécom.

[69] *Le Monde* 8.596 and 11.5.96, and debates of the National Assembly.

[70] *Le Tribune Desfossés* 1.10.93, *Le Monde* 8.5.96, Fillon, 'Réussir la révolution des télécommunications', *Le Monde* 7.5.96, Chevallier, 'La nouvelle réforme des télécommunications', 931–2; interview, France Télécom.

[71] DGPT, *Quelle réglementation pour les télécommunications françaises*; interview, PTT Ministry/DRT/DGPT.

[72] *Le Monde* 8.5.96.

[73] For reviews of the reasons for change, see: M. Roulet, (Président de France Télécom), *Rapport sur l'avenir du groupe France Télécom* (Paris: Ministère de l'Industrie, des Télécommunications et du Commerce extérieur, 1994) and Dandelot, *Le secteur des Télécommunications en France*; Senate reports by Gérard Larcher, UDF Senator, notably, *L'Avenir du secteur des télécommunications*, rapport du Sénat no. 129 (Paris: Sénat, 1993) and *L'avenir de France Télécom: un défi national*, rapport du Sénat no. 260 (Paris: Sénat, 1996).

[74] Bouygues obtained the third mobile telephjony licence in 1993; there was talk of Alcatel entering network operation by taking a stake in France Télécom—*Les Echos* 8.10.93 and *Le Monde* 28.12.93.

to fund public sector 'lame ducks' in 1992–3,[75] and the continuation of special levies (*prélèvements*) until 1994; moreover, tariff rebalancing, which was necessary to prevent 'cream-skimming' of profitable services by competitors but was politically unpopular as it involved increases in rental charges, had been hindered by the government.[76] There was discussion of a partial break-up of France Télécom, notably through privatization of its mobile subsidiaries, even though mobile communications were a rapidly expanding, profitable market.[77] France Télécom also faced rising pension costs (due to heavy recruitment in the 1970s).[78] For the government, partial privatization would bring much needed fiscal receipts (the operator was valued at perhaps 200 billion francs), a factor that led Edouard Balladur (Prime Minister 1993–5), and the Direction du Trésor, and the Direction du Budget to support a sale.[79] In addition, on becoming a company, France Télécom would pay a lump sum to the general budget to cover the cost of future pensions of its civil servants; the sum would be large and might help in meeting the Maastricht criteria.[80]

Internationally, France Télécom's strategy was to form alliances, both with Deutsche Telekom and with American PTOs.[81] However, its approach was said to be threatened by its institutional position. Modification of France Télécom's *statut* was almost set as a condition for co-operation by the Germans, given that Deutsche Telekom was to be privatised (partially) and that future cross-holdings between the two operators were envisaged.[82] Moreover, in 1993 France Télécom experienced defeat in its attempted alliance with the US operator MCI, being beaten by its rival BT; MCI's decision was due, in large measure, to France Télécom's institutional position within the public sector.[83] France Télécom then turned to another American operator, Sprint, but the US Federal Communications Commission and investors linked approval of the alliance to regulatory reforms being undertaken in France.[84]

The reforms of France Télécom's *statut* faced determined opposition from the trade unions, notably the CGT and PTT-SUD, supported by the Socialist and Communist parties. They set their face against the principle of privatization; even the sale of a minority stake would lead eventually to a complete sale.

---

[75] Notably being forced to take stakes in Bull and Thomson, and then the insurance companies AGF and UAP—*Le Monde*, 25.12.92 and 31.1.93; *Les Echos*, 1.1.93; *La Tribune Desfossés* 13.5.93 and 18.1.95.

[76] Most explicitly, in 1992, just ahead of legislative elections—*Le Figaro* 2.3.93.

[77] *La Tribune Desfossés* 30.4.93 and 3.5.93.   [78] *Le Figaro Economique* 2.12.95.

[79] Interview, PTT Ministry/DRG/DGPT.

[80] In the event, 37 billion francs were paid, and enabled France to meet the 3 per cent budget deficit criterion.

[81] *Le Monde* 21.7.93; Dandelot, *Le Secteur des télécommunications en France*.

[82] *Le Monde* 21.7.93; comments by Gunter Rexrodt, German Finance Minister—*La Tribune Desfossés* 30.11.93; *Les Echos* 1.9.94.

[83] Interview with Roulet, *Le Monde* 6.7.93.

[84] *Le Monde* 3.8.94; *La Tribune Desfossés* 18.7.9; *Le Monde* 22.7.95.

They feared that France Télécom employees would lose their civil service status and pointed to heavy job losses after privatization in other countries. Instead, they claimed that the existing *statut* had in fact proved remarkably successful and that France Télécom could obtain greater autonomy and flexibility within existing institutional arrangements.

Modification of France Télécom's *statut* became a lengthy struggle. After the Dandelot Report in July 1993, the Minister, Gérard Longuet, sought to reassure the unions and employees: although France Télécom would become a limited company with a partial sale of shares (the word 'privatisation' was carefully avoided in favour of 'opening of capital'), the state would keep at least a 51 per cent stake in France Télécom and existing staff could remain civil servants.[85] Nevertheless, the unions organized a successful strike against the proposals: no less than 74 per cent of France Télécom employees participated in a one-day strike in October 1993.

Longuet therefore decided to delay legislation in order to allow a major 'debate' on reform.[86] France Télécom's senior management launched a new set of 'consultations', and a 'charm offensive' with its staff and unions in 1994.[87] In July 1994, Marcel Roulet, President of France Télécom published a report setting out the reasons for change, reiterating the 'guarantees' offered by Longuet and suggesting that 5 per cent of the capital of the new company be set aside for its staff.[88] However, in the face of continuing union opposition and with politics dominated by the forthcoming Presidential elections (due in 1995), Longuet and Balladur again postponed a new law.[89]

After the 1995 presidential election, the pace of events quickened. The government and France Télécom's management engaged in complex manoeuvres to ensure that change took place. In July 1995, the government adopted a new strategy: liberalization would be introduced in 1996, but alteration of France Télécom's *statut* would be postponed until later; Marcel Roulet, seen as the main proponent of change, would be replaced.[90] France Télécom's senior management strongly resisted the separation of liberalization and a new *statut*. The extent of pressure on the government was revealed in September 1995: Roulet's publicly designated successor as chairman of France Télécom, François Henrot, declined the post because of lack of guarantees that the *statut* would be altered rapidly.[91] When the government published a new law on

---

[85] *Le Monde* 21.7.93; a ruling by the Conseil d'État confirmed that the proposed reforms of France Télécom would not prevent it employing civil servants—L. Richer, 'Note: Avis du 18 novembre 1993', *Actualité Juridique–Droit Administratif*, 1993, 463.

[86] *Le Monde* 26.11.93.

[87] *La Tribune de l'Expansion* 8.7.94.

[88] Roulet, *Rapport sur l'avenir du groupe France Télécom*.

[89] *Les Echos* 1.9.94, 9.9.94 and 13.9.94; interview, *Mission à la réglementation*.

[90] *Le Monde* 12.7.95 and 13.7.95; *Les Echos* 13.7.95.

[91] *Le Monde* 10–11.9.95; *Les Echos* 11.9.95.

liberalization in early 1996, the new chairman, Michel Bon argued that France Télécom's *statut* had to be altered at the same time.[92]

Caught between a rock and a hard place, the Prime Minister, Alain Juppé asked Bon to negotiate with the trade unions.[93] The latter responded by calling a one-day 'warning' strike. It was largely unsuccessful, as participation was much lower than in 1993.[94] Opposition to reform now weakened and differences among the unions appeared, allowing the reform process to move ahead. Unions accepting a degree of change (notably Force Ouvrière and the CGC) negotiated an agreement with France Télécom's senior management. Its key elements included an early retirement scheme, with replacements by younger staff and the continued recruitment by France Télécom of civil servants until the year 2002.[95] The government then announced that a second law, dealing with France Télécom's *statut* would follow the liberalization law. A final strike in June 1996 by unions opposed to change saw 31.9 per cent of staff taking part and was seen as a failure.[96]

The government therefore proceeded to pass two laws in rapid succession in June 1996, one on competition and regulation, and the second on France Télécom's *statut*. The Left, led by the PS, strongly opposed the laws in Parliament, but could not block them. It also referred them to the Conseil constitutionnel, which ruled that they did not violate the constitution; in particular, the sale of a minority stake in France Télécom was not unconstitutional.[97] Thus the two bills became law: La Loi no. 96–659 du 26 juillet 1996 de réglementation des télécommunications and La Loi no. 96–660 du 26 juillet 1996 relative à l'entreprise France Télécom.[98]

Partial Privatization under the Left 1997

Alain Juppé's government prepared to sell 30 per cent of France Télécom's shares in May 1997. However, the National Assembly elections of June 1997 saw the return of the Left. During the election campaign, the PS–PCF 'platform', and Dominique Strauss-Kahn (who became Finance Minister in June 1997), appeared to rule out even partial privatisation.[99] Once in government, the Left faced difficulties over the budget deficit and pressure from France Télécom's senior management armed with arguments that partial privatization was needed for internationalization (particularly through its alliance with Deutsche Telekom).[100] The new Government rapidly changed tack, and com-

[92]   *La Tribune Desfossés* 2.2.96; cf. Larcher, *L'Avenir de France Télécom.*
[93]   *Le Monde* 20.3.96 and 21.2.96.   [94]   45 per cent participation—*Les Echos* 12–13.4.96.
[95]   *Le Monde* 25.5.96 and *Les Echos* 28.5.96.   [96]   *Le Monde* 6.6.96.
[97]   Conseil Constitutionnel, 23 juillet 1996, déc. no. 96–378 DC: *Journal Officiel* 27 juillet 1997, 11408.
[98]   *Journal Officiel* 27 juillet 1996, 11384.
[99]   *Le Monde* 30.5.97, *La Croix* 5.6.97, *Le Monde* 27.6.97.
[100]   *Libération* 5.6.97, *Le Monde* 7.6.97.

missioned a report by a former Socialist Minister, Michel Delebarre.[101] It soon became clear that Delebarre's task was to prepare for partial 'opening of France Télécom's capital', a conclusion that several trade unions (Force Ouvrière and the CFDT) either supported or were resigned to.[102] The report supported a partial sale, mainly to permit international alliances, particularly a cross-holding with Deutsche Telekom, and to allow France Télécom to meet international competition.[103] A strike called by SUD-PTT and the CGT mobilized only 16 per cent of the workforce.[104] In October 1997, the 23.2 per cent of France Télécom's shares were sold (2.5 per cent to its staff); a further 7.5 per cent would be exchanged with Deutsche Telekom in 1998, with an increase in capital (of 5–6 per cent), thereby reducing the State's share to 62–63 per cent.[105] The issue was heavily over-subscribed, brought in 42 billion francs, led to instant profits for investors (including the 3.9 million individuals who bought shares) and saw France Télécom instantly become the largest firm by share value on the Paris Bourse.[106] In 1998, the cross-holding with Deutsche Telekom was reduced to 2 per cent; nevertheless, it was planned to sell 8 per cent of the shares and a new issue of shares, thereby still reducing the public holding in France Télécom to 62 per cent.[107]

The Reforms of 1996–1997

The two laws of 1996 represented comprehensive reforms of the institutional framework of telecommunications. They altered France Télécom's organizational position, established new regulatory bodies, defined the functions, powers, and duties of operators, regulatory bodies, and the government and established rules governing licensing, competition, and *service public*. The laws were frequently detailed and specific, dealing with substantive matters such as interconnection, the definition and financing of universal service, and the services covered by licensing requirements and the conditions for granting of licences. The majority of provisions were covered by law no. 96–559 (on liberalization and competition, hereafter referred to as 'the law'), whereas law no. 96–660 dealt almost solely with France Télécom's organizational position.

France Télécom's Organizational Status and Ownership[108]

Under the law no. 96–660, France Télécom became a 'national company' (*entreprise nationale*) from 31 December 1996; in practice, this meant a limited

---

[101] *Le Monde* 19.7.97.   [102] *Le Figaro-Économie* 31.7.97.
[103] *Le Monde* 7–8.9.97.   [104] *La Tribune* 1.10.97, *Le Monde* 1.10.97.
[105] *Le Monde* 10.9.97, *La Tribune* 20.10.97, *Le Monde* 18.10.97.
[106] *La Tribune* 20.10.97, 21.10.97, *Le Monde* 21.10.97.   [107] *Financial Times* 21.7.98.
[108] For detailed commentaries, see: J. Chevallier, 'La Nouvelle Réforme des télécommunications: ruptures et continuités', *Revue Française de Droit Administrative*, 12(5) (1996), 909–51, and C. Boiteau, 'L'entreprise nationale France Télécom', *La Semaine Juridique*, 41 (1996), 379–84.

company operating under private law.[109] Partial privatisation was allowed: 10 per cent of capital was set aside for staff and up to another 39 per cent could be disposed of. However, the State had to keep a minimum stake of 51 per cent.

Despite the reforms and partial privatization, France Télécom's institutional autonomy from the government remained circumscribed. Its chairman (*président*) was nominated by decree (issued by the President and Prime Minister), although he/she was proposed by the France Télécom Board. When the state holding fell below 90 per cent of shares, the composition of the Board altered: one third were elected staff representatives; the remainder were representatives of the state nominated by decree and persons elected by shareholders at the Annual General Meeting (at which the state had a majority, thanks to its shareholding). France Télécom was given obligations specified in licence conditions (the *cahier des charges*), including those of *service public*. In addition, France Télécom continued to have a non-legally binding *contrat de plan* with the government, albeit much weakened since it no longer covered tariffs.

The most important constraints arose from the position of France Télécom personnel. Existing and new civil servants retained their rights—notably security of employment, career progression based on length of service, and membership of their *corps*. Furthermore, a joint staff–management committee was created to represent staff and deal with matters such as disagreements over promotions and related staff matters. Only over the longer-term would France Télécom obtain greater flexibility over personnel, as the recruitment of civil servants was to end in 2002, so that staff employed on private law contracts would gradually replace civil servants.

The Government

The government kept many powers over the overall framework of regulation. It issued licences for public networks and public voice telephone services and, by decree, laid down the obligations imposed on those licensees (the *cahiers des charges*). Moreover, the rules for universal service, including methods of evaluating its costs and their distribution, were laid down by government decree. In addition, representation of France in international bodies remained part of the PTT Ministry's domain. A majority of the members of the new independent regulatory body, the Autorité de régulation des télécommunications (ART) were appointed by government decree. The government retained its powers to pass laws, regulations and decrees, which, the 1996 law stated, the ART was to implement.

---

[109] Legally, the position was much more complex—see Chevallier, 'La Nouvelle Réforme des télécommunications', 939.

The Autorité de Régulation des Télécommunications

An 'independent administrative authority' was created, the ART. It was headed by five members, with three (including its head) being nominated by the government and two by the presidents of the National Assembly and the Senate respectively. ART members were to be chosen for their legal, economic and technical expertise. They enjoyed non-renewable six-year terms, with a third of the members leaving every two years, and were to benefit from the employment conditions of the most senior civil servants. The ART was funded from fees paid for its services, licence charges and by public monies.

The ART was to ensure the good functioning of competition and to preserve the interests of users as a whole.[110] The law laid down the purposes of regulation, enumerating the pursuit of seven 'essential objectives', both for the ART and for the PTT Minister (Article 2):

- the supply and financing of *service public*;
- fair and effective competition;
- the development of employment, innovation, and competitiveness;
- establishment of terms for access and interconnection to networks;
- respect for confidentiality of messages and neutrality of networks;
- fulfilment of obligations concerning defence and public security;
- protection of all the geographical areas of France and of users.

The ART's power to issue licences was limited, being largely concerned with closed-user group networks. On the other hand, its powers over the operation of competition were extensive. It was to ensure that operators fulfilled the obligations placed on them and was to monitor operators with 'significant market power'. Moreover, it could determine: the technical and financial terms of interconnection; technical rules over networks and terminals; rules governing the operation of closed-user group networks and other networks that did not require a licence. It was empowered to settle disputes, notably those concerning interconnection and the shared use of facilities on public land, and to demand information from suppliers. To ensure the 'continuity of the network', the ART could issue temporary orders and could also inflict penalities on operators if they breached legislation or regulations, including fines, a shortening of a licence, or even its withdrawal.

Important consultative functions were given to the ART. It was to offer its advice on tariffs for universal service and on the level of contributions to the universal service fund, and had the right to be consulted on all draft bills, decrees and regulations in telecommunications. It was also to produce an annual report addressed to the government, Parliament, and Commission supérieure du service public.

---

[110] *Exposé des motifs*, 5—see Chevallier, 'La Nouvelle Réforme des télécommunications', 932.

Other Regulators and the Courts

Management of the airwaves was given to a National Agency for the Airwaves (l'Agence nationale des fréquences), whilst audiovisual broadcasting remained regulated by the Conseil supérieur de l'audiovisuel (CSA). Telecommunications remained subject to general competition law and hence to the powers of the competition authority, the Conseil de la concurrence. To facilitate co-operation, the President of the ART was to inform the Conseil of any abuse of a dominant position and anti-competitive behaviour, whilst the latter was to ask the ART's advice on cases in the ART's field and to communicate information about telecomunications cases.

The courts were given specific powers over the ART, in addition to their general role through administrative law. In particular, challenges to decisions of the ART concerning disputes and temporary measures (such as injunctions) to preserve the running of networks were to be made before the Paris Cour d'appel, whilst fines and penalties imposed by the ART for breaches of the regulations were open to challenge before the Conseil d'État.

Parliament

The legislation gave few powers to Parliament, whose role was largely consultative. The Public Service Commission (Commission supérieure du service public), composed of seven *deputés* and seven *sénateurs*, gave its views and recommendations, and Parliament received the annual report of the ART.

Users

Two specialized consultative committees were created, one for radio communications and the other for networks and services, with representatives of users (business and domestic), as well as suppliers and experts. They were to be consulted by the Minister and the ART, on matter such as licensing procedures and conditions, and technical requirements, but they had no powers of their own.

Competition in Supply and Licensing[111]

The law no. 96–659 ended the remaining elements of France Télécom's monopoly, notably over public voice telephony and the infrastructure. A framework for providing licences (*autorisations*) to suppliers throughout telecommunications was established. It distinguished between three types of service/ network. First, there were public telecommunications networks (defined as those established or used to supply services to the public) and public telephone

---

[111] See: D. Berlin, 'L'Accès au marché français', *Actualité Juridique–Droit Administratif*, 20 mars 1997, 229–45; W. J. Maxwell, 'Regulation and Competition: French Telecommunications Licensing', *Communications et Stratégies*, 22 (1996), 145–60.

services.[112] Competition was permitted from 1 January 1998, but suppliers required a individual licence issued by the PTT Minister. A licence could only be refused for specific reasons: safeguarding public order, security and safety; technical constraints arising from shortages of radiospectrum; the technical or financial inability of the operator to meet his obligations; the existence of previous penalties imposed on the operator under the PTT Code. Reasons had to be given for a refusal. The second group of services mainly concerned 'closed user' or 'independent' networks, which had already been opened to competition. Licences were issued by the ART and could only be refused under a number of tightly-defined conditions. The third group consisted of services and networks that did not require a licence. The law expanded this group; it included most public value-added data services.

Licences for public networks and voice telephony services were subject to conditions—a *cahier des charges*. The legislative framework set out a wide-ranging and potentially onerous set of conditions, with details to be provided by decree.[113] They included: confidentiality, and 'neutrality'; protection of defence and public security; interconnection; interoperability of services; funding of *service public*. Moreover, non-EU and EFTA bodies could only control (directly or indirectly) 20 per cent of the share capital of an operator, subject to reciprocity requirements established by France's international obligations.

Fair Competition

The law no. 96–559 included several provisions designed to ensure that competition was 'fair and effective'. If an operator enjoyed a dominant position or public subsidies, licence conditions were to include accounting transparency and, if necessary, separation. Licensed operators of public networks were to provide interconnection on demand with other licensees of public networks or public voice telephony services. Refusal was only permitted because of capacity constraints and reasons had to be given. Although interconnection was a private law agreement between operators, it had to be offered on 'objective, transparent, and non-discriminatory' terms, prices were to be based on the costs of using the network and operators with 'significant market power' had to publish those terms. The ART was to be informed of interconnection terms and its approval was required for the published terms of operators with 'significant market power'; it could ask for their modification and adjudicated on interconnection disputes.

Provisions were made to ensure 'unbundling' of tariffs: operators with a

[112] Many of the provisions are contained in Articles L.33 and L.34 of the law 96–559 of 1996.
[113] See Décret no. 96–1175 du 27 décembre 1996 relatif aux clauses types des cahiers des charges associés aux autorisations attribuées en application des articles L.33-1 and L34-1.

telecommunications turnover above a threshold (fixed by decree) were obliged to provide accounting separation for the licensed telecommunications services. Moreover, operators with a monopoly or dominant position in another sector (for instance, energy) with an infrastructure that could be physically separated from that for telecommunications, had to establish separate subsidiaries for their telecommunications operations.

The law also insisted that a national numbering plan be introduced by the ART that would 'allow' equal access' amongst different operators. Numbers were to be attributed on 'objective, transparent, and non-discriminatory' terms. Limited number portability was to begin in 1998, being extended to all users from 2001.

Service Public

The increasing legislative definition of *service public* was taken further by the law of 1996 (especially Article L35), which stated that the concept comprised the principles of equality, continuity, and adaptability and was to include universal service and 'obligatory services'. Universal service was defined as the supply of telephone services of sufficient quality throughout France, available to all at an affordable price. The services consisted of fixed-line telephony and related services (free emergency calls, directory enquiries, a directory of subscribers, and public call boxes). Although universal service obligations relating to matter such as standards of quality and tariffs could be entrusted to any operator (through licence conditions), that operator had to be able to meet them throughout France and the law also stated that 'France Télécom is the public operator entrusted with universal service'.

The universal service obligation was to be financed in two ways. First, there was 'extra funding' to cover the costs arising from cross-subsidization amongst services and between geographical areas. It was levied through additional interconnection costs for usage of France Télécom's network payable directly to France Télécom by all operators except mobile operators. It was a transitional levy, ending in December 2001 when France Télécom was to finish rebalancing its tariffs to bring them closer to costs. The second element was permanent, to cover the other costs of universal service; it consisted of payments to a universal service fund, was levied on each operator in proportion to its share of total telecommunications traffic and was paid to operators undertaking universal service functions.

'Obligatory services', referred to important services such as packet switched networks, leased lines and ISDN. Operators were to follow the principles of *service public*, but 'obligatory services' did not have to be supplied at an affordable price and operators could vary tariffs between users if due to 'objective criteria'. The duties relating to obligatory services were imposed on France Télécom, but could also be imposed on other operators through their licence conditions.

Conclusion: Institutional Divergence, Differences, and Change

In the 1980s and 1990s, Britain and France experienced very different institutional arrangements in telecommunications. Between 1981 and 1990, institutional divergence took place as the differences that existed after 1969 increased. In France, the DGT/France Télécom remained part of the civil service within the PTT Ministry, lacking even a separate legal identity in the public sector but keeping its monopoly over supply. In Britain, the Post Office was split into two public corporations in 1981, allowing telecommunications to be separated from postal services with the creation of BT. Comprehensive reforms in 1984 saw the contrasts between the two countries grow further. BT was privatized and lost its statutory privileges over network operation, and the supply of 'other services and networks' and CPE. A new regulatory framework was established. The government's direct role in decisions over the running of the network and the supply of services was greatly modified; its main instrument was no longer ownership but the setting of licence conditions. Moreover, policy making now involved two major participants, as important powers were given to the Director General for Telecommunications, notably over licence enforcement and modification. The powers and spheres of each were fairly clearly defined and also separated, with both enjoying considerable autonomy in their respective spheres. The duties of each were also laid down, although their general objectives were often couched in wide terms. The role of Parliament was further diminished.

Increasing divergence between Britain and France ended in the 1990s due to institutional reforms in the latter. A few differences were ended by changes in 1990, but only in 1996–7 was comprehensive reform introduced which led to several institutional features becoming common to the two countries. France Télécom was separated from postal services, obtained its own legal identity, operated under private law, and was partially privatized. Its statutory special rights over supply were ended and a licensing system was introduced, with most licences being issued by the PTT Minister. An independent regulatory body was established to enforce licence obligations. Parliament's formal role was diminished.

Nevertheless, even after the changes of 1996/7 in France, significant institutional differences remained with Britain. BT was entirely privately-owned, whereas in France, the state was obliged by law to keep at least 51 per cent of France Télécom. Moreover, BT staff were employed under ordinary contracts, whereas most of France Télécom's personnel were civil servants and able to keep that status until retirement. There were dissimilarities in the position and powers of the government and independent regulator. The ART was headed by five members, with nominations being shared between government and Parliament, whereas in Britain, the DG was an individual appointed solely by the government. Attempts were made to separate clearly the roles and spheres of the DG and the Secretary of State, whereas in France the division of responsibilities between the ART and PTT Minister was less sharply defined (for instance, both had roles in interconnection and universal service). Little detail was provided by British legislation over the exercise of powers by the DG and Secretary of State in matters such as licensing, universal service and interconnection, leaving much scope for discretion. In contrast, in France the laws of 1996 offered a much greater degree of detail and specificity, including the rules for licensing for different categories of service and network, definitions of universal service, mechanisms for its funding and principles for interconnection. Moreover, the ART did not have powers to modify licence conditions, whereas in Britain the DG had powers to alter licences. The role of the government in setting overall policy was made more explicit in France than in Britain, where the institutional framework for the determination of overarching policy remained very broad.

Institutional divergence and dissimilarities in the 1980s and 1990s arose from contrasting patterns of institutional change in Britain and France. There were important differences between the two countries in the timing, processes, and nature of institutional change. Analysis of the conditions for reform, and the obstacles to it, is therefore crucial in explaining cross-national institutional differences. Comparison of their experiences, and contrasts with the 1970s, a period of stability despite pressures for change, points to the importance of three major sets of factors. First, dissatisfaction with existing arrangements was needed; however, as the 1970s showed, this alone was insufficient. A second element in successful institutional modification was the support (either tacit or enthusiastic) of senior PTO management. The third and most important factor was active and sustained participation by the political leaders of the government/political executive. Co-operation between the government and PTO leaders was essential to overcome powerful opposition by trade unions and employees.

In Britain, the Conservatives were able to introduce major reforms in a short space of time. Pressures for change arose from frustrations over public sector accounting rules, the fiscal advantages of privatization, and the party political interests and strategy of the Conservatives. The general election result of 1983, with its overwhelming Conservative majority, allowed the government to overcome trade union opposition, itself hampered by legal constraints. Nevertheless, the Government had to compromise; in particular, it had to obtain support for privatization from BT's senior management, notably by keeping BT intact.

In contrast, institutional change in France was a slow and tortuous process. Pressures for reform came later than in Britain, due to the successes of the 1970s and the flexibility of public sector finance rules following new mechanisms for raising capital (see Chs. 5 and 6). However, over time, the forces for reform grew stronger, becoming intense in the mid-1990s. The central arguments for change were the evolving nature of telecommunications markets, the weakening of national monopolies, the need for internationalization for operators to prosper and expanding supra-national regulation, allied to fiscal advantages of sale receipts. Powerful pressure for new institutional arrangements (notably privatization) was led by France Télécom's management in the mid-1990s, but met equally vehement opposition by unions, employees and parts of the political left. During the 1980s and early 1990s, governments of the Right were weak, waiting for forthcoming presidential elections and unwilling to engage in a dangerous struggle with the trade unions over France Télécom's *statut*. Only when there were no immediate elections in sight, with governments that appeared to be durable, did change take place: under the Left in 1990 and then under the Right in 1996. Furthermore, reformers had to pay close attention to the demands of powerful groups, especially the unions and France Télécom employees. Nevertheless, the strength of pressures for change was finally tested in 1997: a newly-elected government of the Left introduced partial privatization, contrary to its own election promises.

The experience of institutional reform in the 1980s and 1990s offers several important implications for national institutionalist claims that countries have different and often stable organizational frameworks, and that insofar as change occurs, it follows dissimilar national paths. The 1980s and 1990s were a period of intensifying transnational pressures for change in telecommunications that were common to Britain and France, due to the combination of technological and economic developments, and the international regulatory environment.[114] The maintenance of differing and indeed often divergent institutions in the sector lends powerful support to arguments that nations can and do have dissimilar institutions. Yet cross-national differences arose from contrasting patterns of institutional change implemented by policy-makers, thereby weakening claims of institutional stability and indeed weakening the distinction between policy and institutions. Moreover, the mid-1990s saw a degree of convergence, as entrenched opposition was overcome and comprehensive institutional reform was implemented in France (although significant differences remained between the two countries). At the same time, modification of the institutional framework was not easy, and depended on the existence of certain conditions favourable to reform. Hence the overall picture is one of national institutions that could be altered from time to time, under favourable circumstances, with differences in these conditions giving rise to contrasts in the path of reform in the two countries.

[114] See Chs. 3 and 4.

8

The Impacts of Institutional Change and Divergence on Policy Making: The Network Operators in Britain and France during the 1980s

The 1980s offer an excellent opportunity to study the impact of national institutions on telecommunications policy making. On the one hand, transnational forces for change common to Britain and France grew more powerful.[1] On the other hand, not only did the organization of the sector differ in the two countries, but it diverged, due to institutional reforms. The period therefore allows the influence of institutional arrangements in the two countries to be studied in three ways. First, the major features of policy making are established and then compared, to see if the two countries experienced differing patterns despite facing common powerful transnational pressures. Second, the ways in which particular institutional features influenced policy making are examined, with particular attention being paid to those characteristics that differed between the two countries, such as ownership of the dominant network operator, the existence of a sectoral regulatory body and the rules governing powers, duties and financial arrangements. Third, the effects of institutional reform are analysed, particularly in Britain, which saw comprehensive changes in 1984.

The chapter finds that policy differences between the two countries continued in the network operation subsector, and indeed became more marked after 1984. It argues that the dissimilarities found were influenced by the institutional contrasts between the two countries and shows how specific institutional features impacted on policy making in each country, resulting in differing national policy patterns. Moreover, it demonstrates how institutional reforms in Britain in 1984 resulted in a significant break with the previous features of policy making.

Analysis begins with consideration of policy-making processes and major areas of substantive policy (competition, retail tariffs and relations between operators and their equipment suppliers) in each country, so that national patterns can be seen; the same areas are analysed in both and the concluding

---

[1] See Chs. 3 and 4.

section compares the two countries directly and offers explicit analysis of the ways in which cross-national institutional differences led to the contrasts in policy making that were identified. In both countries, attention is focused on policy concerning the dominant network operator: British Telecom in Britain; the Direction Générale des Télécommunications, renamed France Télécom in 1988 (referred to as the DGT/FT), in France. Policy remained centred around these suppliers, who comprised the heart of the industry: they accounted for all or almost all of network operation, which itself represented the prepouderant element of the telecommunications sector in the two countries in the 1980s.

Britain

Decision-Making Processes and the Overall Pattern of Policy in the 1980s

Decision-making processes for matters concerning the network between 1980 and 1984 remained dominated by BT, the DoI/DTI (Department of Industry/Trade) and the Treasury, whilst those relating to equipment supply involved the DTI, BT, and three largest British suppliers. As in the 1970s, the Treasury's main concern was the effect of the PO/BT's finances on the Public Sector Borrowing Requirement. BT consulted the DoI on matters concerning investment, general plans for modernization and prices, but enjoyed considerable autonomy within the financial framework established.[2] The government and BT did not formulate general co-ordinated plans concerning expansion, modernization, prices, investment and the equipment-manufacturing subsector. The early 1980s were, however, also a period of strategic decisions over institutional reform, competition and licensing that involved the structure of the sector. Such strategic decisions differed from the pattern of routine policy making in the degree of conflict, the DoI formulating a more overarching view of telecommunications, and the use of outsiders for policy advice.[3]

After the institutional reforms in 1984, a new pattern in the processes of policy making emerged. Three actors occupied the centre stage of the 'regulatory space' in telecommunications: the DTI; Oftel; BT.[4] The Treasury ceased to play almost any direct role, now that BT's expenditure no longer formed part of public spending totals and borrowing. Users became more influential, but relied on the sensitivities to their views of BT and Oftel. The pattern of

---

[2] Interviews, PO/BT staff.   [3] See also Ch. 7 for comments on institutional reform.
[4] C. Hall, C. Scott, and C. Hood, 'Regulatory Space and Institutional reform: The Case of Telecommunications', *CRI Regulatory Review* 1997; cf. L. Hancher and M. Moran, 'Organizing Regulatory Space', in L. Hancher and M. Moran (eds.), *Capitalism, Culture and Regulation* (Oxford: Oxford University Press, 1989) for a discussion of regulatory space.

relations among participants in policy making was strongly marked by the institutional arrangements of the sector.

The DoI/DTI determined the framework of competition and regulation through use of its licensing powers under the Telecommunications Act 1984—both through its decisions over the number of licences issued and by the terms of BT's licence which were set in 1984, and only began to be altered later during the 1980s. The DoI/DTI did not undertake day-to-day regulation of telecommunications, which was left to Oftel. It supported Oftel's decisions, and refused to intervene in disputes between Oftel and BT lying within the former's competence, even when lobbied by BT.[5] Despite its large stake in BT until 1993, the government's participation in BT's internal life was largely ended: BT generally did not even consult the government before making crucial commercial choices, over prices, investment, choice of supplier and senior appointments.[6] The government's role in relations between BT and its equipment suppliers was greatly diminished, being largely confined to the application of general competition regulation over mergers and takeovers.

Oftel came to assume a central role in regulation. Using the looseness of the statutory framework concerning its objectives, Sir Bryan Carsberg, its Director General between 1984 and 1992, developed a 'conceptual framework' based on competition.[7] It had two main 'legs'. The first was promoting 'effective competition' as the highest priority for Oftel, from the list of duties specified in §3 of the Telecommunications Act 1984. Oftel claimed that competition would benefit consumers and was compatible with its other duties. The second 'leg' was developing 'incentive regulation'. It applied where competition was not possible and involved establishing a regulatory framework that 'mimicked' a competitive market, seeking to produce similar incentives and pressures to those offered by competition. The conceptual framework provided a basis to interpret the broad legislative framework and to justify regulatory action by Oftel, either to ensure that competition was 'fair and effective' or to 'mimic' a competitive market.[8]

In regulating suppliers, Oftel utilized its institutional powers, notably over the enforcement and modification of licences. Most of Oftel's activity concerned BT, with which Oftel engaged in almost constant communication and sparring. Using its licence modification powers, Oftel made numerous alterations to BT's licence. A form of 'game' developed:[9] BT and Oftel undertook

---

[5] Examples include questions concerning interconnection, prices and rates of return; interviews, DTI Ministers and officials, Oftel and PO/BT senior staff.

[6] Interviews, DTI Ministers and officials, and PO/BT staff.

[7] See Oftel, *Annual Reports*, especially those of 1984 and 1985; B. Carsberg, 'Injecting Competition into Telecommunications', in C. Veljanovski (ed.), *Privatisation and Competition* (London: IEA, 1989), and Carsberg, B., 'Office of Telecommunications: Competition and the Duopoly Review', in C. Veljanovski (ed.), *Regulators and the Market* (London: IEA, 1991).

[8] Interview, Oftel.

[9] Cf. C. Veljanovski, 'The Regulation Game', in id. (ed.), *Regulators and the Market*.

detailed discussions on possible licence amendments; in the background, and sometimes in the foreground for contentious issues, existed the threat that if they did not reach agreement, the DG would refer the matter to the Monopolies and Mergers Commission (MMC); a reference would result in a period of uncertainty for BT and carry the danger that a broad reference might be made, or even that the issue of breaking up BT would reappear; hence, almost all licence modifications were agreed between Oftel and BT.[10] Oftel also used its institutional powers and discretion to establish decision-making procedures designed to offer 'transparency' and attract public attention and support.[11] Thus, for instance, before taking decisions, it published consultative documents and proposals, and invited comments before taking measures. Oftel developed a recognized specialist expertise in telecommunications regulation, overcoming an initial dependence on BT for information.[12]

After privatization, BT found itself freed from many government constraints over its internal decision making, but instead, regulated by a detailed licence and embroiled in close relations with Oftel. For most of the 1980s, it was largely protected from greater competition in network operation by government policy on licensing. It used the period to move away from its inheritance as a public sector supplier, restructuring its relations with its equipment suppliers and preparing for competition through internal reforms, investment and tariff rebalancing. Rather than attacking the principle of wider competition, BT sought removal of controls over its behaviour and argued that its competitors should not enjoy unfair advantages. As the dominant, vertically-integrated supplier, BT found itself at the core of policy and regulation.

Competition and Licensing

The development of competition was slow in the 1980s, being constrained by BT's institutional position. Sir Keith Joseph, Secretary of State for Industry (1979–81), sought to extend competition to network operation. In 1980, he commissioned an independent economic assessment on the liberalization of value-added network services. The report in January 1981, by Professor Michael Beesley,[13] went considerably further than its terms of reference. Drawing on experience of competition in the US and new ideas concerning 'natural monopolies', in telecommunications, he recommended that competition be allowed in network operation in two ways: resale of spare capacity of lines leased from BT for all uses, including voice telephony; the creation of alternative public telecommunications networks.

---

[10] Interviews, Oftel and BT.

[11] See T. Prosser, *Law and the Regulators* (Oxford: Clarendon Press, 1997), 83–6.

[12] Interviews, PO/BT and DoI/Oftel officials.

[13] M. Beesley, *Liberalization of the Use of British Telecommunications Network* (London: HMSO, 1981).

Conservative back-bench opinion was in favour of greater competition, as was Joseph.[14] However, BT was strongly opposed, claiming that it would lead to 'cream-skimming' of profitable services, and hence sharp price rises for residential customers.[15] The BT unions were also opposed, whilst business users, including the TMA (Telecommunications Managers Association, formed in 1980) were more concerned with private circuits than competition in network operation.[16] Faced with strong opposition, Joseph believed that he could only pursue one of Beesley's suggestions and in July 1981 he invited proposals for an alternative network.[17] The sole response came from 'Mercury', a consortium of Cable and Wireless, Barclays Merchant Bank and BP.[18] The Secretary of State used his powers under section 15 of the 1981 British Telecommunications Act to license Mercury as a second network operator in February 1982. However, Mercury's role was unclear: its 1982 licence was limited and in practice appeared to be primarily concerned with the supply of leased lines.[19]

The privatization of BT saw the government caught between the desire for a successful, speedy sale and the danger of BT being sold as a private monopoly.[20] In response, it chose limited competition in network operation. At the same time, it rejected BT's initial argument that existing fair trading rules in general competition law were sufficient,[21] and issued a detailed licence for BT. It argued that since BT would continue to dominate the British market for some years, regulation was needed to balance the interests of customers, competitors, employees, investors, and suppliers.[22] The government's decision followed the views of Patrick Jenkin (Sir Keith Joseph's successor at the DoI), who, looking at the American experience of competition, believed that a privatized BT would still require regulation; moreover, one element in persuading Margaret Thatcher against breaking up BT was that BT's predominant position would be regulated.[23] In the absence of 'structural regulation', behavioural

[14]   Interview, DoI/Oftel official; *Financial Times* 15.7.81 and 24.2.82.

[15]   *Financial Times* 24.4.81, 29.6.81, and 3.7.81.

[16]   A. Cawson, P. Holmes, D. Webber, K. Morgan, and A. Stevens, *Hostile Brothers* (Oxford: Clarendon Press, 1990), 93; *Financial Times* 15.4.80 and 24.4.81.

[17]   Interview, DoI/Oftel official.

[18]   *Financial Times* 3.7.81; Mercury was originally owned 40 per cent by Cable and Wireless, 40 per cent by BP and 20 per cent by Barclays Merchant Bank; in May 1984, Barclays sold its 20 per cent share equally to the other two—*Financial Times* 11.5.84; later in 1984, BP agreed to sell its share to Cable and Wireless—*Financial Times* 15.8.84.

[19]   The licence did not provide for an international switched service and restricted Mercury to 3 per cent of the UK telecommunications market—*Financial Times* 31.7.84.

[20]   Interview, DTI Minister; Cawson *et al.*, *Hostile Brothers*, 96, M. Beesley and B. Laidlaw, *The Future of Telecommunications* (London: IEA, 1989), 21–2.

[21]   Interview, BT.

[22]   Department of Industry, *The Future of Telecommunications in Britain*, Cmnd. 8610 (London: HMSO, 1982).   [23]   Interview, DTI Minister.

regulation was needed to prevent BT from abusing its dominant position as a single, vertically integrated company with a dominant position.[24]

Teams from the DTI and BT negotiated the terms of BT's licence. Events took place close to the 1983 general election and the government was sensitive to the popularity of privatization and the balance between consumer interests, a successful sale and its dependence on BT's senior management for support for privatization.[25] The outcome was that in June 1984, BT's licence was published; its conditions covered all major aspects of supply from 'universal service' to tariffs and interconnection.[26] The licence showed that privatization, far from ending public policy in telecommunications, had replaced public ownership with sector-specific regulation of privately-owned suppliers.

BT was obliged by its licence to meet all reasonable demand for voice telephony and other services to convey messages (condition 1), including to rural areas (condition 2); it was also obliged to provide a Directory Enquiries service (condition 3), the same level of public call boxes as existed in 1984, and apparatus and facilities for the disabled (conditions 31–3), albeit subject to a test of 'reasonableness' (condition 53). The DG could require BT to provide information to him in order to be able to carry out his duties.

Price controls were a key element in BT's 1984 licence. The DoI commissioned a report from Professor Stephan Littlechild, which examined various forms of price regulation.[27] Drawing on American experience, it specifically rejected 'rate of return regulation'. Instead, it recommended a price cap which, it claimed, offered significant advantages. It would provide a stable framework, ending constant intervention by policy-makers in price decisions. It would create incentives for efficiency, since BT could keep productivity gains and prevent unnecessary expenditure ('gold-plating') undertaken only to reduce rates of return. It reduced the need for information by regulators and accompanying 'intrusion' into detailed decisions over allowable spending. Finally, vigorous competition was expected to develop in the near future: Littlechild argued that unrestricted resale of leased lines and licensing new network operators, such as cable television networks, mobile networks and a third satellite operator, would make price control of long-distance services unnecessary. Thus the price cap should only cover local calls, rental charges, and call box charges.

In the event, a price cap was included as a condition in BT's licence (condition 24). However, since only limited competition was introduced in network

---

[24] For an economic critique, see J. Vickers and G. Yarrow, *Privatization: An Economic Analysis* (Cambridge: MIT Press, 1988).

[25] Interview, BT.

[26] Department of Trade and Industry, *Licence granted by the Secretary of State for Trade and Industry to British Telecommunications under Section 7 of the Telecommunications Act 1984* (London: HMSO, 1984); for a detailed discussion, see C. Long, *Telecommunications Law and Practice* (London: Sweet and Maxwell, 2nd edn., 1995), esp. 63–95; the specific conditions are analysed below.

[27] S. Littlechild, *Regulation of British Telecommunications Profitability* (London: DoI, 1983).

operation, its scope was widened to a basket of services, covering local and trunk calls, and rentals; call-box charges, connection, and international services were excluded. The use of a 'basket' permitted tariff 'rebalancing' among the services within the basket. BT feared 'cream-skimming' by Mercury if unrestricted resale of capacity were permitted. Hence in the licence negotiations it opposed separate price caps for individual services in order to be able to continue rebalancing.[28] The formula applied to the basket was the Retail Price Index (RPI) minus 3 per cent per annum for the maximum rise in the basket, weighted by BT's revenues from each service; it became known as 'RPI – 3 per cent' and applied until 1989. BT gave a separate 'voluntary' undertaking that the rise for rentals would be limited to RPI + 2 per cent pa.

The government used its power over the issue of licences to establish regulatory protection for a BT–Mercury duopoly in network operation for a minimum period of time. Unrestricted resale of spare capacity for voice telephony would not be permitted until 1989 whilst the BT–Mercury duopoly in network operation would continue until at least 1990. On the other hand, assistance was also provided for Mercury to become a fully-fledged network operator. It was given a new 25-year licence, whose terms were less constraining than the licence given to BT.[29] BT's licence contained several conditions designed to ensure 'fair competition' in network operation. In particular, BT had to provide connection with all other PTOs (such as Mercury) and licensed systems (conditions 13 and 14). In addition, it was forbidden from showing 'undue preference or discrimination' (condition 17), and in engaging in other practices using its position as network operator, such as linked sales and exclusive dealing arrangements, and the anti-competitive use of intellectual property rights, are prohibited (conditions 35 and 36). The Director General was given powers to enforce these conditions; in addition, he/she could determine interconnection terms under condition 13 if there were a dispute.

Competition 1984–1990

Soon after privatization, Oftel's powers and role in competition were tested.[30] Mercury and BT failed to agree on the terms of interconnection in 1984 and Sir Bryan Carsberg therefore made a 'Determination' of interconnection conditions.[31] It was firmly in favour of competition. There should be full

[28] Interviews, DoI/DTI and BT staff.
[29] Mercury's prices were not controlled and no 'universal service' obligation was placed on it—J. Hills, *Deregulating Telecoms: Competition and Control in the United States, Japan and Britain* (London: Pinter, 1986), 133, and *Financial Times* 31.7.84.
[30] Cf. M. Cave, 'Competition in Telecommunications: Lessons from the British Experience', *Communications & Strategies*, 13 (1994), 61–78.
[31] Oftel, *Determination of Terms and Conditions for the Purposes of an Agreement on the Interconnection of the BT System and the Mercury Communications Ltd System* (London: Oftel, 1985).

interconnection between the two networks, so that any person could call any other person, and any customer should be able to choose which network carried his call, even if this meant that BT's local network was used at both ends and Mercury's network only for the trunk section. The tariffs charged by BT for use of its network should be based on its costs plus a percentage determined by Oftel, not BT's public tariffs, greatly assisting the economic viability of competition. Further Oftel action followed, notably to support Mercury's expansion into the highly profitable overseas market by pressing for direct connection with overseas PTOs.[32]

Mercury grew in the 1980s. Nevertheless, it accounted for a tiny proportion of the total UK telecommunications market, reaching only a 5 per cent market share by revenue and handling approximately 2.6 per cent of total calls by 1991.[33] Mercury only won significant shares of certain market segments, notably international telephony and very large business customers. When the prohibition on unrestricted resale of spare capacity of leased lines expired in 1989, Carsberg made a strong and influential recommendation to the Secretary of State, Lord Young, in favour of its abolition.[34] He argued that the original restriction had been justified only by BT's leased line prices being far from costs, a problem much reduced by price changes since 1984.[35] In June 1989, Lord Young announced that the restriction would not be renewed for lines within the UK, allowing firms to buy capacity from BT or Mercury and then resell it as they wished, including for voice telephony. Further liberalization took place in the 1990s.

BT's position as Network Operator and Commercial Organization

Before 1984, many of the features on the pattern of relations between BT and the DoI seen in the 1970s continued. The DoI rarely intervened in detail over BT's internal organization and business strategy, although it was important in senior appointments, notably that of the Chairman (Sir George Jefferson in 1981).[36] Its approval was sought for overall investment and modernization programmes, but BT enjoyed considerable autonomy in these 'technical' decisions. Discontent over BT's services grew, both by the public and business users, due to lengthy waiting lists and the failure to use digital switches and optical fibre cables. Expansion and modernization were constrained by external financing limits and delays in the availability of the British digital switch (System X). In 1984 only two of the 459 trunk exchanges in use were digital, and only one out

---

[32] Interview, DoI/Oftel official.
[33] Oftel, *Annual Report 1991*.
[34] Interviews, DoI/DTI and DoI/Oftel officials.
[35] Carsberg, 'Injecting Competition in Telecommunications'.
[36] Interview, PO/BT; cf. N. Lawson, *The View from No.11* (London: Corgi edn., 1993), 222.

of the 6,292 local exchanges.[37] BT did not plan the mass introduction of System X until the late 1980s.

After privatization, BT's position changed. Despite its 49 per cent stake, the government did not intervene in BT's internal affairs, including strategic commercial decisions.[38] The clearest example came in 1988, when the DTI was not informed, even by the government Directors, that Iain Vallance had been chosen to replace Sir George Jefferson as Chairman.[39] BT undertook measures designed to transform itself into a competitive private sector firm. It increased capital spending to modernize its network; in particular, worried by Mercury's ability to 'cream-skim', it introduced digital switches and optical fibre cables into the international and trunk network, before turning to the local network.[40] By 1990 almost the entire trunk network and 47 per cent of customer lines were switched by time division exchanges.[41] Staff numbers were reduced, and a series of organizational changes were introduced to improve BT's competitive performance.[42]

Direct government intervention and oversight were replaced by licence conditions and Oftel regulation. Oftel took action to enforce BT licence provisions (notably over call boxes and apparatus for the disabled). Moreover, it extended its activities. It examined quality of service following large reductions in BT employee numbers in the mid-1980s, a strike by engineers at BT in 1986, and a series of critical reports (notably one in July 1987 by the National Consumer Council).[43] In 1986, it began to undertake its own surveys of BT's service and in 1987 it published BT's quality of service figures that BT had ceased to make publicly available. Oftel put strong pressure on BT to publish internal quality figures, to set targets and to give subscribers a contractual right to compensation.[44] It threatened to refer these matters to the MMC and to impose financial penalties on BT, for instance, by making price rises depend on quality,[45] but in 1987 and 1989 BT rapidly agreed to comply with Oftel's wishes on all three points.[46]

---

[37]   Vickers and Yarrow, *Privatization*, using figures from the 1984 BT sale prospectus.

[38]   Interviews, DoI/DTI Minister and official; interview, BT.

[39]   Interview, DTI Minister.   [40]   Interviews, BT.

[41]   British Telecom, *Annual Review* 1992 (London: BT, 1992) and figures supplied by BT.

[42]   D. Pitt, 'An Essentially Contestable Organisation: BT and the Privatization Debate', in J. J. Richardson (ed.), *Privatisation and Deregulation in Canada and Britain* (Aldershot: Dartmouth, 1990); P. Willman, 'Negotiating Structural and Technological Change in the Telecommunications Services of the United Kingdom', in B. Bolton (ed.), *Telecommunications Services: Negotiating Structural and Technological Change* (Geneva: ILO, 1994).

[43]   Oftel, *The Quality Of Telecommunication Services* (London: Oftel, 1986).

[44]   Oftel obtained legislative powers to take these measures under the Competition and Service (Utilities) Act 1992.

[45]   Interview, BT; Oftel, *Annual Report 1987* (London: Oftel, 1987); Oftel, *British Telecom's Quality of Service* (London: Oftel, 1987).   [46]   Interviews, BT and Oftel.

Relations between BT and its Equipment Suppliers

Despite strong pressures for change, policy-makers were unable to substantially alter relations between BT and its equipment suppliers within the institutional framework that existed before 1984, and several features of the 1970s persisted. Policy remained focused on public switches. In 1980 the PO/BT had three public switching suppliers (GEC, Plessey, and STC), but was developing only one time division switch, System X, in which all three firms were participants. The supply of System X suffered from considerable delays in the early 1980s.[47] BT had long wanted to reduce the number of firms involved and the need for change in its production was increasingly accepted within the DoI.[48] Soon after the formation of BT, the new Chairman, Sir George Jefferson, pressed for a new contractual arrangement with suppliers. Senior BT executives discussed a new scheme with senior DoI civil servants and ministers (notably Kenneth Baker), whereby one firm would become prime contractor, with the others reduced to subcontractors; ministerial support was promised. In 1982 BT sought submissions to be prime contractor from the three firms involved (GEC, Plessey, and STC). BT, not the DoI, examined the proposals and the record of the three companies. It chose Plessey, on commercial grounds with respect to its efficiency.

GEC and STC fought a major battle against the new arrangements. Led by Lord Weinstock, Chairman of GEC, they lobbied ministers, especially Patrick Jenkin, who appeared not to know of Baker's promise of support for BT and who told BT that he must take the matter to the Cabinet's Economic Committee. The latter wanted a less controversial reorganization, and referred the matter back to BT. A deal was then brokered between BT and its suppliers by Jenkin's special adviser, Sir Jeffrey Sterling.[49] Plessey would be the prime contractor for development work, with GEC as subcontractor, but procurement would be by competitive tendering. STC was to leave the project, and hence cease to supply public switches to BT when System X became available, but as 'compensation' STC would become sole supplier of TXE4A exchanges, estimated to be worth £100m. p.a. for five years.[50]

Throughout the 1980s, the DoI/DTI very much wished that GEC and Plessey would merge their public switching manufacturing operations.[51] Furthermore, from the early 1980s, BT wished to introduce a second, foreign source of time division switches in order to run a 'pacing horse' for System X,

---

[47] This section draws strongly on an interview with a senior BT executive and on Cawson et al., *Hostile Brothers*, 112–13.

[48] Interviews, DoI Minister and senior executive, Plessey.

[49] Interviews, DoI Minister and BT.

[50] *Financial Times* 5.10.82, Cawson et al., *Hostile Brothers*, 113.

[51] Interviews, DoI/DTI Ministers.

drive down System X prices, and enjoy greater security of supply. However, BT and the DTI were unable to implement further changes before 1984, because they failed to produce a co-ordinated plan of action and the suppliers were able to resist further changes. Thus, although hopes rose at BT and the DoI of greater co-operation between GEC and Plessey during the 1982 eviction of STC, these were not realized due to opposition by the two firms (whose heads greatly disliked each other), the fear of job losses in the North of England from a merger, and BT's ambivalence, as it feared that it would be unable to import time division switches, leaving it totally dependent on one supplier.[52] Furthermore, when BT began discussions for a second time division switch with a number of foreign suppliers, including Siemens, Ericsson, and Alcatel, the DoI put pressure on BT to delay its move until after the 1983 general election and privatization were secure; only in 1984 could BT properly assess its strategy.[53]

After years of immobility, the pattern of relations between BT and its suppliers rapidly altered after institutional reforms in 1984. The DTI was no longer a direct participant and BT was now a private company facing competition from Mercury, which was developing a digital trunk network and was able to buy network equipment from foreign suppliers at a lower price per line than BT.[54] In July 1984, BT announced that it would seek overseas tenders for a foreign time division switch to compete with System X. It invited tenders from eight manufacturers, and then short-listed three, ATT/Philips, Northern Telecom, and Thorn–Ericsson, a joint company, 51 per cent owned by Thorn and 49 per cent by Ericsson. It chose Thorn–Ericsson, which had offered Ericsson's AXE 10 (known as System Y in Britain), on commercial grounds, namely price and delivery, and Ericsson's knowledge of UK signalling systems (it had supplied international exchanges from the 1970s).[55] Nevertheless, its choice was aided by the participation of a 'British' company, Thorn, and the AXE 10 being produced at Thorn–Ericsson's factory at Scunthorpe.[56]

GEC and Plessey had been excluded from bidding for the BT tenders, which specified a different exchange from System X. They protested, as did trade unions and MPs. Nevertheless, the government took little part in BT decisions (although it did insist that the AXE be manufactured in Scunthorpe).[57] In its refusal to act, the government was aided by the fact that BT was a 'private company' and the promise by Norman Tebbit (DTI Secretary of State 1983–4) in the BT prospectus that the government would not intervene in BT's internal operations.[58]

Instead, complaints were made to Oftel, which conducted an investigation. Carsberg's report,[59] set out clearly the conflict between his different duties

---

[52] Interview, DoI Minister.   [53] Interviews, BT; Cawson et al., *Hostile Brothers*, 99.
[54] Interviews, BT.   [55] Interview, BT.   [56] Cawson et al., *Hostile Brothers*, 99–100.
[57] Interviews, BT and DoI/DTI official.   [58] Interview, DoI/DTI official.
[59] Oftel, *British Telecom's Procurement of Digital Exchanges* (London: Oftel, 1985).

under the 1984 Act (in particular, the promotion of competition) and the interests of GEC and Plessey. He gave priority to competition and the protection
of the interests of the consumer.[60] Therefore he generally supported BT's
decision, since it introduced competitive pressure on the price and delivery
of switches and increased security of supply. Nevertheless, he suggested a
number of safeguards, including a maximum limit of 20 per cent of BT orders
for System Y until 1987–8, no further increase in orders for System Y without
a full competitive tender against System X and increases in the proportion
of local components. However, Oftel had no power to enforce its recommendations, and BT was swift to reject them, especially any limit on purchases of System Y.[61] In practice, from 1987, BT orders for digital exchanges
were open to competitive bidding between System X and System Y and only
a limited proportion of orders went to the AXE.[62] Its decisions were, nevertheless, made without intervention by Oftel or the government, and no
action was taken when Thorn ended its participation in Thorn–Ericsson in
1988.[63]

The entry of Ercisson acted as a catalyst for further change. After 1984,
the DTI continued to believe that GEC and Plessey should merge their
public switching production.[64] However, its policy was that it was not the
government's business to ensure restructuring, and that it lacked the tools to
do so.[65] Instead, the initiative came from the suppliers. The entry of Ericsson
led Plessey to initiate discussions with GEC on joint production of System X;
when these broke down, GEC launched a bid for Plessey in December 1985.[66]
Lord Weinstock cited the need to improve the efficiency of telecommunications equipment manufacturing as the primary reason for the move; in particular, the British market was small relative to the costs of a time division
switch.[67]

The Trade and Industry Secretary referred the takeover bid to the MMC on
competition grounds. In its submission, the DTI supported the merger, arguing
that it would rationalise the electronics industry. BT was not opposed to the
takeover in public switching manufacture, but argued that international partners were needed, as the UK market was too small to amortize research and
development expenditure. Privately, BT feared that either GEC or Plessey might
pull out of the public switching business, perhaps resulting in the ending of
System X which BT had largely designed.[68] Carsberg supported a merger of

[60] Ibid., paragraphs 9, 22, and 43.   [61] *Financial Times* 25.7.85.
[62] *Financial Times* 25.3.87; one estimate was that 25 per cent of BT's time division switch orders
went to Ericsson—*Independent* 20.9.90.
[63] Interviews, BT.
[64] Interview, DTI Minister; see also speech by the Junior Trade Minister, Lord Lucas in the
House of Lords, on the rationale for a merger—*Financial Times* 15.6.85.
[65] Interview, DTI Minister.   [66] *Financial Times* 5.12.85 and interview, Plessey.
[67] *Financial Times* 4.12.85.   [68] Interview, BT.

GEC's and Plessey's System X interests, arguing that world-wide the telecommunications industry was highly competitive and that in public switching overcapacity resulted in weak prices and slim margins for time division exchanges. A merger of the two companies' interests was necessary to gain full efficiency gains and for System X to compete in world markets. The MMC recommended that the overall bid be blocked (mainly due to the effects on competition in the defence sector), but that the two firms be allowed to merge their interests in System X.[69] The Secretary of State for Trade and Industry accepted the MMC recommendations, and the bid was blocked. However, in 1987 GEC and Plessey decided to merge all their telecommunications interests, including not only System X, but also transmission equipment, PABXs, and data equipment. The agreement was approved by the Secretary of State, Lord Young, without another reference to the MMC, and a joint company, GPT, was formed in early 1988.

A further bid for Plessey was made in November 1988, by GEC and the West German firm, Siemens, whose activities included large-scale public switching manufacture (it was the main supplier for the *Deutsches Bundespost*). Under the offer, GEC would take 60 per cent of GPT, and Siemens 40 per cent. Oftel did not oppose the bid, arguing that the telecommunication industry was international, and that economies of scale would be expected.[70] BT also supported the sale of all or part of GPT to a foreign company, stating that its main concern was continuation of the supply of existing products and that it believed that GPT would be unable to fund the production of the next generation of switches on its own.[71] Within the DTI, there was concern about the entry of Siemens into GPT, but given that the companies were privately owned and that Oftel and BT did not raise major concerns, the telecommunications aspects of the bid were not referred to the MMC. In any case, the overall bid was cleared by the MMC and was successful in 1989.

Thus between 1984 and 1989, relations between BT and its suppliers had been radically reshaped. BT introduced a second, foreign supplier of time division switches. Equipment manufacturing in Britain had been highly concentrated and saw the entry of a large powerful foreign firm, Siemens, as a partner.

Network Operation Finances: Profits, Investment, Borrowing, and Retail Tariffs

Before privatization, financial decision making largely followed the same pattern established in the 1970s. The Treasury laid down external financing

[69] Monopolies and Mergers Commission, *The General Electric Company PLC and The Plessey Company PLC: A Report on the Proposed Merger*, Cmnd. 9867, (London: HMSO, 1986).
[70] *Financial Times* 7.12.88.   [71] *Financial Times* 3.1.89.

limits for BT, together with target rates of return,[72] its main concern being implications for the public sector borrowing requirement (PSBR). Faced with unmet demand and modernization costs, considerable public disagreement took place: the BT chairman, Sir George Jefferson, attacked Government-imposed EFLs as damaging investment and BT pressed for higher EFLs, notably for 1981–2, when it asked for £650m. and obtained £380m.[73]

Profitability was important for keeping down the EFL whilst maintaining investment; hence tariff changes followed Treasury targets. After the election of the Conservatives in May 1979, the target of a 5 per cent fall in tariffs in real terms set out in the 1978 White Paper, was abandoned. Sharp rises took place between October 1979 and November 1981.[74] The main reason for the rises was the need to generate income for the large investment programme without increasing borrowing which would breach the EFLs.[75] However, as the threat of competition developed, BT also began to 'rebalance' tariffs, increasing rental and local charges and reducing (in real terms at least) trunk and international calls in order to bring prices closer to costs.[76]

After privatization, financial policy making altered sharply. BT accelerated its investment and modernization due to the cost advantages of new technologies, its ability as a private firm to increase investment expenditure and the advent of competition.[77] The government no longer limited investment through EFLs, nor it did set targets for borrowing or profits; tariff decisions were taken without government involvement. Oftel did not intervene in BT's investment decisions. However, it did examine BT's capital costs and profits in relation to decisions over price controls.

Financial regulation of BT continued, but it was undertaken by Oftel and centred on price controls, which, as a licence condition, were subject to its enforcement and modification powers. Rapidly Oftel faced pressures to act: BT used the scope of the RPI − X (Retail Price Index minus X) formula to put up prices within the controlled basket in nominal terms, in November 1984, 1985 and 1986; increases were particularly sharp for local calls, whilst BT's profits rose.[78] The tariff and profit increases provoked public complaints and Oftel investigated them.[79] Its main concern with respect to the overall price increases was that BT's overall rate of return should not become 'excessive'—i.e. it

---

[72] 5 per cent for 1979–82, 5.5 per cent for 1982–3, and 6.5 per cent for 1983–4.

[73] *The Times* 28.11.80; *Financial Times* 7.3.81, 20.3.81, 7.5.81, and 3.6.81.

[74] *British Telecommunications Statistics.*

[75] *The Times* 11.7.80, 1.8.80; interview, PO/BT.

[76] *Financial Times* 15.7.81, 25.7.81, 30.12.81, 6.7.82; interviews, BT.

[77] Interviews, PO/BT.

[78] For a full list of changes in prices controlled by Oftel, see Oftel, *The Regulation of BT's Prices* (London: Oftel, 1992), 7.

[79] See Oftel, *British Telecom's Price Changes, November 1985*, (London: Oftel, 1985) and Oftel, *Review of British Telecom's Tariff Changes* (London: Oftel, 1986).

examined whether 'X' had been set at the right level. Oftel looked at BT's rate of return and compared it with that of other large industrial companies.[80] Carsberg found that BT's 19 per cent rate of return on capital was 'not excessive', but warned that a significant increase in the rate would lead him to reconsider the position. He reached a similar conclusion concerning BT's price rises of November 1986.[81] Therefore he did not seek to alter the price formula prematurely; he emphasized the virtues of a stable regulatory regime and the need to set economic incentives for network operators to increase efficiency.[82] However, in 1987 BT's rate of return climbed above 20 per cent; it chose to make no price rise. Carsberg stated that but for BT's decision to freeze prices in 1987, he would have referred the RPI − 3 per cent formula to the MMC to seek a licence change; he also sought assurances that any price rises in 1988 would avoid 'excessive profits'.[83] In response, BT agreed to leave prices unchanged in 1988 as part of the new RPI − X agreement with Oftel.

When the first price cap expired in 1989, capping was continued. A series of licence modifications were agreed between BT and Oftel over the period 1988 to 1990 (coming into effect in 1989, 1990, and 1991). The caps were tightened; thus 'X' was increased to 4.5 per cent per annum in 1989 and to 6.25 per cent in 1991. The scope of price caps were also widened—in 1989 operator-assisted calls and directory enquiries were added to the basket, followed by international calls in 1991, and a separate cap on rentals (RPI − Z) began in 1989.

Each modification of the price controls was preceded by prolonged discussions between Oftel and BT. In the absence of detailed substantive rules governing the renewal of price controls, Oftel enjoyed considerable discretion in establishing a framework for its decisions. It argued that regulation should 'mimic' a competitive market, creating incentives for BT to increase its efficiency without allowing it to earn 'excessive' profits: BT should earn only 'normal' profits in the long run; between price reviews, it could exceed this level by producing additional efficiency gains, but at the following review of the RPI − X formula, the benefits would be shared between it and consumers in the form of lower prices, as would occur in a competitive market by new firms entering due to the attraction of high profits.[84] Thus the conceptual dis-

[80] Oftel, *British Telecom's Price Changes, November 1985* (London: Oftel, December 1985), esp. paragraphs 29–31.

[81] Oftel, *Review of British Telecom's Tariff Changes* (1986).

[82] Oftel, *The Regulation of British Telecom's Prices. A Consultative Document* (London: Oftel, 1988), 2–4.

[83] *Financial Times* 1.12.87 and Carsberg Statement, 'Telephone Services and Prices', 4, (London: Oftel, 1987).

[84] For a discussion of Oftel's approach to the regulation of BT's profitability, see: Carsberg, 'Injecting Competition into Telecommunications'; N. Hartley and P. Culham, Telecommunications Prices under Monopoly and Competition', *Oxford Review of Economic Policy*,

tinction between 'rate of return regulation', and price cap regulation was much less clear cut in practice, as BT's profitability, costs of capital and future efficiency gains became entangled in questions of price rises. In discussions with BT, Oftel sought to implement its approach by threatening to refer the proposed licence change to the MMC. BT, concerned at the uncertainty, loss of management time, and the danger of being broken up, came to agreements on each occasion with Oftel.[85]

Oftel also became involved in the setting of tariffs for individual services. Within the basket of controlled prices, BT implemented considerable rebalancing. Tariffs for local calls rose,[86] as did those for off-peak trunk calls and for less-used trunk routes, whereas charges for more popular and cheaper trunk routes were reduced for peak and standard times. Rental charges also saw sharp increases, taking place in every year except 1987 and 1988. International charges, especially with North America, were reduced. The effects were to favour high spending users, especially businesses.

Oftel explicitly supported tariff rebalancing by BT so that prices moved closer to costs (generally marginal costs) and indeed was even informally consulted by BT on proposed changes.[87] Oftel believed that cross-subsidization of services was not economically efficient and that telecommunications prices should not be used as an indirect method of redistributing income. Hence its role was ensure that rebalancing did not proceed too suddenly and did not go beyond levels justified by costs. In 1986, it indicated that price rebalancing had advanced a great deal and should not proceed rapidly in the future; in response, and faced with public disapproval of the price changes of 1985–86 and difficulties over quality of service, BT paused the rebalancing process.[88] Moreover, BT wished to raise rental charges faster than the RPI − 2 per cent agreed 'voluntarily' in 1984, but Oftel refused to alter its position, and BT decided not to break the informal undertaking and risk a reference to the MMC.[89] In the late 1980s, Oftel's involvement in BT's tariff setting grew: it persuaded BT to establish 'low user' schemes from 1988, introduced a cap on rentals of RPI + 2 per cent for 1989–93, as well as an informal RPI + 2 per cent cap on connections.

4(2) (1988), 1–19; Oftel, *Review of British Telecom's Tariff Changes* (1986), 12; Oftel, *The Regulation of British Telecom's Prices. A Consultative Document* (1988), 4; Oftel, *The Regulation of BT's Prices* (1992).

[85] Interviews, BT.

[86] Notably peak-rate calls in 1986, with a 18.9 per cent rise, and cheap rate calls in 1990, which rose by 10.1 per cent.

[87] Interviews, BT and Oftel; see B. Carsberg, 'What Are Fair Prices for BT's Services?', *Oftel News*, no. 5 (Dec. 1986), 2 and Oftel, *The Regulation of British Telecom's Prices. A Consultative Document* (1988), 22.

[88] Interviews, BT.   [89] *Financial Times* 22.5.90.

France

Decision-Making Processes and the Overall Pattern of Policy

Decision-making processes reflected institutional arrangements in that the central actors in policy were the DGT (renamed France Télécom in 1988, but referred to here as the DGT) and parts of the political executive, notably the PTT Ministry, Finance Ministry, Matignon and the Élysée. In addition, in matters concerning relations between the DGT and its suppliers, the equipment manufacturers were key participants when publicly owned. In the early 1980s, the Industry Ministry was also important, especially under politically active occupants, notably Jean-Pierre Chevènement (1981–3) and Laurent Fabius (1983–4). Users and the independent regulatory bodies established (the CNCL[90] and then the CSA[91]) were not significant participants, mirroring their lack of institutional powers in telecommunications.

As in the 1970s, the political executive played a direct and central role in policy formation, participating in most types of decision. However, the alliance of the 1970s between the Presidency and the DGT was not continued under Mitterrand and, in contrast to the earlier period, the DGT's lack of institutional autonomy was cruelly exposed. The heads of the DGT, Jacques Dondoux (1981–86), and Marcel Roulet (1986–95), were less influential than Théry.[92] Although PTT Ministers played a more important role, helped by greater continuity in office holders, and the considerable political weight of post holders after 1986 (the Ministers were Louis Mexandeau (1981–6), Gérard Longuet (1986–8), and Paul Quilès (1988–91)), power over telecommunications was dispersed within the political executive. Decision making was fragmented, spheres of action were not clearly defined and hence policy was often the outcome of complex battles within the political executive, involving several ministries, as well as Matignon and the Élysée.

A high degree of conflict existed, especially in the early 1980s: the DGT's senior officials, supported by the PTT Minister, sought to protect its interests and financial health; other ministries, notably Industry and Finance, saw the DGT as a source of funds; elected politicians linked decisions to possible electoral consequences. The institutional dependence of the DGT on the political executive was revealed as the latter used its powers over senior staff appointments, tariff-setting, allocation of administrative and financial responsibilities and financial targets to determine policy, even if opposed by the DGT. The most visible sign of the weaknesses of the DGT lay in its relations with equipment manufacturers between 1981 and 1987, as it found itself consistently defeated

---

[90]   Commission Nationale de la Communication et des Libertés.
[91]   Conseil Supérieur de l'Audiovisuel.
[92]   Interview, PTT Minister's *cabinet*; E. Cohen, *Le Colbertisme 'high tech'* (Paris: Hachette, 1992), 261–2.

by manoeuvres of the publicly-owned firms and members of the political exec-utive and it lost control of the allocation of its own orders. Attempts to create even modest autonomy failed: in 1983, a *Charte de gestion* (management plan) was established to provide a medium-term framework for the DGT for the years 1983–6,[93] but its financial targets were rapidly abandoned in the face of the costs of new responsibilities imposed on the DGT.

A general policy framework did develop, but it was flexible and included potentially contradictory elements, as it accommodated decisions reflecting the balance of forces within the political executive; moreover, that balance that fluc-tuated due to ministerial changes, including the government of the Right under Chirac (1986–8). '*Service public*' was incanted by policy-makers of Left and Right. Although its core was accepted to be provision by the State of a telecommuni-cations service throughout France at the same tariffs, which should be reason-able,[94] it was open to many interpretations.[95] In the early 1980s the Left emphasized protection of employees, the unity of the postal and telecommuni-cations services, but also added that the DGT should be managed as if it were a public enterprise, enjoying operating autonomy and responding to the needs of 'the market'.[96] The liberal Right from the mid-1980s extolled the virtues of the DGT operating as a firm in order to offer efficient and low cost service (includ-ing universal service) and be able to compete.[97] In the late 1980s, Quilès under-lined the ability of France Télécom to operate in profitable markets, and not be merely confined to providing loss-making services.[98] At the same time, the DGT was treated as an instrument for the pursuit of wider policy objectives, relating not only to the telecommunications network, but also to broadcasting, the structure of the equipment manufacturing subsector, industrial policy and fiscal management. Finally, policy involved protection of the DGT from competitors: it was too valuable for the political executive to be damaged; at the same time, it was seen as vulnerable to competition in network operation. Hence the DGT's monopoly was maintained; at the same time, especially after 1986, mea-

[93] See J.-Y. Gouiffès and M. Roulet, 'La Charte de gestion à moyen terme des Télécommuni-cations', in *Revue Française des Télécommunications*, 47 (1983), 14–18.

[94] T. Vedel, 'La Déréglementation des télécommunications en France: politique et jeu poli-tique', in Institut Français des Sciences Politiques, *Les Déréglementations* (Paris: Economica, 1988), and B. Lasserre, 'Service public et télécommunications: une rencontre difficile', *Le Communica-teur*, 2 (1987), 150–9.

[95] See J. Chevallier, 'Quelle définition pour le service public', *Le Communicateur*, 2 (1987), 147–9, Lasserre, 'Service public et télécommunications', and J. Chevallier, 'Les Enjeux juridiques: l'adap-tation du service public des télécommunications', *Revue Française d'Administration Publique*, 52 (1989), 37–52, for a discussion.

[96] See Mexandeau's comments in *Le Monde* 8–9.11.81 and *l'Unité* 5.2.82; *Le Monde* 4.2.83; com-ments by Hirel, Mexandeau's *Directeur de cabinet*, *Le Monde*, 15.6.85; Mexandeau comments, *Le Monde* 31.1.86.

[97] G. Longuet, *Télécoms. La conquête de nouveaux espaces* (Paris: Dunod, 1988), esp. 77–90.

[98] *Libération* 20.7.88.

sures were taken to prepare the DGT for institutional change and possible competition, notably concerning its fiscal position, tariffs, and internal organization.

Competition

There was little support for introducing competition within the Left and the matter was never seriously considered before 1986. After 1988, Quilès as PTT Minister defended the monopoly, including at the EC level.[99] The DGT was believed to have an excellent record in modernizing the network from the 1970s onwards and French business users appeared relatively content with its service.[100] There was a general belief that network operation was a 'natural monopoly' and that a second network operator would not be viable.[101]

The main potential source for challenge to the DGT's position was among economic 'liberals'. In opposition before 1986, the Right was divided over ending the DGT's monopoly.[102] Its manifesto for the 1986 legislative elections was ambiguous, suggesting, on the one hand, wide-ranging competition for communications between firms and international communications, but, on the other hand, competition being limited to value-added services.[103] The three ministers most concerned with telecommunications, Gérard Longuet (PTT Minister 1986–8), Alain Madelin (Industry Minister 1986–8) and François Léotard (Communications and Culture Minister 1986–8), were 'liberals'. Yet competition in network operation was not attempted—instead, Longuet promised a 'very prudent' deregulation,[104] and the extension of competition was limited to selected advanced services and networks (see Ch. 10).

Powerful constraints limited liberalization between 1986 and 1988. First, the Right supported some form of *service public*. This was believed to require cross-subsidization of services, in order to have nationally uniform tariffs and hence equality between users, despite differing costs; cross-subsidization was difficult to reconcile with competition, which would permit 'cream-skimming' of profitable services.[105] Second, the Right wanted the DGT to be able to compete effectively and to operate 'as a firm'.[106] However, this required a number of changes: institutional reform, because the DGT, as an *administration*, was

[99] Interview, PTT Minister's *cabinet*; Quilès interview, *Le Monde* 1.9.90.

[100] F. Essig, 'La Pointe de vue des entreprises' in *Le Communicateur*, 2 (1987), 82–5; Vedel, 'La Déréglementation des télécommunications en France'; Longuet, *Télécoms*, 85–7; Cawson *et al.*, *Hostile Brothers*, 127–8.

[101] Interview, PTT Minister's *cabinet*; *Le Monde des Télécoms*, May 1987, and L. Benzoni, 'Departing from Monopoly', paper presented at a colloquium on 'Asymmetric Deregulation', Red Hall, June 1987.

[102] Parts of the UDF were in favour, but Raymond Barre and much of the RPR were opposed—*Le Matin* 22–23.3.86; interview, *Mission à la réglementation*.

[103] *Le Monde* 16–17.3.86.   [104] Longuet interview, *Le Quotidien de Paris* 16.5.86.

[105] Interview, PTT Minister's *cabinet* and see discussion in Longuet, *Télécoms*, 77–83.

[106] *Tribune de l'Économie* 21.5.86, *Le Quotidien de Paris* 21.5.87, *Le Monde* 3.2.87, and Longuet, *Télécoms*.

believed to be too handicapped by restrictions to be free to compete successfully; a new law to provide a framework for competition; reform of the DGT's
fiscal position and pricing structure.[107] These measures were not fully implemented under the Right, although prices were brought closer to costs and VAT
(TVA) was extended to the DGT in 1987. In particular, trade union opposition
to any breach of the DGT's monopoly or alteration of the DGT's *statut* unions
provided an effective veto on institutional reforms which were seen as precon-
ditions for competition.[108]

The Position of the PTT Ministry and the Functioning of the DGT

The DGT's position as an *administration* within the PTT Ministry provided the
political executive with powerful policy instruments. One was the selection of
senior staff. In 1981, after the election victories of the Left, Théry was sacked,
being too closely identified with Giscard d'Estaing. Jacques Dondoux, a critic
of Théry and of his industrial policy, became the Directeur général des télécommunications. In turn, Dondoux was displaced by Marcel Roulet in 1986,
when the Right came into government, his replacement being demanded by
the Gaullists to underline the change of government.[109]

Modification of the responsibilities and status of the PTT Minister offered
another policy instrument, one that indicated the repercussions of the breakdown of the alliance between the DGT and the heads of the political executive. A series of costly levies (*prélèvements*) were imposed on the DGT, which
it, supported by Mexandeau, strongly resisted, but failed to prevent due to insufficient influence within the political executive; in particular, in battles between
the DGT and Laurent Fabius (Minister of the Budget 1981–3, Industry Minister 1983–4, Prime Minister 1984–6), the Élysée supported the latter.[110] The
prélèvements were bitterly resented by the DGT, not only for their size, but also
for their unpredictability.

The first *prélèvement* was general, designed for the 1982 general Budget; it
was set at 50 per cent of the operating profit of the previous year and amounted
to FF3.2b. It was obtained in Autumn 1981 by Fabius, against the opposition of
Mexandeau, but with the support of Jacques Attali (special adviser to Mitterrand), and by the *arbitrage* of the Prime Minister, Pierre Mauroy.[111] The levy
was meant only to be 'exceptional', promised Mauroy.[112] Nevertheless, another
levy for the general budget was imposed for the year 1983, of FF2b.; it was paid,
despite pushing the DGT into loss. The levy to the general Budget continued
throughout the 1980s and into the 1990s, in the face of continuing DGT
resentment.[113]

[107] *Le Monde* 3.2.87, and Longuet, *Télécoms*, 69–75 and 83–90.
[108] See Chs. 5 and 7 for institutional reforms.   [109] *Le Monde* 10.12.86.
[110] Interviews, DGT and PTT Minister's *cabinet*.
[111] Interviews, DGT and PTT Minister's *cabinet*; *Le Point* 5.10.81.   [112] *Le Monde* 1.10.81.
[113] For figures, see *l'Express* 24–30.8.84, *Le Monde*. 25.7.85, and Longuet, *Télécoms*, 187.

Specific responsibilities were also given to the DGT, and correspondingly, the costs of meeting them (specific *prélèvements*). In 1983, the PTT Ministry was made subordinate to the Industry Ministry, allowing the latter, now headed by Laurent Fabius, to use the DGT as a source of funds.[114] Thus, from 1984, the DGT paid part of the costs of the *filière électronique* (the plan devised in 1982 to relaunch the French electronics computing, and office equipment sectors[115]), as well as providing capital and subsidies to state-owned firms (notably Thomson); it also paid monies in 1985 for the space organization (the CNES), for some of La Poste's losses, and for government-sponsored computing programmes in schools.[116] Even when Mexandeau recovered his status as a full Minister in 1984, when Fabius became Prime Minister, the *prélèvements* continued; moreover, Mexandeau had to dismiss much of his *cabinet* at Fabius's behest and appoint Jean-Claude Hirel, an ally of Fabius, as its head.[117]

In addition to providing funds, the DGT remained at the centre of other industrial policies decided by the political executive. During the early 1980s the DGT was used to boost employment.[118] The division of DGT orders became intimately linked to the restructuring of the telecommunications equipment-manufacturing subsector, whilst the modernization of the infrastructure became part of wider debates on cable television and information superhighways (see Ch. 10). Again, the DGT found itself severely weakened, as its orders and revenues were used in ways that it opposed, due to its lack of support within the political executive.

From the mid-1980s onwards, another strand of policy began to attain greater prominence in the functioning of the DGT: operating as an efficient commercial organization. Increased attention was given to large users, as the DGT became aware of the danger of competition and the fact that a few, very large users accounted for a high proportion of revenue and an even greater share of profits. In 1984, a department for large users was established; moreover, the DGT promised to pay compensation for failure to meet obligations.[119] Commercial methods were introduced into management and sales, and changes were made in the DGT's internal organization to allow the DGT to operate as a business.[120] The relationship between such developments and *service public* was not made explicit: the latter was assumed to be protected by its juridical framework and by public ownership of the DGT, and hence whilst a few targets were set in the *Charte de gestion* (notably for obtaining

[114]   *Le Monde* 26.3.83.

[115]   For a short history, see M. Palmer, and J. Tunstall, *Liberating Communications* (Oxford: Basil Blackwell, 1990), 121–8.

[116]   For details of the composition of the levies, see *l'Express* 24–30.8.84, *Le Monde* 31.10.84, *Le Monde* 25.7.85, and Longuet, *Télécoms*, 187.

[117]   Interview, PTT Minister's *cabinet*; *Le Monde* 7.8.84, and *La Vie Française* 27.8.84–2.9.84.

[118]   *Le Monde* 1.10.81 and interview, DGT.   [119]   *Le Figaro* 21.10.84.

[120]   See *La Tribune de l'Économie* 2.3.87 for a review of the changes.

a line), the DGT was not set binding obligations for performance of 'social obligations'.

In the mid-1980s, preparing the DGT to become a more 'commercial' organization saw further modifications of the PTT Ministry's responsibilities and internal organization. In 1985, Mexandeau argued that the roles and responsibilities of the DGT should be clarified.[121] He therefore gave responsibilities for strategy, regulation, and sectoral responsibilities (*tutelles industrielles*) to a new body created within the PTT Ministry, the *Délégation générale de la stratégie*. After the victory of the Right 1986, the process became more explicit.[122] The PTT Ministry's formal responsibilities for the computing, electronics, space sectors and the telecommunications equipment-manufacturing industry, were all transferred to the Industry Ministry, although the new PTT Minister, Gérard Longuet, failed to end the *prélèvements*, which the Finance and Budget Ministers insisted continue.[123] The *Délégation générale de la stratégie* was replaced in 1986 by the *Mission à la réglementation*, whose tasks were to show that separation of regulation and supply was possible and beneficial and to prepare for institutional change whereby an independent body, the CNCL, would regulate competition.[124] This was continued by the *Mission*'s successor in 1988, the Direction à la Réglementation Générale (DRG), which became the main body within the PTT Ministry responsible for regulation. Hence a process of separating regulation and supply was begun, albeit within the constraints of existing institutional arrangements.

Relations between the DGT and its Equipment Suppliers[125]

The 1974–81 period had seen co-operation between the DGT and the political executive in using DGT orders to restructure the manufacturing subsector. Between 1981 and 1987, the pattern was largely reversed, as the DGT found that the division of its orders was largely determined by the political executive and its suppliers acting together against its wishes.

Policy was concentrated on public switching equipment. The nationalization of CGE, Thomson, and CGCT in 1981–2 meant that all of the DGT's public switching suppliers were publicly-owned and led to the appointment of new heads of each firm.[126] Yet the firms remained separate companies, with their own managers and profit and loss accounts. Soon, they faced pressures for restructuring. Thomson was making heavy losses, due mainly to the high development costs of its MT switch, and DGT penalties for late

---

[121] *Le Quotidien de Paris* 2.12.85; see comments by Hirel, *Libération* 30.1.86.
[122] Cf. Longuet interview, *Le Quotidien de Paris* 16.5.86.
[123] *Le Monde* 29.4.86, 5.4.86 and 23.7.86.   [124] Interview, *Mission à la réglementation*.
[125] A detailed account is offered by J. M. Quatrepoint, *Histoire secrète des dossiers noirs de la Gauche*, (Paris: Moreau, 1986), Part IV; see also Cohen, *Le Colbertisme 'high tech'*, 147–63.
[126] Alain Gomez at Thomson, Pierre Lestrade at CGCT and Georges Pébereau at CGE.

delivery.[127] DGT orders were set to decline in the 1980s, overseas markets were fiercely competitive and other suppliers were forming international alliances (for instance, the American manufacturer ATT and the Dutch firm Philips), which seemed to portend the entry of ATT into European markets.[128]

Two responses to these problems emerged. The Industry Minister between 1981 and 1983, Jean-Pierre Chevènement, favoured the creation of a single French company composed of the telecommunications interests of CGE, Thomson, and CGCT. He claimed that this would create a world-sized group, provide greater funds available for research and developments, increase exports, and end the 'undesirable' rivalry between CGE and Thomson.[129] Mexandeau and the DGT opposed reliance on a single switching supplier, which would have great power over the DGT and end competition that was argued to be beneficial for prices and exports; instead, each French company should form alliances with European partners.[130]

Chevènement made several attempts to create a single French public switching supplier. He presented his suggestions of the merger of the three suppliers to Mitterrand.[131] However, he not only faced resistance by Mexandeau and the DGT, but also suffered from poor relations with key members of the Élysée staff dealing with industrial policy, notably Alain Boublil, who opposed his plans.[132] The Élysée withheld its support from Chevènement's aims, and no decision was taken.

In September 1983, soon after Laurent Fabius became Industry Minister, the situation changed. A sweeping agreement was announced between CGE and Thomson. All of Thomson's telecommunications interests would be transferred to a holding company, Thomson Telecommunications, which would be managed by CGE's telecommunications subsidiary, CIT-Alcatel, in 1984; within three years, the two telecommunications manufacturers would merge, with CGE owning 50 per cent of the shares in the new entity. In return, Thomson would receive CGE's military, consumer goods and micro-chip activities. Moreover, Thomson and CGE agreed not to compete in the activities transferred between them before the end of 1989. The DGT would be left with one supplier of time division switches, controlled by CGE.

The initiative for the restructuring came from Thomson's head, Alain Gomez.[133] He secretly negotiated the agreement with CGE's head, Georges Pébereau, but with the knowledge of Fabius, his *directeur de cabinet*, Louis

---

[127] *Le Nouveau Journal* 16.10.82; interview, DGT.

[128] *Le Figaro* 1.3.83; for a list of co-operation agreements by European telecommunications firms, see Cawson et al., *Hostile Brothers*, 207–14.

[129] *Le Nouveau Journal* 21.12.82.

[130] *Les Echos* 15.10.82, *Le Point* 17.1.83, and *Le Figaro* 1.3.83.

[131] Quatrepoint, *Histoire secrète*, *Le Nouveau Journal* 21.12.82, and *Le Point* 17.1.83.

[132] Quatrepoint, *Histoire secrète*.

[133] Interview, PTT Minister's *cabinet*; Cohen, *Le Colbertisme 'high tech'*, 152–3.

Schweitzer, and of Boublil, who reversed his earlier opposition.[134] Thomson was in deficit, in part due to problems with the MT20 switch, whereas CGE was profitable, and arguments about economies of scale were accepted by Élysée advisers Boublil and Jacques Attali.[135] The government had recently altered its policy to emphasizing the autonomy of publicly-owned firms and the need for them to be profitable.[136] Crucially, Fabius enjoyed great influence in the Élysée, and had friendly relations with Pébereau.[137]

Mexandeau and the DGT fought hard against the plan. In a long memorandum to Mitterrand, the Direction générale des télécommunications, Jacques Dondoux claimed that the merger would worsen the problems of motivation, management and employment in Thomson; it would also increase imports, as a single firm could not control 84 per cent of DGT orders (the sum of the two companies share of DGT switching orders) and prevent an European solution that could maintain two French suppliers.[138] However, Mexandeau and the DGT lost: the Conseil interministériel of 18 September 1983 agreed to the merger, setting certain conditions over maintaining employment and Thomson's MT product range. The Élysée had taken the final decision, and Dondoux was told that if he disagreed with it, he should resign.[139]

The merger was followed by further restructuring, as CGE still faced difficulties. It had surplus capacity, two ranges of public switch and its financial position was weak. It therefore diminished its workforce and number of factories, reduced its product range and obtained government financial aid, disguised in the form of State purchases of shares.[140] These moves were contrary to the conditions laid down in 1983, but the government did not act; without support from the political executive, the DGT was unable to stop the ending of the production of some of the MT range and was forced to accept price rises and a pluri-annual contract with CGE.

However, Pébereau's main concern was CGE's international expansion. DGT orders were falling or about to do so.[141] Pébereau believed that rising costs and fierce international competition would reduce the number of viable manufacturers of public switches.[142] CGE's strategy was to expand in the US market, where the regional Bell operating companies (RBOCs), newly established after the 'Bell settlement', seemed to offer important opportunities for new suppliers. CIT-Alcatel's switches were old, and needed updating; in particular, its E10S switch was unsuitable for the American market, as it was too small and

[134] Quatrepoint, *Histoire secrète*.   [135] *Le Point* 17.1.83, interview, DGT.
[136] Cohen, *Le Colbertisme 'high tech'*, 153–4.   [137] Interview, PTT Minister's *cabinet*.
[138] Quatrepoint, *Histoire secrète*; interview, DGT.
[139] Interviews, PTT Minister's *cabinet* and DGT.
[140] See Quatrepoint, *Histoire secrète*, for details.
[141] Quatrepoint, *Histoire secrète*, and the reports by the Groupe de Stratégie Industrielle, *Les Echos* 3.10.84 and *Le Monde* 2.3.85.
[142] Cohen, *Le Colbertisme 'high tech'*, 159–60 and 169.

did not meet the technical requirements of the RBOCs. Upgrading the E10S would have cost $200m., which the DGT refused to pay and which was beyond CGE's resources, since it was desperately short of capital. Therefore CGE needed foreign partners, preferably ones with access to the US market.

CGE turned to AT&T, the largest switch manufacturer in the world, but whose earlier alliance with Philips had yielded few results. CGE negotiated a 'protocol of intention' with AT&T. The latter would become the DGT's second supplier by buying 70 per cent of CGCT, which would manufacture AT&T's ESS5 public switch to meet CGCT's 16 per cent share of DGT switch orders. In return, AT&T would pay up to $30m. to upgrade the E10S for the US market and would assist in selling a minimum of $100m. p.a. worth of the E10S, with penalty clauses in case of failure; AT&T and Philips would cede a controlling interest in their transmissions activities to CGE.[143]

The pact was remarkable. CGE was determining the ownership of CGCT and the division of DGT orders, neither of which were its property. CGE and Pébereau negotiated the agreement, and only a small group of people around Fabius (now Prime Minister) and in the Élysée staff knew of the negotiations or were influential in them. Jacques Dondoux, (Directeur générale des télécommunications), was involved in discussions over supplies of AT&T's ESS5 switch but not in industrial restructuring matters; Mexandeau and Edith Cresson (Industry Minister 1984–6) were excluded, and remained so until the negotiations were revealed.[144]

When the possible agreement became publicly known in September 1985, the Government and DGT were not committed to it, and reacted cautiously.[145] Pébereau led a campaign to obtain the assent of the government, lobbying Ministers and seeking support from Dondoux and CGCT's management.[146] The proposal was controversial, as AT&T was seen as part of the 'American menace' to French industry, and it was fiercely attacked by the PCF, parts of the Socialist Party, CGCT workers, and the Right. The Socialist Government and Fabius, weakened by the Greenpeace Affair, and facing elections, refused either to accept the deal or to reject it.

On coming into office, the Chirac Government did not give immediate assent to the CGE–AT&T deal. Indeed, having failed to win assent to changes involving AT&T, Pébereau had found a further international partner, ITT, with whom contacts had been continuing during negotiations with AT&T.[147] ITT wished to withdraw from switching manufacture, due to problems with its time division switch, System 12, and the danger of a predatory takeover.[148] In July

---

[143] see Quatrepoint, *Histoire secrète*, for details.
[144] Quatrepoint, *Histoire secrète*, and interview, DGT.
[145] Cf. Mexandeau's comments, *Le Monde* 22–23.9.85, and the DGT's 'technical' appraisal of the ESS5, *Le Monde* 2.1.86.
[146] Quatrepoint, *Histoire secrète*; Cohen, *Le Colbertisme 'high tech'*, 161–3.
[147] Interview, DGT.   [148] Cohen, *Le Colbertisme 'high tech'*, 164.

1986, another agreement was announced whereby CGE would gain control of ITT's subsidiaries in Europe, together with some others in Latin America and Australia.

The proposal required both assent from the government and finance, since the cost was put at $2.8b., far beyond CGE's financial means. After some hesitation, especially by the Finance Ministry, modification of the settlement to reduce the cost and the removal of Pébereau as head of CGE, the Chirac Government accepted the agreement. It had become linked with the privatization of CGE, and hence finance was provided in two ways: a series of holding companies in which CGE held only part of the stake, thereby limiting the cost; on privatization in 1986, CGE's debt was reduced, allowing it to find funds for the purchase.[149] CGE emerged as the second largest telecommunications equipment manufacturer in the world, becoming a French 'international champion'.

This left the question of CGCT. It had no time division switch, and was making large losses, but held 16 per cent of DGT public switch orders. Moreover, the DGT was seeking a strong alternative supplier to CIT-Alcatel. Dondoux, Longuet, and Madelin (Industry Minister 1986–8) favoured the sale of CGCT to AT&T; the US administration applied strong pressure in favour of this.[150] An alternative was Siemens, for which the West German Government lobbied strongly, threatening retaliation against CGE's German subsidiary, SEL.[151] The Prime Minister, Chirac, favoured an European solution, and the Finance Minister, Edouard Balladur, blocked a sale to AT&T. As a compromise, obtaining maximum support within the government and avoiding the risks of the other two solutions, CGCT was sold to a consortium led by the French firm Matra and the Swedish firm Ericsson.[152] CGCT would build Ericsson's time division AXE switch under licence, to meet 16 per cent of DGT orders.

Network Operation Finances: Profits, Investment, Borrowing, and Prices

During the 1980s, only limited policy attention was given to the DGT's profits and little pressure existed to ensure high net profitability. High operating profits were offset by high financial costs (especially on overseas borrowing); nevertheless, the political executive imposed large *prélèvements*.[153] Moreover, investment levels were maintained at a high level in order to modernize the network

---

[149]   Quatrepoint, *Histoire secrète*; interview, DGT.
[150]   Interview, DGT; Cohen, *Le Colbertisme 'high tech'*, 166.
[151]   Cawson *et al.*, *Hostile Brothers*, 135.
[152]   See *Le Figaro* 5.1.88, and *Le Monde* 24.4.87 for details.
[153]   For instance, in nominal terms, FF15.2b. in 1985, FF19.6 in 1986, FF16.8 in 1987, and FF12.5 in 1988.

with time division switches and optical fibre cables and to fund projects such as the Telematics Programme, the Cable Plan, and the satellite programme (see Ch. 10). Low profitability combined with high investment resulted in heavy borrowing. Although the *Plan* for 1982–7 envisaged a fall to FF50b. debt from FF73b. in 1981, the opposite occurred, with the debt rising to over FF120b. by the late 1980s.[154] The DGT continued to borrow both via the *sociétés de financement*, and directly by PTT bonds, outside the general Budget.

The political executive was closely involved in tariff policy, which was driven by two factors: meeting the DGT's financial obligations; protecting the DGT against possible competition in network operation. The first came to the fore in the early 1980s. The VIIth Plan for 1982–7 and the 1983 *Charte de gestion* set a target of a 3 per cent p.a. fall in prices in real terms between 1982 and 1987.[155] The continued imposition of the *prélèvements* on the DGT after 1982 led to negotiations between Dondoux, Mexandeau, the Ministry of Finance, and members of the Élysée (notably Jacques Attali).[156] They decided to increase tariffs, most sharply in 1984, which saw two increases (an average 8.3 per cent in May and then a further rise of 16.3 per cent in August).

After 1984 the political executive and the DGT co-operated to introduce significant rebalancing of tariffs: long-distance call charges, which were priced above costs, were reduced whilst local call charges, which were set below costs, were increased. Under the Left, the aim was to protect the DGT's monopoly, as residential users were cross-subsidized by firms which, it was feared, would lead to pressures for liberalization and competition. Under the Right, rebalancing formed part of Longuet's explicit strategy to prepare the DGT to behave as a firm: cost-based prices (*la vérité des prix*), reducing cross-subsidisation between services and types of users, would allow the DGT to withstand 'cream-skimming' if competition were introduced and prevent it from being handicapped by loss-making services.[157] In addition, there were concerns that the pricing structure disadvantaged French firms and caused network congestion by encouraging excessive local calls.[158] Particular pressures existed concerning international calls: large users could 'bypass' the French network, routing communications via other countries to enjoy lower charges, and competition existed between national network operators to attract traffic and multinational firms. French policy-makers were especially concerned about competition with BT for communications with North America.

Rebalancing began in earnest in 1984. Until then, local calls were charged at one unit per call, regardless of duration. Dondoux proposed that local call

[154] *Les Echos* 28.12.82, 27.1.83, and *Le Monde* 28.1.89.
[155] *Les Echos* 27.1.83, and *Le Monde* 21.6.83.
[156] Interviews, PTT Minister's *cabinet* and DGT.
[157] Cf. Longuet's comments reported in *Le Monde* 22.5.86, Longuet interview in *Le Figaro* 25–26.7.87; *Le Matin* 4.1.88.
[158] Interview, DGT; *Le Matin* 4.1.88; *Libération* 2.5.85; *Le Monde* 11.9.86.

charges should vary with the duration of the call, but he needed Mexandeau's support to have the change approved by the Conseil des ministres in November 1984; President Mitterrand personally questioned the reform, and Dondoux and Mexandeau had to defend the change.[159] In 1985–6 unlimited duration for local calls was ended. In contrast, costs for firms were reduced by the introduction in 1986 of the SIO (*service interurbain optionnel*), whereby firms could pay a subscription fee, and obtain discounts on trunk communications.[160] In addition, transatlantic tariffs were reduced.

Under Longuet, rebalancing was accelerated between 1986 and 1988. There were no fewer than six reductions in the cost of trunk calls, whilst the length of call per unit was steadily reduced, especially for local calls. Furthermore, in 1987, VAT (TVA) was imposed on telephone services, offset by cuts in the price per unit; since firms could reclaim TVA, they benefited from the change. International call prices were lowered; the DGT reduced prices in direct response to price cuts by new US operators, MCI and Sprint, and closely shadowed BT's tariffs.[161] Decisions were made by Longuet acting with the Finance Minister, Edouard Balladur.[162] The latter was attracted by reductions in the overall levels of tariffs (which contrasted with the Socialists' record of increases 1981–6) and which also helped to reduce inflation.[163] After 1988, rebalancing continued, but at a reduced pace: it was unpopular with residential users, whilst the Socialist Government concentrated on institutional reform.

Conclusion

Different patterns of policy making concerning the network operators were seen in Britain and France during the 1980s despite powerful common transnational forces. Analysis shows how the dissimilar institutional arrangements in the two countries influenced national patterns of policy making. Their impact can be seen by comparing policies in Britain and France—both processes of decision making and the substantive decisions taken—and examining how specific institutional features contributed to the differing patterns in each country. In addition, the influence of institutions is visible through the effects of institutional reforms; in particular, comprehensive institutional reforms in Britain in 1984 were followed by major alterations in policy making, widening the differences with France.

Policy making processes offer a good example of the influence of institutions and organisational reform. In Britain, the main participants in decision

---

[159] Interviews, PTT Minister's *cabinet* and DGT.   [160] *Le Monde* 12.3.86.
[161] Interview, DGT; *l'Express* 26.10.84, *Le Monde* 11.2.86; see Longuet, *Télécoms*, 149, who indicates how closely tariffs offered by the DGT, BT and American operators on the North American routes moved together from 1984.
[162] Longuet, *Télécoms*, 12.   [163] *Le Monde* 11.9.86, 4.1.88, 19.4.88.

making in network operation before 1984 were the DoI/DTI, the Treasury and BT. Spheres of activity were relatively well-defined, with a clear leading body in each: the Treasury in setting financial limits for BT, the DoI/DTI in determining the framework of licensing and competition, and BT in taking decisions over the functioning of the network and choices of technology. The exception was the relationship between BT and its equipment suppliers, where the initiative for changes lay with BT and its suppliers, but the government acted as 'umpire' or mediator in disputes. After institutional reform in 1984, the processes of policy formation altered. Oftel emerged as a central actor, dealing with licence enforcement and modification and providing information and advice, whereas the Treasury's direct participation largely ended. The DTI set the overall regulatory framework, through licensing. BT became free to decide how to supply services within the framework of its licence; neither the government nor Oftel participated in its internal company decisions. The government's role in relations between BT and equipment manufacturers was greatly diminished, being largely confined to dealing with the regulation of takeovers.

Decision-making processes in France differed greatly from those in Britain, especially after 1984 when new patterns were emerged in the latter. Unlike BT, the DGT did not enjoy a clearly defined sphere of autonomous decision making. Instead, the political executive was closely involved in a wide range of DGT matters including its responsibilities, *prélèvements*, modernization, internal organization, senior appointments, tariffs and investment. In the equipment-manufacturing subsector, decisions saw the involvement of the Élysée, certain Ministers, the DGT and the top managers of the publicly-owned suppliers. Policy was often the result of negotiations and manoeuvres within the political executive.

Institutional arrangements were important for the patterns found in each country. The division of roles reflected the formal distribution of powers. In France, the processes of decision making matched the DGT's institutional position as part of the civil service: the political executive used its powers to participate actively in many areas of policy and, for its part, as an *administration*, the DGT was formally and in practice, largely under the orders of the political executive. In a change from the 1970s, the DGT's alliance with the political executive did not hold and its lack of institutional autonomy and resulting vulnerability were frequently exposed. The clearest example came in relations with equipment suppliers, who were publicly-owned between 1981–2 and 1987 and thereby became rivals to the DGT within the public sector: the intimate involvement of the political executive in decisions about DGT orders was closely linked to the dependence of both the DGT and equipment suppliers on its support to pursue their objectives.

In contrast to the DGT, BT, as a public corporation before 1984, had an identity as an enterprise, in addition to a virtual monopoly of expertise over complex technological issues; it was therefore well placed to take decisions over how to run its network and its internal functioning. However, in financial matters, BT's borrowing and investment affected the general Budget, and the Treasury had powers to set it financial targets, encouraging and permitting an active government role in these matters. For its part, the DoI/DTI's main policy instruments concerned the regulatory framework, whilst their application required limited technical knowledge; these arrangements allowed and encouraged the Department to focus on matters such as licensing and competition. In relations between BT and its equipment suppliers: the suppliers were privately-owned companies, whereas BT was a publicly-owned purchaser and institutionally separate from the DoI, leading to a situation in which the suppliers turned to the Department as an interested third party. However, the new institutional framework in Britain after 1984 led to changes in decision making, increasing contrasts with France and marking a break with well-established processes, some of which had existed for decades.[164] BT's position as a private firm discouraged government participation in its internal decisions, including the allocation of its equipment orders. The Treasury now lacked institutional powers to control BT, and in any case, the basis for its role had been removed, since BT's borrowing no longer affected public expenditure totals. The DTI's main powers were over licensing; in the 1980s, they were crucial in establishing the framework of competition. Oftel became a central participant in policy making. As a specialist sectoral body, it developed expertise and was responsible for regulating a private dominant supplier; it ended BT's previous virtual monopoly over policy expertise and indeed replaced it as the specialist telecommunications body within the public sector. Oftel used its position and its powers, notably over licence enforcement and modification, to develop a framework for regulation in which it played a central role.

Analysis of substantive policy decisions in network operation also reveals both considerable differences between Britain and France and significant modifications in Britain following institutional reform in 1984. In the latter country, policy before 1984 centred on BT meeting financial targets that were linked to the general budget through BT's external financing limit, constraints on investment, and prices increases to meet EFL targets. However, after 1984, Oftel developed a new overall policy framework, based around the promotion of competition. BT's monopoly was reduced, whilst regulation concerned BT's tariffs, and, to a lesser extent, its rates of return, rather than its investment and borrowing. The overall thrust of French policy differed considerably from that in Britain. It combined traditional elements of *service public* with the pursuit of other objectives: protecting interests of employees; using the DGT as a tool of wider policy; the DGT operating as an efficient enterprise; sheltering the DGT from adverse regulatory changes. Financially, the DGT became a source of

---

[164] See also Chs. 2 and 6.

funds for non-telecommunications purposes, with prices being raised if necessary. Tariff rebalancing shows some greater similarities than other aspects of
policy in the 1980s: in both countries, long-distance prices were reduced and
local charges increased. However, the timing and speed of the change differed,
taking place earlier and faster in Britain than in France.

The dissimilar institutional frameworks in Britain and France contributed to
the contrasting policies choices made in the two countries concerning the role
of the network operator, industrial policy, and competition, whilst in Britain,
institutional reforms aided modification of policy. In the latter country, despite
the desires of ministers, before 1984 the government found it difficult to introduce extensive competition into network operation as long as BT was part of
the public sector. Privatization saw a move to a duopoly, as the government
faced the conflicting pressures of the need for a successful sale of BT, avoidance of a private monopoly and defence of the sale of BT as a vertically-
integrated firm. However, after 1984, Oftel played a key role in the development of a new general policy framework. It exploited the generality of the 1984
Telecommunications Act to establish a conceptual framework that regulation
should ensure that effective competition took place and that otherwise, regulation should mimic a competitive market. In turn, that framework provided
Oftel with a means of reconciling its potentially conflicting statutory duties. It
also offered a rationale for Oftel's extensive and detailed regulatory role: its
activities could be justified either by the need to ensure that competition developed or by the need to substitute for competition. Oftel's stance in favour of
competition and BT's position as a private firm made severe restrictions on
competition more difficult to sustain, and so in 1989 the government began to
reduce the regulatory protection of BT's oligopoly position.

The differing policies pursued in France were also linked to the organizational features of its telecommunications sector. The DGT's multiple functions
reflected its organizational position: it was a public sector monopolist; as an
administration, it provided a tool for the political executive; it produced valuable income for wider policy purposes. In addition, there was no independent
specialist telecommunications regulator to rival the political executive or to
develop an alternative framework for policy. At the same time, the DGT's
position represented an obstacle to competition in network operation: its
monopoly over supply was more defensible than that of BT after 1984, as it
was publicly-owned, preventing private 'exploitation'; it provided funds for the
political executive; for its monopoly to be ended, institutional reform was
required, especially in its *statut* in order for it to be able to compete fairly,
whereas such reform was very difficult; there was no equivalent to Oftel pressing for greater competition.

Analysis of the financial aspects of network operation policy also indicates
the effects of institutional arrangements. The concentration in Britain before
1984 on BT's investment and borrowing was closely linked to public sector

accounting rules and to Treasury powers over BT's external financing limit. The change in the objects of regulation after 1984 reflected BT's new position as a private company operating under a licence that specified tariff controls, together with the Treasury's loss of instruments and the fact that Oftel's powers concerned licence conditions, including price controls. In tariff setting, the threat of competition in Britain was a powerful force for the policy of rebalancing being undertaken earlier and more forcefully than in France. Moreover, Oftel supported rebalancing and BT, as a private company, had considerable autonomy from the government. In contrast, the DGT's tariffs were decided in the Conseil des ministres, where elected politicians, anxious about residential users losing out from tariff changes, had to be persuaded to accept rebalancing. More generally, the DGT's financial arrangements allowed and encouraged the political executive to use it to provide revenue: thanks to the *budget annexe*, the DGT could borrow outside the general budget to pay for continued high investment; being publicly owned, there was less pressure for it to produce high levels of profits than in a private firm.

Analysis of the relations between network operators and their equipment suppliers also indicates the impact of institutions and organizational change. In Britain, before 1984, the government and BT were unable to greatly alter supply arrangements. They failed to co-ordinate their actions, allowing the existing suppliers to restrict change. The organization of the sector made it difficult to pursue a strategic restructuring strategy: BT was a public corporation, with substantial autonomy; the Department lacked technical knowledge and the ability to control BT's orders, but found it difficult to withdraw from decision making since BT was a publicly-owned purchaser. After the institutional reforms of 1984, the position altered. As a private company, BT was free to choose its suppliers; moreover, it faced competition from Mercury. Oftel focused on issues of competition and the interests of the consumer. Thus the government was able to withdraw from relations between BT and its suppliers, leaving BT to take decisions that led to a comprehensive restructuring of the subsector. In contrast, in France, decisions over the distribution of DGT orders were linked to the reshaping the equipment manufacturing subsector, including its internationalization, profitability and choice of overseas partners. Unlike the 1970s, choices ran counter to the wishes of the DGT, which found that its orders were pawns in the hands of other actors, rather than instruments in a strategy it had devised or desired. The pattern of policy again related to the institutional framework. The DGT was an *administration*, under the formal control of the political executive. The DGT's suppliers were publicly-owned, following nationalization in 1981–2, but kept their identities and devised their own commercial paths. The political executive wished to have strong and profitable publicly-owned equipment firms, and no strong independent regulatory bodies existed to emphasize the interests of DGT users. Such institutional factors encouraged and permitted the political executive to play a direct role in the allocation of DGT orders, in pursuit of goals such as creating an international French manufacturing champion and selecting foreign partners for French firms.

Thus the experience of policy towards network operators in the 1980s provides strong support for national institutionalist claims that dissimilar organizational arrangements lead to differing policy patterns. The impact of national institutions is visible in three ways. First, despite powerful transnational pressures (technological and economic changes and an evolving international regulatory environment), Britain and France pursued increasingly contrasting policies for their network operators, especially when institutional reforms increased divergence in the organization of the sector between the two countries. Second, policy patterns can be linked to institutional characteristics. Policy-making followed institutional arrangements. Moreover, the roles of specific institutional features in policy choices can be traced in each country; in particular, analysis reveals the ways in which the formal powers of policymakers, the degree of separation between the network operator and the political executive, ownership of the network operator and equipment suppliers, the existence of a legal monopoly and the creation of an independent sectoral regulator permitted, encouraged or constrained policy-makers. Third, institutional reform, especially in Britain, was followed by policy changes. Hence not only did major cross-national and temporal contrasts exist, but they can be linked to particular institutional characteristics.

9

Competition in Network Operation 1990–1996: Differing National Paths away from Monopoly

The 1990s saw increased external pressures on British and French policy in network operation: in addition to powerful technological and economic developments, supra-national regulation grew, notably by the EC. Yet developments in the institutional frameworks in the two countries followed different paths between 1990 and 1996: in Britain, the institutional framework established in 1984 saw little change; in France, however, significant reforms took place in 1990, which left very considerable institutional differences compared with Britain but narrowed the contrasts between the two countries.

Hence the 1990s allow consideration of the effects both of cross-national institutional differences and also of modifications that reduced those contrasts. Moreover, the pattern of institutional development was the opposite to that seen in the 1980s: reform took place in France rather than Britain, and it led to a degree of institutional convergence rather than divergence. The period 1990–6 therefore provides different comparative cases to the 1980s and hence another set of tests for the impact of national institutions. If institutional arrangements were important for policy making, then several features can be expected: noticeable but not revolutionary change in patterns of policy making in France, but stability in Britain; a reduction in differences between the two nations compared with the 1980s due to policy alteration in France; continuing important dissimilarities between the two countries.

The chapter examines decision-making processes and key areas of substantive policy in the two countries concerning network operation; it applies the same structure for analysis of each country, and also largely follows the framework used in the previous chapter. The structure therefore allows comparison, both cross-nationally and with the policy patterns seen in the 1980s. Institutional factors that differed between Britain and France are looked at in detail, including the ownership and formal position of the network operators (BT and France Télécom[1]), the existence of an independent industry regulator, the ending of the network operator's monopoly and the powers and duties of the political executive, regulatory bodies and network operator. At the same time,

[1] As the DGT had been renamed in 1988.

in examining France, particular attention is given to policy change and to the impact of those institutional features that were altered in 1990, such as the separation of France Télécom and the PTE Ministry, the operator obtaining a legal identity and the Ministry being left with regulatory functions. In the final section, Britain and France are compared directly in order to link institutions to the patterns of policy making found, including differences between the two countries and changes in France following the reforms of 1990.

Britain

Decision-Making Processes and the Overall Direction of Policy

Processes of decision making remained strongly marked by the institutional framework established in 1984. Despite retaining a large stake in BT until 1993, the government did not intervene in BT's internal decision making. The Department of Trade and Industry set the extent of competition through its licensing power, albeit in close co-operation with Oftel, whose advice the DTI often took.[2] Oftel remained a central actor, thanks to its powers and position as specialist regulator with far greater expertise and information than any other public bodies, including the DTI.[3] It enjoyed independence from the government, which did not intervene in Oftel's use of its powers, even in contentious matters such as price controls and possible MMC references.[4]

Oftel's activities remained centred on the regulation of BT, as the dominant vertically-integrated supplier, although the development of greater competition during the 1990s saw new entrants in network operation (such as the cable companies and long-distance operators) become more significant actors in decision making.[5] Relations between Oftel and BT continued to involve an often conflictual 'game' in which Oftel sought licence modifications, threatening to use its power to refer matters to the MMC; unable to control the terms of a reference and fearing wide-ranging references and the uncertainty of an MMC investigation, BT only rejected Oftel's proposed licence modifications once between 1990 and 1996.[6] Moreover, Oftel utilized its discretion over regulatory procedures to further develop its 'transparency' and increase participation by interested parties, including user representatives and experts; thus, for instance, in the mid-1990s, it sought to publish most submissions on consultation docu-

---

[2] Interview, DTI.   [3] Interviews, DTI.   [4] Interviews, Oftel, DTI, BT.
[5] C. Hall, C. Hood, and C. Scott, 'Regulatory Space and Institutional Reform: The Case of Telecommunications', *CRI Regulatory Review* 1997.
[6] The occasion was number portability, when BT knew that the reference would be narrowly-framed—interviews, Oftel and BT; particularly acute conflict took place over the fair trading and price cap conditions in 1995–6; at times, BT even feared that a reference might lead to break-up: interviews, BT and Oftel; *Financial Times* 11.7.91 and 16.7.91.

ments, held public hearings and workshops and established an advisory body to aid the DG in decisions on enforcing fair trading licence conditions.[7] Large, experienced operators such as AT&T and Colt, were particularly useful in providing Oftel with an alternative source of information.[8] At the same time, although consultation took place, in accordance with institutional arrangements, the DG personally took major decisions.[9]

The flexibility of the institutional framework established by the 1984 Telecommunications Act permitted the evolution of policy. The government removed regulatory restrictions to entry, using its powers over licensing. As competition grew, Oftel gave greater weight to 'selective deregulation' and less to the need for detailed regulation to 'mimic' a competitive market.[10] Under Don Cruickshank (DG 1993–8), Oftel sought to transform itself into a sectoral competition authority. It aimed to progressively withdraw from detailed regulation through 'prescriptive' licence conditions and instead to apply 'simple over-arching principles' backed up by guidelines derived from general EC competition law.[11] It thus modified licences to obtain new powers over anti-competitive behaviour and sought, to some extent at least, to replace *ex ante* regulation (via detailed licence conditions) with broader, *ex post* regulation (policing competition as it developed). Oftel claimed that its new interpretation of its role matched changed market conditions since 'the regulator must not meddle more with the market than is justified in ensuring fair competition'; it was also a response to increasing demands on its resources as competition increased.[12] The degree of change was limited, in that Oftel continued to play an extensive role in detailed regulation, especially with respect to BT,[13] but nevertheless it was visible in key areas such as retail price controls and interconnection arrangements.

Competition

The extension of competition greatly accelerated in the 1990s. The major change came when the government's promise to keep the BT–Mercury duopoly over fixed-link public telecommunications networks expired in November 1990. The Duopoly Review was carried out jointly with Oftel, and

---

[7] See Oftel, *Annual Report 1996*; T. Prosser, *Law and the Regulators* (Oxford: Clarendon, 1997), 83–6; interviews, BT and Oftel.

[8] Interviews, Oftel and BT.   [9] Interviews, BT, Oftel, DTI.

[10] Cf. C. Scott, 'The Future of Telecommunications Regulation in the United Kingdom: Tinkering, Regulatory Reform or Deregulation?', *Utilities Law Review*, 6(2) (1995), 13–17.

[11] Oftel, *Annual Report 1995* (London: Oftel, 1996), 1; see esp. the section in Oftel's *Annual Reports* headed 'Oftel as a Competition Authority'.

[12] Oftel, *Annual Report 1996*, 1; cf. *Annual Report 1995*, 1–2; interviews, BT.

[13] See e.g. the chronology of events in Oftel's *Annual Reports* for the frequency and breadth of Oftel action concerning BT.

Carsberg's views appear to have been highly influential.[14] Although Carsberg did not make a formal submission, he indicated in public statements that both greater competition, especially from cable television companies, and more regulation, were needed.[15]

In the Duopoly Review, BT accepted that there should be greater competition, but argued that it should be 'fair'.[16] This entailed the lifting of 'artificial regulatory constraints' on BT, especially concerning prices, requiring reciprocity for overseas entrants, particularly the American RBOCs and allowing BT to transmit television programmes on its networks. Potential new entrants, notably the cable television companies and utilities with their own private networks, argued for competition in local and trunk networks, supported by interconnection rights.[17]

The government issued a Green Paper in November 1990, and then a White Paper in March 1991.[18] It announced that competition would be greatly increased. The duopoly would be ended and applications for further licences for fixed-link systems within the UK would be granted unless there was a good reason to the contrary. Cable television operators would be permitted to become public telecommunications operators (PTOs) offering telephony in their own right. Satellite services not linked to public networks would be allowed; applications from satellite operators for connection to the PSTN and from mobile operators to offer fixed link services would also be favourably considered. Only in international links was the duopoly continued, but in the 1990s international liberalization developed, AT&T lobbied for change, and British restrictions became an obstacle to regulatory approval of BT entry to the US market. The DTI therefore progressively extended international simple resale (i.e. for voice telephony) and then in 1996 decided to allow competition in international facilities.[19]

Thus by 1996 competition was permitted throughout the telecommunications sector in Britain. In practice the Secretary of State followed a policy of accepting licence applications, so that by the end of 1996 twenty-four fixed-link national or regional PTO licences had been granted.[20] The Duopoly Review

---

[14]   Interviews, DTI, Oftel, BT; see also the White Paper, Department of Trade and Industry, *Competition and Choice: Telecommunications Policy for the 1990s*, Cmnd. 1461 (London: HMSO, 1991), which is replete with references to the Director General.

[15]   Oftel, *Annual Report 1989* (London: Oftel, 1990); Carsberg speech, *Independent* 23.11.89; B. Carsberg, 'Office of Telecommunications: Competition and the Duopoly Review' in C. Veljanovski (ed.), *Regulators and the Market* (London: IEA, 1991); B. Carsberg, 'Injecting Competition into Telecommunications' in C. Veljanovski (ed.), *Privatisation and Competition* (London: IEA, 1989).

[16]   *Independent* 2.1.90, 9.8.90, 29.11.89 and I. Vallance, 'A Competitive Role for BT', *Independent* 22.1.91.

[17]   *Independent* 30.7.90 and 7.8.90.

[18]   DTI, with both being entitled *Competition and Choice: Telecommunications Policy for the 1990s* (London: HMSO), the White Paper being Cmnd. 1461.

[19]   Oftel, *Annual Report 1995*, 25 and *Annual Report 1996*, 38; *Independent* 7.3.96.

[20]   DTI, *Telecommunications Liberalisation in the U.K.* (London: DTI, 1997), 6.

was followed by changes in market shares, with significant declines for BT in the mid-1990s; in the financial year 1996–7, BT accounted for 80.2 per cent of all fixed-link operators' revenues.[21] Nevertheless, BT remained the dominant supplier for network operation as a whole, and, as a result, it continued to be the centre of policy and regulation.

Regulating for 'Fair and Effective' Competition

With the extension of competition in the 1990s, Oftel modified its stated purpose, seeking to become a 'competition authority'. In 1994–5 Don Cruickshank decided to alter BT's licence conditions to include a broad prohibition on anti-competitive agreements and abuse of a dominant position; these clauses were modelled on Articles 85 and 86 of the Treaty of Rome. Oftel argued that in a fast-moving competitive market, it was not appropriate to have licence conditions to cover specific individual types of anti-competitive behaviour.[22] Although BT bitterly opposed the licence change, it ultimately chose to accept it, as part of the new 1997 price controls rather than face a 'fundamental' reference to the MMC.[23] Similar conditions were then placed in the licences of other operators. The new clauses marked a move away from detailed *ex post* regulation based on breaches of specific licence conditions, and hence towards a combination of detailed licence prohibitions and a broader set of *ex ante* rules against anti-competitive behaviour. They allowed Oftel to relax detailed restrictions over interconnection and retail tariffs.

Interconnection was crucial to competition. The 1985 interconnection Determination had contained few details of the calculations on which figures were based (notably concerning social costs), had relied on BT's historic cost figures and was largely 'tailor-made' for BT. In the 1990s, Oftel used its powers to adapt interconnection arrangements to increasing competition.

One key issue was the allocation of 'social costs'. BT claimed that its licence obligations imposed burdens of social obligations, especially those relating to universal service. Oftel believed that the costs of BT's universal service obligation were potentially large and agreed with BT that as competition grew, they should be shared by other operators, if necessary through special interconnection payments (ADCs—access deficit contributions). In 1991, the DG modified BT's and Mercury's licences to set out more explicit rules to impose ADCs to cover these costs. However, as part of Oftel's policy of 'entry assistance', the DG was given the power to grant waivers of ADCs for operators with limited

---

[21]   Oftel, *Market Information 1992/93 to 1996/97* (London: Oftel, 1997).

[22]   Oftel, *A Framework for Effective Competition* (London: Oftel, 1994) and *Effective Competition: Framework for Action* (London: Oftel, 1995).

[23]   Although it subsequently unsuccessfully challenged Oftel in an action for judicial review- C. Scott, 'Anti-Competitive Conduct, Licence Modification and Judicial Review in the Telecommunications Sector', *Utilities Law Review*, 8(4) (1997), 120–2; interview, Oftel.

market shares.[24] In practice, the DG continued to waive ADCs for almost all operators.[25]

Oftel then reviewed ADCs in 1994–5, linking them to its work on BT pricing and the cost of universal service. After prolonged discussions, Oftel argued that the costs of universal service borne by BT were low (£65–85 m. in 1995–96 for uneconomic areas, customers, and public call boxes).[26] Moreover, providing universal service offered BT many advantages, such as attracting customers who would become profitable later in their lives, ubiquity and positive corporate reputation. As a result, Oftel asserted that the benefits to BT offset the estimated costs and hence that it was not an undue burden on the company. Oftel therefore decided to end ADCs to BT as part of the new price controls that began in 1997 and not to establish a specific fund or make payments to BT until further study showed the costs and benefits of providing universal service.[27] Moreover, any costs of universal service should be met by a special fund rather than interconnection charges.[28]

As new operators entered the market, Oftel also adapted its role in the setting of interconnection terms. Faced with several operators, Oftel's detailed involvement in price setting through annual Determinations (if the operators failed to agree on interconnection terms) threatened to be slow and was contrary to Oftel's desire to become a 'competition authority'. In response, in 1993 Oftel developed interconnection Determinations with standard terms. In 1995, as part of interconnection and accounting separation, BT was obliged to allocate costs to different parts of its network activities, offering the basis for Oftel to calculate interconnection charges. Then, substantial reforms were introduced as part of price controls beginning in 1997.[29] The basis for interconnection was

---

[24] He could grant waivers to operators with less than 10 per cent of the national market and of international communications and to continue to waive the first 10 per cent until the operator obtained a 25 per cent market share; if BT's market share fell below 85 per cent, it was assured of receiving ADCs on at least the excess over the 15 per cent—see Oftel, *Licence Modification Proposals to Implement Duopoly Review Conclusions* (London: Oftel, 1991) and *Modifications to the Conditions of the Licences of British Telecommunications plc and Mercury Communications Ltd* (London: Oftel, 1991).

[25] The only major contribution was from Mercury in international services, ending in 1996—D. Gillies and R. Marshall, *Telecommunications Law* (London: Butterworths, 1997), 143.

[26] Oftel, *Universal Telecommunication Services. Consultative Document* (London: Oftel, February 1997), 28.

[27] Oftel, *Universal Service. Statement* (London: Oftel, July 1997).

[28] See below; see also Oftel, *Interconnection and Accounting Separation* (London: Oftel, 1993) and *Interconnection and Accounting Separation: The Next Steps* (London: Oftel, 1994).

[29] See: Oftel, *Network Charges from 1997* (London: Oftel, July 1997); Oftel, *Network Charges from 1997. Consultative Document* (London: Oftel, May 1997); Oftel, *Statement. Pricing of Telecommunications Services from 1997. OFTEL's Proposals for Price Control and Fair Trading* (London: Oftel, 1996); Oftel, *Statement. Interconnection and Accounting Separation: The Next Steps* (London: Oftel, 1994).

altered to long-run incremental costs, thereby seeking to 'mimic' an economically efficient competitive market rather than allowing BT to recover its past expenditure. Oftel ended its detailed role in setting particular rates for interconnection in annual Determinations. Price controls were removed from services opened to competition; as a result, Oftel estimated that the network charge cap only covered around 45 per cent of BT's wholesale revenues.[30] For services that were likely to become competitive, price controls would be ended when competition occurred; in the meantime, a cap of RPI − 0 was set.[31] For 'bottleneck' services[32] and services not opened to competition, Oftel set price caps, but in the form of baskets, thereby allowing price rebalancing.[33] BT thus became freer to decide its prices. However, Oftel retained many powers to intervene in disputes between operators or if it believed that anti-competitive behaviour was occurring (notably using its powers under the new 'fair trading' licence condition).[34]

Enforcement of fair competition was highly dependent on appropriate information being available on internal BT practices. This was particularly the case for cross-subsidization, since BT was an integrated company, with operating divisions established for business purposes and producing commercial accounts. Oftel therefore obtained from BT major changes known as 'Interconnection and Accounting Separation', starting in 1995.[35] BT began to produce regulatory accounts ('financial statements'), designed to offer Oftel information in a form suitable for its regulatory decisions. BT had to produce separate accounts for different businesses on a regulatory basis, for instance, distinguishing its access, network, retail, and supplemental services and apparatus supply. Moreover, BT had to 'unbundle' costs, setting out which costs were apportioned to which business and explaining the basis for so doing. Using this information, Oftel determined interconnection charges and checked that BT

[30] A. Bell, 'Governance in the regulation of Telecommunications: the Case of the UK' (paper presented to Telecommunications Workshop, November 1997, European University Institute, Florence).

[31] These services included 'inter-tandem conveyance' (corresponding to transmission between trunk switches as a 'tandem exchange' is one that routes calls between exchanges but is not linked to end users) and international direct dialling services. For a detailed list, see Oftel, *Guidelines on the Operation of Network Charges* (London: Oftel, October 1997), Annex A.

[32] i.e. call termination services—i.e. carrying calls from the local exchange to their destination on the local loop.

[33] There were three separate baskets—for call termination services, general network services and interconnection services; the RPI − X formula was continued, with 'X' set at 8 per cent; for each service, BT was required to publish indicative maximum prices and minimum tariffs ('floors and ceilings') based on costs, according to a methodology established by Oftel.

[34] For details, see Oftel, *Guidelines on the Operation of Network Charges* (1997).

[35] See *Oftel Annual Report 1995* (London: Oftel, 1996), 29–31; Oftel, *Interconnection and Accounting Separation* (London: Oftel, 1993); Oftel, *Interconnection and Accounting Separation: The Next Steps* (London: Oftel, 1994).

was not unfairly discriminating in access to its network against third parties who were competitors downstream.[36]

Oftel also took steps to 'neutralise the advantages of incumbents by removing artificial entry barriers'.[37] It obliged BT to introduce number portability in 1995, a step that involved a long battle with BT about who should bear the burden of costs rather than the principle of portability; it ended in a reference by Oftel of BT's licence condition to the MMC.[38] In addition, Oftel actively enforced BT's 'fair competition' licence conditions, such as restrictions on sales tactics and discounts schemes for selected customers.[39]

The Internal Functioning of Network Operators

The government did not participate in the internal decision making of BT or other operators over tariff setting, investment, appointments or overall commercial strategy. Similarly, it did not intervene in BT's relations with its equipment suppliers. The government's detached role even extended to strategic decisions with implications for the structure of the industry, such as discussions of a takeover of Cable and Wireless (owner of Mercury) by BT or internationalization decisions, most notably BT's attempts to expand overseas by forming 'global alliances'.[40] Nevertheless, the government and Oftel did assist international expansion by British firms, notably BT; they supported liberalization by the EC and the World Trade Organization, believing that British companies would be 'well placed to gain market share'.[41] The clearest example was BT's attempt to enter the US market through its alliance with MCI from 1993, followed by an attempted takeover of MCI in 1996–7, which required regulatory approval by American authorities. Opponents of the move in the US claimed that the British market was insufficiently open. In response, the government removed several regulatory obstacles: it ended its 'golden

[36] The most important example was that BT Network had to offer the same terms for use of the network to BT Retail as to other operators.

[37] Oftel, *Annual Report 1996*, 2.

[38] Monopolies and Mergers Commission, *Telephone number portability* (London: HMSO, 1995), *Oftel News*, no. 39, March 1998, 5; number portability became a licence condition for all public telecommunications operators by 1998.

[39] For details, see Oftel, *Annual Reports* and Oftel, *Competition Bulletins*, which began in the mid-1990s; the number and range of measures increased in the 1990s.

[40] BT took a 20 per cent stake in MCI in 1993, established an alliance named 'Syncordia', and later broadened as 'Concert' and in 1996 sought to buy the remaining 80 per cent in MCI, against the opposition of AT&T—see D. Elixmann, and H. Hermann, 'Strategic Alliances in the Telecommunications Service Sector: Challenges for Corporate Strategy', *Communications & Stratégies*, 24 (1996), 57–88 and *Independent* 1.4.96 and 2.4.96; *Sunday Times* 3.11.96, *Independent* 4.11.96; for previous overseas expansion, see *Financial Times* 29.11.91.

[41] Interviews, BT, Oftel, DTI; Oftel, Annual Report 1996, 102; M. Thatcher, 'Regulatory Reform and Internationalization in Telecommunications', in J. E. S. Hayward (ed), *Industrial Enterprise and European Integration* (Oxford: OUP, 1995).

share' in BT in 1997, licensed US companies as fixed-line network operators (including AT&T in 1994), and introduced international resale as part of a policy of reciprocity.[42] It and Oftel lobbied American authorities in support of BT's cause.[43]

The Social Obligations of Network Operators

Both Carsberg and Cruickshank argued that competition was the best method of protecting users and that social needs should be met in ways that encourage competition.[44] Nevertheless, in practice, Oftel acted to limit the effects of competition and to protect certain groups of users and services. Thus, for instance, after 1989, it persuaded BT to encourage schemes for low-spending customers,[45] to introduce alternatives to disconnection for non-payment and to provide services for the disabled, as well as targeting price controls from 1997 on the lowest spending users. It worked to define the scope of universal service, deciding that it included connection to the fixed-line network, the availability of restricted services at low cost and reasonable geographic access to public call boxes across the UK at affordable prices.[46] It undertook detailed measures to protect consumers (for instance, monitoring the quality of service, complaints procedures, and itemized billing) and reached agreements with BT and other network operators over matters such as deposits, customer appointments, codes of practice and call-barring.[47]

Network Operation Finances: Profits, Investment, and Retail Tariffs

In early 1990s, Oftel pursued its approach of using its powers over BT's licence to regulate directly or indirectly key aspects of BT's financial decisions. Thus, in 1992, a new cap was agreed with BT that covered the period 1993–7. The overall cap was increased to RPI − 7.5 per cent per annum, whilst a sub-cap of RPI + 0 was placed on all services individually, with the exception of rental charges (RPI + 2 per cent per annum); connection charges were also formally

[42] *Independent* 30.3.94 and 9.7.94; Oftel, *Annual Report 1994*, 34.
[43] Interviews, BT, DTI, Oftel.
[44] See e.g. Oftel, *Annual Report 1996*, paragraph 1.4 and Oftel, *Submission by the Director General of Telecommunications to the Department of Trade and Industry Review of Utility Regulation* (London: Oftel, 1997), paragraph 4.19.
[45] Such as the 'low user' and light user' schemes, and the 'lifeline' scheme offering incoming calls only.
[46] Other elements included free emergency services and access to operator assistance, directory information, itemised billing and selective call barring—Oftel, *Universal Service. Statement* (London: Oftel, July 1997); *Universal Telecommunication Services: Proposed Arrangements* (London: Oftel, February 1997); *Universal Telecommunication Services: Proposed Arrangements for Universal Service in the UK from 1997* (London: Oftel, 1995); see also Oftel, *Effective Competition: A Framework for Effective Competition* (London: Oftel, 1994).   [47] See Oftel, *Annual Reports*.

capped.[48] Oftel did not set targets for BT's profits, but in deciding the level of X, it looked at BT's rate of return, future investment, cost of capital, and likely efficiency gains.[49] The extension of tariff licence conditions meant that by the mid-1990s, 64 per cent of BT's revenues were covered by price controls.[50] Moreover, the caps had become increasingly detailed, as sub-caps were placed on individual services.

The mid-1990s saw Oftel, under Don Cruickshank, reverse the trend towards increasingly extensive and specific price controls. In 1996, Oftel and BT agreed to end the specific price cap on residential line rentals (of RPI + 2 per cent), replacing it with reference prices; BT was therefore able to offer a wider range of discount packages, covering both rentals and call charges.[51] The most radical change came in the 1995–6 price review (taking effect in 1997).[52] Using the flexibility of its statutory duties and its powers over licence modification, Oftel was able to alter price control and to link inclusion of the 'fair trading' condition in BT's licence to the altered form of price controls. Oftel argued that high-spending users had 'disproportionally' benefited from previous price controls and were protected because they had access to effective competition.[53] On the other hand, smaller users, notably most residential customers and small businesses, had gained less and still did not enjoy sufficient choice through competition. Oftel therefore, sought to concentrate retail price controls on segments of the market in which competition was weaker. It stated that controls should be ended for other segments in which tariffs were subject to competitive forces, especially since it had new powers under 'fair trading' conditions in operators' licences (which formed part of the agreement with BT on price controls from 1997).[54]

Under the price control agreement, the scope of formal price controls on BT for the period 1997–2001 was reduced. A price cap of RPI − 4.5 per cent applied to BT, but only to its tariffs for residential customers; the cap covered a basket of rental charges and calls based on the spending patterns of the lowest 80 per cent of residential users; hence the reduction in charges would be con-

[48]   See Oftel, *Annual Report 1992*, 12 for a summary; for details, see Oftel, *The Regulation of BT's Prices. A Consultative Document* (London: Oftel, 1992) and Oftel, *Future Controls on British Telecom's Prices: A Statement by the Director General of Telecommunications* (London: Oftel, October 1992).

[49]   Oftel, *Annual Report 1992*, 2–3, Oftel, *Future Control on British Telecom's Prices* (October 1992); interview, Oftel.

[50]   Oftel, *Annual Report 1996*, 3; Oftel, *Statement Pricing of Telecommunications Services from 1997. Oftel's Proposals for Price Control and Fair Trading* (1996).

[51]   See Oftel, *Effective Competition: Framework for Action* (London: Oftel, 1995).

[52]   Oftel issued two consultative documents, both entitled *Pricing of Telecommunications Services from 1997: Consultative Document* (London: Oftel, 1995 and 1996), and then *Pricing of Telecommunications Services from 1997: OFTEL's Proposals for Price Control and Fair Trading* (London: Oftel, 1996).

[53]   See Oftel, *Pricing of Telecommunications Services from 1997: OFTEL's Proposals for Price Control and Fair Trading*, 33.   [54]   Ibid.

centrated on lower-spending users. Moreover, an agreement was sought to ensure that small business users enjoyed reductions in their bills of between RPI − 0 and RPI − 4.5 per cent.[55] The reduced scope of price controls from 1997 meant that only 26 per cent of BT's revenues would be covered. Moreover, Oftel stated that it was 'confident' that effective competition at the retail level was not far away that hence that the 1997–2001 price control would be the last one for BT's retail services.[56] Nevertheless, in setting 'X' at 4.5 per cent, Oftel continued to look at BT's rate of return, and hence at market trends, efficiency gains, asset base, cost of capital and investment—the scope of price control was reduced, but the level of detail was not.[57]

France

The Processes of Policy Making and Overall Pattern of Policy

After the institutional reforms of 1990, significant changes in policy-making processes were seen. Although decisions between 1990 and 1996 remained dominated by France Télécom and the political executive (notably the PTE/ Industry Ministry,[58] the Finance Ministry and Matignon) relations between them altered. There was a clearer separation between France Télécom and the political executive. The participation of elected politicians in France largely ended Télécom's internal organization and its relations with its equipment suppliers; it continued, but in diminished form, over issues which were politically sensitive or required co-operation between France Télécom and the political executive, such as tariffs and internationalization. The duties and objectives given to France Télécom were formalized through two *Contrats de plan* (for 1991–4 and 1995–8),[59] which provided a guiding framework for decisions in practice, in contrast to their predecessor, the 1983 *Charte de gestion*.[60] France Télécom remained dependent on the political executive, but at the same time resisted attempts to use it as an instrument of fiscal and industrial policy, using the *Contrats de plan* as a defence.[61]

---

[55] For details of the complex safeguards, see ibid. 35.   [56] Ibid., paragraph 2.12.

[57] See Oftel, *Pricing of Telecommunications Services from 1997: OFTEL's Proposals for Price Control and Fair Trading*, ch. 6, and interviews, Oftel and BT.

[58] After 1988, the PTT Ministry formed part of the PTE (Postes, Télécommunications et Espace) Ministry; the PTE Minister was under the authority of the Finance Ministry between 1990 and 1991, and then part of the Industry Ministry between 1993 and 1995, and after September 1995. The ministers directly responsible for telecommunications were: Paul Quilès 1988–9; Jean-Marie Rausch 1991–2; Emile Zuccarelli 1992–3; Gérard Longuet (also Industry Minister) 1993–4, José Rossi 1994–5 (also Industry Minister), François Fillon 1995–7.

[59] See A. Delion and M. Durupty, 'La Réforme en suspens du statut de France Télécom', *Revue française d'administration publique*, 73 (1995), 177–81.

[60] Interviews, France Télécom, PTE Ministry.

[61] Interviews, France Télécom, PTE Ministry; for conflicts between Michel Bon and the Minister, see *La Tribune Desfossés* 4.10.95.

Changed relations were most marked between France Télécom and the unit within the PTE Ministry responsible for regulation—the DRG (Direction de Réglementation Générale) and its successor after 1993, the DGPT (Direction Générale de la Poste et des Télécommunications). The DRG (established in 1989, as successor to the Mission à la Réglementation) and the DGPT were both headed by a respected telecommunications expert, Bruno Lasserre. Before 1990, the DRG had been 'invisible';[62] after 1990, it became a driving force in decision making, whereas France Télécom's role in the PTE Ministry greatly diminished. It enjoyed a strong degree of independence from both France Télécom and the PTE Minister.[63] Most of its members were formerly staff within France Télécom.[64] Yet relations between the DRG/DGPT and France Télécom were marked by a sharp separation; indeed, often there was a 'conflictual dialectic' and discussions could be 'very sharp'.[65] For its part, the DRG/DGPT sought a reputation for impartiality, publishing documents outlining its thinking, holding public hearings and consultations, and turning to experts outside France Télécom for advice.[66]

The overall direction of policy was established in the shadow of institutional reform, notably the end of France Télécom's monopoly over network operation and the battle over modification of France Télécom's *statut* (see Ch. 7). The prospect of competition led to a marked modification in priorities compared with the 1980s. The use of France Télécom as an instrument available to the political executive for fiscal and industrial its policies gradually gave way to preparing France Télécom to face competition. The political executive increasingly behaved 'as a shareholder', keen to safeguard the value of its asset.[67] Thus it aided or allowed France Télécom to undertake internationalisation, tariff rebalancing and debt reduction. *Service public* remained an important concept, but was to be reconciled with competition and would be protected through legislation setting out the regulatory framework rather than France Télécom remaining an *administration*, available for use by the political executive.

Competition

Competition in network operation became accepted as inevitable (both because of technological factors and then EC law), especially after the Right won the

---

[62]   Official, PTE Ministry.

[63]   T. Vedel, 'Information Superhighway Policy in France: The End of High Tech Colbertism?', in B. Kahin and E. J. Wilson III (eds.), *National Information Infrastructure Initiatives* (Cambridge, Mass., and London: MIT Press, 1997), 321 and 328; *La Tribune Desfossés* 13.12.96.

[64]   For example, Lasserre was a former head of the DGT's legal service.

[65]   Quotes, France Télécom senior official; interviews, DRG; For interconnection, see, for instance, comments by Fillon and by Lasserre, *La Tribune Desfossés* 30.11.95.

[66]   e.g. over new rules for competition and interconnection.

[67]   Quote, senior France Télécom official.

1993 legislative elections.[68] Nevertheless, France Télécom's monopoly over fixed-line public voice telephony and network infrastructure continued until 1 January 1998, the last date stipulated by EC law. The main obstacle to increased competition was the desire of policy-makers to protect France Télécom: the maximum time was sought for France Télécom to adapt to new market conditions, through institutional reform but also by tariff rebalancing and internal reorganization.[69]

Moves towards greater competition were gradual. In the early 1990s, the steps were small: a number of private 'teleports' providing transmission via satellites and experimental voice telephony services were licensed by the DGPT; the use of 'alternative infrastructures' (such as cable television networks) for services other than public voice telephony was brought forward, being permitted in 1996 under the law of July 1996 rather than 1997 as required by European law;[70] in 1993, Longuet authorized mobile operators to use private networks for transmission in addition to their mobile networks, with SNCF obtaining a licence for its private network in 1995.[71] Nevertheless, infrastructure competition was not vigorously promoted; thus when the publicly-owned Caisse des dépôts et consignation sold its cable subsidiary, Com-dev, in 1994, and the government found itself at the centre of a fierce battle between France Télécom and private companies with cable networks, half Com-dev's cable network was sold to France Télécom and the other half to La Lyonnaise des eaux.[72] However, as 1998 approached, the DRG encouraged the need for 'challengers' to France Télécom, notably French companies such as the large multi-utility companies that possessed cable networks (La Compagnie générale des eaux, La Lyonnaise des eaux, and Bouygues) and state-owned utilities that had extensive private networks (the railway company SNCF and the electricity supplier, Electricité de France); these companies made active preparations to enter the telecoms market after 1998, notably the creation of Cegetel, whose major shareholders included Confédération des cadres (CGE) and BT.[73] Finally, in 1996 the PTE Minister explicitly called for at least three generalist network operators to ensure real competition.[74]

The DRG/DGPT also made progress on vital issues of interconnection

---

[68] Interviews; M. Dandelot, *Le Secteur des Télécommunications en France. Rapport au Ministre de l'Industrie, des Postes et Télécommunications et du Commerce Extérieur* (Paris: Ministère de l'Industrie, des Postes et Télécommunications et du Commerce Extérieur, 1994); comments by Longuet, *Les Echos* 10–11.6.94, and F. Fillon, 'Réussir la révolution des télécommunications', *Le Monde* 7.5.96.

[69] *La Tribune Desfossés* 13.3.93; *Les Echos* 2.12.93; *Le Monde* 3.12.93.

[70] This was part of the agreement with the European Commission to approve the 'Atlas' joint venture between France Télécom and Deutsche Telekom—*Les Echos* 10.3.95; *Le Monde* 22.3.95; W. J. Maxwell, 'Regulation and Competition: French Telecommunications Licensing', *Communications et Stratégies*, 22 (1996), 145–60.

[71] *Libération* 18.5.95; *Le Monde* 19.5.95.

[72] *Le Figaro* 1.1.94, 5.1.94; *La Tribune Desfossés* 13.1.94, 3.2.94, and 22.12.94.

[73] *La Tribune* 20.10.92; *La Tribune Desfossés* 13.7.95; *Les Echos* 11.5.95; *Le Figaro Economique* 12.5.95; *Le Monde* 6.9.96.   [74] *La Tribune Desfossés* 8.10.96; *Le Monde* 9.10.96.

and equal access before 1998. The privately-owned mobile operator, SFR, challenged France Télécom's interconnection terms; the DGPT was asked to arbitrate, and its ruling reducing tariffs for leased lines by between 41 per cent and 61 per cent greatly displeased France Télécom, which took the case to the Conseil d'etat; it was followed by further challenges to France Télécom's interconnection charges by other mobile operators.[75] The DGPT argued that interconnection charge should be based on costs, and set up a consultation over leased line costs and an audit of France Télécom's costs, whilst the government created a study to establish appropriate principles for interconnection after 1998 (the Champsaur committee) which recommended use of long-run incremental costs.[76] The DGPT also increased the availability of numbers (by adding a digit to existing numbers) in order to allow 'equal access': network operators would have a special prefix, so that callers would have to choose amongst them without having to dial a special digit to avoid using France Télécom's network by default.[77] Thus, led by the DGPT, France began to prepare for the introduction of competition.

France Télécom's Internal Decisions

After 1990, France Télécom become significantly more autonomous from the political executive in its internal decisions. Its head resisted attempts to force nominations to senior posts, greatly aided by the fact that these were no longer formally decided in the Conseil des ministres.[78] Moreover, senior managers increasingly answered to the Board, established in 1990; in addition to representatives of the political executive, it included specialists from academia, industry, and finance.[79] Even the political executive's ability to choose the head of France Télécom was called into question. In 1995, the PTE Minister, Fillon, wished to replace Marcel Roulet, arguing that the latter was exerting undue pressure for a change in France Télécom's *statut*.[80] After the failure of a first attempt (due to lack of support from Matignon and the Élysée),[81] in September 1995, Fillon, Matignon and the Élysée chose François Henrot to take the top post; he demanded assurances that the *statut* would be rapidly modified, and, failing to obtain these, resigned after one week.[82] He was replaced by Michel Bon (head of the ANPE, a former businessman and not an *ingénieur des télécommunications*), who was disliked by the unions; his nomina-

[75] DGPT, *Rapport Annuel 1994*, 45; *Le Figaro-Economique* 7.6.94; *Le Figaro* 18.10.94; *La Tribune Desfossés* 15.11.95; the legal case was still proceeding in 1998.
[76] DGPT, *Rapport Annuel 1995*, 15–16; *Les Echos* 14.11.96.
[77] *Les Echos* 16.9.96; *Financial Times* 18.10.96; *Les Echos* 18.10.96.
[78] Interviews, France Télécom.
[79] *La Tribune de l'Expansion* 17.12.90; interviews, France Télécom.
[80] *Libération* 7.7.95; *Le Monde* 12.7.95.
[81] *Libération* 13.7.95; *Le Nouvel Observateur* 26.7.95.
[82] *Le Monde* 10–11.9.95; *Le Canard Enchaîné* 13.9.95.

tion required a positive vote by a majority of the Board and this was only just achieved.[83]

Staffing within France Télécom began to move away from its traditional administrative form. The composition of senior management changed, with a reduction in the weight of the *ingénieurs des télécommunications*, and the increased recruitment of business school graduates.[84] France Télécom undertook a comprehensive regrading of staff between 1990 and 1994, designed to move away from a complex system of 110 grades to one of posts based on functions; the reforms were undertaken in the face of considerable staff anxiety and occasional strikes, and despite the fact that they concerned civil servants.[85] In 1995–6, France Télécom's management negotiated an early retirement scheme, both as part of agreement on the change in the *statut* and because of its worries about an ageing workforce, overcoming opposition from the Ministry of the Budget.[86]

France Télécom's relations with its equipment suppliers also became less a matter of industrial policy and more one of commercial relations.[87] The political executive played little role in the allocation of France Télécom's orders or in Alcatel's internationalization strategy. Orders to companies other than Alcatel increased, including those to non-French suppliers.[88] When allegations of financial impropriety involving overcharging of France Télécom by Alcatel emerged in 1993, the method of allocating orders began to alter, away from three-year contracts that largely guaranteed the division of orders, with the vast majority being held by Alcatel, and towards competitive tenders.[89]

Although France Télécom continued to serve as a source of funds for fiscal purposes and industrial policy, these functions were increasingly opposed by France Télécom. In December 1992, its Board agreed to purchase part of the government's share of Thomson.[90] This was followed by France Télécom again purchasing government shares in two insurance companies, AGF and UAP.[91] The decisions brought sharp condemnation from trade unions and the Right, and France Télécom resisted pressure to increase its share in Thomson and Bull.[92] However, the political executive had to negotiate the moves with Marcel

[83] *Les Echos* 11.9.95; *Le Monde* 13.9.95; *Le Nouvel Observateur* 14.9.95.

[84] Interview, France Télécom; one example was the 'atypical' nomination of the head of human resources in 1991 who was not a member of the *corps des ingénieurs des télécoms* and against the desires of the Ministry of Finance—*La Tribune de l'Expansion* 28.11.91.

[85] Y. Landreau, 'Negotiating Structural and Technological Change in the Technological Services in France', in B. Bolton (ed.), *Telecommunications Services: Negotiating structural and Technological Change* (Geneva: ILO, 1993); *La Tribune Desfossés* 18.1.94; *Le Monde* 27.1.94; *La Tribune Desfossés* 31.1.94.

[86] *La Tribune Desfossés* 18.1.95; *Les Echos* 25.4.96 and 30.4.96.

[87] Interviews, France Télécom, PTE Ministry.

[88] *Les Echos* 26.1.95; *Le Monde* 22.3.91; *La Tribune Desfossés* 26.7.95.

[89] *Les Echos* 16.12.94; *Le Figaro* 12.1.95.   [90] *Le Monde* 25.12.92.

[91] *Les Echos* 1.2.93; *Le Monde* 31.1.93.   [92] *Les Echos* 1.2.93 and *Le Figaro* 2.2.93.

Roulet, who insisted on France Télécom obtaining shares, which it could sell later.[93] When France Télécom became liable for taxes on its profits in 1994, the special levies (*prélèvements*) begun in the 1980s, were altered to 'dividends' to the government.[94] France Télécom was able to defend itself against financial burdens by pointing to increased competition and the objectives of the *Contrat de plan*; its capacity to resist new obligations imposed by the political executive grew, and plans by Edith Cresson as Prime Minister (1991–2) to return to an industrial policy based on France Télécom finance and orders, failed.[95]

France Télécom's Commercial Strategy

Faced with the prospect of competition within France from 1998, France Télécom adopted a two-pronged strategy, which it led, but in which it enjoyed co-operation with the political executive. First, it accelerated its move away from the behaviour of a traditional French *administration*, whilst waiting for a change in its *statut*. Modernization of the network, notably the use of optical fibre, was oriented towards the needs of firms.[96] Quality of service became an explicit target, forming part of the *Contrat de plan* for 1995–8, together with the creation of client 'charters';[97] the DGPT became responsible for monitoring France Télécom's performance.[98]

To offset potential losses of its domestic market and to capture the expanding demand for transnational services, the second element in France Télécom's strategy was to internationalize. Overseas expansion was an objective in France Télécom's *Contrat de plan* for 1995–8 which also aimed to raise the operator's foreign income from 3 per cent in the mid-1990s to 10 per cent by the year 2000.[99] One method was to take holdings in overseas operators; it did so, notably in Argentina and Mexico. However, the main route was through international alliances. France Télécom's key partner was Deutsche Telekom; its feared opponents were BT and, within France, Alcatel, which wished to take a stake in France Télécom, a move fiercely opposed by the latter.[100] Deutsche Telekom and France Télécom formed a joint venture for value-added network

---

[93] Interviews, France Télécom and PTE Ministry; in 1996, France Télécom indicated that it wished to sell its holdings in both Bull and Thomson—*Le Monde* 18.7.96.

[94] *Les Echos* 22.1.95 and *Le Figaro-Economique* 10.9.96.

[95] Interviews, France Télécom/senior civil servants.   [96] *Le Figaro* 25.3.94.

[97] These specified the commitments made by France Télécom, which differed between type of user (residential, professional and firm), and new complaints procedures.

[98] DGPT, *Rapport Annuel 1995*, 85–7; *La Tribune Desfossés* 29.3.95.

[99] Delion and Durupty, 'La Reforme en suspens du statut de France Télécom', 178–9; A. Mouline, 'Les Stratégies internationales des opérateurs des télécommunications', *Communications & Stratégies*, 21 (1996), 77–93, 85–6.

[100] *Quotidien de Paris* 2.7.93; *Le Figaro* 5.8.93, interview with Charles Rozmaryn, Directeur Général of France Télécom, *01 Informatique*, 12.11.93; *Le Monde* 28.12.93.

services in 1992 (Eunetcom),[101] followed by a joint venture for an international network of leased lines and 'global services' ('Atlas').[102] American partners were also sought. Attempts to woo MCI in 1993 were unsuccessful (it chose an alliance with BT, in large measure because of France Télécom's institutional position) and discussions with AT&T did not yield results. However, in 1995 France Télécom and Deutsche Telekom established a strategic alliance (Phoenix, renamed Global One), with joint ventures for international services and networks; they also bought minority stakes (7.5 per cent each) in the American operator, Sprint, in 1996.

France Télécom led efforts at internationalization, but depended on co-operation by the political executive, which played a direct role in its strategy and offered active support. France Télécom had to justify its investment in South America to the political executive, notably the Finance Ministry, whose permission was needed for large investment.[103] The alliance with Deutsche Telekom was approved by ministers of both countries and, indeed, by President Mitterrand and Chancellor Kohl.[104] However, it depended on the political executive introducing institutional reform of France Télécom to allow cross-holdings; indeed, privatization was explicitly demanded by the Germans.[105] Furthermore, the joint ventures between France Télécom and Deutsche Telekom had to obtain approval by regulatory authorities, and in particular, by the European Commission. The French government lobbied the latter to approve the Atlas joint venture; moreover, to obtain agreement, it introduced liberalization of alternative infrastructures in 1996, earlier than was required.[106] Similarly, the joint venture with Sprint needed regulatory approval in the United States (notably from the Federal Communications Commission) and faced opposition; French Ministers went to Washington and in discussions with the FCC, argued (or promised) that the French market was being opened to fair and effective competition, with an independent regulator and that France Télécom's capital would be opened to private investors.[107]

Network Operation Finances

The prospect of competition spurred France Télécom to prepare itself financially. The 1990s saw a shift in policy priorities: higher profits and especially debt reduction came to the fore, whereas less importance was attached to investment. The shift took place in the first *Contrat de plan* for 1991–4, which established a target for debt to fall from 122 billion francs in 1991 to 104 billion in 1994, with the costs of financing it to decline from 11 to 7 per cent of

---

[101] *Libération* 12.3.92; *La Tribune de l'Expansion* 13.3.93 and 17.9.93
[102] *Financial Times* 8.11.93; *Les Echos* 8.11.93; *Le Monde* 9.11.93.
[103] Interviews, France Télécom.   [104] *La Tribune Desfossés* 2.12.93, 29.3.95.
[105] Dandelot, *Le Secteur des Télécommunications en France*; *Le Monde* 1.12.93; see also ch. 7.
[106] *Les Echos* 10.3.95; *Le Monde* 22.3.95.   [107] *La Tribune Desfossés* 15.6.94, 4.12.95.

turnover.[108] The importance attached to reducing debt thus began under the
Left before 1993, when it did not envisage privatization of France Télécom.
The *Contrat de plan* for 1995–8 confirmed the altered priorities: by setting objectives in 1998 of 70 billion francs of debt and financial costs of only 3 per cent
of turnover.[109] Increasingly, comparisons were made between France Télécom
and what became seen as its rivals, especially BT; France Télécom's senior
management pressed hard to strengthen its financial position and achieve the
same levels of debt and financial costs.[110]

One reason for declines in debt was that lower priority was given to investment. Although capital spending remained very high (France Télécom was the
largest or second largest investor in France), capital expenditure experienced
declines in the early 1990s. France Télécom sought to 'target' its investment
expenditure.[111] When a report by Gérard Théry suggested a *grand projet*
approach to create information superhighways for all users through large-scale
spending by France Télécom (francs 5–10b. per annum for 20 years),[112] France
Télécom strongly opposed being obliged to spend large sums on a project that
did not offer clear profits for it and instead emphasized the need to reduce its
debt; Théry's proposal was swiftly rejected in favour of a more limited, experimental approach.[113]

Tariff policy saw an acceleration of rebalancing.[114] France Télécom was able
to implement large-scale changes, even though higher rental and local call
charges were largely borne by residential users (proportionally) and indeed
resulted in some residential users facing increases in their telephone bills.[115] One
reason was that although it was given price caps in the *Contrats de plan* (of 3
per cent per annum declines in real terms between 1991 and 1994, and then
between 4.5 per cent and 6 per cent per annum for 1995–8), these were only
for its overall tariffs, covering the entire basket of services.[116] Within this target,
charges for long distance and international calls were reduced very sharply,
whereas rentals and some local tariffs were increased. Changes were large and
frequent.[117] The process was led by France Télécom, but involved the political

[108] Delion and Derupty, 'La Réforme en suspens du statut de France Télécom', 180; *Le Monde* 7.11.91.
[109] *Les Echos* 30.5.94; *La Tribune Desfossés* 29.3.95.
[110] *Le Figaro* 1.7.93; *La Tribune Desfossés* 21.12.93; interviews, France Télécom and PTE Ministry.
[111] *Les Echos* 30.5.94   [112] See Ch. 10.
[113] *Libération* 29.9.94; *Le Monde* 24.10.94; *La Tribune Desfossés* 26.10.94; *Le Monde* 9.12.94, 2.3.95.
[114] M. Rogy, 'Price Cap Regulation in European Telecommunications', *Communications & Stratégies*, 15 (1994), 47–75, 58–9.
[115] *La Tribune Desfossés* 24.12.92; *Le Monde* 14.7.93; *La Tribune Desfossés* 29.12.93; *Les Echos* 19.1.96; *La Tribune Desfossés* 9.1.96; *Les Echos* 30.8.96; DPGT, *Rapport Annuel 1994*, 61.
[116] *La Tribune Desfossés* 29.3.95.
[117] For instance, reductions in international tariffs took place twice in 1993, whereas local tariffs were restructured in January 1994, generally increasing local costs and decreasing national and

executive. Thus, for instance, the Finance Ministry delayed rebalancing in 1992 in order to limit effects on the retail price index and because of forthcoming parliamentary elections whilst increases in rentals were considered by the Prime Minister personally and were restricted because of their political sensitivity.[118] In January 1994, a major reform of tariff structures was introduced; it was only accepted by Balladur because there were no immediate elections.[119] Nevertheless, ministers facilitated rebalancing by imposing only an overall price target, whilst the DRG/DGPT supported the move towards cost-based prices.[120] France Télécom decided price changes, and justified them on the grounds of needing to be competitive, with prices being brought closer to costs and being comparable with those of other European and North American network operators, who were seen as competitors.

Social Objectives

The development of competition in network operation led to a debate about its compatibility with *service public*, notably universal service, cross-subsidisation of users and services, and regional development.[121] France Télécom pressed for greater freedom to set tariffs according to costs, and hence to end 'equality of tariffs' (the same tariffs for the same service, regardless of the location and type of user) and cross-subsidization.[122] In contrast, trade unions and opponents of competition and institutional reform claimed that *service public* was under threat.[123] In response, ministers argued that competition could be reconciled with *service public* by further defining its content, imposing obligations on France Télécom, and ensuring that competitors paid compensatory sums to France Télécom.[124] Nevertheless, little detailed work was done before 1996; the only significant step was that, in the face of continued rebalancing and following a request by the DGPT, France Télécom instituted a scheme offering reductions in rental charges for low users.[125] The framework of key social obligations (and methods of paying for them) such as universal service, regional development and emergency services were only defined in the laws of 1996, with the details being established thereafter by decree and by the new regulatory authority, the ART.[126]

---

international ones *La Tribune Desfossés* 24.12.92 and 17.12.93—*Libération* 28.12.93; *La Tribune Desfossés* 29.12.93; further sharp reductions in trunk and international calls followed in 1996—*Les Echos* 19–20.1.98; *La Tribune Desfossés* 9.7.96.

[118] *La Tribune de l'Expansion* 5.8.92; *Libération* 15.1.94; interviews, France Télécom/senior civil servants.

[119] Interviews, France Télécom.   [120] DGPT, *Rapport Annuel 1994*, 60.

[121] *Le Monde* 1.1.95.   [122] *Le Monde* 10–11.12.95.   [123] *Les Echos* 9.1.96.

[124] See interview with Fillon, *Le Figaro* 2.10.95; *Les Echos* 4.10.95.

[125] DGPT, *Rapport Annuel*, 60, 64–5; *Les Echos* 19–20.1.96; interview, senior official, PTE Ministry.   [126] See Ch. 7.

Conclusion

French policy making in network operation between 1990 and 1996 altered significantly compared with the 1970s and 1980s, leading to a narrowing of differences with Britain. Changes in the institutional framework in France in 1990, especially the reform of France Télécom's *statut* that gave the operator an independent legal and organizational identity and separated it from the PTE Ministry, contributed to new patterns of policy making. Nevertheless, dissimilarities continued to exist between Britain and France in the processes and instruments of policy making and in substantive decisions. These dissimilarities can be linked to the institutional contrasts between the two countries that persisted between 1990 and 1996 (ownership of the network operator, the presence of an independent industry regulator and the distribution of powers among public bodies).

Study of the processes of policy making reveals the impact of institutional arrangements both on national patterns and cross-national differences. In Britain, the division of roles largely followed the 1984 Telecommunications Act. The DTI set the general framework of competition through its licensing powers, but did not participate in BT's internal decision making; it respected Oftel's independence. As a specialist sectoral regulator, Oftel played a central role. It applied its institutional powers of licence enforcement and modification, notably its ability to make a reference to the MMC if a licence modification was not agreed with a supplier. Its activity remained focused on BT as the dominant vertically-integrated operator. Oftel exploited its discretion under the 1984 Telecommunications Act to establish new, more open decision-making procedures. In France, the reforms of 1990 inaugurated a greater separation between the PTE Ministry and France Télécom in policy making. The duties of France Télécom were formalized and the political executive's role in its internal decision making diminished. Within the PTE Ministry, the DRG/DGPT developed a relationship with France Télécom that was frequently conflictual; it also sought to appear impartial and made policy making somewhat more open. The limited institutional detachment of France Télécom from the political executive was thus reflected in practice. As a result, differences in the processes of decision making with Britain became a little less marked. Nevertheless, important dissimilarities remained that reflected organizational contrasts between the two countries. Thus, as a publicly-owned supplier, France Télécom's autonomy from elected politicians was much smaller than BT's. Similarly, the DGPT was less separate from other parts of the political executive than Oftel from the British government, a situation that matched the institutional arrangements whereby the DGPT was a unit within the PTE Ministry and not an independent regulator.

Analysis of substantive policy decisions (competition, the network operators' strategies, internal life, and industrial functions, and the treatment of social obligations) reveals evolution in Britain, but following the same path as that taken after 1984. The promotion of competition continued to be central to British policy. Thus extensive liberalization took place after 1990, so that by 1996 the entire network operation subsector was open to competition. The government maintained its non-interventionist approach to BT's internal decision making, albeit that it provided support for BT's internationalization; Oftel continued to regulate service delivery through licence conditions. As network operation was increasingly liberalized, Oftel took measures that were designed to ensure effective competition and to move away from detailed licence *ex post* regulation; in particular, it modified interconnection terms, introduced 'fair trading' licence conditions and, in the mid-1990s, reduced the scope of retail price regulation. The regulation of social policy obligations was considered in detail during the 1990s, particularly by Oftel, which sought to ensure that they did not damage the development of competition.

Policies in France saw significant changes compared with those pursued before 1990, that reduced differences with Britain. Ending France Télécom's monopoly in network operation was accepted as inevitable and/or beneficial. Compared with the 1970s and 1980s, France Télécom enjoyed greater autonomy from elected politicians and the political executive found it more difficult to control France Télécom, as the operator offered increased resistance to being used as a source of funds for ministries. Instead, more indirect methods of steering were applied, notably through the *Contrats de plan* which established a framework for France Télécom. The operator, for its part, moved increasingly away from its traditional operating style as an *administration* within the civil service and towards that of a firm facing competition. Staffing changed, and the power of the traditional elite in telecommunications, the *corps des ingénieurs des télécommunications*, fell; conversely, the role of senior staff with a business background grew, increasing the similarities with BT. Moreover, in sharp contrast to the 1970s and most of the 1980s, relations between France Télécom and its equipment suppliers saw little role for the political executive; instead, they became increasingly commercial.

Whilst significant, the changes in France involved important elements of continuity and did not end the considerable dissimilarities with policy in Britain. Thus, for instance, full competition in network operation was only undertaken in 1998, later than in Britain. No equivalent framework for regulating competition to that developed by Oftel was put in place, leaving future entrants very dependent on the detailed decisions of the new regulatory body established after 1997, the ART. The political executive remained directly involved in France Télécom's decisions over internationalization and tariffs, and still sought to use it as a policy tool for its wider industrial policy. Unlike Britain in the 1990s, retail price controls were broad, allowing extensive rebalancing, whilst the treatment of social policy objectives remained implicit, with little detail concerning the scope and methods of financing *service public* and their compatibility with competition.

Policy developments in both Britain and France were related to the institutional frameworks in each country. Although organizational stability existed after 1990, the evolution of policy in Britain was possible thanks to the flexibility of the arrangements established in 1984. In particular, Oftel exploited its institutional powers and discretion over licence modifications to alter interconnection charges or the regulation of anti-competitive behaviour. Policy changes in France were much greater; they were linked to the institutional reforms of 1990. The separation of France Télécom and the PTE Ministry and the creation of the DGPT were important for the extension of competition: the DGPT played an active role in promoting liberalization and prepared the ground for competition to be effective (for example, over cost-based interconnection charges and numbering changes for equal access). France Télécom's new *statut* was followed by a restructuring of its internal practices and its relations with elected politicians and its suppliers; the operator achieved greater distance from the political executive and moved towards operating as a commercial firm. Reflecting its new institutional position and the imminent ending of its monopoly, as well as the desire of its senior management to form international alliances and achieve some form of privatization,[127] France Télécom also reshaped its financial priorities: in another marked break with the policies of the previous two decades, it moved away from long-established objectives of maximizing investment and towards aims of reduction of debt and financial costs, increased profitability, and continuous large-scale tariff rebalancing.

The substantial policy contrasts that remained between Britain and France after 1990 were linked to continuing cross-national institutional dissimilarities. The more direct and extensive role taken by the political executive in France Télécom's internal decisions compared with that of the British government reflected public ownership of the former. Similarly, organizational features in each country played a part in liberalization taking place later and more slowly in France than Britain. BT was a private company that had had several years to adjust to competition, whilst Oftel acted as an agent of change, pressing for liberalization, offering advice and shaping opinion. France Télécom was a publicly-owned organization only beginning to move away from its long history as an *administration*, whilst the DRG/DGPT was only a newly-established unit within the PTE Ministry. Similar organizational factors applied to the application of narrower and more focused price controls in Britain than in France: BT had had time to rebalance tariffs and faced competition, whereas France Télécom was preparing to face entrants and needed a broader price cap to

---

[127] See Ch. 7.

continue to restructure its prices. The development of only a limited regulatory framework for competition and social policy in France compared with Britain largely arose from the fact that the DGPT could only begin the task of regulating competition, given that France Télécom's monopoly remained largely intact in network operation, that it did not possess Oftel's powers over licence modification and that crucial decisions over interconnection and *service public* were to be defined by the laws of 1996 rather than being left to its discretion.

Thus the institutional framework of telecommunications left its imprint in the 1990s, despite technological and economic pressures and the development of an increasingly intrusive supranational regulatory environment. The role of institutions was seen in three related ways that support national institutionalist arguments linking organizational arrangements and policy making. First, specific institutional features such as ownership of the network operator, the existence of an independent regulator and the distribution of regulatory powers influenced policy patterns. Second, policy changes offer important evidence for the impact of institutions. The reforms of 1990 in France contributed to a modification of policies, an argument supported by evidence under the first heading showing how new institutional features affected decision making. In Britain, institutional stability was matched by strong continuities in policy but also a degree of evolution. Its experience indicates that policies are not static within a set organizational framework; nevertheless, the policy developments followed the same direction as taken after 1984, were made possible by institutional arrangements and were marked by those arrangements. Cross-national comparison offers the third source of evidence for the role of national institutions. Following the institutional changes in France in 1990 that brought the two countries somewhat closer, the alterations in policy making in France saw a narrowing of differences with Britain. At the same time, substantial dissimilarities in policy making persisted that related to continuing institutional contrasts. Despite the increasingly powerful forces for convergence in the 1990s, differing institutional frameworks played their part in ensuring that policy in network operation in Britain and France between 1990 and 1996 was not the same.

10

Policy Making in a New Field of Telecommunications: Advanced Networks and Services and Customer Premises Equipment from the Late 1970s to the Mid-1990s

From the late 1970s onwards, technological and economic developments allowed the practical and commercial development of advanced networks and services, used with suitable customer premises equipment. They thereby transformed the nature of the subsector from being an insignificant adjunct to network operation to a diverse, rapidly-expanding field of telecommunications, often at the cutting edge of 'new technology' for firms and residential users. As with network operation, the subsector was subject to powerful transnational forces for change that challenged traditional policies, notably monopoly supply by PTOs. However, its technological and economic characteristics were very dissimilar. Its size, cost structure, network characteristics, relationship with networks, and range of products all differed from network operation: it was largely a new subsector, it was closely linked with computing and sometimes broadcasting, its services and users were highly diverse and it was not a natural monopoly.[1] Moreover, pressures from the international regulatory environment (notably liberalization in the US and from the extension of EC law) arose earlier than in network operation. Thus advanced networks and services and CPE offer a field with very different characteristics to network operation to test the influence of national institutions on policy making in the face of powerful transnational pressures.

The period from the late 1970s until 1996 is examined, thereby covering institutional changes in Britain in the 1980s and those in France in 1990. The impact of institutional arrangements is revealed in three ways. First, the role of specific institutional features in producing policy patterns within each country is analysed. Second, the effects of institutional change on patterns within each country are studied. Third, cross-national comparison shows how increasing

---

[1] See Ch. 3.

institutional divergence between Britain and France in the 1980s was followed by policy divergence, and then that the reduction in such institutional dissimilarities after 1990 led to a lessening of policy disparities without causing them to disappear.

Advanced services and networks became a highly diverse group in the 1980s and 1990s, ranging from simple services for residential users available with ordinary handsets to very specialized services requiring expensive customer equipment or usable in conjunction with computers. Six key areas are therefore selected as examples, chosen for their importance and as diverse illustrations of policy: broadband networks; leased lines and specialized networks; videotex services and other 'value-added' network services (VANS); satellite services; public mobile telephony and paging networks/services; customer premises equipment (CPE).

Britain

Decision-Making Processes and General Policy

Until 1981, the Post Office had a monopoly over the supply of all services and CPE that could be attached to its network. Although it was empowered by the 1969 Post Office Act to license other suppliers, it only authorized highly specialized CPE and advanced services. Under the 1981 British Telecommunications Act, the Secretary of State obtained the power to issue licences. He used his new position to begin a process of extending competition. However, BT strongly opposed liberalization and the government, lacking detailed technical expertise, was only able to introduce limited change.

After the institutional reforms of 1984, patterns of policy making altered considerably: the Secretary of State set the general framework of policy (notably by using his licensing power), BT became a regulated supplier operating under a licence and the role of other parties (new suppliers and users) grew. Oftel became the most important body in regulating competition and the supply of services. It offered expert advice to the DTI, especially on the licence conditions needed for competition to be effective and on the potentially controversial task of awarding licences when only a limited number were available.[2] It enforced and modified licence conditions, particularly those of BT.

The pursuit of competition was at the core of policy after 1984. BT's monopolies were ended and licences were granted for services and CPE. Entry was encouraged by attempts to remove restrictive licence conditions and the gradual replacement of individual licences with class licences and general approvals. Measures were taken to ensure that competition was effective and

---

[2] Interviews Oftel, DoI/DTI officials.

230 INSTITUTIONS AND POLICY MAKING 1980–1997

'fair', through licence conditions. Although BT's market share of advanced services and CPE diminished after 1984, regulation was concentrated on its licence due to concerns about possible abuse of its position as a vertically-integrated supplier. BT's licence contained several important conditions affecting competition in the supply of advanced services and CPE:

- users and other suppliers of services and CPE had the right of connection or use of BT's network (conditions 14 and 15);
- BT could not exercise 'undue preference or undue discrimination' (condition 17);
- cross-subsidisation of BT's VANS and CPE businesses from other parts of the company was prohibited (condition 18);
- separated accounts for BT's Systems Business (covering many 'other services and networks') and CPE supply had to be instituted from April 1987 (condition 20);
- BT could not show preferential treatment in the supply of services for customers using CPE supplied by it (condition 22);
- linked sales of services or CPE were banned, as were exclusive dealing arrangements for CPE supply (conditions 35 and 36).

Policy was largely limited to the regulation of competition. Co-ordinated large-scale programmes involving public-private co-operation, to supply services, create unified networks, stimulate demand for services and CPE, or to link the supply of telecommunications services with other related sectors were avoided. Competition was given priority, even at the expense of the interests of existing suppliers, especially equipment manufacturers and, increasingly, BT.

Creating a National Broadband Network

Modernization of the telecommunications network offered the technological possibility of creating a national broadband network or 'information superhighway', composed of optical fibre, and able to transmit telecommunications services, cable television and new services. Pressures for a co-ordinated plan to develop such a network existed throughout the 1980s and 1990s. Yet institutional factors acted as important obstacles to an overall plan for a national network.

In the early 1980s, BT lobbied for the creation of an integrated national broadband network. Ministers, especially the Information Technology Minister at the DoI 1981–3, Kenneth Baker, appeared sympathetic.[3] However, responsibilities were divided between the Home Office (broadcasting) and the DoI/DTI (telecommunications) and the former was concerned to ensure diver-

[3] Interview, DoI/DTI; *Financial Times* 17.5.82, 19.5.82, and 19.6.82.

sity in cable provision and protection of the BBC and ITV.[4] Furthermore, building a broadband network required massive investment, which was unlikely to be accommodated within BT's external financing limit.[5] As a result, policy separated telecommunications and cable development. Thus a 1982 report by the Information Technology Advisory Panel (ITAP), a unit within the Cabinet Office, recommended that cable networks should be financed by private funds; it rejected a publicly-funded network led by BT.[6] The Home Office also established a committee, chaired by Lord Hunt; its report in 1982 largely followed the views expressed by ITAP, recommending that cable networks capable of offering multi-channel television should be allowed to proceed with a minimum of regulation.[7] The ensuing White Paper in 1983[8] and the 1984 Cable and Broadcasting Act contained no plans for an integrated network. Instead, franchises to build and own networks were to be awarded to private cable operators, who could choose the type of cable (coaxial or optical fibre) and the form of the network.

After 1984, pressures for a concerted plan for a national broadband network persisted. The Peacock Report on the future of broadcasting,[9] recommended that BT and Mercury be allowed to act as a national 'common carrier' with a cable grid, but that there be competition in the provision of services, and that BT be banned from owning local cable franchises. BT claimed that Britain risked falling behind in modernization and argued that it should be allowed to transmit television programmes in order to make an optical fibre network more commercially viable.[10] The Government's Advisory Council for Science and Technology and the House of Commons Trade and Industry Select Committee warned of the lost opportunities if no co-ordinated plan were developed. In 1994, the latter issued a report claiming that Britain risked falling behind in network infrastructure; a national broadband optical fibre network by BT should be encouraged by appropriate regulation, notably by allowing BT to use it to supply telecommunications, broadcasting, and advanced services.[11] Then,

---

[4] *Financial Times* 3.12.82; interview, DoI/DTI; for a more general discussion of the Home Office and media policy in the 1980s, see M. Palmer and J. Tunstall, *Liberating Communications* (Oxford: Basil Blackwell, 1990), and R. Negrine, 'Cable TV in Great Britain', in R. Negrine (ed.), *Cable Television* (London and Sydney: Croom Helm, 1985).

[5] *Financial Times* 28.3.82 and 19.5.82.

[6] Cabinet Office, ITAP, *Cable Systems* (London: HMSO, 1982).

[7] Home Office, *Report of the Inquiry into Cable Expansion and Broadcasting Policy*, Cmnd. 8679 (London: HMSO, 1982).

[8] Home Office, *The Development of Cable Systems and Services*, Cmnd. 8866 (London: HMSO, 1983).

[9] Sir A. Peacock, *Report of the Committee on Financing the BBC*, Cmnd. 9824 (London: HMSO, 1986).

[10] *Independent* 21.9.89 and 23.11.89.

[11] House of Commons Trade and Industry Select Committee, *Optical Fibre Networks*, Third Report, Session 1993–4 (London: HMSO, 1994).

232 INSTITUTIONS AND POLICY MAKING 1980–1997

in the mid-1990s, BT and the Labour Party Leader, Tony Blair developed a plan for an 'information superhighway' which appeared to involve using BT's network for broadcasting in return for BT establishing a national high capacity network, with free connection for public bodies such as schools and hospitals.[12]

However, powerful institutional obstacles militated against a national, co-ordinated plan for a single broadband network, and, in particular, BT's position as a privatized firm, the end of BT's monopoly in telecommunications, and Oftel's position as regulator. BT's and Mercury's 1984 licences prohibited them from delivering cable television programmes on the public switched telephone network.[13] Proposals for a national grid after 1984 met the problems of finance: public subsidies would have to be paid to BT, a private company; alternatively, providing sufficient economic incentive for BT to build such a network appeared to require a licence modification allowing BT to deliver television on the PSTN, a decision which would have given BT enormous power over broadcasting and ran counter to the policy of encouraging greater competition supported by Oftel and the government.[14] The 1991 Duopoly Review decided to maintain the prohibition on BT broadcasting public entertainment services until at least 2001. Instead, a policy of infrastructure competition was followed by both the government and Oftel.[15] Indeed, the Duopoly Review adopted an 'asymmetric' approach in that it allowed cable franchisees to become public telecommunications operators as part of the policy of increasing competition by offering alternative infrastructures, especially in the local network, whilst protecting them from competition in broadcasting in their franchises. More generally, competition among different types of infrastructure was supported. Thus, for instance, a report in 1988 by an advisory DTI committee that included Sir Bryan Carsberg, opposed a co-ordinated plan for a national optical fibre network as incompatible with allowing the market and profitability to determine network development; it argued that competition in the provision both of networks and services should be maximized, without prescribing a particular technology.[16] The need for experimentation and competition among different infrastructure technologies was again underlined by the government in 1994.[17] Oftel argued that the same principles should apply to broadband as had been used for narrowband telecommunications: competition, private finance,

---

[12] *Independent* 6.10.95.

[13] See Schedule 3 (1)(b) of BT's licence for the definition of the 'applicable system' authorized by the licence.

[14] Interviews, DoI/DTI and Oftel; see the discussion in Department of Trade and Industry, *The Infrastructure for Tomorrow* (London: HMSO, 1988) and Palmer and Tunstall, *Liberating Communications*, 308–9.

[15] C. Scott, 'The UK Information Superhighway', *Utilities Law Review*, 6(3) (1995), 70–2.

[16] DTI, *The Infrastructure for Tomorrow*.

[17] DTI, *Creating the Superhighways of the Future: Developing Broadband Communications in the UK*, Cmnd. 2734 (London: HMSO, 1994).

and regulation of dominant suppliers.[18] It opposed an early end to the broad-casting restrictions on BT and supported competition in providing access to the internet and information 'superhighway'.[19]

Leased Lines and Specialized Networks

Leased lines (also known as private circuits) and advanced networks were often used by large users to build private networks and to support value-added networks services. In the early 1980s, BT's supply of private circuits was poor: there were long delays in their provision, particularly for digital lines in the City of London, leading to considerable discontent by business users.[20] BT's approach was to wait for new technology to become available, notably System X digital exchanges. However, after 1984, faced by competition from Mercury and the danger of resale of leased line capacity, this altered.[21] During the mid-1980s, BT targeted large business users, especially in the City of London, offering high speed digital circuit services and a special optical fibre system (Flexible Access System), with much shorter delays in service provision.[22] At the same time, it undertook sharp price rebalancing, with increases for short-distance circuits and for analogue circuits, but price cuts in the highly competitive international circuit market.[23] It concentrated on private circuits: although it launched its PSS packet-switched network in 1981 and began a full integrated services digital network (ISDN) from 1989, with more advanced ISDN services in the early 1990s, no concerted policy to encourage use of these public networks was promoted.

Policy centred on the regulation of BT, and comprised extending competition and preventing BT from abusing its market dominance. Following complaints concerning BT's price rebalancing after 1984 and the quality of BT's private circuits, Oftel launched several investigations of BT's services.[24] It concluded that BT was bringing prices closer to costs, and was not making 'excessive profits'; hence it took no action. After further complaints following BT's March 1988 price rise and a new investigation, Carsberg decided to act, on the grounds that BT's continued market dominance meant that it 'lacked sufficient incentive to provide circuits efficiently', and that customers were receiving a

---

[18] Oftel, *Annual Report 1995*, 41–2; Oftel, *Beyond the Telephone, the Television and the PC* (London: Oftel, 1995).

[19] *Financial Times* 9.1.97.   [20] Ibid. 15.4.80, 24.4.81, and 1.10.82.

[21] Ibid. 22.7.87, and 19.1.88; interview, Oftel.   [22] *Financial Times* 3.3.83 and 18.1.88.

[23] *Financial Times* 25.7.81, 29.8.81, 19.2.85, 5.9.85, 28.7.86, 19.1.88; 29.1.88, and Oftel, *The Control of the Quality and Prices of BT's Private Circuits* (London: Oftel, 1989), 10, for a detailed summary of price rises 1984–9 for various types of circuit.

[24] Notably into 'access lines' (a special type of private circuit) in February 1985, private circuits generally in September 1985 and private circuit prices and returns in 1987–8—see *Financial Times* 19.2.85 and 5.9.85 and Oftel, *Prices of Access Lines and Private Circuits* (London: Oftel, 1986).

poor service.[25] A price cap of the increase in the RPI (RPI – 0) for domestic private circuit prices as a whole was imposed for the period 1989–93; it thus allowed rebalancing between types of circuit. Moreover, BT would have to publish quality of service figures, set targets for quality and introduce a contractual compensation scheme for failure to provide or repair a private circuit within certain time periods. Faced with the threat of a reference to the MMC, BT accepted the amendments to its licence required for the new regulation of private circuits.[26]

In line with residential tariffs, price controls were extended and tightened in the early 1990s.[27] However, as Oftel sought to become a competition authority in the mid-1990s, price controls were reduced. Under the agreement with BT for price controls for 1997–2001, high-capacity inland private circuits were removed from controls, since it was argued that competition existed, whilst subcaps were loosened, in order to permit cost-based tariffs and hence wider competition.[28] Moreover, when complaints were made over BT's ISDN tariffs, which were said to be high, Oftel decided not to place a price cap on the services, but instead ordered BT to end discriminatory and anti-competitive elements to its pricing structure, thereby acting as a 'competition authority.'[29]

Value-Added Network Services

Until 1984, institutional factors constricted the development of policy towards VANS. On the one hand, policy-makers lacked the capacity or the incentives to establish large-scale co-ordinated plans. On the other hand, BT resisted rapid moves towards competition. These two aspects of policy can be illustrated by the examples of public videotex services (VANS) and the general regulation of VANS.

'Interactive videotex' was invented by the Post Office in the 1970s. A mass market was believed to exist for videotex services which seemed to offer the Post Office the advantages of greater use of the telephone network by residential subscribers, entry into the electronics market and a worldwide market, especially if British norms were adopted abroad.[30] The Post Office thus hurried

[25] Oftel, The Control of the Quality and Prices of BT's Private Circuits, paragraph 3.

[26] Interview, Oftel; Financial Times 8.7.88 and 10.10.88.

[27] In 1991, international private circuits were included in the RPI + 0 control and when the formula was renewed for 1993–7, sub-caps were placed on rises for particular types of circuit to prevent abrupt rebalancing—Oftel, Annual Report 1991, 22, Annual Report 1993, 35; Oftel, Statement, Future Controls on BT's Private Circuit Prices (London: Oftel, 1993).

[28] Oftel, Statement, Pricing of Telecommunications Services from 1997. Oftel's proposals for Price Control and Fair Trading (London: Oftel, 1996), paragraphs 5.54–5.63.

[29] Financial Times 10.6.96; Oftel, Annual Report 1996, 60; Oftel, Statement. Pricing of Telecommunications Services from 1997, paragraphs 5.41–5.45.

[30] G. Dang Nguyen and E. Arnold, 'Videotex: Much Ado about Nothing?', in M. Sharp (ed.), Europe and the New Technologies (London: Frances Pinter, 1985) and Financial Times 27.3.79.

to launch its Prestel service in 1979, with the aim of a mass residential market. Services would be provided by it and other suppliers, including private firms.

No co-ordinated plan linking the Post Office, government, manufacturers, and service suppliers was drawn up. Initially, the PO/BT was not closely involved in the supply of terminals, due largely to the PO's belief that the private manufacturers feared that it might enter the equipment market and compete with them; similarly, there was little co-operation between the PO and possible service suppliers. The Post Office and equipment manufacturers aimed for rapid profitability, and no long-term public subsidy. As a result, at first, Prestel services could only be received on modified colour television screens, which cost £1,000 each, charges for rental and usage were high and few services were offered. Prestel failed to meet its objectives: by September in 1981, there were only 13,000 terminals, as against a target of 50,000 by the end of 1980.[31] The DoI's role increased, as it held meetings in 1981 and 1982 with equipment manufacturers, retail firms, broadcasters, and BT.[32] Yet no overall plan whereby BT would supply cheap terminals was drawn up. Prestel remained very small and whilst BT added new services facilities, it also changed strategy to focus on business users, rather than residential ones, abandoning the objective of a mass residential market.[33]

In the early 1980s, the government sought to alter the general regulation of VANS by introducing competition, beginning with advanced services. Before 1980, the Post Office, which was responsible for licensing services under the 1969 Post Office Act, had restricted the number and scope of advanced services in order to protect its own markets.[34] In July 1980, Sir Keith Joseph announced that private firms would be given more freedom to use PO/BT circuits to offer services not currently provided by the PO/BT, for example in data processing. At the same time, he commissioned an independent economic assessment of liberalization of VANS by Professor Michael Beesley. The report recommended removing all restrictions on the use of BT private circuits, and that BT be permitted to set leased line prices and to compete in the supply of VANS.[35] In response, BT lobbied hard against unrestricted resale, but accepted competition in 'real' VANS, seeing them as a source of new business, and hence agreed with the DoI in November 1981 to license services which created 'genuine additional value'.[36]

In October 1982, armed with its new licensing powers under the 1981 British Telecommunications Act, the government issued the first general VANS

---

[31] *Financial Times* 18.9.81.   [32] Ibid. 6.2.81 and 5.2.82.
[33] Ibid. 6.2.81, 27.4.81, and 18.9.81.
[34] P. Gist, 'The Role of Oftel', *Telecommunications Policy*, 14(1) (1990), 26–51.
[35] M. Beesley, *Liberalisation of the use of British Telecommunications network* (London: HMSO, 1981); see ch. 8 for its wider recommendations concerning unrestricted resale of capacity.
[36] Interview, DoI Minister; *Financial Times* 3.7.81 and 4.7.81; Gist, 'The Role of Oftel'.

licence.[37] Competitors to BT obtained the right to supply VANS on BT's network. In order to qualify as a VANS, an operator had to 'enhance' the message of another person, by storing it, distributing it throughout the network, or processing it. VANS covered by the licence included: public videotex services, data communications, e-mail, protocol conversion services, message store, conversion, and forwarding services, and answering services. Nevertheless, important restrictions remained, which left VANS operators dependent on BT and made commercial viability more difficult to achieve; in particular, BT determined the conditions of access to its network, international private circuits could not be used and simple resale of capacity for transmission continued to be prohibited.

After 1984, the policy of 'fair competition' in VANS was pursued more vigorously, with action both by the government and by Oftel. Limits on the supply of VANS were progressively removed. Following criticism of the scope and restrictions of the 1982 VANS licence, the DTI began a long consultation period, in which Oftel and VANS suppliers and users took part. Major suppliers such as IBM, together with Carsberg supported wider competition.[38] The DTI then issued a new, 12-year general value added and data services (VADS) licence in 1987.[39] Competition in the supply of all VANS, except telex, was permitted, including managed data networks and services using international leased lines. The resale of spare capacity of leased lines for data transmission (but not for voice transmission) was allowed. Moreover, another licence issued by the DTI in 1987[40] liberalized the use of 'branch telecommunications systems'[41] to provide VANS and other services for internal network use. Then in 1989, unrestricted resale of leased line capacity was permitted, so that VANS operators could sell spare capacity from their leased lines for voice telephony; a new class licence was therefore issued that covered both networks composed of leased lines and 'private branch systems'.[42] In 1991 resale of international capacity for non-voice telephony was allowed and a new, less restrictive telecommunications services licence (TSL) was issued in 1992.[43] For operators

[37] Department of Industry, *General Licence under section 15(1) for telecommunications systems used in providing value added network services* (London: DoI, 1982).

[38] See *Oftel News* no. 1, December 1985, and no. 2, March 1986; *Financial Times* 10.9.85 and 17.12.85.

[39] DTI, *Class Licence for the running of telecommunications systems providing value added and data services* (London: DTI, 1987).

[40] The Branch Systems General Licence (BGSL), first issued in 1984.

[41] Networks almost entirely on private property and not containing leased lines on the PSTN; they were usually switched by PABXs.

[42] DTI, *Class licence for the running of branch telecommunications systems granted by the Secretary of State for Trade and Industry under Section 7 of the Telecommunications Act 1984* (London: Department of Trade and Industry, 1989).

[43] Oftel, *Annual Report 1992*, 23–4.

of networks not selling services to third parties, individual licences were no longer needed, as a self provision licence (SPL) was issued in 1991. Further, simplified TSL and SPL licences which removed almost all remaining restrictions were issued in 1996.[44]

The licensing system was used to ensure that competition was 'fair and effective'. The first test came in 1984, when BT and IBM proposed to set up JOVE, a 'managed data network', to consist of BT private circuits linked to customers' IBM computers and designed to offer advanced services from e-mail to electronic payments and financial market services. The system would have used IBM's proprietary SNA (Systems Network Architecture) standard, rather than the internationally agreed OSI (Open Systems Interconnection) standards, which are compatible with a range of equipment. Oftel recommended that the Secretary of State refuse a licence, on the grounds that the project would restrict competition and inhibit entry into the VANS market, advice that he followed.[45] Thereafter, licence conditions were used to protect competition. Thus, for instance, the 1987 VADS licence imposed conditions on 'major service providers' of VADS, including a prohibition on anti-competitive conduct, requirements to notify charges to Oftel and a general obligation to use open systems interconnection (OSI) standards.[46] Oftel's activities also involved enforcement of licence conditions, especially those of BT; it concentrated its attention on cross-subsidization, as part of ensuring that competition was 'fair'.[47]

Oftel's activities were primarily centred on competition. Exceptions were rare and even when they occurred, Oftel sought to minimize their scope. Thus, for instance, in the late 1980s, there was public and Parliamentary concern about premium rate services, notably regarding obscenity and misuse of chatlines by children.[48] Although Oftel took action, including referring BT and Mercury's licences to the MMC in 1989, it rapidly reduced its role to regulating competition and informing customers; it transferred responsibilities for issues such as compensation and codes of practice to an independent industry body and promoted 'self-regulation'.[49]

---

[44] Oftel, *Annual Report 1996*, 100.

[45] Interview, Oftel; J. Vickers and G. Yarrow, *Privatization: An Economic Analysis* (Cambridge, Mass.: MIT, 1988).

[46] The provisions on anti-competitive conduct were relaxed in the 1992 BSGL licence revision.

[47] For instance, it issued orders/directions to BT to end cross-subsidization of its VANS operations in 1985 and 1996 and of its managed network services in 1995, and investigated Prestel charges to ensure that they were 'justified in relation to costs'—see Oftel, *Annual Reports* and *Oftel News*, no. 13, June 1989 for details.

[48] *Financial Times* 28.1.88.

[49] For a summary, see L. Woods, 'Regulation of Premium Rate and Similar Services: The Proposals', *Utilities Law Review*, 7(2) (1996), 44–7.

Public Mobile Communications Services and Satellites Services

In 1980, the PO's radio-telephone service was small, over-subscribed, and still manually operated; the PO held a monopoly over satellite services. The following decade saw the extension of competition, even when opposed by BT, as the government used its licensing powers under the 1981 British Telecommunications Act and then the 1984 Telecommunications Act to permit other suppliers to enter the markets. In 1982, Patrick Jenkin (then Secretary of State at the DoI) announced that he would license two rival cellular networks and allocate appropriate radio frequencies. The licences specified that the networks would use an American-based standard; no attempt was made to develop a British standard.[50] Moreover, licence conditions sought to ensure effective competition—for instance, equipment had to be usable on both networks and vertical integration by network operators was prohibited or controlled. One licence was awarded to BT, on condition that it formed a partnership with a private firm; BT established Cellnet, with Securicor taking a 40 per cent stake, but bitterly resented its enforced partnership. Following applications, the government awarded the second licence to a consortium 'Racal-Vodafone', led by Racal Electronics. The government then sought to extend competition by issuing four licences for new one-way 'Telepoint' services in 1988 and three licences for digital two-way PCN personal communications networks (PCN) in 1991. Moreover, the government, on advice from Oftel, decided to exclude BT/Cellnet and Racal from seeking PCN licences in order to increase competition, despite protests by BT and Racal.[51] Competition to BT was also introduced into paging from 1983 by the DTI issuing licences.[52]

Satellite policy also centred on competition. In the early 1980s, attempts to link satellite transmission in telecommunications and broadcasting failed. BT was a member of the 'Unisat' consortium formed to launch a satellite for telecommunications and direct satellite broadcasting (DBS) of television. The DTI was involved in planning, but offered no public money nor sought to lead the project, which collapsed in 1985 when neither the BBC or independent television companies decided to participate.[53] Instead, services saw liberalization from the late 1980s onwards, often in response to international pressures by firms and the US government.[54] The American firm PanAmSat launched the first independent intercontinental telecommunications satellite in 1988 and

---

[50] The TACS (Total Access Cellular System) norm, based on the American AMPS (Advanced Mobile Phone System) standard was used—*Financial Times* 22.2.83 and G. Dang Nguyen, *Analyzing the Competitive Process in a New Industry: Mobile Telephony* (Bretagne: ENST, 1990).

[51] Interviews Oftel, DTI Minister, BT; *The Independent* 21.7.89.

[52] *Financial Times* 20.2.84.

[53] Tunstall and Palmer, *Liberating Communications*, 283–8; *Financial Times* 15.12.83 and 18.1.85.

[54] See I. Komiya, 'Intelsat and the Debate about Satellite Competition', in K. Dyson and P. Humphreys (eds.), *The Political Economy of Telecommunications* (London and New York: Routledge, 1990).

demanded the right to transmit directly to earth stations in Britain, with the supported of the American administration.[55] Lord Young (Trade and Industry Secretary 1986–9) decided to issue six licences for point to multi-point transmission by satellite.[56] Despite the strong opposition of BT, the scope of the licences was widened in 1989 to allow the licensees to transmit to Europe, and also to receive any satellite signal and re-broadcast it.[57] In 1991, a class licence allowing operation of earth stations for voice, data, and image satellites services that did not use the public switched telephone network at either end was issued.[58] Then in 1992 licences were granted that allowed satellite services linked to the public switched telephone network.[59]

Oftel played a key role in the development of competition after 1984. It strongly supported the extension of competition, and offered influential advice on the number of licences to be awarded and which applicants should be selected, an important method of 'depoliticizing' the allocation of licences.[60] Moreover, it regulated competition through the enforcement of licence conditions of network operators (BT and mobile network operators).[61] Reflecting concerns about BT as a vertically-integrated operator, Oftel acted against unfair cross-subsidization in mobile services and undue preference by BT in the provision of private circuits to its own satellite business: it issued Directions that such practices be ended and introduced detailed financial monitoring.[62] Moreover, Oftel investigated complaints of excess profits and poor quality, notably in mobile services and published figures over quality of service.[63]

Customer Premises Equipment

Strong pressures for liberalization of CPE supply developed in the early 1980s. There was fierce business criticism of BT's supply of CPE, particularly PABXs,

---

[55] *Financial Times* 17.2.88; interview, DTI Minister.

[56] *Financial Times* 18.2.88 and 19.2.88.

[57] *Independent* 29.11.89 and 2.12.89; *Oftel News*, no. 15, March 1990.

[58] Oftel, *Annual Report 1991*, 28–9.   [59] Oftel, *Annual Report 1992*, 26.

[60] Interviews, DTI Minister and official, and Oftel; *Independent* 29.11.89; *Oftel News*, no. 15, March 1990; *Financial Times* 4.1.89.

[61] Thus, for instance, it ruled that BT was obliged to provide transmission links ('uplinks') between customers in the UK and PanAmSat's satellite under the new licences, and to connect earth stations to BT's networks; it also agreed procedures with BT, to separate allocation of leased satellite capacity from BT's operational and commercial activities and over the operation of BT's 'signatory affairs office' that allocated space segment reservations—see: Oftel, *Representation on behalf of PanAmSat* (London: Oftel, 1988); *Oftel News*, no. 15, March 1990; Oftel, *Annual Report 1994*, 44; cf. *Annual Report 1995*, 51.

[62] Oftel, *Annual Report 1994*, 30–2; *Annual Report 1995*, 49.

[63] Cf. Oftel, *Quality of Service on the Cellular Networks* (London: Oftel, 1989); Oftel, *Annual Report 1992*, 14–15; *Annual Report 1993*, 59.

which suffered from long delays; the PO merely rented most equipment, refusing to sell it; user associations, such as the Telephone Users' Association, called for the end of the PO's monopoly over the supply of CPE, a position that the Conservatives had supported in Opposition.[64] In July 1980, Sir Keith Joseph announced that the PO's monopoly over the supply of CPE would end over a period of three years, although CPE would have to meet mandatory standards and be licensed.[65] The Government decided that the British Standards Institute (BSI) was to determine the standards, and the British Electro-Technical Approvals Board (BEAB), replaced in 1982 by the newly established British Approvals Board for Telecommunications (BABT), would certify that equipment met these standards, so that the DTI could license it.[66]

Despite the pressures for greater competition, the process of change was slow until 1984. The DoI intervened directly, taking over the approvals process itself in 1982.[67] Liberalization accelerated after 1984, as Oftel rapidly took an active role in CPE regulation. The DTI delegated the responsibility for approving equipment and designating telecommunications standards to Oftel in 1986.[68] Oftel extended competition to types of equipment that remained under BT's monopoly, such as wiring and installing sockets and payphones. Following complaints that the BSI was very slow in setting standards, and that these were too high, Oftel led the process of relaxing mandatory standards for equipment: in 1988 it ended them for equipment attached to private networks; in 1990 restrictions applicable to equipment attached to public networks were loosened; it issued general approvals whereby CPE meeting their requirements did not need individual approval.[69] Moreover, from 1990, BABT became the main body responsible for granting approvals for individual types of CPE.[70] Oftel also acted to ensure that competition was 'fair and effective'. Thus, for instance, it gave influential advice to the DTI in 1986 to refer vertical integration by BT (through a takeover of an equipment manufacturer, Mitel) to the MMC and issued Directions to BT to stop favouring its own equipment manufacturing business in its purchases and to end unfair cross-subsidization of its CPE business.[71]

---

[64] The Times 15.4.80, 21.4.80 and 15.10.80.
[65] Other than the first telephone set, over which BT's monopoly was ended in 1985.
[66] Financial Times 27.11.81 and Oftel News, no. 1, Dec. 1985.
[67] Financial Times 17.2.82 and 28.5.82.
[68] Oftel News, no. 6, March 1987.
[69] Oftel, Statement on the Telecommunications Standards Review Committee (London: Oftel, 1988); Oftel News, no. 16, Oct. 1990; Oftel, Annual Report 1992, 33.
[70] Oftel, Annual Report 1990, 33.
[71] Oftel News, no. 6, March 1987 and Financial Times 26.11.86; Oftel, Annual Report 1991, 23–4 and Annual Report 1995, 48; following the MMC report, the Mitel takeover was approved in 1986, but subject to conditions.

France

Processes of Decision Making and Overall Policy

In the late 1970s and 1980s, decision making was highly closed, being dominated by the interaction between the DGT and members of the political executive. Both were closely involved in choices over which advanced services should be developed and in deciding industrial and commercial strategy, but the DGT depended on the political executive for support. After the institutional reforms of 1990, the two continued to be the central actors in policy making, but their roles became more distinct and the importance of other participants grew. Policy instruments altered, with a move away from direct commands by the political executive to France Télécom and greater use of the *Contrat de plan* and enforcement of France Télécom's licence conditions (*cahiers des charges*). The changes after 1990 reflected France Télécom's new institutional position and the separation of regulation and supply, especially the establishment of a regulatory and policy unit within the PTE Ministry, namely the Direction de la réglementation générale (DRG), reconstituted as the Direction générale des postes et télécommunications (DGPT) in 1994.

General policy until the 1990s involved protection of the DGT's position (especially its monopoly over network operation), encouragement of the use of public networks to supply services and the pursuit of wider policy aims linked to other telecommunications subsectors or to other sectors. The last element often took the form of *grands projets*: the DGT engaged in large-scale investment in pursuit of long-term objectives, including those not directly benefiting itself, such as regional development and the establishment of powerful French firms in expanding markets of the future.[72] The telematics plan was the clearest example, but elements of the *grand projet* approach were found in other advanced services and networks, notably the Cable Plan and mobile communications.

A limited degree of competition was also introduced during the 1980s, but it was only in the 1990s that general policy was significantly modified. Greater emphasis was given to the extension of competition, to its fairness and transparency and to the rights of third parties. The institutional reforms of 1990 were influential in the evolution of policy. As a supplier with its own legal identity, France Télécom operated under a licence whose conditions regulated France Télécom's competitive behaviour and relationship with other suppliers. The DRG/DGPT participated in the allocation of licences and supported the extension of competition.[73] It sought to ensure 'fair competition', developing two complementary regulatory strategies, namely a 'preventative' approach to

[72] For a discussion, see E. Cohen, *Le Colbertisme 'high tech'* (Paris: Hachette, 1992), 96–100.
[73] For instance in satellite services—see DRG, *Rapport d'Activité 1992*, 57.

unfair practices and an *a posteriori* function of dealing with complaints.[74] The former involved insertion of appropriate licence conditions and the establishment by the DGPT of principles of 'fair competition', notably for France Télécom.[75] In particular, licensed service operators had the right to interconnect with France Télécom's network and, if terms could not be agreed, either party could ask the DRG/DGPT to arbitrate. Accounting separation became required for France Télécom's activities in competitive fields and cross-subsidisation for such activities was prohibited.[76] *A posteriori* regulation consisted of enforcement of suppliers' licence conditions, especially those of France Télécom.

With the change in France Télécom's *statut* in 1990 and the progressive ending of its monopoly, policy moved away from the *grand projet* model of development. France Télécom focused on the financial viability of services; the clearest example came in the debate on information superhighways, in which Gérard Théry's attempt to transpose the *grand projet* approach he had used in the 1970s and early 1980s for digital switching and videotex was largely rejected. Even the public rhetoric of elected politicians altered, towards 'liberal leadership'[77] and a 'pragmatic approach' towards information superhighways, involving 'experimentation' and 'modest public action'.[78]

A Broadband Network

Broadband policy offers an excellent illustration of the effects of changing institutional structures on policy, and, in particular, on the strategy of *grands projets*. In 1981–2, the PTT Minister, Louis Mexandeau, in close association with the Elysée and several Ministers (notably Jack Lang, Minister of Culture, and Georges Filoud, Minister of Communications), decided to launch a Cable Plan (*Plan Câble*).[79] The 1982 Cable Plan envisaged that a national broadband and interactive network would be created, using optical fibre in both local and trunk networks; it would reach 6.4 million households by 1992.

The Cable Plan was a *grand projet*, designed to offer a coherent strategy covering telecommunications, broadcasting and electronics, in pursuit of economic, cultural and political objectives and involving public and private sector

---

[74] DGPT, *Rapport Annuel 1994*, 51.

[75] See DGPT, *Intervention de France Télécom dans le secteur concurrentiel* (Paris: DGPT, 1994) and DGPT, *Rapport Annuel 1994*, 50.

[76] DRG, *Rapport d'Activité 1991*, 77–9.

[77] '*Voluntarisme libérale*', interview with Longuet, *Le Figaro* 24.6.94.

[78] Comments, José Rossi (PTT/Industry Minister), *Le Monde* 2.3.95.

[79] Interviews, PTT Minister's *cabinet* and DGT; *Le Point* 15.11.82; for a general history of the Plan and the strategies of the various actors, see E. Brenac, B. Jobert, P. Mallein, P. Payen, and Y. Toussaint, 'L'Entreprise comme acteur politique: la DGT et la genèse du plan câble', *Sociologie du Travail*, 27(3) (1985), 304–15, and E. Brenac and G. Payen, *Une politique en dérive. La DGT et le Plan Câble* (Grenoble: Université de Grenoble, 1988).

actors.[80] One aim was a modern, high capacity telecommunications network for the DGT, able to transmit existing telecommunications services, and, 'downstream', stimulating new, wideband services, such as ISDN, the visiophone, and other interactive services involving images that would increase usage of the DGT's network.[81] 'Upstream', the Plan would create large orders for French equipment manufacturers, enabling them to win a world lead in the expanding opto-electronics business, and compensating for declining DGT public switching orders.[82] In broadcasting, the advent of satellite broadcasting entailed the danger of 'television programmes without identity or cultural ambition', threatening French culture, national control over the media, and French programme-making; cable networks would offer a cheaper, better alternative with French programmes.[83] Moreover, cable networks would encourage freedom of expression, wider access to the media and decentralization. Finally, by carrying television, voice telephony, data, and new interactive services, the new networks would be profitable.

The arrangements of the Plan reflected these varied aims and the interests of the actors involved. A distinction was drawn between the infrastructure and telecommunications services, which remained under the DGT's monopoly and control, and non-telecommunications services, for which competition and diversity would be encouraged. Local authorities would initiate cabling of their area. They would establish Sociétés locales d'exploitation commerciale (SLECs), in partnership with other organizations (public and private), which would manage cable services, including choosing public and private providers of cable services, paying rents to the DGT and dealing with subscribers. Financing of the building of networks would be on a national basis, with a very large contribution by the DGT (francs 7b. 1983–5), but also payments by local authorities and rents for use of the networks paid to the DGT.

Rapidly, however, the Cable Plan encountered major problems.[84] Costs were higher than anticipated. Much of the equipment for opto-electronics was not available, the building of networks was delayed and new interactive services were not developed or offered. New airwave television channels were licensed in the mid-1980s and provided an alternative to television, the sole real cable service. Only a tiny minority of those cabled actually chose to subscribe to cable services. The DGT was concerned about the cost of the Plan and especially any threat to its telecommunications monopoly from use of cable networks for

[80] Cohen, Le Colbertisme 'high tech', esp. 175–80 and 191–7.

[81] Le Monde 3–4.10.82; Brenac and Payen, Une politique en dérive, 48–50, 54, and Mexandeau Report, 4–5, reprinted ibid.

[82] Le Monde 5.11.82, Brenac and Payen, Une politique en dérive, 33, Cohen, Le Colbertisme 'high tech', 139.

[83] Mexandeau Report, 2–3.

[84] See Brenac and Payen, Une politique en dérive, 10–17 and 33–58 for a detailed history, and Cohen, Le Colbertisme 'high tech', 140–6 and 191–7 for a summary of events.

telecommunications services; soon it began to press for a switch away from optical fibre networks. Meanwhile, the local authorities attacked the framework of the Plan, including the DGT's monopoly over the construction and operation of cable networks, financial arrangements, French programme quotas, and ministerial opposition to the entry of large private sector firms (such as the water companies) into the SLECs.

In the face of such pressures, the Cable Plan was modified; the political executive played a central role in the evolution of policy, together with the DGT. Mexandeau favoured the use of optical fibre cable, a choice that was upheld in 1983–4 by increasing the financial burden borne by the DGT.[85] However, as costs rose and Mexandeau's position was weakened, the DGT increasingly abandoned optical fibre; by the end of 1986, only 10 out of 50 networks built or in the process of being built were in optical fibre.[86] Moreover, in January 1985, after a long battle within the political executive, decrees governing the operation of the SLECs relaxed programme quotas and restrictions on the entry of private firms into SLECs.[87] Following the Right's victory in 1986, the DGT's monopoly over the building and operation of cable networks was ended; this formed part of Longuet's policy of introducing greater competition into telecommunications. The counterpart was that the DGT also became much freer in deciding whether to accept requests for cable networks, and to make such decisions on commercial grounds. Since cable networks were largely unprofitable,[88] the result in practice, was the end of the Cable Plan. By 1990, cable networks remained small, were mostly in coaxial and focused on cable television.[89]

In the mid-1990s, the possibility of creating a broadband network arose again, as part of a policy debate on 'information superhighways'. At first, a similar path to that of earlier *grands projets* appeared possible. In February 1994 the government asked Gérard Théry (head of the DGT 1974–81) to examine 'information superhighways'. His report[90] urged concerted public action to create a fibre optic network of 4–5 million lines as soon as possible and reaching all households and firms by 2015; France Télécom should lead the Plan by investing 150 billion francs over twenty years, and public and private sectors would then supply services over the new, broadband network.

The response to Théry's proposals differed greatly from those to his earlier plans for videotex (discussed below). France Télécom's reaction was guarded

[85]   Its share was raised from 70 to 90 per cent in 1984—*Le Figaro* 9–10.6.84.
[86]   Brenac and Payen, *Une politique en dérive*, 35.   [87]   Ibid. 16.
[88]   Cf. the report by the Cour des comptes—Inspection général des finances, *Rapport d'enquête de MM Capron, d'Hinnin et Rubinowicz* (Paris: Inspection général des finances, 1987).
[89]   15,000 subscribers in 1987 to networks established under the Plan, with a take-up rate of 10 per cent in September 1989 and in 1988, only 29 per cent of sockets used optical fibre—Inspection général des finances, *Rapport d'enquête* and *Le Monde* 16.11.89.
[90]   G. Théry, *Les Autoroutes de l'information. Rapport au Premier Ministre* (Paris: La Documentation Française, 1994).

and indeed largely hostile. It emphasized the need for profitability, especially as its remaining telecommunications monopolies would end in 1998. It opposed the expensive blanket cabling of France, especially for residential users; instead, it favoured a more 'market-driven', experimental approach, relying on specific services and focused on users with definite needs, particularly companies.[91] The government adopted a cautious approach and explicitly rejected the *grand projet* approach of the Cable Plan.[92] It sought to involve public and private actors in a 'liberal *voluntariste*' strategy, avoiding a centralized approach and therefore decided to begin with 'experiments'.[93] It took care in choosing pilot projects to safeguard the publicly-owned network operator: many involved France Télécom as a partner, and in the first batch chosen in 1995, only those that did not require regulatory derogations (i.e. did not threaten FT's telecommunications monopoly) or public funds were accepted.[94] Thus the government adopted a limited approach, involving stimulation of debates and experiments, but steered away from an expensive national plan or encouraging competition to France Télécom.

Leased Lines and Specialised Networks

The DGT pursued a policy of encouraging use of public networks, rather than leased lines in the 1970s and 1980s, a choice linked to wider objectives such as making full use of network capacity, introducing modern technology, and creating national networks that promoted regional development.[95] A switched circuit system for data transmission, Caducée, was opened in 1972. Then, in 1978, a packet switched network, Transpac, was established; it utilized a transmission technique particularly suitable for data and whose charges depended on volume of data sent and time of transmission, not distance. Transpac was vigorously promoted by the DGT, and was used in the 1980s for transmission of the telematic services offered on Minitel terminals. In the late 1980s, an ISDN was opened which was also strongly supported by France Télécom; by 1993, France had the largest number of ISDN connections in Europe.[96] Although the

[91] *Libération* 29.9.94; *Le Figaro-Economique* 10.3.95; *Le Monde* 24.10.94; T. Vedel, 'Information Superhighway Policy in France', in B. Kahin and E. J. Wilson III (eds.), *National Information Infrastructure Initiatives* (Cambridge, Mass., and London: MIT Press, 1996), 321–2.

[92] *Les Echos* 28.10.94, 8.12.94.

[93] Vedel, 'Information Superhighway Policy in France', 319–320; *Le Monde* 30–31.10.94; *Le Figaro* 8.12.94.

[94] *Libération* 1.3.95; only later was small-scale public funding made available and were projects from cable companies involving telephony accepted, linked to regulatory reform in 1996—Vedel, 'Information Superhighway Policy in France', 320.

[95] *Les Echos* 20.9.84, 15.2.72, and 4.3.74; see also J.-C. Mailhan, E. Huret, M. Tréheux, and A. Gheysen, 'Communication d'entreprise: la nouvelle donne', *Revue Française des Télécommunications*, 73 (1990), 38–63.

[96] P. Gailhardis, 'Numéris: le réseau du futur simple', *Revue Française des Télécommunications*, 69 (1989), 30–49; *Le Figaro* 21.5.90; *Financial Times* 23.7.91; *Les Echos* 19.8.93.

DGT established modern, high capacity private circuits for firms in the 1980s,[97] policy (notably tariffs) encouraged use of public networks.[98]

The period after 1990 saw a degree of policy change, influenced by the growth of competition, France Télécom's new institutional position and the role of the DGPT. The principle of cost-based tariffs for leased lines and advanced networks and concomitant rebalancing of prices were accepted by both the DGPT and France Télécom: for the latter, they were necessary to face competition, whilst for the former they formed part of 'fair competition' and its attack on cross-subsidies and abuse of a dominant position, as well as complying with the EC's 1990 Open Network Provision (ONP) Directive that included the principle of cost-oriented tariffs.[99] The principle of cost-based pricing was enshrined in a decree of 28 July 1993 on leased lines (which transposed the EC Directive on Leased Lines of 1992 into French law) and reductions in leased line prices and targets for quality of service formed part of a three year plan for 1992-5 and France Télécom's *Contrat de plan* for 1995-8. Substantial rebalancing of tariffs and reductions in leased line prices took place in the mid-1990s.[100] The DRG/DGPT sought to enforce 'fair competition', examining matters such as France Télécom's tariffs and cross-subsidisation of specialised public networks, the effects of long-term discounts on entry, financial and technical conditions of access to networks and publication of tariffs.[101] It sought to break its dependence on France Télécom for information and in 1994 commissioned an independent audit of tariffs and a consultation of leased line users.[102]

Value-Added Network Services

Policy towards VANS saw the concerted use of policy instruments offered by the institutional framework in pursuit of a *grand projet*, in sharp contrast to Britain. It also involved protection of France Télécom, notably its monopoly over network operation. Only in the 1990s did moves away from both strands of policy take place, as competition to France Télécom was permitted. The development of policy is best illustrated by two cases: telematics, with the well-known Minitel programme; the general regulation of VANS.

From his election as President in 1974, Giscard d'Estaing had been interested in the computerization of society and in 1976, he set up a commission to

[97] Notably the 'Trans' series of high capacity digital links.
[98] A.-M. Roussel, 'French Telecom Opens Up to Competition (Slowly)', *Data Communications*, Oct. 1993.
[99] *La Tribune Desfossés* 20.10.93; Roussel, 'French Telecom Opens Up'; DGPT, *Rapport Annuel 1994*, 60.
[100] Cf. *La Tribune Desfossés* 20.10.93; DGPT, *Rapport Annuel 1994*, 66, *Rapport Annuel 1995*, 82.
[101] See e.g. DGPT, *Rapport Annuel 1994*, 54-6, *Rapport Annuel 1995*, 53-6, 82.
[102] DGPT, *Rapport Annuel 1994*, 66-7.

examine the issue. Two of its members produced the highly influential 'Nora–Minc Report', *L'Informatisation de la société*.[103] It argued that different forms of communications, computing, telecommunications, and broadcasting, were converging into one, giving rise to a new and strategic form of service, 'telematics'. The report warned of the danger of dominance by American computer firms, especially IBM, and claimed that only concerted State action, led by public telecommunications operators, could prevent the extension of such firms' power over new forms of communication.

In 1978, a Conseil interministériel, chaired by President Giscard d'Estaing, decided to adopt two programmes for interactive videotex services, one for electronic telephone directories and another for a telematics programme. After initial experiments, the two programmes were merged into the Telematics Plan (the *Plan télématique*): both the electronic telephone directory and other telematic services (*Télétel* services) would be offered on cheap terminals, known as 'Minitel' terminals.[104] The Telematics Plan was to follow a *grand projet* strategy whereby the DGT committed large sums to develop a national network on which telematic services would be supplied.[105] From 1981, 3.5 m. terminals were to be ordered every year. They were to be given free of charge to subscribers, and would replace (compulsorily) the free paper telephone directories.

The Plan had a variety of aims, relating well beyond telematics, and sought to satisfy a correspondingly wide range of public and private interests. It would create powerful French telematics service suppliers, creating a world lead for French firms and pre-empting other countries, especially Britain's Prestel system.[106] It would provide revenue and profits for the DGT by developing new commercial telematic services, increasing residential usage of the telecommunications network, which was low, and replacing costly paper telephone directories.[107] Moreover, the *Plan de rattrapage du téléphone* was nearing completion; the Telematics Plan offered the DGT an opportunity to justify further high levels of investment, and also continuing development of its autonomy and power within the State.[108] Similarly, DGT public switching investment would soon peak; telematics appeared to offer a source of orders for French equipment manufacturers and a springboard for exports. Finally, the Plan would aid France's struggling microchip industry.[109]

---

[103] S. Nora and A. Minc, *L'Informatisation de la société* (Paris, La Documentation Française, 1978).

[104] G. Dang Nguyen and E. Arnold, 'Videotex: Much Ado about Nothing?', in Sharp, *Strategies for New Technology*.

[105] Cohen, *Le Colbertisme 'high tech'*, 124–30.

[106] P. Humphreys, 'France: A Case Study of "Telematics"', in Dyson and Humphreys, *The Political Economy of Telecommunications*, 216.

[107] Interview, Direction des Affaires Industrielles et Internationales; Dang Nguyen and Arnold, 'Videotex'.

[108] Argued in Cawson *et al.*, *Hostile Brothers*, 124.

[109] Palmer and Tunstall, *Liberating Communications*; Forum International 13.9.79.

The Telematics Plan ran into considerable opposition: the enforced replacement of paper directories by 'Minitel' terminals was criticized as authoritarian; the cost was high; the written press was strongly opposed, seeing a threat to its advertising revenues, and waged a vigorous campaign at local and national level; there was parliamentary resistance to the project.[110] Jacques Dondoux had criticized it and on becoming Directeur général des télécommunications in 1981 announced that he would end it.[111]

Nevertheless, the project was continued after 1981, thanks in large measure to the strong personal support of Mexandeau, together with Lang and Filoud. Changes were made, which reduced opposition: subscribers were given the choice between paper directories and terminals; the local press was given a monopoly over small advertisements and financial aid to develop telematic services; the agreement of local politicians was required before Minitel terminals would be distributed in a region.[112] Moreover, the DGT was to have a monopoly over the network, but not over services on it. Instead, a 'liberal regime' of freedom in the supply of services was established under the Law on Audiovisual Communication of 29 July 1982: to supply a telematics service on Minitel, a supplier only had to register and give a brief description of the service. Several 'technical' decisions followed, which proved vital to the project: the network was made 'open', so that all kinds of computers could be linked to it, and was in 'real time' so that users could send messages directly back to computer databases; payment was made easier by the 'Kiosque' system, whereby the DGT calculated and collected charges levied by the service suppliers as part of telephone bills; telematic services were transmitted on the Transpac network which was more suitable than the PSTN.

The Minitel programme gradually grew, so that France had the largest number of public videotex terminals in the world. By the late 1980s there were five million terminals and several thousand services were supplied, ranging over all sectors and types of service, from airline reservation systems to telematic chatlines.[113] However, new challenges to French telematics policy arose. The cost of Minitel was criticized in a report by the Cour des comptes in 1989, which claimed that total costs exceeded revenue by 5.3 billion francs.[114] Although the report was based on figures for 1987 and its arguments were vigorously opposed, from the late 1980s, greater emphasis was laid on profitability. New, more sophisticated terminals were offered, for which charges were levied and

[110]   Interview, PTT Minister's *cabinet*; Humphreys, 'France: A Case Study of "Telematics"'; Cawson *et al.*, *Hostile Brothers*, 124–5.

[111]   Interview, PTT Minister's *cabinet*; Cohen, *Le Colbertisme 'high tech'*, 128.

[112]   Cohen, *Le Colbertisme 'high tech'*, 128–9, Humphreys, 'France: A Case Study of "telematics"', 218–19.

[113]   See ch. 11 for figures.

[114]   Cour des Comptes, *Rapport de la Cour des comptes au président de la République 1989* (Paris: Cour des comptes).

which were often aimed at firms.[115] The mid-1990s saw policy move away from creating a national network of terminals led by France Télécom, to be replaced by competition among internet service providers (including France Télécom) linking both upgraded Minitel terminals and personal computers bought by customers; profitability became the main criterion guiding France Télécom's choices.[116]

Competition also became increasingly central to the general regulation of VANS. Minitel represented the first breach in the DGT's monopoly over VANS. During the mid-1980s, further pressures for change existed: VANS such as services for travel agents and credit card transactions began to be established; large companies including IBM, a group led by Olivetti, Bull, and several large banks, planned to develop VANS and pressed for regulatory change.[117] After 1986, Longuet made liberalization of VANS part of his overall policy of introducing greater competition into telecommunications, whilst the DGT wished to expand its supply of VANS and accepted the need for some competition to be allowed.[118]

Despite forces for change, reform in the mid-late 1980s was slow and cautious as policy-makers sought to reconcile the interests of several actors, notably users and the DGT; indeed, the latter negotiated over change with the unit responsible for regulation within the PTT Ministry, the Mission à la réglementation.[119] In particular, the DGT feared that lines leased for VANS could be used simply for the transmission of signals or for voice telephony, 'bypassing' the PSTN and weakening its monopoly over network operation.[120] Software and hardware suppliers were concerned that VANS suppliers could set up services with proprietary norms, incompatible with certain types of hardware or software; in particular, they were worried about IBM, which was proposing to offer a 'universal' or 'horizontal' VANS linking users' computers, to supply services.[121]

The VANS decree of 24 September 1987 reflected these concerns.[122] It permitted the sale of services on leased lines and of telematic services to third parties, but laid down a number of conditions. Ministerial authorization for large VANS was required. The DGT's monopoly was protected: the use of

---

[115] N. Mougenot, *State Intervention in the French Telecommunications Sector: Analysis of a Success, Minitel, and Current Evolution* (Sandvica: Norwegian School of Management, 1998), 7; *Libération* 12.11.93; *Le Monde* 21.1.95.

[116] *Le Figaro-Economie* 13.1.96; *Le Monde* 14–15.1.96, 10–11.3.96; *La Tribune* 13.2.97.

[117] *Le Figaro* 21.5.86; *Tribune de l'Economie* 16.9.86; *Le Monde* 25.9.87.

[118] Interview with Marcel Roulet, *Le Monde* 24.9.86; interview, Mission à la Réglementation.

[119] Interview, Mission à la Réglementation.

[120] *Tribune de l'Economie* 16.9.86.

[121] *Le Monde* 1.7.87 and interview, Jacques Stern, head of Bull, *Le Monde* 5.11.86.

[122] See G. Longuet, *Télécoms. La conquête de nouveaux espaces* (Paris: Dunod, 1988), Annexe 20, and P. Conruyt, 'Réseaux à valeur ajoutée: une demande évolutive', *Revue Française des Télécommunications*, no. 65 (1988), 70–7, for summaries of the decree.

VANS for voice telephony was banned; the amount charged to customers for the mere transmission of data could not exceed 15 per cent of a VANS' turnover; the Minister was given the power to impose 'access charges' for connecting a private network to the PSTN, in case the DGT suffered heavy revenue losses from 'bypassing'. Moreover, the decree declared its aim to be the encouragement of 'open' OSI norms and restricted a VANS supplier's ability to impose proprietary norms.[123]

In the 1990s, under the direction of the DRG/DGPT, policy gradually evolved, becoming more centred on competition. A decree in 1991 removed some of the restrictions and conditions on VANS supply; thus, for instance, the 15 per cent limit on transmission charges was ended, the size of VANS requiring authorization was raised and the purpose of licensing was circumscribed, being merely to ensure that the VANS was not merely a data transmission service (which remained a France Télécom monopoly) and met technical 'essential requirements' (as allowed under EC law), notably interoperability of services.[124] Moreover, France Télécom was placed under the same obligations as other suppliers. Then in December 1992, as also required by the EC 1990 Services Directive, a decree allowed competition in data transmission services (including bearer services' involving simple data transmission), subject again only to meeting 'essential requirements'. The DRG/DGPT laid emphasis on 'light regulation' aimed at ensuring that competition was 'fair'; in particular, it included provisions to give interconnection rights for 'bearer services' (with the DGPT being asked to arbitrate if no agreement was reached) and to ensure transparency in France Télécom's supply conditions.[125] In drawing up the decrees and decisions (arrêtés), the DRG undertook a consultation of users and interested parties, including France Télécom's rivals such as BT and AT&T; these companies were then successful in obtaining licences to supply services.[126]

Mobile Communications Networks and Services

In the late 1970s the DGT faced long waiting lists for its small and technologically backward mobile telephone system.[127] It chose Thomson to produce a

[123] VANS above a certain capacity specified by the Minister had to be offered with OSI norms, at the same price and conditions as with other norms; the Minister was empowered to order all VANS not using OSI norms to cease operating in two years.

[124] Décret no. 92-286 du 27 mars 1992 relatif aux services de télécommunications relevant de l'article L34–5 du code des postes et télécommunications; DRG, Rapport d'Activité 1991–1992, 21–2.

[125] DRG, Rapport d'Activité 1992–1993, 35–7; DGPT, Rapport Annuel 1994, 13.

[126] DRG, Rapport d'Activité 1992, 35–7, 88–9; e.g. by 1995, seven companies had obtained licences for bearer services—DGPT, Rapport Annuel 1995, 51.

[127] Les Echos 2.6.80.

new system, Corpac 400. When Thomson could not produce the system to meet the DGT's timetable and withdrew it, the DGT refused to import foreign technology; instead, it turned to another French company, Matra, to develop equipment. The resulting Radiocom 2000 service, an analogue cellular system, only began operating in 1986.[128] Furthermore, although demand was rising rapidly in the 1980s, with increasing waiting lists, the PTT minister, Mexandeau and the DGT decided to concentrate on the next generation of mobile systems, digital cellular systems, which would be supplied using European-wide GSM norms but would be available in the early 1990s, rather than expand the intermediate technology analogue system to meet excess demand.[129]

Under the Right between 1986 and 1988, it appeared that policy would change. As part of his policy of illustrating the merits of competition, Longuet used his power under Article L33 of the PTT Code to license a second analogue cellular service.[130] After a public tender, La Société française du radiotéléphone (SFR), a consortium led by the Compagnie générale des eaux with Alcatel, was chosen.[131] Its network used foreign technology produced by Nokia and Motorola and began operating in March 1989. Moreover, competition was introduced into paging by Longuet authorizing the publicly-owned firm Télédiffusion de France (TDF) to establish a service. Nevertheless, the degree of change was limited. The threat to the DGT from TDF was ended when it took a 49 per cent stake in the latter in January 1989. A 'telepoint' service (Pointel) was planned, but, unlike Britain, it was to be a monopoly service run by France Télécom.[132] In 1990 SFR equipment could still not be used on Radiocom's network, which itself remained technologically backward and faced a waiting list of ten thousand.[133]

Only in the 1990s did greater change take place. In 1991, France Télécom and SFR were licensed to offer GSM mobile telephony. Desiring better performance, Longuet threatened to sell France Télécom's mobiles business, causing great alarm for the operator.[134] Although this was not implemented, a third GSM licence was made available in 1994 with the aims of increasing competition and ending the comfortable SFR–France Télécom duopoly; it was awarded to a consortium led by Bouygues, but which included several foreign operators (such as Cable and Wireless). Competition was reintroduced in paging, with three operators (including France Télécom) being licensed for new digital services in 1993.[135] By the mid-1990s, France Télécom was pursuing a vigorous

[128] La Vie Française 18–24.5.87.
[129] Cohen, Le Colbertisme 'high tech', 276; Le Monde 29.1.87.
[130] La Vie Française 18–24.5.87; Longuet, Télécoms, 49.
[131] For the full list of participants in the consortium, see La Tribune de l'Expansion 25.2.88.
[132] The service was indeed launched in 1993. Although open to competition after 1990, no other operator asked for a licence—DRG, Rappport d'Activité 1992–93, 50.
[133] Le Figaro-Economie 21.5.90.   [134] La Tribune Desfossés 3.5.93 and 13.5.93.
[135] Le Figaro 21.9.94.

policy of investment and lower tariffs, whilst its competitors were growing rapidly.[136]

Measures were also taken to ensure that competition was 'fair'. SFR complaints over France Télécom's interconnection charges led the DGPT to arbitrate and lower charges by 40–60 per cent; further arbitrations for other mobile services followed in 1995.[137] Moreover, Longuet authorized SFR to use 'alternative infrastructures' (such as cable networks) instead of France Télécom's leased lines to link network 'cells'.[138] France Télécom's licence prohibited cross-subsidization between its mobile business and other activities; concern by the DGPT over enforcement and lack of sufficient accounting separation led to an agreement to transform France Télécom's mobile business into a legally-separate subsidiary.[139] Finally, the close links between France Télécom and French manufacturers began to weaken: in particular, Alcatel did not take part in developing equipment for Pointel, was a candidate for the third GSM licence to compete with France Télécome and took a 20 per cent share in France Télécom's rival, SFR, in 1994.[140]

Ministers and the DGPT played central roles in the evolution of policy. The decisions to licence competitors to France Télécom and the threat to privatise its mobile activities were part of Longuet's policy of increasing competition; they were not required by EC law. The allocation of licences remained highly controversial. In particular, the choice of Bouygues in 1994 involved several ministers, including the Prime Minister, Balladur; it appeared linked to wider industrial political concerns, notably the financial strength and independence of operators from foreign takeovers and the position of Bouygues and its media interests in the forthcoming presidential election.[141] The DGPT played a major role in its decisions over interconnection fees and requiring the separation of mobile activities, acting in opposition to France Télécom.

Satellites

Satellite policy offered another field for the *grand projet* strategy, in this case, linking telecommunications and broadcasting through the DGT/France Télécom in pursuit of national independence and a world lead for French suppliers. In 1979, two satellite projects were accepted by the political executive; the Élysée played a key role in both decisions.[142] The DGT proposed to launch a series of telecommunications satellites, Télécom 1, in response to IBM's

---

[136] *Libération* 3.6.94; DGPT, *Rapport Annuel 1995*, 43–6.

[137] DGPT, *Rapport Annuel 1994*, 44–5, *Rapport Annuel 1995*, 55–6.

[138] *Communications Week International* 11.10.93.   [139] DGPT, *Rapport Annuel 1995*, 48–9.

[140] *Le Figaro* 28.4.94; *Le Monde* 4.5.94; *Le Tribune Desfossés* 28.10.94.

[141] *Libération* 3.6.94; *Le Canard Enchaîné* 5.10.94; *La Tribune Desfossés* 30.9.94; *Le Monde* 30.9.94.

[142] For a brief history, see Cohen, *Le Colbertisme 'high tech'*, 130–7 and Palmer and Tunstall, *Liberating Communications*, 27–45.

announcement that it would launch private satellites for data transmission. The other project was for two satellites, TDF1 and 2, for broadcasting of television in collaboration with West Germany; it was proposed by TDF (Télédiffusion de France), the publicly-owned body responsible for broadcasting transmission, which was a strong rival of the DGT.

The telecommunications satellite Télécom 1 was put into orbit in 1984, followed by Télécom 1B in 1985 and 1C in 1988. The satellite series was operated by the DGT and used to provide links with France's overseas territories and for a range of advanced data and image transmission services; however, it was also used for some television broadcasting, although not direct satellite broadcasting to homes.[143] Meanwhile, the TDF project went ahead, albeit in altered form: it was presented first as an alternative to the other European satellite television operator, SES, with its Astra satellites, which was accused by France of being a 'trojan horse' for non-European television broadcasters, notably Rupert Murdoch; then it became part of the French contribution to the European high definition television programme based on the MAC norm.[144] TDF 1 was finally launched, after many delays, in 1988.[145]

The late 1980s saw increasing linkage between telecommunications and broadcasting. France Télécom took a 49 per cent stake in TDF in January 1989 and hence found itself responsible for the TDF satellite programme which was now clearly an expensive white elephant, suffering from technical problems and insufficient demand. In response, France Télécom and the PTT Ministry announced that there would be no successors to the TDF satellites. Instead, digital broadcasting of television would be undertaken by the new generation of telecommunications satellites, Télécom 2. Nevertheless, the policy of national independence was maintained: the Télécom 2 satellites were to rival both SES and the European satellite operator Eutelsat. Moreover, attempts to use the satellite programme to aid French broadcasting continued, with the PTT Minister playing a central role in matters such as the allocation of channels amongst broadcasters and setting low tariffs to aid the latter.[146]

The 1990s, however, saw a gradual breakdown of the *grand projet* approach in satellites. The DRG/DGPT supported increased competition in satellite telecommunications services[147] and France Télécom's monopoly over satellite telecommunications services was gradually ended. In 1991, VSAT (very small aperture terminals) networks and 'satellite newsgathering' services were licensed and hence opened to competition; connection to the PSTN was allowed provided that the service remained a closed one, excluding sales to

---

[143] See P. Gailhardis, C. Bacot, M. Beugin, and J.-P. Brillaud, 'Satellites "Télécom 1": bilan et perspectives', *Revue Française des Télécomunications*, 70 (1989), 44–61.

[144] Cf. Cohen, *Le Colbertisme 'high tech'*, 130–7 and 307–51.

[145] Ibid. and *Le Figaro* 9–10.6.84.   [146] *La Tribune de l'Expansion* 21.8.92.

[147] Cf. DRG, *Rapport d'Activité 1991–1992*, 56.

third parties.[148] In 1995, France prepared to implement the 1994 European Satellite Directive, thereby extending competition to public satellite networks and services.[149] Under pressures from the PTT Minister and the need to limit investment and costs, the policy of independent satellites was also gradually abandoned: France Télécom prepared to cease competing with SES and Eutelsat, notably by not launching successors to Télécom 2 and by entering the SES consortium.[150]

Customer Premises Equipment

During the 1960s and 1970s, a degree of competition had been permitted in almost all CPE supply; during the 1980s, remaining restrictions were ended.[151] Nevertheless, the DGT and Government pursued an active policy of aiding French manufacturers. Using its position as the largest supplier of CPE, the DGT placed orders with French firms such as Alcatel and Matra.[152] The DGT sought to create economies of scale for manufacturers by placing large order for types of equipment such as answering machines or videotex terminals;[153] indeed, developing markets for equipment suppliers was one of the aims of *grands projets* such as the telematics programme. Finally, although competition was permitted, equipment needed approval (*agrément*) by the DGT/PTT Ministry. This was used, especially in the early/mid-1980s, to restrict entry by foreign firms, by laying down norms favouring French manufacturers and refusing approvals to foreign products.[154]

In the late 1980s and 1990s, regulatory constraints on entry were gradually loosened, although France Télécom continued to favour French suppliers and the DRG/DGPT enforced prohibitions on non-approved equipment.[155] When France Télécom was separated from the PTT Ministry in 1990, the DRG/DGPT became responsible for approvals. As part of transposition of the 1991 EC Directive on mutual recognition for CPE,[156] new procedures for approval were introduced, which limited requirements to those deemed 'essen-

---

[148] DRG, *Rapport d'Activité 1992–93*, 64–5.   [149] DGPT, *Rapport Annuel 1995*, 53.

[150] *Le Figaro-Economie* 1.9.95; *Les Echos* 23.10.95; *Le Monde* 6.1.96; *La Tribune Desfossés* 14.11.96.

[151] J.-P. Voge, 'A Summary of French Regulatory policy', in M. Snow (ed.), *Marketplace for Telecommunications: Telecommunications Regulation and Deregulation in Industrialized Democracies* (New York: Longman, 1986); G. Dang Nguyen, 'Telecommunications in France', in J. Foreman-Peck and J. Müller (eds.), *European Telecommunication Organisation* (Baden-Baden: Nomos, 1988).

[152] For a list of suppliers of various types of equipment to the DGT, showing that almost all were French, see *Financial Times* 24.10.84.

[153] Cf. *Le Monde* 14.3.81, 11.9.83; *La Vie Française* 24–30.9.84.

[154] Dang Nguyen, 'Telecommunications in France', 144; for examples concerning cordless phones and handsets, see *Le Figaro* 31.1.85 and *Libération* 20.9.85.

[155] *Libération* 7.4.95 and 17.11.95; DRG/DGT, *Rapport d'Activités/Rapports Annuel*.

[156] Directive 91/263/EEC.

tial' under EC law; moreover, procedures were clarified and for a few products, especially in mobile telephony, requirements only related to their use of the radio-spectrum.[157]

Conclusion

In both Britain and France, public bodies were closely involved in the advanced services and networks, and CPE subsector, but their roles differed both cross-nationally and over time. The impacts of national institutions can be seen by analysing two sets of features in both decision-making processes and substantive policy choices. First, within Britain and France, institutional reforms were followed by policy modification. Second, cross-national dissimilarities developed in the 1980s, especially after 1984; there was a degree of convergence after 1990, but significant differences remained. Both sets of characteristics can be related to institutional arrangements and to specific features of the organisation of the sector in each country.

In Britain, the main participants in decision making were the DoI/DTI and BT before 1984; thereafter, following institutional reform, Oftel became a central actor in regulatory change. The division of roles largely followed that set down in the 1984 Telecommunications Act, as each actor used its formal policy instruments. Thus, the DTI set the regulatory framework by issuing licences and determining their conditions. For its part, Oftel offered influential advice to the DTI and enforced and modified licences, notably that of BT. The government and Oftel took almost no direct part in commercial decisions over which services and CPE should be supplied and how they should be provided—such matters were left to private suppliers.

In France, policy-making processes also reflected formal institutional arrangements. Prior to 1990, the central actors in policy formation were the DGT, PTT Minister, and other elements of the political executive. In contrast to Britain, the political executive was often closely involved in decisions about which services were supplied by the DGT and how they were made available, as well as the regulatory framework applicable. The institutional reforms of 1990 saw a greater separation of roles between France Télécom and the PTT Ministry; moreover, the DRG/DGPT became a central participant in decision making. The institutional separation of France Télécom from the PTT Ministry as a legally distinct supplier was therefore followed by modifications of decision-making practices.

From the 1980s onwards, BT's monopolies were ended and British policy centred on the regulation of competition. Although the process began before 1984, there was a marked acceleration after the privatization of BT, and by the

---

[157] DRG, *Rapport d'Activité 1992–93*, 67–70.

late 1980s competition was permitted in almost all services. Moreover, other barriers to entry, such as restrictive conditions in VANS licences or for CPE supply, were reduced. The government and Oftel took measures in favour of 'fair competition' through the definition, enforcement and modification of licence conditions. Much regulation concerned BT specifically, to ensure that it did not benefit from 'unfair' advantages as the dominant supplier and vertically-integrated network operator; examples included BT's licence conditions, controls on BT's supply of leased lines, VANS licences, the insistence on separate subsidiaries for mobiles and action on satellite services and CPE sales. The policy of promoting competition was followed even when strongly opposed by BT or apparently damaging to BT, as, for instance, in the allocation of new mobile licences or decisions to permit cable television companies to compete in telecommunications without allowing BT to use its network for cable television. Policy-makers did not attempt to encourage use of BT's 'public networks' (for instance, packet switched networks, videotex networks, or the PSTN for broadcasting). Instead, they introduced competition and prevented the PSTN from being used for broadcasting. The government and Oftel focused on regulatory framework. Large-scale programmes involving public expenditure, the co-ordination of public and private actors or the linkage of telecommunications with computing and broadcasting, were not undertaken, despite calls for action over broadband networks and videotex services.

Unlike BT, the DGT played several roles in France before the 1990s: supplier of services, equipment purchaser, regulator, and provider of finance. Frequently, the political executive followed a *grand projet* approach, seeking to co-ordinate public and private actors; the most striking examples concerned cable networks, videotex services and satellites. It used the DGT (sometimes willingly, but on occasion against its wishes) to pursue wide-ranging objectives, including the creation of markets for equipment manufacturers, 'freedom of communication', regional development, national economic and cultural independence, and benefiting from the 'convergence' of telecommunications with broadcasting and computing. Policies were designed to encourage the development and maximum use of public networks: hence DGT investment in cable networks, packet switched networks and videotex terminals was undertaken. Moreover, a distinction was drawn between network operation and advanced services. On the one hand, regulation protected the DGT's monopoly over networks and voice telephony, through restrictions on the creation of networks, limits on cable networks and VANS and prohibitions on the resale of capacity; mobile communications represented a only very limited exception to this policy. On the other hand, competition was allowed in services supplied on the DGT's networks (for example in videotex services, advanced cable services and after 1987, VANS). The distinction aided a policy of supporting the transmission of advanced services on public networks and discouraging the use of private circuits.

During the 1990s, policy in France moved away from the *grands projets* approach. Large-scale French satellites programmes were abandoned, the idea of a national broadband network to be built by France Télécom was rejected and, even in videotex, France Télécom focused on supplying profitable services. Instead, competition became more important for policy. France Télécom's remaining monopolies were ended (notably, in data transmission networks and satellite services), whilst the number of suppliers in the mobile market increased. Greater emphasis was placed on ensuring that competition was 'fair', especially by the DRG/DGPT, which enforced France Télécom's licence conditions, even when opposed by France Télécom (for instance, in interconnection charges and the separation of mobile activities). For its part, France Télécom gave high priority to the needs of business users and to its ability to compete (for example, by rebalancing its leased line tariffs, and modifying its Minitel strategy towards profitability), changes which were not obstructed by the political executive and DRG/DGPT.

The institutional framework contributed to policy differences between Britain and France concerning competition, *grands projets* and industrial strategy, whilst institutional reforms (those of 1984 in Britain and 1990 in France) contributed to modifications in policy. The influence of specific institutional features can be analysed, notably the ownership and position of the network operator, the existence of an independent regulator, continuing public monopolies over other parts of the telecommunications sector and the powers of the government/political executive and any independent regulator.

The differing institutional positions of BT and the DGT/France Télécom influenced the pace of liberalization and the regulatory protection given to their monopolies. Before 1984, the government in Britain sought to increase competition, but made only limited progress in the face of opposition by BT, which utilised its position as a public sector corporation and a participant in decision making to obstruct change. After 1984, BT's new status as a private firm aided the move to greater competition: a private monopoly was difficult to justify and it was more of an outsider in licensing decisions. Although BT's position made a move towards competition easier, conversely, it stood in the way of *grands projets*: BT was not available as a tool under government control for direct application in industrial policy. In contrast, in France, the DGT's position as an *administration* meant that the various roles of regulation, industrial policy, and supply were not institutionally separated and that the DGT lacked institutional autonomy. These features provided the political executive with the opportunity and the means to utilise the DGT as a policy instrument to pursue wider objectives. Hence it could link DGT decisions to policies for manufacturing firms and other sectors and undertake projects with objectives other than direct returns for the operator and whose profitability could only, at the very best, be very long run (videotex, cable, and satellites).

After 1990, however, policy in France changed as the institutional framework was altered. France Télécom's new position as a corporation with its own legal identity resulted in a clearer separation of the PTT Ministry/DGT's various roles; it also provided the operator with a degree of institutional autonomy from the political executive and a licence that made explicit its duties and that contained important conditions that pointed to a 'fair competition' model of telecommunications (for instance, its provisions over cross-subsidization of competitive and monopoly activities). France Télécom became less available as a policy tool for the political executive in pursuit of its industrial policy objectives, notably unprofitable *grands projets*.

Licensing powers and the continuation of BT's and the DGT's/France Télécom's legal monopoly outside advanced services (over the infrastructure and voice telephony) constituted other organisational factors that contributed to differing national policy patterns. In Britain before 1981, the powers to issue licences and break the Post Office's monopoly lay in the hands of the Post Office itself. Under the 1981 British Telecommunications Act, it was transferred to the Secretary of State, who used it to license competitors to BT. Furthermore, after 1984, BT's position as a private firm in competition with other firms, made it difficult for the government or Oftel to pursue public policies to encourage usage of public networks, to co-ordinate programmes or to decide which services were provided and how they should be supplied (even if they had wished to do so): such policies would have meant singling BT out from its competitors for special treatment, and hence, whether advantageous for BT or not, would have resulted in 'unfair competition'. In France, in contrast, the DGT's continuing monopoly over network operation required regulatory protection, leading to controls over cable networks and VANS to prevent 'bypass' of the PSTN (in particular, of voice telephony). Furthermore, the DGT's monopoly over networks allowed policies that encouraged use of public networks to be pursued, without difficulties of favouring one supplier over others. However, modifications in policy followed the French institutional reforms in 1990. The development of competition made the *grand projet* approach of maximizing use of a publicly-owned monopoly network difficult to continue; instead, France Télécom increasingly concentrated on profitable services and selected market segments.

Another important institutional factor was the existence of a regulatory body that was separate from the network operator. In Britain before 1984, the government found it difficult to muster the expertise to implement the detailed regulatory reforms needed for competition to develop; its difficulties were seen, for instance, in the 1982 VANS licence or CPE liberalization. After 1984, Oftel acted as an influential actor in increased competition. Its functions and powers allowed it to enforce and modify licences and to develop a specialized competence in regulating telecommunciations. In contrast, in France until 1990, regulation and supply were not separated, with both being undertaken by the PTT Ministry. There was no strong body responsible for regulation and promotion of 'fair competition' independent of the dominant operator. Change took place after 1990, when supply and regulation were separated and France Télécom ceased to be part of the PTT Ministry. Although the DRG/DGPT was not an independent regulator, it was a body seperate from France Télécome, and rapidly assumed a major role in pressing for 'fair' competition.

Thus dissimilar institutional arrangements contributed towards the increasing contrasts found in the policy-making process and the policies adopted in the 'advanced services and networks' and CPE subsector until 1990, aiding, encouraging, and providing instruments for differences. Thereafter, dissimilarities between the two countries diminished, as the French organizational reforms of 1990 took effect. Examination of institutional arrangements aids explanation both of national policy patterns, including change, and of cross-national differences. Moreover, the role of specific institutional features in policy patterns can be traced. Advanced services and networks, and CPE allow the impact of national institutions to be seen in a subsector of telecommunications with different technological and economic characteristics than network operation (which was examined in previous chapters), and one subject to earlier and more powerful forces arising from the international regulatory environment. The findings therefore provide valuable support for national institutionalist claims that national institutions influence policy.

PART IV

**Economic Outcomes in Telecommunications
1970–1997**

11

Economic Outcomes in the Telecommunications Sector in Britain and France 1970–1997: Convergence Despite Institutional Divergence

National institutionalism suggests that contrasting institutions result in important differences not only in policy making but also in the economic performance of countries. In the face of common technological and economic developments, Britain and France maintained dissimilar institutional arrangements over the period 1969–97. If economic performance were strongly influenced by a country's institutions, then differences should also be seen over that period. Moreover, it might be expected to show variations corresponding to changing institutional patterns: hence it might diverge over the period 1969–90, reflecting increasing institutional dissimilarities between the two countries before 1990 and then some degree of convergence, following a narrowing of institutional contrasts. In addition, the effects of institutional reforms in Britain in 1984 and in France in 1990 should be visible.

Previous chapters have shown that differences in policy making existed between the two countries, albeit with a lessening of differences after 1990. However, this chapter looks at economic results. An automatic link between institutions, public policy, and economic performance cannot be assumed: policies may not be implemented or may be formulated in nominal financial terms, whereas it is real outcomes that are more significant for economic performance; the effects of public decisions may be counterbalanced by those of private actors; public policy may be unimportant for economic outcomes relative to other factors; dissimilar public policies may result in similar economic performances by nations, due to interactions with other national factors (for instance, culture or industrial structure); vice versa, similar policies may not produce equivalent outcomes due to differing national environments.

To assess the possible impact of national institutions on economic performance, the chapter examines indicators of 'economic outcomes'—quantifiable results concerning the supply of telecommunications services and equipment in the policy areas analysed in previous chapters. Its function is to establish whether, in terms of economic outcomes, the two countries were similar or different in the period 1970–97. Hence it seeks either data that runs counter to institutionalist claims or evidence that is congruent with institutionalist arguments. After analysing the overall economic size of the British and French telecommunications sectors in international and national terms, it studies network operation, the equipment manufacturing subsector and 'other networks and services'. A wide range of indicators are considered—size, revenue, modernization, profitability, investment, the date of availability of new services and tariffs.

The central finding is that a wide variety of economic indicators were characterized by similar trends in both Britain and France. Furthermore, many of the differences that existed between the two countries in the 1970s had narrowed by the mid-1990s. Contrasts did exist, but they often lay in the pace and timing of change. Insofar as dissimilarities continued to exist between Britain and France, they were overshadowed in size and importance by the similar directions of change that applied to the two countries.

The evidence in terms of economic outcomes therefore contradicts institutionalist predictions. The finding of similarities and often convergence thus represents a challenge and indeed a rebuttal of national institutionalist claims. However, the chapter does *not* seek to explain the economic results that are found: this would involve examination of econometric evidence and a market survey of suppliers, both public and private. Similarly, it does not attempt to analyse economic efficiency. Instead, it limits itself to providing a host of data comparing trends in the two countries and, where possible, also comparing levels directly. It confines itself to testing national institutionalist claims, rather than offering explanation of its economic findings.

Methodology

Quantitative indicators are studied that relate to the policy areas analysed in earlier chapters. Two types of comparison between Britain and France are used. First, the main features and trends over time in each of the two countries are determined and then compared; features may be similar or different, and the directions of change may be similar or different. Second, direct comparison of absolute levels may be undertaken where possible in the two countries although in a more tentative manner than trends over time due to greater obstacles concerning comparability of data; absolute levels may converge, diverge, show unchanging similarities or differences, or be characterized by trendless fluctuation.

The period from 1970 until 1996/7 is examined. Figures are given for selected years, mostly 1970, 1980, 1984, and 1990 and the mid-1990s. Tariff figures for 1997 are those of July 1997. The choice of 1980, 1984, and 1990 is due to major institutional change occurring in Britain in 1984 and in France in

1990: if institutional arrangements made a major impact on economic performance, this might be seen in figures for periods before and after the institutional modifications.

All monetary figures are in 1970 pounds sterling or 1970 pence, in order to allow comparison over time and between Britain and France; figures for France have been converted into nominal pounds sterling, using purchasing power parities, and then the UK GDP deflator has been applied to figures to obtain 1970 prices. Furthermore, indices with 1970 as base 100 are provided to facilitate comparison of trends. In comparative tables, figures for the UK are placed on the left-hand side of tables and those for France on the right-hand side. In network operation and the supply of 'other services and networks', only figures for the PO/BT and the DGT/FT are considered: although competition was permitted in the 1980s and 1990s, notably in Britain, both organizations kept a preponderant market share, with the exception of cellular radio in Britain.[1] However, by 1995, other suppliers were attaining significant size, and hence certain figures for market size are underestimates. Unless otherwise stated, the sources for figures for the UK are: PO/BT, British Telecommunications Statistics (London: HMSO, annual), Post Office/British Telecom, Annual Reports and Accounts (London: PO/BT, annual), and Oftel, Annual Report (London: HMSO, annual); and for France, DGT/FT, Statistique Annuelle (Paris: DGT/FT, annual) and France Télécom's Rapport Annuel (Paris: FT, annual) for France.

Analysing statistics confronts various problems which need to be recognized from the outset. First, not all figures are available, especially for 1996–7. Second, some years may be abnormal; this applies particularly if an annual 'flow' is examined, such as profits or investment; hence more figures are provided or a check has been undertaken that the years selected did not greatly differ from other recent years. However, the most important problems concern comparison. Time series may suffer from changing categories or methods of data collection. Cross-national comparison is even more vulnerable to differences in definitions, categories and data collection, as well as the conversion of monetary figures. Given these problems, the overall picture is sought and conclusions are not based on small differences. Moreover, the problems outlined tend to affect cross-national comparison more than trends over time within a country, and hence the first method of comparison (features and trends between countries) may be regarded as more reliable than direct cross-national comparison of absolute levels. Finally, no attempt is made to explain the pattern of outcomes found nor to tackle issues of efficiency, which would require

[1] In France, little competition was allowed until the 1990s; in Britain, when competition was permitted, overall, BT kept a market share of over 97 per cent until the mid-1990s; even in specialized segments such as international traffic or packet switching, BT enjoyed market shares of over 80 per cent until the mid-1990s; for figures, see Oftel, Annual Reports (London: Oftel, annual), Oftel, Market Information (London: Oftel, annual), and BZW, Telephone Sector Networks Review, (London: BZW, 1990).

TABLE 1: Total telecommunications services income in selected countries as a per cent of OECD toal telecommunications services income

Year	Britain	France	USA	Japan
1970	7.0	4.5	48.8	11.6
1975	8.4	5.1	47.0	10.7
1980	6.7	6.2	45.6	12.7
1985	6.6	6.0	50.5	10.4
1990	7.2	5.1	43.9	10.6
1995	6.1	4.7	41.3	11.6

Source: ITU (International Telecommunications Union), *Annual Statistics* (Geneva: ITU, annual); calculation using purchasing power parities from OECD, *Principal Economic Indicators* (Paris: OECD, quarterly).

a detailed econometric analysis. The Appendix contains details of the method used in calculation of figures and the problems with the use and interpretation of statistics.

The Overall Position of the Telecommunications Sector

Analysis of the size of the entire British and French telecommunications sectors indicates similar positions in international and national terms throughout the period 1970–96 (see Table 1). The sectors accounted for only relatively small shares of the total world market and were much smaller than the telecommunications sectors in the United States and Japan. Whilst the French telecommunications sector was somewhat smaller in 1970 than the British one, differences had largely disappeared by the late 1980s.

The limited size of the British and French telecommunications sectors in international terms can also be seen (Table 2) by looking at the income and investment of the network operators in the two countries as a proportion of that in the OECD (markets in the OECD represented 85–90 per cent of the entire world market[2]). Although telecommunications in France were somewhat smaller than in Britain during the 1970s, they had largely caught-up by 1980 and, in world terms, the two countries were of similar size.[3]

[2] OECD, *Telecommunications Network Based. Services* (Paris: OECD, 1989) and *Pressures and Policies for Change* (Paris: OECD, 1983).

[3] The ITU figures in Tables 1 and 2 somewhat overstate the gap between Britain and France, due to the COGECOM subsidiaries of France Télécom being excluded; direct comparison of BT and France Télécom in the 1990s indicates that the two companies were of comparable size. See Table 6.

TABLE 2: Total gross investment by network operators as per cent
of total by OECD network operators

Year	Britain	France	USA	Japan
1970	8.1	4.3	43.6	15.4
1975	8.1	5.5	36.0	15.9
1980	6.3	7.4	41.1	13.5
1985	5.6	7.9	36.0	13.0
1990	5.7	4.9	25.6	14.5
1995	5.6	4.6	25.6	20.4

Source: (and calculation) as in Table 1.

In national terms, the British and French telecommunications sectors as a whole grew rapidly, both in absolute size and as a percentage of GDP. This can be seen by looking at the combined revenue of network operation and equipment supply (Table 3); moreover, such figures underes-timate volume growth due to falling real prices, especially during the 1980s and 1990s.

The French telecommunications sector was considerably smaller than the British one in 1970, in absolute terms and as a proportion of GDP, but had largely caught-up by 1980; the gap is slightly over-estimated due to the existence of DGT subsidiaries, whose turnover is not included

TABLE 3: The economic size of the telecommunications sector

Year	Britain			France		
	total income	1970 = 100	per cent of GDP	total income	1970 = 100	per cent of GDP
1970	1,028	100	2.0	568	100	1.2
1975	1,439	140	2.5	907	160	1.6
1980	1,488	145	2.4	1,268	223	1.9
1984	1,856	181	2.8	1,492	263	2.1
1988	2,155	210	2.8	1,549	273	2.0
1990	2,279	217	2.8	1,632	287	2.0
1992	2,005	195	2.5	1,895	334	2.1
1995	2,090	203	2.4	1,920	338	2.0

Sources: CSO, National Accounts (London: HMSO, annual); BT, British Telecommunications Statistics and BT Reports and Accounts; DGT/FT, Statistique Annuelle; CSO, Business Monitors PQ 81, PQ 363, PQ 3441 (London: HMSO, quarterly) for UK equipment, and INSEE, NAP (Nomenclature d'Activités et de Produits) 2911 (Paris: INSEE, annual), for French equipment manufacturing; 'other services and networks' are excluded, but they were small relative to network operation and equipment manufacturing; figures for the mid-1990s are considerably less accurate than for previous years as they exclude service suppliers other than BT and FT, which had attained significant size by 1995.

TABLE 4: The income of the PO/BT and the DGT/FT as proportion of total telecommunications income

Year	Britain		France	
	PO/BT income (£1,970m.)	PO/BT income per cent total sector income	DGT/FT income (£1,970m.)	DGT/FT income per cent total sector income
1970	786	76	432	75
1974	955	77	561	67
1978	1,201	84	833	72
1980	1,272	83	967	76
1984	1,568	84	1,135	76
1988	1,856	86	1,151	74
1990	1,938	85	1,296	79
1992	1,760	88	1,562	82
1995	1,780	85	1,659	86

Note: Figures for the mid-1990s are considerably less accurate than for previous years as they exclude service suppliers other than BT and FT, which had attained significant size by 1995.

(Table 4).[4] In both Britain and France, the sector was dominated by the network operator—the PO/BT and the DGT/FT, who accounted for the majority of sector income (See Table 4), as well as providing orders to domestic equipment suppliers.

Network Operation

Analysis of network operation indicates strong similarities in the direction of change in the two countries. These findings apply to the key features of national operation—size, modernization, investment, quality, financial characteristics, and tariffs. The telephone networks were expanded and modernized. High levels of investment were undertaken, labour productivity rose and quality of service improved. In general, network operators were highly profitable; they derived a disproportionally large share of their profits and revenues from national (trunk) and international calls. Tariffs saw very substantial changes, with large declines in real terms for certain services, and rebalancing of relative prices of local and long distance communications.

[4] Due to double-counting problems, since consolidated accounts of the DGT and its subsidiaries were not produced; COGECOM, the holding company for the subsidiaries since 1984, had an income (£1970) of £65m. in 1987 and £156m. in 1990.

Most directions of change were highly pronounced in the two countries, being sustained over many years. They were much more significant than the differences that existed between Britain and France, which mostly related to the timing and speed of change, not its direction. Moreover, whilst considerable contrasts existed between the DGT and the Post Office in 1970, by the mid-1990s, the dissimilarities had greatly narrowed, as economic outcomes in the two countries converged.

Size of Network Operators

In both countries, the network operators the PO/BT and the DGT/FT experienced large-scale and sustained expansion (Table 5 and 6). Growth can be seen both in terms of revenues (which more than doubled over the period in real terms, despite reductions in most tariffs in real terms) and numbers of main lines (total numbers and connections per 100 inhabitants). Moreover, the size of the two networks converged: whereas the French telephone system was approximately half the size of the British one, by the early 1980s it was of very similar size in terms of numbers of main lines (and indeed exceeded it by the mid-1980s), whilst the gap in revenues narrowed sharply (Table 6).

Figures for the volume of traffic ought to allow measurement of usage. Unfortunately, until the 1990s, Britain and France produced different measures. The PO/BT measured the number of 'originated effective calls', but with no indication of the length of calls or number of units consumed. The figures indicate that the number of calls grew rapidly over the period: from 10,766m in 1970, to 20,291 in 1980, to 38,855m in 1990. The DGT/FT measured the number of chargeable units consumed (until 1988), which rose from 15,574m in 1970 to 56,468m in 1980, and then 98,161m in 1988. In the 1990s, both countries produced figures for the number of minutes of traffic, which indicated

TABLE 5: The telephone network

Year	Britain		France	
	main lines (m.)	main lines per 100 inhabitants	main lines (m.)	main lines per 100 inhabitants
1970	9.2	16.6	4.2	8.2
1980	18.4	33.1	15.6	29.7
1984	20.9	37.0	21.6	39.2
1990	25.9	45.5	28.0	47.0
1995	29.4	50.3	32.4	55.8

Includes Mercury in Britain, unlike other tables.

TABLE 6: Network operators' revenues

Year	PO/BT		DGT/FT	
	real income (£1970m.)	1970 = 100	real income (£1970m.)	1970 = 100
1970	786	100	432	100
1975	1,171	149	607	140
1980	1,232	157	967	224
1985	1,627	207	1,271	294
1990	1,938	247	1,296	300
1996	1,781	227	1,805	418

Note: Figures somewhat understate the DGT/FT's revenues before 1996, due to its COGECOM subsidiaries being excluded.

comparable sizes in the two countries (in 1995, there was usage of 116,747m minutes within the UK and 104,400m minutes in France).[5]

Modernization, Investment, Employment, Labour Productivity, and Quality of Service

In both Britain and France, new technology was rapidly introduced into network operation, thanks to large-scale investment. Employment fell, labour productivity rose and quality of service improved. Differences did exist between the PO/BT and the DGT/FT, but these related more to the speed and timing of changes, rather than to their direction.

The technological nature of network operation was transformed in both Britain and France: in 1970, most switching was undertaken by electro-mechanical exchanges, but by 1995 all or almost all was being done by time division (i.e. fully digital) switches (Table 7). The main differences between the two countries lay in the use of the intermediate space division exchanges and the timing of the introduction of time division exchanges: in France, the DGT began to move directly to time division exchanges from the late 1970s, whereas in Britain space division exchanges were introduced from the late 1970s and time division switches were used on a large scale only after 1986. Thereafter, however, the implementation of time division switching was extremely rapid and by the mid-1990s, time division switching predominated.

In both Britain and France, optical fibre cable became widely used in the network during the 1980s. The main difference between them was that in France under the Plan Câble it was used in the local network, with 85,000 kilo-

---

[5] See ITU, Annual Statistics.

TABLE 7: Percentage of PSTN customer lines switched by different types of exchange

Year	Britain			France		
	electromechanical	space division	time division	electromechanical	space division	time division
1970	98.0	0.2	0.0	78.0	0.0	0.0
1980	85.3	14.7	0.0	87.3	5.6	8.7
1984	67.0	32.9	0.1	50.3	15.0	34.8
1990	16.1	37.1	46.9	13.5	13.4	73.0
1996	0	7.4	92.6	0	7.0	93.0

Note: Manual exchanges are not included; they accounted for 1.2 per cent of switching in Britain in 1970 and 22 per cent in France, but by 1980 no manual switches remained in use in either country; sources for 1996: BT, *Annual Reports* and FT, *Rapport Annuel.*

metres laid by 1987,[6] but was less used in the trunk network until the late 1980s, whilst it was extensively used in BT's trunk network in the 1980s, and was only introduced into the local network on a large-scale in the late 1980s. However, by the 1990s, differences narrowed: France Télécom established a large-scale optical fibre trunk network, with 1.3 million kilometres of optical fibre cable; BT had 3.3 million kilometres of optical fibre cable by March 1997, but was also using optical fibre cable for both trunk networks and local networks for large business customers.[7]

Very considerable investment, representing a significant share of national investment was undertaken by both the PO/BT and the DGT/FT throughout the period 1970–1990s (Table 8). French investment in telecommunications in the early 1970s was considerably smaller than in Britain. This pattern changed during the mid- to late 1970s through a series of substantial increases, and from the mid-1970s to the mid-1980s, DGT investment was somewhat larger than PO/BT investment, which fell in real terms from its 1970 level. However, increases in BT's investment in the 1980s meant that by the late 1980s the level of investment in the two countries was similar.

In both the PO/BT and the DGT/FT, employment rose in the 1970s, before declining slightly in the 1980s (Table 9). However, employment in the DGT/France Télécom remained at a considerably lower level than in the PO/BT until the mid-1990s. Throughout the period, labour productivity, as measured by the number of main lines per employee or revenue per employee, grew steadily for both operators, as can be seen in Table 10.

Quality of service greatly improved over the period 1970–96, although the measurements used in Britain and France are not comparable. The waiting list for a telephone in Britain was 108,000 in 1970 and after fluctuations in the 1970s,

[6] FT, *Rapport d'Activité 1989.*   [7] FT, *Rapport Annuel 1996*, 7. BT, *Annual Report 1997*, 69, 8.

TABLE 8: Fixed asset investment by the PO/BT and DGT/FT

Year	PO/BT			DGT/FT		
	investment (£1970m)	1970 = 100	per cent gross fixed capital formation	investment (£1970m)	1970 = 100	per cent gross fixed capital formation
1970	426	100	4.4	231	100	2.0
1974	541	127	4.5	384	166	1.8
1978	369	87	3.2	484	210	3.6
1980	353	83	3.1	498	216	3.3
1984	376	88	3.3	484	210	3.6
1988	494	116	3.3	492	213	3.2
1990	406	95	2.6	415	180	2.4
1994	380	89	2.9	429	186	2.5
1996	325	76	2.6	312	135	1.8

Note: Comparability over time for FT is reduced by the exclusion of indirect taxes after 1990 and the exclusion of subsidiaries before 1996.

TABLE 9: Employment

Year	PO/BT (000)	DGT/FT (000)
1970	232	106
1980	247	161
1984	235	167
1990	227	156
1996	127	165

Note: DGT/FT figures exclude subsidiaries until 1996.

TABLE 10: Labour productivity

Year	PO/BT		DGT/FT	
	no. of main lines per employee	revenue per employee (£1970)	no. of main lines per employee	revenue per employee (£1970)
1970	39.7	3,387	39.6	3,789
1980	74.5	4,989	98.9	6,006
1984	88.9	6,672	134.7	6,794
1990	100.4	7,608	156.3	7,193
1996	231.5	14,024	196.4	10,939

reached 500,000 in 1980.[8] The list then rapidly diminished, so that by 1984 supply was sufficient to meet demand, a position that continued thereafter.[9] Call quality improved: the percentage of trunk calls failing to get through due to reasons attributable to the PO/BT fell from 4.3 per cent in 1970 to 3 per cent by 1983, whilst the figures for local calls were 2.5 per cent in 1970 and 1 per cent in 1983.[10] After 1983, a new (and non-comparable) method of measurement showed that the percentage of BT local calls that failed due to defective equipment or congestion declined from 2.7 per cent in 1983 to 0.4 per cent by March 1991 and then to 0.09 in March 1994, and the percentage of trunk calls failing also fell from 5.9 per cent in 1983 to 0.5 per cent by 1991 and then 0.12 in March 1994.[11]

In France, waiting lists decreased dramatically, from 792,000 on the list in 1972 to 28,000 in 1985, whilst the average wait for a main line declined from an average 18 months in 1972 to under two weeks in 1990. Call quality also showed great improvement: a global index of quality, covering congestion, length of wait for a dialling tone, reporting of faults and speed of repair, showed an increase from 57 in 1975 to 96 in 1986.[12] The number of faults per 100 main lines fell from 20.9 in 1986 to 6.3 in 1995.[13] In the 1990s improvements continued: by end 1993, the waiting time for telephone line was 8 days, whilst only 0.33 per cent of calls failed due to network defects or congestion.[14]

Profitability and the Sources of Costs, Revenues, and Profits

Comparing financial indicators, especially those relating to profits, is fraught with greater difficulty than for other figures: categories differ between countries or change over time; annual fluctuations can be large; limited data are available on sensitive matters. However, circumscribed conclusions can be drawn, provided that reliance is placed on broad features. Telecommunications operators have generally been very profitable, albeit with significant fluctuations in net profits. Revenues and profits in both countries have disproportionately derived from long-distance (trunk and international) communications rather than charges for local calls and access to the network.

Table 11 shows that in Britain the net profits and profitability of the PO dropped markedly between 1970 and 1974, but then recovered sharply during the mid-late 1970s. After a decline in 1980, profitability continued to appreciate during the 1980s and then declined somewhat in the early 1990s. In France, DGT/*France Télécom* profitability fell from the very high levels that existed in the 1970s and especially the early 1980s, but then recovered somewhat in the late 1980s and 1990s.

---

[8] *The Times* 22.4.70 and 15.10.80.
[9] J. M. Harper, *The Third Way* (Stevenage: IEE, 1990).   [10] Ibid. 22.
[11] Oftel, *Annual Reports*.   [12] For individual indices, see DGT, *Statistique Annuelle*.
[13] ITU, *Annual Statistics*.   [14] DGPT, *Rapport Annuel 1994*, 72.

TABLE 11: The profits and profitability of the PO/BT and DGT/FT ('profit on ordinary activities'—excluding taxes, exceptional items, and '*prélèvements*')[a]

Year	PO/BT		DGT/FT	
	historic cost profit	as per cent of total	net profit	as per cent of total
1970	130	16.5	166	32.9
1972	49	5.8	108	19.4
1974	−49	−5.1	167	26.2
1976	291	23.3	148	21.9
1978	261	21.7	185	19.7
1980	154	12.5	201	18.4
1982	233	16.2	56	5.6
1984[b]	303	19.3	147	8.8
1986	387	22.1	184	14.1
1988	409	22.0	153	12.9
1990	453	23.4	229	16.6
1992	262	14.9	197	12.6
1994	352	19.2	178	10.7
1995	312	20.9	182	11.1

[a] Difficulties with direct comparison of the PO/BT and the DGT/FT should be noted, 1996 is excluded due to changes in FT's accounting rules and the consolidation of subsidiaries; accounting changes have taken place, notably in France in 1990.
[b] BT switched to historic cost accounting in 1984; figures for the period before then are own calculation using PO/BT accounts.

Cross-national comparison of net profitability is hazardous given differing accounting rules and conventions, especially concerning depreciation (notably historic cost accounting, which distorts profits due to the effects of inflation and the different timing of investment). The changing patterns of profitability over time and differences between the two operators can be better understood by looking at the a break down of costs. Both the PO/BT and the DGT/FT had similar proportions of income devoted to staff costs, and both saw declines in the 1980s and 1990s. However, BT had considerably lower levels of depreciation than the DGT/FT, a factor increasing the PO/BT's levels of operating profitability and ordinary profitability. During the 1970s, the DGT had significantly lower levels of interest and other financial costs, increasing its profitability on ordinary activities (but not affecting operating profits, which exclude interest payments). After 1984, the position was reversed, as BT enjoyed much lower interest charges, but in the 1990s, differences between the two operators narrowed as France Télécom's interest costs fell sharply. These factors can be seen in Table 12.

Table 13a/b shows that for both the PO/BT and the DGT/FT, network operation (i.e. the fixed-line public switched telephone network) accounted for the bulk of their revenue, although this fell somewhat in the 1990s; within

TABLE 12: Major categories of costs as % of the total revenue of the PO/BT and DGT/FT

Year	PO/BT			DGT/FT		
	staff	depreciation	interest/financial	staff	depreciation	interest/financial
1970	46.6	15.4	14.8	44.7	20.8	1.2
1974	61.2	17.6	20.6	35.1	16.9	3.4
1978	41.7	12.5	13.8	35.1	20.2	8.5
1980	46.3	13.9	12.1	33.6	25.5	12.9
1984	36.7	12.2	5.2	32.6	27.8	19.1
1988	35.3	14.5	3.1	32.1	42.7	14.8
1990	29.7	14.7	3.2	26.5	27.8	10.7
1994	27.9	15.4	2.4	27.7	27.6	7.5
1995	25.5	15.2	1.2	28.1	27.7	6.2

TABLE 13a: Income from network operation

Year	PO/BT		DGT/FT	
	Total PSTN income	PSTN as per cent of total income	Total PSTN income	PSTN as per cent of total income
1970	691	88	377	87
1980	1,069	87	874	90
1984	1,366	87	1,029	91
1990	1,305	67	1,104	85
1996	1,135	64	1,222	68

Sources: ITU, *Annual Statistics*, BT, *Reports and Accounts*, DGT, *Statistiques Annuelles*, France Télécom, *Rapport Annuel*; strict comparability of figures is limited by: inclusion of public callboxes in France; inclusion of 'other income from the telephone service' until 1984 by BT, so that access and call charges do not account for 100 per cent of total PSTN income; changes in BT's accounting bases in 1984.

TABLE 13b: Composition of network income revenue

Year	PO/BT		DGT/FT	
	per cent from calls	per cent from connection and rental charges	per cent from calls	per cent from connection and rental charges
1970	59	36	75	25
1980	57	36	76	24
1984	62	38	81	19
1986	62	38	83	17
1990	79	21	n/a	n/a
1996	70	30	72	28

this, calls provided the majority of revenue and only a minority of network operation income came from charges for access to the network (i.e. connection and rental charges). Although a somewhat higher proportion of PSTN income in Britain arose from access charges than in France, where call income was more important, in the 1970s and 1980s, this situation was largely ended by the mid-1990s, as the share of PSTN income derived from access charges increased.[15]

Further analysis of sources of revenue indicates that long-distance calls, especially international traffic, provided a disproportionately large share of revenues for the network operators. Thus, for instance, international calls accounted for only 0.2 per cent of the total number of calls in 1970, but provided 22 per cent of the Post Office's call revenue; in 1980, the figures were 0.6 per cent of calls and 27 per cent of revenue. In 1995–6, the figures for traffic volumes and shares of BT's total call revenues were:[16]

Type of call	per cent total call minutes	per cent BT's total call revenues
local	63 per cent	32 per cent
national	30 per cent	27 per cent
international	3.2 per cent	16 per cent

In France, in 1989, the composition of traffic (by minutes) was:

local	65.0 per cent
trunk	31.0 per cent
international	2.2 per cent.

However, one estimate[17] of the composition of call revenues in 1986 was:

local traffic	17 per cent
interurban traffic	73 per cent
international traffic	10 per cent

In 1995, outgoing international calls represented 2.6 per cent of total national telephone traffic in France, but international telephone services provided 15.4 per cent of France Télécom's PSTN income.[18]

---

[15] This is linked to changes in tariffs—see below.

[16] Source: Oftel, *Market Update* (London: Oftel, annual).

[17] M. Feynerol, 'Télécommunications: un nouvel environnement', in *Revue Française des Télécommunications*, 62 (1987), 17–23.

[18] ITU, *Annual Statistics*, France Télécom, *Rapport Annuel 1996*, 27; the position for international traffic is complicated, due to the international settlements system, whereby monies are also paid to the operator receiving the international call and the existence of international bothway traffic; nevertheless, the sheer size of the differences between usage and income remains.

TABLE 14a: The profitability of PO services (per cent of revenue from charges for each service)

Year	Access to PSTN profit margin	Inland calls profit margin	International calls profit margin
1970	−6.2	22.1	26.3
1980	−31.7	25.2	24.9
1982	−13.1	21.3	n/a

TABLE 14b: DGT/FT revenue and call costs for 1986, by type of call

Service	per cent of call revenues	per cent costs
local	17	56
interurban	73	38
international	10	6

Analysis of the type of user also indicates that both the PO/BT and the DGT/FT derived a large proportion of their income from a few large corporate customers, who tended to use trunk and international communications heavily: one estimate claimed that in the early 1980s, 300 clients produced 20 per cent of BT's revenue,[19] whilst a figure of 10 per cent of DGT income being derived from 2000 corporate clients has been put forward.[20]

Not only were revenues disproportionate to usage, but so were profits. Whilst figures are particularly difficult to analyse in detail, since data are confidential and the allocation of costs to types of service involves a considerable degree of judgement, it does appear that cross-subsidisation between services took place in both Britain and France: trunk and especially international traffic were highly profitable, and subsidised access to the telephone network, whilst local calls were unprofitable or less profitable than long-distance calls.

Table 14a sets out the profit/losses and profit margins for access to the telephone network, inland calls and international calls in Britain. Figures produced by Oftel and by BT itself in the 1990s appear to indicate that different profit levels by service and cross-subsidization of access to the network continued in

[19] A. Cawson, P. Holmes, D. Webber, K. Morgan, and A. Stevens, *Hostile Brothers* (Oxford: Clarendon Press, 1990), 102.
[20] L. Benzoni, 'Departing from Monopoly' (paper presented to Red Hall colloquium, June 1987); 2 per cent of main lines provided 20 per cent of total traffic in the late 1980s—see also OECD, *Telecommunications Network Based Services*.

the late 1980s and 1990s. In particular, network access (connection and rental charges) was loss making, whilst calls were profitable.[21]

In France, Feynerol[22] produced the figures given in Table 14*b* for costs and revenues by telephony service. Another study, by Curien and de la Bonnetière[23] estimated that revenue from access charges only covered 40 per cent of costs, that from local telephony met 79 per cent of costs, whereas that from international traffic represented 230 per cent of costs.

Tariffs

Two central features of tariffs have been common to both Britain and France. First, there have been massive declines in real terms for most services, especially long-distance calls. Second, there has a been a 'rebalancing' of prices, most markedly in the 1980s and 1990s: declines for rental have been much less than for trunk and international calls, and some local calls have risen in real terms. Comparison between Britain and France indicates a narrowing of many differences in absolute levels, but in any case, the trends common to the two countries have been much greater than any differences between them in tariffs.

Two methods of analysing and comparing prices are possible: examination of the prices of individual services; construction of 'baskets' reflecting the usage of different services. Both approaches are used below, but each suffers from a number of problems.[24] Analysis of individual services allows 'rebalancing' to be identified, but faces the distorting effects of changes over time and differences between countries concerning:

- usage of services
- size of telephone areas
- the steps between local, lower rate trunk and full rate trunk calls
- the times and size of reductions for off-peak usage
- the minimum cost of a call—i.e. the cost per unit.

---

[21] Oftel, *The Regulation of BT's prices* (London: Oftel, 1992) provides figures for 1990 showing that profits as a percentage of turnover were −15.5 per cent and −38.6 per cent for business and residential access, but 52 per cent for local calls, 65 per cent for trunk calls and 46.6 per cent for international calls; for the 1997–8 financial year, BT's *Financial Statements for the Businesses and Activities 1998 and Restated 1997 Financial Statements* (London: BT, annual after 1997) offers figures of an 8.3 per cent return on turnover for business access, −7.8 per cent for residential access, but 46 per cent for local calls, 56 per cent for national ones and 37 per cent for international calls.

[22] 'Télécommunications: un nouvel environnement'; see also Longuet, *Télécoms. La Conquête de nouveaux espaces, op. cit.*, Annexe 1, for similar figures.

[23] N. Curien and G. de la Bonnetière, 'Les Transferts de revenus induits par la tarification téléphonique entre catégories d'abonnés et entre types de prestations', *Annals des Télécommunications*, 39(11–12) (1984), 469–86.

[24] For a fuller exposition, see M. E. McDowell, *Oftel Working Paper no. 2, International Comparison of Telephone Charges* (London: Oftel 1987), and Appendix.

- the quality of service
- the different fiscal treatment of services (VAT was not payable in France until 1987).

Moreover, examining charges for individual services faces the difficulty that in the mid-1990s, payment option plans, offering many reduction packages.[25] Thus figures for individual services in the 1990s underestimate price declines for calls.

Basket comparisons can offset the aforementioned limitations, but very few rigorous studies exist, especially covering periods of time, thus preventing the development of time series, data concerning usage of various services are limited and results tend to cover only the 'average' user. Although integration of payment options is possible, the process is complex and requires many assumptions to be made.

TABLE 15: Connection charges in Britain and France (£1970)

Year	Britain		France	
	cost	1970 = 100	cost	1970 = 100
1970	25.00	100	36.47	100
1980	14.88	60	11.72	32
1984	15.37	61	3.19	11
1990	19.04	76	3.15	9
1997	11.52	46	2.98	8

Connection Charges

Over the 25 year period, connection charges fell somewhat in Britain, although this included an increase in the 1980s. In France, connection charges fell dramatically and by the 1980s were much lower than those of BT.

TABLE 16: Rental charges (including supply of basic telephone handset)

Year	Britain		France	
	rental (£1970 p.a.)	1970 = 100	rental (£1970 p.a.)	1970 = 100
1970	20.00	100	17.93	100
1980	13.31	67	11.26	63
1984	12.60	63	7.29	41
1990	12.33	62	6.80	38
1997	10.55	53	7.63	43

Note: Rental charges in Britain are those for residential customers.

[25] e.g. BT's 'Family and Friends' scheme and 'Business Choice' levels, or France Télécom's local calling plan.

Table 17: Local call charges in the UK (1970 pence per minute)

Year	Peak rate	1970 = 100	Standard rate	Cheap rate	1970 = 100
1970	0.160	100	none	0.083	100
1980	0.554	346	0.369	0.122	147
1984	0.641	401	0.481	0.120	145
1990	0.648	405	0.457	0.162	195
1997	0.391	244	0.163	0.099	119

Table 18: The cost of the telephone unit in France (1970 pence)

Year	Cost	1970 = 100
1970	1.82	100
1980	1.17	64
1984	1.20	66

Rental Charges

Rental charges in Britain declined, especially during the 1970s and slightly in the early 1990s. French rental charges also dropped in real terms during both the 1970s and 1980s, but to a greater extent than in the UK, and in 1990 were lower than BT's charges; thereafter, however, they rose, reducing the gap between the two countries.

Local Call Charges

Table 17 shows that local call charges in Britain rose considerably in real terms over both the 1970s and 1980s, particularly peak rates. The 1990s saw a reversal of the trend, with reductions in local rates. In France the cost of local calls in France was not based on duration until 1985/6—one unit bought an unlimited length of time. Thus local calls were very cheap, aided by a drop in the real price of the unit (Table 18). In 1984–5 the tariff structure was altered, with the introduction of limited call duration varying with time of day. This meant a very large price increase, especially for longer length calls (Table 19). In the 1990s, local tariffs continued to rise, although a major revision of local call areas and distances in 1994 makes direct comparison more difficult.

In both Britain and France, local call charges rose sharply between 1970 and 1997. Comparison of absolute levels of local call charges between Britain and France is difficult, as French local call areas are generally smaller than British ones, in terms of area and subscribers. Nevertheless, it appears that charges in

TABLE 19: French local rates (1970p per minute)

Year	Red tariff	White tariff	Blue tariff	Blue night tariff
1986	0.19	0.11	0.09	0.07
1990	0.13	0.08	0.07	0.05
1997	0.24	0.16	0.12	0.08

TABLE 20a: UK trunk calls over 56 km. (1970 pence per minute)

Year	Peak rate	1970 = 100	Standard rate	1970 = 100	Cheap rate	1970 = 100
1970	7.50	100	6.00	100	1.67	100
1980	6.65	89	4.44	74	1.39	83
1984	3.85	51	2.29	38	1.20	72
1990	2.09	28	1.57	26	0.93	56
1997	0.78	10	0.46	8	0.33	20

France were much lower than in Britain before 1985/6; the gap then greatly narrowed in the period to 1997.

UK Trunk Calls (b-routes) and French Inter-Urban Calls[26]

Very large decreases occurred in trunk call tariffs in Britain, especially in the 1980s and 1990s, as can be seen in Table 20a.

A similar pattern of falling real prices applied to French interurban calls (Table 20b), although the introduction in 1984 of the 'red-white-blue' tariff structure[27] makes comparison with pre-1985 difficult, whilst alterations in the size of local calling areas in 1994 again represent a difficulty for data equivalence. In Table 22 'red' is treated as the equivalent of the 'normal' tariff and 'blue' as equivalent of the reduced tariff of pre-1985.

Direct comparison of British and French charges for trunk calls confronts the problems of different distances (over 56 km. in the UK, but 100 km. in France), off-peak reductions and times. Nevertheless, it can be seen that if the 'peak' period in Britain is taken as the equivalent to the normal/'red' period in France,

[26] Tariffs for UK trunk calls under 56 km., UK cheap trunk routes ('b1' routes) and French inter-départemental call prices are not considered as they followed a very similar evolution to the services considered in Table 20a; figures for 1997 are those for July 1997.

[27] Red is full tariff at peak times, white offers a 30 per cent reduction, blue offers a 50 per cent reduction, blue night provides a 65 per cent reduction.

TABLE 20b: French interurban calls over 100 km. (1970p per minute)

Year	Full rate	1970 = 100	Reduced rate			1970 = 100	
1970	9.12	100	4.56			100	
1980	5.86	64	2.93			64	
1983	5.20	57	2.60			57	

	red rate	1970 = 100	white rate	blue rate	1970 = 100	blue night
1984	5.98	66	4.20	3	66	2.09
1990	3.25	36	2.28	1.62	36	1.13
1995	2.19	24	1.53	1.10	24	0.77
1997	1.36	15	0.97	0.68	15	0.48

the standard rate to the white period and the cheap rate to the reduced/blue tariff, French prices were somewhat higher than those in Britain in the early 1970s and after 1984. However, the most striking feature is the sharp fall in real prices in both countries over the period.

International Telephony

In both Britain and France, prices of international telephony fell rapidly, notably in the 1980s and 1990s. Moreover, the figures indicate that although French charges were above British ones in the early 1970s, convergence of prices took place, most markedly in terms of price structures and levels for communications with the US in the mid-late 1980s.

Three international rates for telephony are set out as examples, in Tables 21–3: between Britain and France, a rate which also applied from the early/mid 1970s to other major countries within the EEC/EU; to the USA; and to Japan.

Basket Comparisons

Various studies analysing baskets of services for international comparison were carried out in the 1970s and 1980s. The majority of these indicated that charges were higher in France than in Britain.[28] However, these studies suffer from a number of methodological weaknesses.[29]

The most rigorous analysis has been McDowell's study.[30] Examining inland services only, he estimated that in 1986 telephone costs in France for the average residential consumer were 94 per cent of those in the UK, and 112 per cent for

[28] For instance: Post Office, Report and Accounts 1977–78; BEUC (Bureau européen des consommateurs), Telephoning in Europe (Brussels: BEUC, 1985); B. M. Mitchell, 'The Cost of the Telephone Service', Telecommunications Policy, 7(1) (1983), and Oftel, Review of BT's Tariff Changes (London: Oftel, 1986).

[29] See McDowell, Oftel Working Paper no. 2, for detailed criticisms.   [30] Ibid.

TABLE 21: UK–France and France–UK telephony rates (1970p per minute)

Year	PO/BT			DGT/FT		
	full rate	1970 = 100	reduced rate	full rate	1970 = 100	reduced rate
1970	11.9	100	none	9.8	100	none
1980	9.0	77	6.8	6.4	65	none
1984	7.7	65	62	7.2	73	4.8
1990	5.4	45	4.3	4.8	49	3.2
1997	2.8	24	2.6[a]	2.4	24	1.9

[a] Additional weekend rate of 2.3.

TABLE 22: UK and French call charges to Japan

Year	Britain			France		
	Full rate	1970 = 100	Reduced rate	Full rate	1970 = 100	Reduced rate
1970	83.0	100	none	99.6	100	none
1980	32.5	39	21.6	54.2	54	none
1984	18.3	22	13.8	44.8	45	none
1990	18.1	22	none	20.3	20	16.2
1997	7.6	9	7.2[a]	6.4	6	5.1

[a] Additional weekend rate of 6.9.

TABLE 23: UK and French rates to the USA

Year	UK rates				French rates			
	Full rate	1970 = 100	Reduced rate	Reduced rate 2	Full rate	1970 = 100	Reduced rate	Reduced rate 2
1970	50.0	100	none	n.a.	99.6	100	none	n.a.
1980	21.6	43	16.2	n.a.	54.2	54	none	n.a.
1985	12.5	25	11.5	9.9	19.4	27	13.2	11.6
1990	9.8	20	8.9	7.6	9.9	14	7.6	6.1
1997	2.3	5	2.2	none	2.9	3	2.3	none

the average business subscriber. Oftel updated his study: in January 1990, it estimated that French residential subscriber costs were 76 per cent of those in
Britain, and business costs were 83 per cent.[31] However, a study by the DGPT
in 1994, using baskets of services for 'households' and for 'firms' constructed

[31] Oftel, *Press Notice*, January 1990.

TABLE 24: Equipment sales by UK and French manufacturers

Year	Britain		France	
	Total sales (£1970m)	1970 = 100	Total sales (£1970m)	1970 = 100
1970	242	100	136	100
1980	256	106	301	221
1984	288	119	357	263
1988	299	124	332	245
1995	310	128	355	261

TABLE 25: Employment

Year	Britain (000)	France (000)
1974	87	69
1980	68	61
1984	51	52
1995	n/a	26

by Oftel, concluded that for calls within each country (i.e. local and trunk calls), the basket cost for France Télécom was 96 per cent that of BT for firms and 83 per cent that of BT for households (using purchasing power parities).[32] These findings are congruent with figures set out for individual services. It appears that during the 1970s, French telephone tariffs were higher than those in Britain. However, during the 1980s and 1990s, *overall* costs converged.

Equipment Manufacturing and Supply[33]

The equipment-manufacturing subsector in Britain and France experienced similar trends over the period 1970–95. Although growth occurred, it was much slower than for telecommunications services and employment in the subsector declined. Whilst the French equipment manufacturing subsector was much smaller than its British counterpart in 1970, it enjoyed rapid growth to become of similar size or slightly larger by 1980; thereafter, however, it too suffered from slow or negative growth.

[32] DGPT, *Rapport d'Activité 1994*, 62–3.
[33] Sources: CSO, *Business Monitors* PQ 81, 363, and 3441 (London: CSO, quarterly) for Britain; NAP 2911 (Paris: INSEE, annual) and SI3T/SIT (Syndicat des Industries de Télécommunication), *Rapports d'Activité* (Paris: SI3T/SIT, annual); the figures include the manufacture of customer premises equipment.

TABLE 26: The composition of equipment sales (per cent of total)

Year	Britain[a]				France			
	Public switching	Private switching	Transmission	Terminals/ CPE	Public and private switching	Transmission	Terminals/ CPE	Other
1970[b]	43	8	14	26	64	20	12	4
1980	49	9	13	24	58	16	17	9
1984	33	11	24	30	47	12	27	14
1988[b]	28	16	29	23	45	21	33	—
1990[b]	28	18	18	31	53	19	26	—

[a] Changes in definitions and counting methods in 1987; further alterations in 1990 make comparison impossible.
[b] The figures for France were taken from the years 1971, 1989, and 1993 respectively.

TABLE 27: Destinations of sales by manufacturers (per cent of total)

Year	PO/BT	Domestic non-PO/BT	Exports	DGT/FT	Domestic non-DGT/FT	Exports
1974	65	17	13	65	24	11
1980	71	16	9	57	30	13
1984	75	15	13	49	32	19
1988	58	27	16	49	37	14
1993	(60)		41	45	37	28
1995	(27)		73	41	26	33

In both Britain and France, switching equipment accounted for a very large proportion of sales (Table 26). However, this share decreased in the 1980s, whereas that of customer premises equipment and terminals rose. The major source of orders (Table 27) in both countries remained the domestic network operator, but this too decreased over the period 1970–95.

The greatest difference between Britain and France in equipment manufacturing lay in the balance of trade, which moved in opposite directions: in the former it passed from surplus in the 1970s to growing deficit in the 1980s, whereas France enjoyed some growth in its surplus. However, British exports expanded rapidly in the 1990s, and indeed in 1996, the deficit was down to £36m. (£1970).

The Supply of Advanced Networks and Services and Customer Premises Equipment

Advanced networks and services are highly diverse and often only began to be supplied commercially from the 1980s onwards. Nevertheless, in both Britain

TABLE 28: Equipment exports and imports (1970m.)

Year	Britain			France		
	exports	imports	trade balance	exports	imports	trade balance
1974	37.6	21.1	16.5	30.1	12.0	18.2
1980	22.1	19.0	3.1	34.9	12.1	22.8
1984	37.5	48.0	−10.5	66.1	13.7	52.3
1988	47.5	107.3	−59.9	44.5	20.2	24.3
1995	226.0	280.0	−54.1	117.0	63.6	53.6

and France, trends have been for the development and expansion of new services and advanced networks and for declining prices in real terms; moreover, figures for prices underestimate the real changes because quality has generally greatly improved. Whilst differences have existed between Britain and France, they have been less significant for most networks and services than the features common to the two countries, notably the appearance of similar services at similar times in both countries.

Four groups of networks/services are analysed, chosen due to their size and/or importance in policy making: leased lines and specialised networks; examples of 'value-added network services' (VANS); mobile networks and services; customer premises equipment. The difficulties of analysing data are particularly acute for advanced services and networks, and related customer premises equipment: most markets are competitive; data are confidential; tariffs have changed frequently and are often subject to a host of permutations and reduction packages; developments alter the nature and importance of a service or network. Thus figures are sometimes incomplete and must be treated with especial caution.

Leased Lines and Specialized Networks

Leased lines/private circuits are used not only for voice telephony, but also as an important method of data transmission and the main basis for creating VANS. Most of the large services that involve data transmission, such as on-line databases, reservation systems and financial transfer systems, require the security of transmission offered by leased lines and although little detailed work has been done, the vast majority of data transmission would appear to have taken place using leased lines. In France, 71 per cent of network termination points used for data transmission in 1972 used leased lines, and the figure reached 87 per cent in 1980. In 1990 leased lines still carried the vast majority of data: a study of major sectors[34] found that a very high proportion of data

[34]   C. Rofe and F. Rowe, *Data Transmission Flows Assessment: Application to the French Economy* (ITU international conference paper, 1990).

TABLE 29: PO/BT and DGT/FT revenues from private circuits

Year	PO/BT		DGT/FT	
	Revenue (£1,970m.)	1970 = 100	Revenue (£1,970m.)	1970 = 100
1970	31.8	100	14.7	100
1980	36.5	115	36.7	291
1982	59.8	188	45.1	307
1989	117.4	369	62.8	427
1996	113.0	355	66.1	450

Note: 1989 BT figures supplied by BT.

flows in most sectors, and especially in those sectors transmitting large quantities of data, were carried on leased lines. In Britain, the main alternative to leased lines, namely packet switching networks, has been tiny compared to private leased lines.[35] Thus the price and availability of private circuits were important for data transmission and VANS.

In both Britain and France, the real income of the PO/BT and the DGT/FT from private circuits (Table 29) grew in real terms over the 1970s and 1980s, before reaching a plateau in the 1990s; given the decline in the real prices of most private circuits, this suggests a growth in private circuit usage.

Two-wire analogue/telephone circuits, which have limited bandwidth, were available throughout the 1970s and 1980s. During the early/mid-1980s new digital private circuit services became available; they were better suited for data transmission and offered a larger bandwidth. Equivalent services were introduced in both Britain and France, at approximately similar times (the mid-1980s).[36] In both countries, digital leased lines have gradually replaced analogue ones: in March 1997, 71.5 per cent of BT's total number of leased lines were digital, whilst by end 1996, the figure for France Télécom was 55.1 per cent.[37]

The prices of private circuits have varied according to several factors, including transmission capacity, length, and services provided by the network operator. The figures show that charges in real terms for analogue private circuits declined in both Britain and France during the 1970s, before rising in the former after 1980 and in the latter after 1990. However, tariffs for digital leased lines have fallen over the period 1984–96, particularly for longer distances. The prices

[35] BZW put total packet switching revenue at £2.3m. in 1984 and £6.7m. in 1989 (£1,970) BZW, *Telephone Sector Network Review 1990* (London: BZW, 1990).

[36] Notably BT's KiloStream and MegaStream services and the 'Trans' series in France.

[37] Figures for BT calculated from Oftel, *The UK Telecommunications Industry: Market Information 1992/93–1996/97* (London: Oftel, 1997); for FT, from its *Rapport Annuel*.

TABLE 30: Rental for two-wire telephone/analogue standard private circuit (£1970)

Year	PO/BT			DGT/FT		
	8 km.	40 km.	80 km.	5 km.	25 km.	100 km.
1970	90	(250)	695	112	308	637
1980	55	203	260	91	272	796
1984	86	168	322	85	243	692
1989	105	201	330	81	261	716
1997	130	245	315	107	285	554

Sources: CEPT, Statistiques Annuelles, BT and Eurodata, T-Guide Tariffs (London: Eurodata, annual).

TABLE 31: Rentals for a 9.6 kbit/s private circuits (£1970)

Year	PO/BT			DGT/FT		
	5 km.	25 km.	100 km.	5 km.	25 km.	100 km.
1984	307	440	545	—	—	—
1986	309	470	565	1,291	3,325	6,767
1990	280	422	497	169	494	907
1997	251	390	449	143	355	531

Note: French prices are for the Transfix service.

for rental of four types of private circuits (chosen as the most commonly used), are set out in Table 30.[38]

Three types of digital circuits are examined in Tables 31–3.[39] The figures indicate that prices were somewhat higher in France than in Britain, a conclusion supported by comparative studies.[40] However, the figures also indicate some narrowing of differences over the 1980s and especially in the 1990s.

Packet switched networks and ISDN offer alternative methods of data transmission to leased lines,[41] with charges in Britain and France being based on usage rather than being a fixed sum. Packet switched networks were opened

[38] Comparison is complicated by BT charging for the actual length of private circuits, whereas the DGT/FT charges for distance as the crow flies between the two ends of the circuit; connection charges vary greatly depending on factors such as location and existing facilities, and hence are excluded.

[39] Sources: BT and Logica, European Telecommunications (London: Logica, annual) 1986 and 1990 editions.

[40] See Oftel, The Control of the Quality and Prices of BT's Private Circuits (London: Oftel, 1989); DGPT, Rapport Annuel 1995, 82.

[41] ISDN can also be used for voice and image services.

TABLE 32: Rentals for 64 kbit/s private circuits (£1970)

Year	PO/BT			DGT/FT		
	5 km.	25 km.	100 km.	5 km.	25 km.	100 km.
1984	512	781	866	—	—	—
1986	516	808	903	717	1,852	4,259
1990	406	635	709	512	1,258	2,715
1997	284	421	481	286	401	531

Note: Prices for BT's high speed KiloStream service and the French Trans-fix service.

TABLE 33: Rentals for 2 Mbit/s private circuits (£1970)

Year	PO/BT			DGT/FT		
	5 km.	25 km.	100 km.	5 km.	25 km.	100 km.
1984	917	1,634	4,323	—	—	—
1986	1,031	1,734	3,913	1,474	4,344	12,652
1990	1,208	2,012	4,221	1,117	3,107	9,047
1997	694	1,055	2,798	1,195	2,122	3,799

Note: Prices for BT's MegaStream service and the French Transfix service.

at similar times in both Britain and France: BT opened its PSS (Packet Switch Stream) in 1981, while the Transpac service began in France on an experimental basis in 1978, and began operating fully in 1981. Similarly, BT and FT began an ISDN service in the late 1980s (the French 'Numéris' service began in 1989, and BT's full ISDN service began in 1990).

Transpac grew rapidly in the 1980s, both in the number of direct links and in revenues (see Table 34). Packet switching in Britain also grew, but appears to have been smaller than in France (total revenue was put at £2.3m. in 1984 and £6.7m. in 1989).[42] However, ISDN expansion has been very similar in both countries, as Table 35 shows.

Charges for packet switching comprise four elements: connection; rental; usage by volume of data sent; usage by duration of connection.[43] Data indicate a mixed pattern: BT's connection and rental charges declined whereas decreases in volume charges during the 1980s were reversed in the 1990s; France Télécom's connection charges rose, whilst its rental tariffs were stable (except

[42]   BZW, Telephone Networks Review 1990.
[43]   Sources: BT, Summary of Charges and Logica, European Telecommunications; charges for duration of connection were negligible.

TABLE 34: Transpac's direct links and revenues

Year	Direct links	Revenues (£1970m.)
1981	5,273	1.6
1985	13,410	5.9
1990	81,693	40.4
1995	128,000[a]	61.1

[a] France Télécom, *Rapport Annuel 1995*, p.20.

TABLE 35: Number of ISDN subscribers

Year	Britain	France
1990	2,000	2,000
1995	260,000	250,000

Source: ITU *Annual Statistics*.

for falls for high capacity links) and volume charges fell. The result of differing price movements appears, however, often to have led to a narrowing of differences between the two operators over the period between 1986 and 1997. See Table 36a–c.

TABLE 36a: Packet switching prices: Connection charges (£1970)

Year	BT			FT		
	2.4 kbit/s	9.6 kbit/s	48 kbit/s	2.4 kbit/s	9.6 kbit/s	48 kbit/s
1986	84	800	variable	48	48	48
1990	141	141	221	44	44	44
1997	n/a	111	175	68	68	175

TABLE 36b: Packet switching prices: Rental charges (£1970)

Year	BT			FT		
	2.4 kbit/s	9.6 kbit/s	48 kbit/s	2.4 kbit/s	9.6 kbit/s	48 kbit/s
1986	328	619	1,500	215	281	1,334
1990	348	574	1,473	194	194	1,168
1997	289	468	1,164	219	230	417

TABLE 36c: Packet switching prices: Volume charges pence per kilosegment (1970p)

Year	BT			FT		
	standard rate	low rate	cheap rate	peak rate	standard rate	cheap rate
1984	5.1	3.1	3.1	n/a	n/a	n/a
1986	4.7	2.8	2.8	8.4	5.1	1.7
1990	4.4	2.9	2.7	5.2	3.6	1.6
1997	5.8	3.1	3.1	3.8	2.7	1.1

Value-Added Network Services (VANS)

VANS are highly diverse; they include message / e-mail systems, protocol conversion services, customer databases, electronic data interchange services, videotex services, and electronic financial transactions at point of sale (EFTPOS). They have been supplied by a wide range of companies, although the travel and financial sectors have been important users.[44] Comparison of VANS in Britain and France is difficult, not only due to limits on the availability of data, but also to determining equivalent services, especially as several can be delivered in different ways.[45] Nevertheless, VANS constitute the field of greatest difference in economic outcomes between Britain and France, notably over public videotex networks.

Estimating the size of VANS is difficult due to their diversity and differing definitions of services included. However, it appears that they were small but growing—for instance, one estimate was that the total UK market in 1986 amounted to £47.4m. and reached £98.9m. by 1989, whilst the French one was £15.5m. in 1986 and £35.9m. in 1989.[46] Other studies also indicate rapid growth (rates of 20–25 per cent) in VANS in Western Europe.[47]

---

[44] Registrations in Britain and France during the 1980s illustrate the diversity and development of VANS by the late 1980s; under the UK VANS General Licence, 164 companies had registered 688 VANS as at 18.10.85; the largest categories included message systems (89), electronic mailboxes (71), protocol conversion services (71), customer data bases (54), videotex services (49) and multi-address routing (49); in France, 100 VANS were declared in 1987 under the decree of 24 Sept. 1987, of which one-third were by computer companies and one-fifth by banks—see *Oftel News*, no.1, Dec. 1985 and *Le Communicateur*, no. 20, April 1989.

[45] e.g. e-mail services can be offered on public vidoetex networks or via personal computers linked to the internet or specialized public e-mail services.

[46] P. Purton, 'Slow Progress of VANS', *Communications International*,15(7) (1989), 27–32.

[47] Commission of the European Communities, *The Single Market Review*. Subseries II, vol. 6, *Telecommunications: Liberalized Services* (Luxembourg: European Communities, 1998); see also *Fintech*, no.159, April 1990.

TABLE 37: Freephone service prices

Year	BT	DGT/FT
1985	Connection: £48.50 Rental: £27.16 p.a. plus rental per km. between subscriber's local exchange and nearest specially equipped 'Linkline exchange' of: 0–5 km.: £17.65 p.a. per km. 5–15 km.: £8.92 p.a. per km. 15–50 km.: £2.52 p.a. per km. 50+ km.: £2.13 p.a. per km. Usage (per minute) Calls in local Linkline area: peak: 3.1p; standard: 2.3p; cheap rates: 1.7p Calls in other areas: peak: 3.9p; standard: 2.9p; cheap: 2.3p	Connection: £10.67 Rental: £90.79 p.a. Usage (per minute) within same zone: 2.9p other: 5.9p
1990	Connection: £36.82 Rental: £58.91 p.a. Usage (per minute) peak: 2.4p; standard: 1.8p; cheap rates: 1.3p (volume reductions for 30,000+ calls per month)	Connection: £7.22 Rental: £61.86 p.a. Usage (per minute) Intra-regional: red: 1.3p; white: 0.9p; blue: 0.6p Inter-regional: red: 2.7p; white: 1.9p; blue: 1.2p
1997[a]	Connection: £29.10 Rental: £40.74 p.a. Usage per minute: Daytime: 1.4p; Cheap: 1.0p	Connection: £6.95 Rental: £59.54 p.a. Usage (per minute): Inter-regional red: 2.55p; white: 1.79p; blue: 1.28p; deep-blue: 0.89p Intra-regional: red: 1.21p; white: 0.85p; blue: 0.61p; deep-blue: 0.42p

[a] Of the many choices available, standard rates for 0800 services are used.

Detailed examination of all types of VANS is not possible, given the variety of services. Instead, three illustrative examples are chosen: videotex networks and e-mail and freefone services.

In both Britain and France, directly connected 'freephone' numbers became available from the early 1980s. The number of *numéros verts* in France expanded swiftly during the 1980s—from 953 in 1983 to 14,196 in 1990. No figures are available for BT's 0800 service, but even its much less attractive operator-connected service grew from 4,755 customers in 1986/7 to 5,807 in

TABLE 38: Videotex development

Year	Prestel	Télétel			
	number of terminals	number of terminals	traffic[a] (m. of hours)	total revenue £m	no of services
1984	47,000	530,000	n/a	n/a	n/a
1986	70,000	2,239,983	31	156	4,200
1989	95,000	5,064,958	85	322	12,377
1995	n/a	7,400,000	107	n/a	n/a

[a] Excluding use of the electronic telephone directory.
Sources: OECD, New Telecommunications Services; BT, Summary of Charges 1989 (London: BT, 1989); France Télécom, Rapports d'Activité 1986 and 1989.

1989/90.[48] Table 37 illustrates how prices declined in both the UK and France over the 1980s.[49]

The Post Office launched its 'Prestel service in 1979, while the DGT's 'Télétel' service (better known as Minitel) began in 1983. Although numbers rose in both countries, the development of videotex in the two countries was marked by important differences in size: in Britain, Prestel failed to grow, and videotex networks were used private as part of, closed user services (such as ticket reservation systems or intra-company systems), whereas in France, the network of Minitel terminals and services greatly expanded.

The cost of Prestel and Minitel terminals differed greatly in two countries. The DGT gave Minitel terminals free of charge to residential subscribers, in return for which free paper directories were no longer supplied. Moreover, the cost of hire of the range of Minitel terminals (mostly by businesses) was low—for instance, in 1990 the basic terminal could be hired for £1.51. In contrast, terminals had to be purchased in Britain, and initially were expensive.[50] Tariff structures for usage differed between Prestel and Télétel. Charges for the former consisted of an annual subscription charge (in 1990, £4.71 for residential customers and £10.60 for businesses), plus usage costs (in 1990, 1.0p per minute during peak times, and 0.1p per minute off-peak). There are no subscription charges for public Télétel services, although providers of closed user group services (access to which is by a special code) can charge one. Usage charges were determined by the service provider, but to simplify charging,

[48] Source: BT.
[49] Source: Tarifica, European Telecommunications Services (London: Tarifica, annual), 1986 and 1990 editions; Eurodata, T-Guide Tariffs.
[50] G. Dang Nguyen 'Telecommunications: A Challenge to the Old Order', in M. Sharp (ed.), Europe and the New Technologies (London: Pinter, 1985).

which was done by the DGT/FT through telephone bills, a fixed range of charges existed, from Télétel 1 services (0.2p per minute in 1990) to Télétel 7 services (11.3p per minute in 1990). It is not possible to draw any conclusions about price trends, except that the upper range of charges rose following the addition of the more expensive Télétel 4, 6, and 7 bands.

For e-mail, BT began its Telecom Gold service in 1981, which provided subscribers with an electronic mailbox to send and receive messages using existing terminals such as micro-processors, word processors and VDUs (Visual Display Units). Then in 1988 it launched the Telecom Gold 400 service, whose 'X400' standard and protocol conversion enabled all electronic messaging systems, regardless of type, to communicate with each other—terminals, telex, and fax machines. Similar services were offered in the 1980s in France: FCR, a DGT subsidiary began its 'Missive' service in the mid-1980s, while in the late 1980s Transpac established its 'X400' service, Atlas 400, with facilities corresponding to those of Telecom Gold 400.

E-mail spread rapidly in Britain: Telecom Gold had approximately 35,000 subscribers in 1985 and 76,000 in 1986,[51] whilst in December 1988 it was estimated by Octogan[52] to have 138,000 mailboxes. French e-mail services also grew rapidly: in 1988, Atlas 400 was estimated to have 450 individual subscribers and to be handling 700 messages a day,[53] while by December 1989 it had 3,000 individual subscribers and was handling 10,000 messages per day. Although e-mail appears to have been smaller in France than in Britain, other services existed, offered by private firms (notably Cometex, which had 10,000 mailboxes in 1989), whilst the figures exclude alternative methods of electronic messaging, such as through Minitel.[54]

In the 1990s, both BT and France Télécom launched mass internet access services—BT Internet in February 1996 and France Télécom's Wanadoo service in May 1996.[55]

Mobile Communications

During the 1970s, mobile telephony was very small (for instance, there were 1,000 subscribers in Britain in 1970, and even in 1980 only 7,000), service quality was poor, and 'automatic handover' was not offered, so that a call had to be redialled every time a new transmission/reception cell was entered. The situation was transformed with the introduction of analogue cellular radio systems in the 1980s. This occurred in 1984 in Britain, and in 1988 in France, when a full cellular service with automatic handover was introduced. Then in early

[51] BT, *Report and Accounts 1986*.

[52] Octogan, *Octogan Guide to Electronic Messaging Services, 1989* (London: Octogan, annual).

[53] 'Les Services de France Télécom', *Télécom Magazine* May 1988.

[54] France Télécom, *Rapport d'Activité 1989*.

[55] See BT, *Annual Report 1996* and France Télécom, *Rapport Annuel 1996*.

TABLE 39: Cellular mobile telephony subscribers—total (analogue and digital)

Year	UK	France
1986	130,000	9,000
1990	1,114,000	283,000
1995	5,736,000	1,379,000

Source: ITU, Annual Statistics.

TABLE 40: Digital cellular subscribers—numbers and per cent of total cellular subscribers

Year	UK	France
1993	23,000 (1.0)	88,000 (15.4)
1995	1,771,000 (30.9)	1,000,000 (72.5)

TABLE 41: Cellular radio service tariffs (analogue service)

Year	Cellnet[a]	Radiocom 2000
1986	Connection: £12.18 Rental p.a.: £56.23 Usage: Inner London: 6.56p per min.; elsewhere: 4.69p per min.	Connection: £6.54 Rental p.a.: £43.59 (regional), £78.46 (national) Usage: Paris, Lyon, Marseille: 9.0p per min.; elsewhere: 5.62p per min.
1990	Connection: £9.57 Rental: £44.18 Usage: Greater London: 5.15p per min.; elsewhere: 3.68p per min.	Connection: £2.60 Rental: £24.99 (Paris area), £74.83 (national) Usage: Paris, Lyon, Marseille: 7.81p per min. elsewhere: 4.71p per min.
1997	Connection: £5.82 Rental: £76.82 p.a. Usage: Daytime: 2.68p per min.; other: 1.40p per min.	Connection: £2.47 Rental: £70.62 p.a. (national), £35.31 (local) Usage: Standard: 3.62p per min.; low: 2.53p; cheap: 1.09p Inside Paris: Standard: 7.24p per min. low: 5.07p; cheap: 2.16p.

[a] Vodafone charges were similar.

Note: Discounts and tariff reduction options, sometimes substantial, were offered by France Télécom and in Britain by the many specialist retailers who sold capacity which they bought from the network operators; charges for calls to mobiles are not included.

Sources: Tarifica, European Telecommunications Services; BT, Summary of Charges; France Télécom, Produits et Services (Paris: France Télécom, annual); Eurodata, T-Guide Tariffs.

TABLE 42: Number of subscribers to wide-area paging services

Year	UK	France
1986	390,000	69,000
1990	640,000	242,000
1994	800,000	370,000

Source: ITU, Annual Statistics.

1990s (1992–3), digital cellular systems were introduced, offering much higher quality services. In both countries cellular services grew rapidly, although more so in Britain than in France; however, in both countries the trends were rapid expansion and an increasing proportion of subscribers using digital services. Since competition was permitted in both countries and entrants captured significant market shares (unlike other markets), numbers include operators other than BT and France Télécom.[56] See Tables 39 and 40.

Prices for cellular radio services declined in real terms over the late 1980s in both countries. Tariffs for usage appear to have been higher in France than in Britain, but connection charges lower (Table 41).

Wide-area radiopaging shows a similar pattern to cellular telephony (Table 42): rapid growth during the 1980s and 1990s in both countries, but with the British networks being considerably larger than the French ones.

Customer Premises Equipment

The CPE market has developed in both Britain and France. As services such as mobile telephony, paging and videotex, have developed, appropriate terminal equipment has been needed. Moreover, the growth of company networks has seen the extended use of PABXs- analogue and later digital- and of terminal equipment combining telecommunications and computing facilities. Digitalization of the PSTN has allowed use of more advanced forms of fax machines, answerphones, and handsets. The numbers of units of terminals sold appears to have grown. One example is fax machines, whose numbers rose sharply in both countries, as Table 43 shows. However, falling prices have offset increases in the number of units sold. One indication is provided by the value of sales by manufacturers in each country (Table 44).[57]

It is extremely difficult to provide prices for CPE over the period owing to the diversity of equipment, suppliers, and terms and conditions, and to the

[56] Notably Vodafone, One2One and Orange in Britain and SFR in France.
[57] Although this includes exports and excludes imports; however, reliable data on total domestic market size are unavailable.

TABLE 43: Number of fax machines

Year	UK	France
1986	8,000	60,000
1990	750,000	283,000
1995	1,800,000	1,900,000

Source: ITU, Annual Statistics.

TABLE 44: Value of CPE/terminal equipment sold by British and French equipment manufacturers (£1970)

Year	Britain	France
1970/71	63	16
1980	61	51
1984	86	96
1988	69	n/a
1995	n/a	92

rapid change in the products supplied, as new and more advanced products were marketed and many older ones were discontinued. However, from interviews, market surveys, and the few prices available, it would appear that real prices, and often also nominal prices, fell, especially in the 1980s; this seems to apply particularly to products which have begun to be sold in very large numbers, such as fax machines and answering machines.[58]

Conclusion

Examining indicators of economic outcomes calls for caution, especially concerning the comparability of data over time and between countries. Nevertheless, certain general conclusions can be drawn, which do not depend on pin-point accuracy of the figures analysed. Moreover, two forms of comparison have been applied: comparison of trends in each country and direct comparison of absolute levels in the two countries. Furthermore, a 25 year analysis

[58] For instance, Plessey's PDF fax cost £4,950 when launched in 1981 (*Financial Times* 30.11.81), whereas in 1990 fax machines cost a few hundred pounds and in 1996, a fax machine could be bought retail for between £200 and £300; the cost of a mobile phone dropped sharply, in nominal terms, from £1,420 in 1981 to £354 in May 1989 (*Financial Times* 5.8.89); between 1970 and 1980 the average price of telecommunications equipment rose by 6.6% p.a., compared to 9.4% for manufactured goods generally—OECD, *Telecommunications. Pressures and Policies for Change*.

allows trends to be identified and short-term fluctuations in indicators to be considered in a longer-term context. Finally, use of a wide range of indicators reduces dependence on a particular set of figures. This section therefore analyses and underlines the twin features of similar trends in both Britain and France and convergence in absolute terms between the two countries over the period 1970–97.

Overall, the indicators examined show that economic outcomes in the two countries were characterized by similar directions of change. Moreover, the trends common to the two countries were often much more significant than differences in absolute levels between them and such differences mostly concerned the timing and pace of change. Many of the trends applied throughout the period and did not appear after institutional reforms in either Britain or France; at most, trends accelerated after changes in Britain in 1984 and in France in 1990. Although contrasts in absolute levels remained in 1996/7, several indicators show convergence between the two countries over the period 1970–97 as differences that existed in 1970 narrowed. The evidence for these conclusions applies to the telecommunications sector in aggregate in Britain and France and to all three subsectors—network operation, the supply of advanced networks and services, and customer premises equipment, and equipment manufacturing.

The British and French telecommunications sectors were small/medium-sized in world terms in the period examined. They both experienced considerable growth in absolute size and as a proportion of GDP, and the difference in size between them that existed in 1970 had been greatly reduced by the 1980s. The sector was dominated by network operation in terms of revenue.

In network operation, both countries saw strong growth in the size of the telephone network, in terms of its coverage, revenues, and traffic. Switching and transmission were modernized, and high levels of investment took place. Employment rose in the 1970s, but declined in the 1980s, whilst labour productivity increased and quality improved. Most network operation revenue continued to be derived from calls rather than access charges. Data indicate cross-subsidization among services, at least until 1990, notably between highly profitable long-distance traffic and access charges. Long-distance traffic contributed a disproportionate share of revenue and profits and large users were responsible for a high percentage of revenue and profits. Staff and interest/financial costs fell as a proportion of both BT's and France Télécom's revenues. Most tariffs fell in real terms, although 'rebalancing' also took place between local calls, whose prices increased between 1970 and 1997, and trunk and international calls, whose prices decreased sharply.

Over the period 1970–97, there was marked convergence between Britain and France in network operation. In 1970 the French telecommunications system was substantially smaller and more backward than the British one, with lower levels of investment and higher prices for most services. By the 1990s,

this situation had changed very considerably. The networks in the two countries were of similar size, investment levels were comparable, both networks
had been modernized and call charges were generally similar or were much
less dissimilar than in 1970.

Differences in network operation between Britain and France mainly
consisted of contrasts in the pace and timing of change, and in certain differences in absolute levels that remained by the 1990s. The speed of growth
was higher in France than in Britain in the 1970s, as the French network caught
up in size with its British counterpart. The DGT introduced time division
switching more rapidly than BT in the late 1970s and early 1980s, but BT
had closed the gap by the 1990s. Initially, the DGT also used optical fibre cable
more in the local network whereas BT focused on the trunk network, before
each operator adopted a similar cabling strategy in the 1990s. Numbers of
employees at the PO and BT remained higher than at the DGT/FT until the
mid-1990s. There were dissimilarities in the composition of revenues, with
the DGT/FT deriving a smaller proportion of revenues from access charges
than the PO/BT, although this largely ended in the mid-1990s. Investment
in France rose above British levels in the mid-1970s to the mid-1980s, before
being at similar levels and declining for the two operators. For most of the 1970s
and 1980s, access charges and local call charges were lower in France than in
Britain, whilst trunk call tariffs remained higher; however, such differences
greatly diminished in the later 1980s and in the 1990s. The most significant contrasts throughout the period lay in net profitability and financial costs: the
former fluctuated sharply for the Post Office in the 1970s, before increases
in the 1980s, whereas it fell sharply for the DGT in the 1980s; the costs of depreciation and interest/finance were higher in France than Britain. Nevertheless,
even for these areas of difference, similar trends were seen towards the end of
the period studied: operating profits show fewer differences, France Télécom's
interest and financial costs declined sharply from the late 1980s and both
BT and France Télécom experienced modest declines in profitability in the
1990s.

Analysis of the supply of 'advanced networks and services' and CPE also
reveals important common features in Britain and France. In both countries, a
similar range of new or greatly modified services became available, mostly in
the 1980s and 1990s, at approximately similar times; examples included packet-
switching, digital private circuit services, e-mail, internet access, analogue and
then digital cellular telephony and paging. Services and networks grew rapidly
in both countries, notably leased lines, ISDN services, value-added network services, mobile telephony, paging, and CPE. In both countries, tariffs fell in real
terms for most services, networks, and CPE, including analogue leased lines
until the 1980s, digital leased lines, free-phone services, mobile telephony, and
common types of CPE.

The main contrasts that existed in advanced services and networks between

Britain and France lay in the speed of growth and the size of certain services and networks: leased line revenues and mobile telephony and paging networks grew faster in Britain than in France. Certain differences in tariffs existed, notably in leased lines, but these mostly narrowed over the period, and in general, dissimilarities in prices were less important than similar trends. The greatest contrast between the two countries lay in public videotex networks and associated services: the Minitel system in France was much larger than Prestel in Britain.

The equipment manufacturing subsector in both Britain and France also experienced similar trends and features, especially during the 1980s and 1990s. Growth of sales was low in the 1980s and 1990s, unlike the rest of the sector. Public switching orders declined, counterbalanced by rising CPE and transmission orders. The proportion of orders arising from the domestic network operators gradually decreased or was static, but remained large. Employment in the subsector fell or was stagnant. Furthermore, rapid growth in France in the 1970s meant that the subsector was of comparable size in both countries in the 1980s and 1990s. External trade provides the area of greatest difference between the two countries, in terms of the balance of trade and the composition of exports. However, exports accounted for only a small proportion of orders in both Britain and France.

Thus many trends of change were similar in Britain and France. Furthermore, they were generally larger than the remaining differences in absolute levels between the two countries. This applies to network expansion, modernisation, changes in call charges, to growth and declining tariffs in many 'other services and networks' and CPE, and to slow growth in equipment manufacturing.

Not only do the figures show similar features and directions of change in Britain and France, but they also reveal that institutional reforms in Britain in 1984 and in France in 1990 were not followed by reversals of in the direction of change. On the contrary, many developments had begun in the 1970s or 1980s and continued regardless of institutional reforms. Examples include growth, modernization, rising labour productivity, and rebalancing of tariffs. Even financial indicators, for which institutional reforms would be expected to have maximum impact, saw trends that pre-dated institutional reforms; thus, for example, BT's net profits were rising since 1980, whilst interest/financial costs (as a share of total revenue) were falling for BT before privatization and, similarly, declining for France Télécom before its new *statut* in 1990. At most, institutional alterations were followed by an acceleration in existing trends, such as modernization and tariff rebalancing.

Thus overall, despite dissimilar institutional arrangements, economic outcomes in the telecommunications sector in Britain and France between 1970 and 1997 were marked by similar trends and developments. The main contrasts were in the pace and timing of change, but even so, most differences narrowed.

In addition, institutional reforms in 1984 in Britain and 1990 in France were not followed by changes in the direction of change in terms of economic outcomes. The current study does not attempt to explain how and why the dissimilarities in economic outcomes identified in this chapter came about. Instead, it uses them to show that national institutionalist claims that different institutional arrangements result in dissimilar economic performance did not hold in the British and French telecommunications sector between 1970 and 1997.

PART V

Conclusions

12

National Institutions, Policy, and Change

Telecommunications in Britain and France between 1969 and 1997 were studied as a case to examine the impact of national institutions on policy making. National institutionalism was used to establish the wider issues at stake, namely whether nations maintain differing and stable institutional frameworks, whether dissimilar national institutions result in contrasting patterns of policy making and economic performance, and why and how national institutions influence (or fail to influence) a country's policy formation.

The task of this final chapter is therefore to relate the empirical conclusions of the previous chapters to the analytical issues and questions concerning national institutions that were posed initially. After summarizing the findings of the study in relation to the specific questions posed initially, the discussion turns to national institutionalism. In the light of the empirical findings of the study, the chapter develops national institutionalist analysis by seeking to specify the conditions under which claims concerning the stability of national institutions and the existence of persistent differences among countries held true in the case of British and French telecommunications. It also examines arguments concerning the impact of institutions, offering important limits and distinctions, most notably between policy making and economic outcomes. Thus the case study offers a basis for refining national institutionalism by clarifying and delimiting its arguments and ambit.

National Institutions in British and French Telecommunications

To examine and test national institutionalist claims, two central questions were posed in the selected case of telecommunications in Britain and France between 1969 and 1997: in the face of powerful, external forces for change common to the two countries, did Britain and France maintain differing institutional frameworks in telecommunications? Did these frameworks result in dissimilar patterns of policy making and economic outcomes?

Before 1969, institutional arrangements in Britain and France shared many similar features. A monopoly operator, the Post Office and the Direction générale des télécommunications, was linked with postal services within a government department, with employees being civil servants. Moreover, both countries faced similar and long-standing policy issues, including the organizational position of the operator, excess demand, constrained investment, opposition by the Treasury/Finance Ministry to rapid expansion, and perceived failings by the manufacturing subsector.

Telecommunications policies and institutions in Britain and France were subjected to sweeping external forces for change from the late 1960s. It is not an exaggeration to state that the industry was revolutionized, as technological and economic developments transformed the nature of telecommunications and comprehensive regulatory reforms were introduced in the United States and by the European Community, with repercussions for policy in Western Europe. The changes were not only common to Britain and France but also largely exogenous to them.

Nevertheless, just as common external pressures for change became increasingly powerful, and despite similar institutional and policy starting points, between 1969 and 1990, the two countries experienced not only differing but increasingly divergent institutional frameworks. In Britain, the Post Office ceasing to be part of the civil service in 1969, becoming a public corporation with its own legal identity and powers. Then in 1981, telecommunications were separated from postal services through the creation of BT. Most remarkably for Western Europe at the time, BT was privatized in 1984. An independent regulatory body, Oftel, was established, and its head was given statutory powers over licence enforcement and modification. A new regime based on licences was established for services, with the allocation of powers and functions between different public institutions (notably Oftel and ministers) being laid down by law. In France, the DGT remained an *administration*, within the general civil service, as part of the PTT Ministry. In contrast to institutional arrangements in Britain before 1984, however, its finances were increasingly separated from those of the general budget, with the creation of new instruments in the late 1960s for raising investment capital. Special institutional mechanisms for distributing DGT orders to selected equipment manufacturers were also continued, whilst in the early 1980s, those firms were nationalized, thereby increasing the institutional contrast with the other side of the Channel.

Britain and France were thus able to maintain considerable institutional differences for more than twenty years. However, the 1990s saw the end of institutional divergence, as institutional reforms took place in France during the 1990s. In 1990, France Télécom acquired many of the features that the Post Office had obtained in 1969, including legal identity and a degree of institutional autonomy. Further changes took place in France in 1996–7, when France Télécom was partially privatized, and a licensing regime and an independent regulatory body were established. This significant institutional dissimilarity between Britain and France still existed in 1997, but they were much reduced compared with the previous period.

National institutions did not rapidly alter in the face of pressures for change. On the contrary, institutional reform was far from easy in both Britain and

France. In the former, the modifications of 1969 followed decades of discussion, whilst modest changes were blocked in the 1970s. Privatization and the establishment of a new regulatory regime in 1984 took place rapidly, but they were driven by a determined, newly re-elected government; furthermore, despite favourable circumstances for institutional change, more radical ideas of breaking up BT had to be withdrawn for the reforms to proceed. In France, modification of the DGT's organizational position (its *statut*) enjoyed active support amongst elite policy-makers from the mid-1960s until the mid-1970s, but was not implemented, in large measure because of trade union opposition. Reform in 1990 and 1996–7 in France was difficult, relatively slow and preceded by extensive 'consultation' and debate; even so, it required determined support by the political executive and considerable compromises, especially over the employment conditions of staff.

Different national institutions gave rise to distinct patterns of policy making in the two countries. Processes of decision making differed: the participants in policy making, their spheres of action, degrees of autonomy and relationships. In Britain, policy making became increasingly segmented, with a division of roles and spheres of action. Between 1969 and 1984 policy tended to be narrowly conceived, with the government and the Post Office enjoying their own, relatively autonomous spheres of competence (the former being mostly concerned with general policy and financial outcomes that affected the budget and the latter with other areas such as modernisation and growth); in relations between the Post Office and its equipment suppliers, the government acted as 'umpire'. After the institutional changes of 1984, participants in policy making altered, as Oftel became a central actor, whereas the Treasury's role was greatly diminished. The separation of roles was accentuated: the government dealt with licensing and ceased to be directly involved in BT's internal affairs as a company (including its relations with equipment manufacturers) whilst Oftel was concerned with licence enforcement and modification.

The policy-making process in France until 1990 involved intense interaction among the DGT/PTT Ministry and other parts of the political executive (and within it, often the Élysée, Matignon, and the Finance Ministry), the network operator, and, in questions of equipment supply, manufacturers. In contrast to Britain, the political executive was closely involved in a broad range of network operation decisions, including modernization, growth, the distribution of orders, relations with equipment manufacturers, senior appointments, and financial matters. In many of these matters, the political executive took the lead or its active assent was required; the DGT was highly dependent on support from the political executive, a fact cruelly exposed in battles over its financial contributions in the 1980s. Policy-makers within the political executive sought to co-ordinate decisions in different spheres and to use them to pursue wider objectives, such as restructuring the equipment subsector, aiding other sectors and supporting the general budget; such coordination was most explicit in the *grands projets* relating to expansion, modernization and cable networks. However, after the institutional reforms of 1990, policy processes in France altered. A degree of segmentation among actors took place, reducing the contrasts with Britain. In particular, there was an important move towards a division of responsibilities between the political executive and France Télécom, as the latter became more autonomous in its internal decisions.

The institutional frameworks also contributed to differences between the two countries in the nature of policy—the ambitions and objectives pursued and the policy instruments applied. Divergence took place in the 1970s and 1980s, before being followed by a limited degree of convergence between 1990 and 1996. In Britain, policy before 1984 was focused on ensuring Post Office profitability, operating efficiency, and fulfilment of government-imposed financial targets. The equipment-manufacturing subsector was not restructured, despite persistent pressures for change. After 1984, policy centred on the pursuit of 'fair competition' and regulation mimicking a competitive market when competition did not exist or was judged insufficient. BT's monopolies were progressively ended, whilst regulation developed to curb its market power. The government withdrew from BT's internal affairs, allowing a restructuring of the equipment subsector.

In contrast to the PO/BT, the DGT was seen as an instrument of broader policy. Thus France undertook ambitious *grands projets* in the 1970s and 1980s (digital switching, Minitel, and the Cable Plan), linking telecommunications with other industrial sectors, and seeking to use domestic orders as a springboard for developing a global lead in different areas of telecommunications. The manufacturing subsector was extensively restructured. Policy goals were pursued by the use of special financial instruments for borrowing on private capital markets, the allocation of DGT orders, and tariff setting. In the 1980s, the DGT continued to serve as part of wider industrial and economic policy, albeit now often against its wishes (financing the general budget and providing orders for Alcatel). Following the institutional reforms of 1990, the pattern of public policy altered. Competition became more important, *grands projets* were rejected, and France Télécom increasingly operated as a commercial organization. Even so, significant differences with Britain remained. In particular, competition was introduced later as policy-makers sought to ensure that France Télécom could prepare for it; France Télécom used the period to reduce its debt and financial costs, continue tariff rebalancing and form international alliances.

Thus Britain and France had dissimilar national institutions and patterns of policy making during the 1970s and 1980s, with differences diminishing in the 1990s. Such a finding is consistent with claims for the impact of national institutions, since it matches increasing institutional divergence between 1969 and 1990 and then a degree of convergence after 1990. Nevertheless, the patterns of policy making in Britain and France and the differences between them, need to be linked to national institutional frameworks: the role of institutions must be shown, not merely assumed. The study identified four key institutional features for national patterns of policy making in telecommunications: the organisational position of the network operator, including the creation of autonomous spheres of decision making and ownership; the powers of elected politicians; financial instruments and rules applicable to public policy in the sector; the existence and powers of an independent regulator. It related these to policy making, providing several evidential routes to establish their influence.

The first linkage between national institutions and policy is that institutional reform in each country was rapidly followed by changes in policy making. Alterations were most marked in the processes of decision making; they sometimes involved the end of very well-established patterns of relations. Thus, for example, the Treasury's role almost disappeared in Britain after privatisation in 1984, despite it having been the centre of policy for an entire century.[1] In France, the distance seen between France Télécom and the DRG/DGPT (the regulatory unit within the PTT and Industry Ministry) after the reforms of 1990, followed decades in which France Télécom had been part of that Ministry; there was no tradition of the DGT/FT acting independently of the Ministry. The speed and extent of change in policy making after institutional reform offer powerful evidence of the impact of institutional frameworks.

A second source of evidence for the role of institutional arrangements is that their requirements, objectives and instruments were often followed and used in practice. Thus, for instance, the division of roles between the Post Office and the government laid down in the 1969 Post Office Act was largely respected, whilst statutory objectives such as avoiding losses by the Post Office were pursued. After 1984, the separation between Oftel and the government established under the 1984 Telecommunications Act and the independence of the former were respected. Equally, in France, the DGT's institutional position as an *administration* was reflected in decision-making processes and in its use for broader policy goals. The reforms of 1990 were largely implemented in practice: policy and regulation were indeed separated from supply, whilst decisions were taken to enforce France Télécom's licence conditions, notably over access to its network. Moreover, institutionally-created policy instruments were central in the distinct paths followed in the two countries. The differing investment, borrowing and tariff policies took place through dissimilar financial instruments. In France before 1990, the political executive used the DGT to pursue wider policy objectives by exercising powers over an *administration*. In the 1980s and 1990s, Oftel applied its position and powers as a specialist telecommunications regulator to enforce and modify licences and to develop

---

[1] See D. Pitt, *The Telecommunications Function in the Post Office: A Case Study in Bureaucratic Adaption* (Hampshire: Saxon House, 1980).

policy around competition. Thus, at the very least, policy making took place through institutional powers, procedures and actors.

The ways in which institutions permitted, constrained, encouraged or discouraged directions of policy offers a third, more causally-based, method of showing the impact of national institutions. The institutional autonomy of the network operator was important in its use by elected politicians. The DGT's position as an *administration* before 1990 made it dependent on the political executive and hence aided its role as an instrument of broad industrial and budgetary policy objectives. In contrast, when the network operator had a degree of institutional separation, as in the case of the Post Office after 1969, France Télécom after 1990, and most clearly for BT as a private company, it became more difficult to utilize the network operators as a direct tool of government policy. Financial rules and instruments also played a major role in contrasting national policies: the DGT's separate budget and instruments for borrowing outside the general budget allowed large-scale borrowing for expansion in the 1970s; equally, in the 1980s, they permitted use of DGT funds to aid the general budget or to support public-owned enterprises. In Britain in the period before privatization, public sector accounting rules offered the government incentives to reduce Post Office borrowing to meet general budgetary targets rather than to invest to meet demand, whilst the Treasury had institutional powers over BT's investment and financial targets; as a result, policy focused on BT's financial outcomes that affected the general budget. Once those incentives were removed, together with many instruments of direct control, thanks to BT's privatization, so too were policies of control. Instead, in Britain after 1984, the existence of Oftel as an independent regulator, together with private ownership of BT, greatly encouraged the development of competition and regulation to ensure its 'fairness' and effectiveness. In contrast, competition was extended much more slowly in France, where there was no independent regulator before 1997 and the publicly-owned DGT/FT was given considerable protection by policy-makers, especially before 1990 when it was part of the PTT Ministry.

Thus, the study provides strong evidence for the importance of national institutions. In the face of powerful, common external pressures for change, Britain and France were able to maintain differing, and indeed diverging, institutional frameworks for more than two decades. Distinct patterns of policy making existed in the two countries in terms of decision-making processes and the nature of policy. These patterns and differences between them can be linked to the institutional contrasts between Britain and France.

Nevertheless, the case examined also indicates the limits to the importance of stable national institutions in policy making. First, institutional divergence ended in 1990, and convergence took place in the 1990s. Second, a degree of policy change took place within the same institutional framework. Thus in France, the DGT's favourable position of the 1970s was followed by the imposition of unwelcome decisions in the 1980s over matters such as financial contributions to the general budget and industrial policy. Although the institutionally-based pattern of DGT dependence on the political executive remained unaltered, that relationship could be used to privilege the DGT or to subordinate it. In Britain, Oftel was able to significantly develop and define its role, choosing competition as its primary objective and in the 1990s seeking to become a sectoral competition authority. The ability of policy-makers to alter the substance of policy indicates that institutions were flexible in terms of policy content, which cannot be 'read off' institutional arrangements.

The third and most important limitation on the role of national institutions shown by the study concerns economic outcomes. Despite differing institutions and patterns of policy making, a wide variety of economic outcomes were marked by strong similarities in terms of the directions of change. Moreover, differences between the two countries in 1970 had lessened by 1997, as outcomes converged. Contrasts did exist, especially in the pace and timing of change, but they were less important than the similarities. Moreover, it is not certain that institutions were responsible for even those differences that were found, especially as many trends began before the institutional reforms of 1984 in Britain and 1990 in France. Those reforms were, therefore not followed by new directions of change in economic outcomes.

The Limits of the Arguments Advanced in the Study

It is important to note the limits of the arguments advanced in the study. In concluding that differing national institutions contributed to contrasting policies and policy-making processes, but did not prevent similar paths of economic development, only one sector in two countries over a particular time period has been studied. The telecommunications sector between the late 1960s and the 1990s was marked by very powerful technological and economic forces: in other sectors less marked by transnational technological and economic changes, or in the telecommunications sector at other periods of history, national institutions might have had a greater impact on economic outcomes. For more general conclusions to be drawn, it would be necessary, using the same schema as adopted in the current work, to undertake studies of other sectors, both those with different technological and economic characteristics to telecommunications and those with similar ones.

Furthermore, only two countries have been analysed. A comparison of the telecommunications sector in other small/medium-sized countries in Western Europe, such as Germany or Italy, would allow consideration of a greater range of institutional arrangements established together with the evolution of the same economic outcomes as analysed in Britain and France. Examination of various forms of institutions, different degrees of institutional variance, and many countries would allow wider conclusions to be drawn as to the effects of institutions in Western Europe. Moreover, the two countries chosen were small/medium-sized economies in the telecommunications sector. It is possible that institutional arrangements for telecommunications in very large nations, such as the USA, which accounted for approximately 40–50 per cent of world telecommunications expenditure and over a third of investment in the period 1970–97, might have been important for economic outcomes; in particular, they could have affected technological and economic developments and international regulation, which would therefore not have been exogenous to American policy-makers.

Finally, only a limited time period has been studied: institutional differences might have led to greater economic contrasts over a longer time period, or conversely, even those disparities identified between the two countries might have disappeared.

National Institutions, Change, and National Differences

The analytical framework of national institutionalism was used to identify three empirically testable propositions that lay at the core of claims for the importance of national institutions: first, that national institutions were stable, with change being rare and/or very slow, and marked by past national institutional arrangements; second, that institutions differed considerably among countries and that, insofar as institutional change took place, its path differed from country to country; third, that differing national institutions produced dissimilar patterns of policy making and economic performance from one country to another.

The study has shown the explanatory strengths of the national institutionalist framework, notably in generating empirically applicable and testable propositions, in allowing sensitivity to time and place and in offering causal mechanisms for the impact of institutions. The empirical evidence invites a return to that framework in order to improve it and to develop more sophisticated arguments about national institutions. Hence national institutionalism can fulfil its theoretical functions of relating the particular findings of the critical case study to wider issues concerning national institutions and of producing new hypotheses or lines of enquiry.

Analysis of telecommunications in Britain and France between 1969 and 1997 as a form of critical case has offered powerful support for the importance of national institutions and certain national institutionalist claims. Yet its conclusions also indicate that other institutionalist arguments do not hold or, at least, need to be reconsidered carefully. In particular, the findings point to two possible modifications of national institutionalism, although many other studies will be needed, as only one example, albeit one designed as a critical case, has been used. First, they suggest that certain explanatory boundaries must be affirmed more clearly or distinctions drawn more finely. In particular, whereas national institutionalism has tended to assert the wide-ranging effects of a nation's organizational arrangements, 'policy making and economic performance' need to be separated, as institutions may have different impacts on various aspects of policy making and on economic performance. Second, and more importantly, the findings of the case study suggest that the conditions under which institutionalist propositions hold need to be defined. National institutionalism offers few limits to the role of institutions and fails to define when institutions do influence policy, and hence the circumstances under which they do not do so. The case study of telecommunications offers occasions when institutions did not produce their anticipated impacts or when their effects were counterbalanced by more powerful non-institutional factors.

Thus, in the light of the empirical findings of the case study, the three central themes of national institutionalism are reconsidered: institutional stability and reform; cross-national institutional differences; national institutions giving rise to continuing patterns of policy making and economic performance that differ across nations.

Institutional Stability and Reform

Claims that national institutions are stable receive strong support from the critical case of telecommunications in Britain and France. Despite powerful international and indeed also internal pressures for change, institutional arrangements endured for long periods of time, with comprehensive reforms being rare. Thus in Britain, there were decades of great stability from 1911 and large-scale changes were restricted to those of 1969 and 1984; in France, significant financial reforms occurred in 1923 and the late 1960s, but the overall institutional framework only underwent comprehensive reform in the 1990s. Moreover, institutional modification was difficult and slow. There were long periods of dissatisfaction with existing arrangements and serious problems ascribed to the organization of the sector—for example, in Britain before 1969 and then in the mid-1970s, and in France, during the years between the mid-1960s and the mid-1970s—without major changes being successfully introduced. Moreover, institutional reform involved long consultation processes or determined action by governments to overcome strong opposition. The failure of institutional frameworks to alter rapidly in response to very strong external and internal pressures for change in Britain and France, and the difficulty of institutional reform in both countries, suggest that institutions are, in part at least, an exogenous factor in national policy making: they influence public policy but policy-makers are not able to alter them rapidly.

Nevertheless, institutional reform was undertaken in both countries, albeit at different times and after considerable periods of stability. Hence, over a substantial time period such as thirty years, the distinction between 'institutions' and 'policy' is less clear-cut: institutions can be modified in pursuit of policy objectives. The circumstances under which policy-makers are able to introduce institutional reform and the types of change that are possible are therefore crucial in analysing the balance between institutions operating as an exogenous factor, conditioning policy making but not open to modification in pursuit of policy objectives, and national institutions constituting an endogenous factor, being amenable to alteration as part of policy change. Reform is particularly important if institutional arrangements are in fact rarely open to modification and 'instantiate' policy objectives, norms and a distribution of power[2] and/or if path dependency operates, so that the timing and form of reorganization affect the long-term path of a country's institutional and policy development.[3]

In telecommunications in Britain and France, the pattern of enduring arrangements subject to rare but rapid and substantial alteration matches a model of 'punctuated equilibrium' rather than institutional reform taking place in a gradual, piecemeal manner.[4] However, consensual reforms required long gestation periods: thus whilst the reforms of the Post Office in 1969 and of France Télécom in 1990 attracted widespread support, they represented the culmination of years of discussion. Sharp breaks with pre-existing reform debates involved intense conflicts with a more brutal, impositional approach by governments: far-reaching and rapid institutional modifications, such as the privatization of BT in 1984 and the reform and partial sale of France Télécom in 1997, were controversial and bitterly fought.

[2] P. A. Hall, *Governing the Economy* (Cambridge: Polity Press, 1986); P. A. Hall and R. C. R. Taylor, 'Political Science and the Three New Institutionalisms', *Political Studies*, 44(4) (1996), 936–57; E. M. Immergut, *Health Politics: Interests and Institutions in Western Europe* (Cambridge: Cambridge University Press, 1992); V. C. Hattam, *Labor Visions and State Power: The Origins of Business Unionism in the United States* (Princeton: Princeton University Press, 1993); M. Weir, *Politics and Jobs: The Boundaries of Employment Policy in the United States* (Princeton: Princeton University Press, 1992); S. Steinmo, *Taxation and Democracy* (New Haven and London: Yale University Press, 1993).

[3] P. Pierson, 'When Effect Becomes Cause: Policy Feedback and Political Change', *World Politics*, 45 (1993), 595–628, and 'Not Just What but When: Issues of Timing and Sequence in Comparative Politics' (Boston: APSA conference paper, 1998); R. Berins Collier and D. Collier, *Shaping the Political Arena* (Princeton: Princeton University Press, 1991); J. G. March and J. P. Olsen, 'Institutional Perspectives on Political Institutions', *Governance*, 9(3) (1996), 247–64; cf. D. C. North, *Institutions, Institutional Change and Economic Performance* (Cambridge: Cambridge University Press, 1990).

[4] The former being argued to hold for general national institutions by S. Krasner, 'Approaches to the State: Alternative Conceptions and Historical Dynamics', *Comparative Politics*, 16 (1984), 223–46, and the latter being suggested by K. Thelen and S. Steinmo, 'Historical institutionalism in comparative politics', in S. Steinmo, K. Thelen, and F. Longstreth (eds.), *Structuring Politics: Historical Institutionalism in Comparative Analysis* (Cambridge: Cambridge University Press, 1992).

Although reform did not take place on a blank canvas, the case of telecommunications indicates that major institutional innovation can be undertaken and that policy-makers are not always trapped within national institutional isomorphism when redesigning institutions.[5] Hence, for example, the privatization of BT in 1984 was a radical discontinuity compared with the model of telecommunications that had existed since 1911 in Britain; in France, partial privatization and the establishment of an independent regulatory body in 1996/7 represented considerable departures with long-standing French arrangements for telecommunications and other utilities. Policy-makers were able to create arrangements that drew on new ideas and overseas examples, as well as being influenced by past national frameworks.

Transnational factors played an important part in institutional reform, especially in the 1980s and 1990s. In particular, new ideas from the United States and the example of the break up of AT&T were significant in discussions of change in Britain in the early 1980s, whilst in France, the challenges of competition, the development of EC regulation and global alliances amongst network operators formed part of reform debates in the 1990s. Detailed examination of the French case in the 1990s suggests that transnational pressures for institutional reform grew stronger in the 1990s (or at least, policy-makers perceived them as more pressing), as does the evidence of increasing frequency of institutional changes, not only in telecommunications in France but also in other countries and in other, hitherto stable sectors.[6]

Nevertheless, domestic politics were central in institutional modification. Transnational forces largely operated through the national arena. Thus, domestic policy-makers looked abroad for new ideas, but only imported some of them into the process of institutional reform, as well as adapting them to national circumstances. Operators and users responded to changing technological and economic conditions by pressing for change at the national level. Hence, for example, France Télécom's senior management pressed French policy-makers

---

[5] For claims of isomorphism/copying of existing institutions, see J. G. March and J. P. Olsen, *Rediscovering Institutions: The Organizational Basis of Politics* (New York: The Free Press, 1989); F. Dobbin, *Forging industrial policy: The United States, Britain, and France in the Railway Age* (Cambridge: Cambridge University Press, 1994); K. Thelen, 'Historical Institutionalism in Comparative Politics', *The Annual Review of Political Science 1999* (Palo Alto: Annual Reviews, 1999); P. J. DiMaggio and W. W. Powell, 'Introduction', in W. W. Powell and P. J. DiMaggio (eds.), *The New Institutionalism in Organizational Analysis* (Chicago and London: University of Chicago Press, 1991); Weir, *Politics and Jobs*.

[6] Cf. the literature on privatization or on regulatory reform of the utilities: J. Vickers and V. Wright (eds.), *The Politics of Privatisation in Western Europe* (London: Frank Cass, 1989); V. Wright (ed.), *Privatization in Western Europe: Pressures, Problems and Paradoxes* (London and New York: Pinter, 1994); M. Thatcher, 'Regulatory Reform and Internationalisation in Telecommunications', in J. E. S. Hayward (ed.), *Industrial Enterprise and European Integration: From National to Internationalized Champions: Firms and Governments in the West European Economy* (Oxford University Press, 1995).

very hard for alteration in its organizational position; its key argument for the reforms of 1996/7 was the need to prepare the 'national champion' for international expansion. Even EC regulation, which demanded institutional compliance from member states, produced its impacts through the domestic processes of institutional reform in France.

No automatic link existed between transnational pressures for change and institutional reform. On the contrary, institutional modification was difficult and required an appropriate set of domestic conditions. New arrangements in the 1960s in the two countries were introduced only after the failure of past attempts at reform and the increasing problems of excess demand, user dissatisfaction and lobbying for new arrangements by the network operator. Privatization in Britain in 1984 and in France in 1996/7 took place under considerable fiscal pressure and with a determined political executive. It required the failure of trade union opposition and major concessions by governments, notably in Britain to BT's management over keeping the company intact and in France to the unions over civil service status for employees. The active participation of the political executive was essential for change. In Britain, reforms in 1984 followed the re-election of the Conservative government in 1983, and formed part of beliefs that privatization would alter the role of the state and create future Conservative voters. In France, reforms in 1996 only took place after the presidential election of 1995 and required considerable determination by the Juppé government.

Existing national arrangements also influenced the process of institutional change, notably its timing and path. Thus, for instance, they created incentives for or against certain types of reform, notably privatization. In Britain, public sector accounting rules limited investment by BT and meant that privatization reduced public expenditure and borrowing totals. Moreover, as a public corporation, separated from postal services, BT was suitable for a rapid sale, but was also well-placed to resist being broken-up. In contrast, French financial arrangements allowed the DGT to borrow outside the general budget, reducing the conflict between telecommunications investment and other expenditure. Moreover, the DGT's *statut* presented significant obstacles to privatization: employees were civil servants; internal accounts were not in commercial form; the DGT was linked to postal services. Hence an intermediate step of reform in 1990 was needed, together with extensive preparation, before privatization was undertaken.

Thus national institutions in telecommunications exhibited considerable resistance to alteration. Major institutional changes required the confluence of several factors, notably technological and economic forces, new ideas and, crucially, domestic interests and political leadership by governments: generalised dissatisfaction was not sufficient. Whilst international factors contributed to change, through being translated into national pressures for change, domestic factors remained central in the reform process.

Cross-National Institutional Differences

National institutionalist claims that countries maintain different organizational arrangements receive considerable confirmation from the critical case of the British and French telecommunications sector. In the face of powerful, common external pressures for change, the two countries had differing, and indeed diverging, institutional frameworks. The case study indicates that there is no one unique, matching institutional equilibrium: Britain and France shared many economic similarities and faced similar and very strong external environmental pressures, but nevertheless maintained differing institutional arrangements between 1969 and 1997.[7]

Moreover, the path of institutional evolution differed between Britain and France in terms of its timing, form, processes, and extent. Thus, the two countries followed their own 'adjustment paths' in the 1970s and 1980s.[8] Reforms, such as the move away from civil service status for the network operator, the separation of postal and telecommunications supply, the ending of public monopolies, the sale of shares in the network operator and the creation of an independent regulator, took place later in France than in Britain, with a much shorter period of transition from a civil service monopoly to a competitive market with a partially privatized operator and an independent regulator. Certain institutional forms were unique to one of the countries throughout the period examined—for instance, the methods of funding public investment in France or public sector accounting rules in Britain. The processes whereby reforms were undertaken differed, with greater use of public consultations in France than in Britain. Finally, even after the reforms of 1996/7 in France, significant institutional contrasts remained between the two countries.

Institutional difference and divergence can be explained by analysis of the domestic politics of the two countries, as powerful external factors intersected with national characteristics and processes.[9] Important domestic factors in the interaction included political leadership, views of the performance of existing arrangements, openness to imported ideas, the role of interests, the translation of international pressures into domestic forces for change, and existing institutional arrangements. The position of political leaderships was dissimilar in the two countries for much of the period between the 1960s and 1990s, especially in the 1980s, in terms of political hue, strength, time horizons, and

[7] Cf. March, and Olsen, 'Institutional Perspectives on Political Institutions', 255–6.

[8] P. A. Hall, 'The Political Economy of Europe in an Era of Interdependence', in Kitschelt et al., Continuity and Change in Contemporary Capitalism; cf. P. A. Hall, 'The Role of Interests, Institutions, and Ideas in the Comparative Political Economy of the Industrialized Nations', in M. I. Lichbach and A. S. Zuckerman (eds.), Comparative Politics: Rationality, Culture and Structure (Cambridge: Cambridge University Press, 1997).

[9] For analyses of intersections between factors common to several countries and their domestic politics concerning more macro-level institutional structures, see Berins Collier and Collier, Shaping the Political Arena.

perceived interests. In Britain, a forceful and newly re-elected Conservative government existed in 1984 which enjoyed a large parliamentary majority and believed its electoral interests would be well served by privatization. In contrast, in France, there were governments of the Left between 1981 and 1986 and 1988 and 1993, and weak governments of the Right, which were often waiting for forthcoming presidential elections. In Britain, the performance of the PO/BT was seen as poor, together with that of public utilities in general in the 1970s and 1980s, whereas by the 1980s France had a highly modern network, the DGT/FT was regarded as efficient and strong support existed for the concept of *service public*. In addition, policy-makers in Britain were receptive to new ideas from the United States,[10] whereas in France, American 'liberalism' was not so readily welcomed. In Britain, Conservative Governments were able to overcome trade union opposition to reform, whilst business users, especially in the City, pressed for liberalization of competition and better service; in France, the trade unions were well mobilized, and enjoyed a measure of public support, whilst business users were less influential and slower to argue for institutional reform. Finally, existing differing institutional arrangements in each country affected the evolution of change by creating dissimilar incentives and obstacles to reform. In particular, the French system of funding investment allowed financial adaptation to pressures for greater capital expenditure following the reforms of the 1960s, whereas the British one remained a straitjacket for public enterprises, a factor that was important first in the transformation of the Post Office into a public corporation in 1969 and then in the privatization of BT in 1984.

However, in the 1990s, and especially the mid-1990s, a significant degree of institutional convergence took place, as France adopted several reforms that were the same or similar to those introduced earlier in Britain (France Télécom becoming the equivalent of a public corporation in 1990, followed by the end of its monopoly over network operation, sale of shares, and the establishment of an independent regulatory body in 1996–7). Institutional 'path dependency'[11] appears to have been limited, as past differences did not lead to dissimilar directions of change: on the contrary, France was able to follow many of the institutional steps taken by Britain despite doing so later and in different national circumstances. The 1990s can therefore be contrasted with the period 1969–90 to analyse why institutional convergence took place despite differing institutional histories, and to consider the conditions that encourage or permit cross-

[10]   Cf. D. S. King and S. Wood, 'The Political Economy of Neoliberalism: Britain and the United States in the 1980s', in H. Kitschelt, G. Marks, P. Lange, and J. Stephens (eds.), *Change and Continuity in Contemporary Capitalism* (Cambridge: Cambridge University Press, 1999).

[11]   Cf. Pierson, 'When Effect Becomes Cause', and 'Not Just What but When'; Thelen, 'Historical Institutionalism in Comparative Politics'; see also the literature on 'critical junctures—Berins-Collier and Collier, *Shaping the Political Arena*; S. D. Krasner, 'Sovereignty: An Institutional Perspective', *Comparative Political Studies*, 21(1) (1988), 66–94.

national contrasts in the organization of a sector. Three important related factors can be highlighted in the case of telecommunications: the strength of transnational forces for change; the degree of insulation of nations from policies pursued in other countries; market integration and competitive pressures, or at least, beliefs about these.

During the 1990s transnational forces for convergence in telecommunications appear to have become stronger; thus, for example, technological and economic developments increasingly undermined traditional institutional arrangements such as monopoly and cross-subsidisation. Moreover, regulation by supranational organizations, notably the European Community, grew. National insulation of policy making was further reduced by explicit international copying and learning (in Britain from American experiences and in France from events in Britain) and through the third factor of market integration and competitive pressures. Lucrative international telecommunications services expanded but became increasingly tradeable; direct and indirect competition developed, notably thanks to technological and economic developments; operators began to internationalize. In response, pressures for institutional changes grew, particularly from operators and users. The combination of these related factors in the process of institutional reform can be seen at work most clearly in France where it became sufficient to overcome opposition to reforms, in contrast to the 1970s and 1980s.

Thus the case study of telecommunications indicates that differences in cross-national institutional paths of development arise from contrasts in historical experiences and inheritances, distributions of power, political leadership, propensities to import ideas, themselves intimately linked to previous institutional arrangements. However, although national institutions are resistant to change and convergence, it also shows that resistance can be overcome if countries become closely interlinked through ideas, supranational institutions, and market integration. Such factors have been limited in twentieth century Western Europe, and their impact has been restricted by domestic factors. Nevertheless, the case of British and French telecommunications during the 1990s suggests that when very powerful transnational forces do in fact overcome resistance to reform of national institutions, the past differences of those nations does not prevent institutional convergence. Such forces can prevent countries being 'locked' into institutional dissimilarities by their past histories.

National Institutions and National Patterns of Policy Making and Economic Performance

National institutionalist claims that a country's institutional framework influences policy making and hence that cross-national institutional differences lead to contrasts in policy making find considerable support in telecommunications in Britain and France between 1969 and 1997. Not only did dissimilar patterns of policy formation exist, but also institutional change was followed by modification of policy-making patterns in each country. Moreover, specific key institutional features for national patterns were identified, which helped to explain cross-national differences. Explanation was based on several evidential routes that established the influence of these national institutional characteristics on policy making.

National institutionalism does not claim absolute institutional determinism, nor is it totally static; rather, it argues that insofar as policy patterns evolve, their development is marked by the institutional framework. These assertions are also offered confirmation by the case study. The history of telecommunications in Britain and France over twenty-five years reveals that national institutional frameworks were adaptable: they were able to accommodate policy change. However, they influenced the evolution of policy, constraining certain forms of change, whilst permitting and even at times, assisting its alteration. Thus, dissimilar patterns of policy development were seen, creating national 'policy paths' in the face of common external pressures for change.

Three routes whereby institutions affected policy evolution can be identified. First, institutionally-created organizations participated in modifying policy. Thus, for example, in Britain, Oftel pressed for the extension of competition and established a conceptual framework for liberalisation. Second, institutional frameworks permitted or constrained change. Hence, for instance, the 1984 Telecommunications Act in Britain provided Oftel with great institutional discretion to mould its regulatory role: it could therefore develop new processes of decision making, choose competition as its priority and reposition itself as a sectoral competition authority in the 1990s. In France, the DGT's institutional position as an *administration* made it dependent on the political executive and hence vulnerable to changed priorities by the latter, which did indeed apply its powers to aid the DGT's development in the 1970s but then switched to using them to extract funds from the DGT in the 1980s. Nevertheless, at the same time, institutions could restrict change: they were not infinitely malleable by policy-makers. Thus, for example, despite widespread agreement in Britain during the 1970s and early 1980s that the manufacturing subsector needed reorganization, attempts to restructure it comprehensively before 1984 were constrained by the institutional separation of BT and the government, and by the latter's lack of levers. In France, one of the obstacles to the extension of competition to network operation before 1996 was the DGT/FT's *statut*. Third, the path of policy change within a set of institutions was strongly marked by the features of those institutions. Thus, for example, in Britain, the process of ending BT's monoplies, the creation of new decision-making procedures and moves away from detailed sectoral regulation were intimately related to Oftel's position as an independent regulator, the powers of its Director General and the existence of a privately-owned BT.[12] In France, the processes and timing of liberalization differed, being marked by the French institutional framework of telecommunications.

Whilst clear linkages between national institutions and patterns of policy making have been found, the opposite holds true for economic outcomes. National institutionalist assertions that different institutional frameworks lead to dissimilar economic performance, including outcomes and trajectories, due to their effects on market structures, economic equilibria, firm behaviour, and path dependencies,[13] confront a host of indicators to the contrary. The study finds similarities between Britain and France in directions of change in economic outcomes, and often convergence, despite differing and indeed divergent institutions. In both countries, suppliers took decisions that resulted in similar directions of change; although significant differences existed, they related to the timing and pace of changes, and even then, cannot necessarily be ascribed to institutional factors. The PO/BT as a public corporation and then BT as a privatized company chose the same courses of action as the DGT/FT despite the dissimilar institutional arrangements and forms of public policy that existed in the two countries; thus, for instance, the two operators modernized their network, increased investment and rebalanced prices. In both Britain and France, equipment manufacturing declined in the 1980s, especially relative to network operation, whilst 'other services and networks' grew rapidly and experienced falling real prices. Significant differences existed between the telephone networks in Britain and France in 1970; by the 1990s, these had almost disappeared, and in any case, were much less important than the similarities in the direction of change that were common to the two countries.

Several possible non-institutional national factors, such as State traditions and cultures, the character of the political executive, or the ideas and programmes of policy-makers, differed considerably between Britain and France, and cannot explain the similarities found. Instead, the most likely explanation lies in the external factors that were common to the two countries—technological and economic developments, new ideas, and the international

[12] For the effects of these features on the evolution of independent regulatory agencies in the privatized utilities in Britain, see M. Thatcher, 'Regulation, Institutions and Change: Independent Regulatory Agencies in the British Privatised Utilities', *West European Politics*, 21(1) (1998), 120–47.

[13] See e.g. Hall, *Governing the Economy* and 'The Role of Interests, Institutions, and Ideas'; J. Zysman, 'How Institutions Create Historically Rooted Trajectories of Growth', *Industrial and Corporate Change*, 3(1) (1994), 243–83; D. Soskice, 'The Institutional Infrastructure for International Competitiveness: A Comparative Analysis of the UK and Germany', in A. B. Atkinson and R. Brunetta (eds.), *Economics for the New Europe* (Basingstoke: Macmillan, 1991); D. Soskice, *German Technology Policy: Innovation, and National Institutional Frameworks* (Berlin: WIS Discussion paper, 1996); Hall, The Political Economy of Europe in an Era of Interdependence'; cf. North, *Institutions, Institutional Change and Economic Performance*.

regulatory and market environment—although any conclusion must be highly tentative, as econometric evidence and a survey of public and private actors would be needed for more definite conclusions.

The role of external factors in the decisions of suppliers was evident in several instances, although they have not formed the focus of the present study. In the 1980s and especially the 1990s, the senior management of BT and France Télécom became convinced that competition would be extended in telecommunications. Events in the United States acted as an example of the future path of the sector; they were also a spur to BT and France Télécom in terms of providing likely competitors (most notably, AT&T) and a potential new market. EC regulation reinforced beliefs that firms needed to prepare themselves for competition and bring prices closer to costs. However, it is the strength of technological and economic factors that appears most clearly to explain the common economic outcomes in Britain and France. This can be seen in two ways. First, the pattern of economic outcomes in the two countries was congruent with the technological and economic forces for change described in Chapter 3. The latter included pressures and incentives for expansion, modernization, and the rebalancing of tariffs in network operation and expansion of new services and customer premises equipment, and concentration and internationalization in the network equipment-manufacturing subsector. Second, the specific decisions of actors—policy-makers and private firms—can be related to the technological and economic context. Expansion of the telephone network was related to rising demand, whilst decisions to invest and introduce new technology in switching and transmission were driven by the cost and quality advantages to be gained. In turn, investment affected cost structures, labour requirements, and productivity. Price rebalancing was underpinned by the altered cost structure and the danger of competition or 'bypass' of the PSTN. The expansion of 'other services on the network' and associated customer premises equipment, and declines in their prices, were responses to rising demand and the decreasing costs of supply, both being largely driven by developments in micro-electronics; suppliers in the two countries, whether public or private, responded to these changes in supply and demand conditions. In public switching, the rising fixed cost of developing exchanges, was a central concern in decisions over concentration and internationalization by manufacturers, irrespective of institutional factors such as ownership. Thus the power of technological and economic pressures and opportunities appear to have been felt by public and private decision-makers in both Britain and France.

Diverging institutions failed to result in differing economic outcomes because suppliers in dissimilar institutional settings took similar decisions or decisions with similar economic results. Thus Britain and France followed dissimilar routes to similar economic outcomes: public policy differed, in the sense of the activities of public bodies (the processes of public decision making, the instruments used and the objectives pursued), but strong, common factors, notably technological and economic forces, limited the impact of national institutional variance on economic outcomes. The many similarities found in economic outcomes represent an intriguing puzzle, as well as an anti-dote to claims for the importance of public policies for national economic performance. They suggest that in analysing economic outcomes, greater attention needs to be paid to the interests and strategies of suppliers and their relationship with the wider economic and technological context, as well as to national institutions.[14]

Concluding Comments on National Institutions

The case of telecommunications in Britain and France between 1969 and 1997 indicates that national institutions can influence policy making, even in the face of very powerful international forces. Institutional frameworks differed and remained stable for considerable periods of time in the face of strong pressures for change, giving rise to contrasting patterns of policy making. However, the case also indicates that national institutions can be altered, albeit that their reform is affected by previous institutional arrangements, is difficult, and requires the right configuration of circumstances. Moreover, policy change is possible without institutional alteration, although national institutions affect, constrain, or may indeed even encourage policy development. Finally, the importance of national institutions can vary according to type of phenomena: in the case of telecommunications in Britain and France over the period 1970–97, their effects were much greater on policy making than on economic outcomes. The study thus points to the importance of national institutions for public policy, but also to the need to consider the conditions under which institutions are stable, differ from one nation to another and influence policy formation.

---

[14] For discussions of the place of interests in institutionalist analytical frameworks, see J. Pontusson, 'From Comparative Public Policy to Political Economy: Putting Political Institutions in Their Place and Taking Interests Seriously', *Comparative Political Studies*, 28(1) (1995), 117–47, and Hall, 'The Role of Interests, Institutions, and Ideas'.

Appendix I

Persons Interviewed

Britain

Sir Peter Carey, Permanent Secretary, DTI 1974–85

Sir Bryan Carsberg, Director General of Telecommunications 1984–92

Rt. Hon. Christopher Chataway, Minister of Posts and Telecommunications 1970–2; Minister of State, DTI 1972–4

Sir John Clarke, Chairman of Plessey 1969–89

Don Cruickshank, Director General of Telecommunications 1993–8

Sir Edward Fennessey, Managing Director, telecommunications 1969–77; PO Board member 1969–77; PO Deputy Chairman 1975–7

John Harper, PO North-East telecommunications Region Manager 1969–71; Head of PO telecommunications procurement division 1972–7; Head of business, investment, network planning, and field operations 1975–81; Managing Director inland telecommunications and BT Board member 1981–3

Nigel Inman, BT 'Star' services

Lord Patrick Jenkin, Secretary of State for Industry 1981–3

John King, BT Board member 1983–8

Peter Macarthy-Ward, deputy head of BT's regulatory affairs department 1992–8 and head 1998

Alistair Macdonald, Deputy Secretary and head of the telecommunications division, DTI 1984–90

William MacIntyre, head of telecommunications division 1994–6 and head of Directorate on Information Society Issues 1994– , DTI

Jonathan Rickford, DTI official and senior BT official

David Saville, senior Post Ofice and British Telecom management 1969– ; Deputy Secretary BT, 1991

Derek Sibley, head of BT pricing division 1990

John Whyte, PO Deputy Director of Engineering 1968–71; Director of Operational Planning, PO telecommunications, 1971–5; Director of Purchasing and Supply, PO telecommunications 1975–6; Senior Director of Development, PO telecommunications, 1977–9; Deputy Managing Director, PO telecommunications 1979–81; Managing Director, British Telecommunications and member of Board 1981–3

Bill Wrigglesworth, senior civil servant, telecommunications matters, DoI/DTI, 1978–84; Oftel Deputy Director General 1984–92; Oftel Director General 1992–3

Lord David Young, Secretary of State, DTI 1987–9

France

Philippe Bodin, member of Mexandeau's cabinet 1981–4; Directeur régional des télé-communications for Brest

Jean-Pierre Chamoux, head of the Mission à la Réglementation 1986–8

Jacques Dondoux, *Directeur* of the CNET 1971–74, Directeur général des télécommunications 1981–6

Yves Fargette, Directeur général des télécommunications for Ile de France 1987–

Yves Guéna, PTT Minister 1967–9

Bruno Lasserre, head of the mission à la réglementation 1989–90, of the Direction de la Réglementation 1990–3 and of the DGPT 1993–6

Pierre Lestrade, Directeur général des télécommunications for Lorraine 1969–72; Chef de Service des installations de Paris 1972–4; Directeur des télécommunications for Paris 1974–80; Directeur des télécommunications for Ile de France 1980–2; Chairman and Chief Executive CGCT 1982–4; PTT senior management 1984–

Jean-Louis Libois, Directeur of the CNET 1967–71; Directeur général des télécommunications 1971–4; Président of the CNT 1971–

Gérard Moine, chef de cabinet, Prime Minister (1991–2); Head of DAI, France Télécom 1995–

Hubert Prévot, head of the Prévot Commission on the future of France Télécom 1989–90

Marcel Roulet, Directeur général des télécommunications/France Télécom, 1986–95

Jean-Pierre Souviron, Directeur of the DAI and from 1977 the DAII, PTT Ministry 1974–8

Jean Syrota, Directeur of the DAII, PTT Ministry 1978–81

Gérard Théry, Directeur général des télécommunications de Paris, 1972–4; Directeur général des télécommunications 1974–81

Appendix II

The Use and Interpretation of Statistics in Chapter 11

Methodology Used in Chapter 11

The figures presented need to be set out in a form which permits evaluation of trends over time and also comparison between Britain and France. The following methodology has therefore been used.

1. Figures in nominal French francs have been converted into nominal pounds sterling using purchasing power parities (PPPs). The PPP for GDP deflators is applied, calculated from figures provided by the OECD.[1] The use of PPPs is preferable to that of current exchange rates which have fluctuated rapidly during the period 1970–97, often without a close short-term correlation with inflation rate differentials, and hence would produce apparent changes in values which would be due largely or entirely to short-term currency movements.

2. In order to trace trends over time, monetary values calculated in nominal pounds are then converted into 1970 prices using the UK GDP deflator.[2] The British GDP deflator is used; this should be accurate for France as any general price inflation differential between Britain and France should already have been taken into account via the PPP figure. Thus real values and prices in 1970 pounds are determined and can then be compared. To aid evaluation, an index with 1970 = 100 can also be constructed. The choice of any year as a base year for monetary values is to some extent arbitrary, but 1970 appears suitable as it was a period of relatively stable telecommunications prices and costs, before the effects of major technological and economic changes were felt, and more generally, price inflation and exchange rates were fairly stable in comparison with the 1970s and 1980s.

3. Prices exclude indirect taxes (VAT in Britain and TVA in France) and are those applying at the end of each year unless specified otherwise.

4. UK figures: the Post Office's/British Telecom's financial years have run from April to April, and many figures are taken as at 31 March, whereas in France years run from 1 January to 31 December. Therefore to permit comparison, UK figures have been treated as applying to the year in which the majority of the financial year fell—for instance, figures for the year 1970 are those of the financial year 1970–1, while figures as at 31 March 1971 are compared with those as at 31 December 1970 in France.

---

[1] OECD, *Principal Economic Indicators* (Paris: OECD, quarterly).
[2] Source: *UK National Accounts* (London: HMSO/Stationary Office, annual).

Difficulties in the Use and Interpretation of Statistics in Telecommunications

A number of problems exist in the use and interpretation of statistics, arising either from lack of statistical sources or inherent in analysis of economic developments and comparisons over time and between countries. Chapter 11 has attempted to minimize difficulties by devices such as PPPs, real prices, construction of time series, and comparison of trends within each countries as well as of levels between countries. Nevertheless, remaining major problems should be set out and serve as a caveat in interpreting the figures provided.

1. *Value and Volume.* This is the most serious difficulty in analysing size, where it is measured by monetary values, such as revenue or expenditure. A reduction in the nominal or real prices of telecommunications services or goods reduces monetary values, either in absolute terms or relative to some other total figure. Thus lower prices of telecommunication services and goods lead to an underestimate of actual growth. Frequently it is impossible to correct this underestimate, since 'volume' measures do not exist, are not statistically available or are themselves questionable indicators (for instance, the number of telephone calls as an indicator of telephone usage).

This 'value–volume' problem is particularly important in telecommunications during the period 1970–97 because of falling real and often nominal telecommunications prices. Hence economic size, growth and usage are underestimated when measured by figures such as percentages of GDP. More obvious perverse effects also occur—for example, the reduction in prices by the DGT in 1987 to offset the imposition of TVA (VAT) on telecommunications services led to an apparent reduction in the economic size of the sector in 1988.

2. *Comparison of Figures.* Comparison of figures between Britain and France presents many difficulties, arising from different accounting methods, financial years, data collection, definitions etc. Direct comparison, especially in absolute terms and particularly of monetary values, must therefore be indicative and tentative. Comparison of trends over time within a country is less problematical, but even so, definitions and data collection methods do alter.

3. *Prices.* Analysis of prices presents several particular problems:

- Conditions under which services and products are supplied vary over time and between countries, thus affecting the service or product that is being purchased.
- More specifically, the range of reductions and the conditions for their applicability (for instance, the times and sizes for off-peak usage) differ over time and between countries.
- The usage of services varies over time and between countries; thus following the price of a particular service may become misleading if customers have switched to another one or if usage patterns vary in the other country and customers use an alternative service.

- VAT was imposed on telecommunications services in Britain in 1973, but not until 1987 for most services in France.
- Prices for specialized services for previous years are difficult to obtain.

Specific problems apply to analysis of telephone call charges; these are set out in the text.

4. *PPPs, Currency Conversion, and Real Prices.* Telecommunication prices and costs may be expected to have followed a different trend from the overall GDP deflator, and therefore a narrower deflator, such as the price of services, might be preferable; ultimately, an index of world telecommunications prices would be exceedingly useful in assessing the extent to which Britain and France had diverged from world trends. Unfortunately few specialized indices exist, and no PPPs can be found for those that do.

5. *Changes in Quality.* Changes in quality raise three major problems. First, when do qualitative changes result in a different service/product? One example is provided by mobile communications—can cellular radio be considered as the same service as mobile radio in the 1970s, which lacked many of the features of the former? Second, when examining price movements, changes in quality must be remembered. Thus falling prices underestimate the increased benefits if quality has risen, whilst higher prices may be accompanied by higher quality. Qualitative changes are highly relevant in telecommunications, where enormous improvements have occurred. Third, comparison between countries is rendered even more difficult by differences in quality between them. The analysis has assumed that the quality of services was the same in the two countries.

Appendix III

Conversion Rates Used in Chapter 11

Purchasing Power Parities: French Francs per Pound Sterling[1]

1970	16.45	1981	11.53	1989	11.95
1972	15.94	1982	11.87	1990	11.70
1974	15.61	1983	12.36	1992	10.31
1975	13.95	1984	12.84	1994	10.25
1976	13.51	1985	12.75	1995	9.88
1978	12.93	1986	12.90	1996	10.02
1980	11.54	1988	12.43	1997	9.89

GDP Deflator Figures used to convert nominal pounds sterling into 1970 pounds in chapter 11[2]

1970	100	1981	411.3	1989	638.7
1972	118.0	1982	442.8	1990	678.9
1974	145.4	1983	466.5	1992	752.6
1975	185.0	1984	488.1	1994	756.7
1976	212.9	1985	515.5	1995	811.6
1978	270.1	1986	533.5	1996	836.7
1980	369.6	1988	596.4	1997	859.1

[1] Source: OECD, *Principle Economic Indicators* (Paris: OECD, quarterly); the puchasing power parity for GDP deflators is used.

[2] Source: *UK National Accounts* (London: HMSO/Stationary Office, annual).

Bibliography

Adams, W., and Brock, J. W., 'Integrated Monopoly and Market Power: System Selling, Compatibility Standards, and Market Control', *The Quarterly Review of Economics and Business*, 22(4) (1983), 29–42.

AIT, *Des structures nouvelles pour les télécommunications?* (Paris: AIT, 1985).

Almond, G., 'The Return to the State', *American Political Science Review*, 82(3) (1988), 853–74.

Antonelli, C., 'Externalities, Complementarities and Industrial Dynamics in Telecommunications', working paper, University of Turin, Economics Department, 1990.

—— 'La Dynamique des interrelations technologiques: le cas des technologies de l'information et de la communications', in D. Foray and C. Freeman (eds.), *Technologie et richesses des nations* (Paris: Economica, 1992).

Arthur, W. B., 'Competing Technologies, Increasing Returns and Lock-in by Historical Events', *The Economic Journal*, 99(1) (1989), 116–31.

Ashford, D. E. (ed.), *Comparing Public Policies: New Concepts and Methods* (Beverly Hills, Calif.: Sage, 1978).

—— 'Introduction: Of Cases and Contexts', in D. E. Ashford (ed.), *History and Context in Comparative Public Policy* (Pittsburgh and London: University of Pittsburgh Press, 1992).

Atkinson, M., and Coleman, W., 'Corporatism and Industrial Policy', in A. Cawson (ed.), *Organized Interests and the State. Studies in Meso-Corporatism* (London: Sage, 1985).

—————— 'Strong States and Weak States: Sectoral Policy Networks in Capitalist Economies', *British Journal of Political Science*, 19(1) (1989), 47–67.

Aurelle, B., *Les Télécommunications* (Paris: La Découverte, 1986).

Bar, F., and Borus, M., 'From Public Access to Private Connections: National Policy and National Advantage', paper presented at 15th Telecommunications Policy Conference, Airlie House, 1987.

Bates, R. H., 'Contra Contractarianism: Some Reflections on the New Institutionalism', *Politics and Society*, 16(2–3) (1988), 387–401.

Batstone, E., Ferner, A., and Terry, M., *Unions on the Board: An Experiment in Industrial Democracy* (Oxford: Blackwell, 1983).

Baumol, W. J., Panzar, J., and Willig, R. D., *Contestable Markets and the Theory of Industry Structure* (New York: Harcourt Brace Jovanovich, 1982).

Bealey, F., *The Post Office Engineering Union* (London: Bachman and Turner, 1976).

Beesley, M., *Liberalisation of the Use of British Telecommunications Network* (London: HMSO, 1981).

—— and Laidlaw, B., *The Future of Telecommunications* (London: IEA, 1989).

Bell, A., 'Governance in the Regulation of Telecommunications: The Case of the UK', paper presented to Telecommunications Workshop, November 1997, European University Institute, Florence.

Benson, D., 'Local Exchange Renewal Strategy: Formulating a Strategy', *Post Office Engineers' Journal*, 67(3) (1974), 130–5.

Bensoussan, A., and Pottier, I., 'Réglementation et concurrence', *Communications & Stratégies*, 2 (1991), 154–71.

Benzoni, L., 'Departing from Monopoly', paper presented at a colloquium on 'Asymmetric Deregulation', Red Hall, June 1987.

—— and Rowe, F., 'Du Téléphone Standard aux Réseaux Stratégiques', in F. Rowe (ed.), *Entreprises et Territoires en Réseaux* (Paris: Presses de l'Ecole Nationale des Ponts et Chaussées, 1991).

—— and Hausman, J. (eds.), *Concurrence, Innovation, Réglementation dans les Télécommunications* (Paris: CNET/ENST, 1991).

Berins Collier, R., and Collier, D., *Shaping the Political Arena* (Princeton: Princeton University Press, 1991).

Berlin, D., 'L'Accès au marché français', *Actualité juridique—Droit administratif*, 20 March 1997, 229–45.

Bertho, C., *Télégraphes et téléphones: de Valmy au microprocesseur* (Paris: Le Livre de Poche, 1981).

—— (ed.), *L'Etat et les Télécommunications en France et à l'étranger* (Geneva: Droz, 1991).

BEUC (Bureau Européen des Consommateurs), *Telephoning in Europe* (Brussels: BEUC, 1985).

Blyth, M., ' "Any more Bright Ideas?" The Ideational Turn of Comparative Political Economy', *Comparative Politics*, 29(2) (1997), 229–50.

Boiteau, C., 'L'Entreprise nationale France Télécom', *La Semaine Juridique*, 41 (1996), 379–84.

Bolter, W. G., McConnaughey, J. W., and Kelsey, F., *Telecommunications Policy for the 1990s and Beyond* (New York: M. E. Sharp, 1990).

Bonnetblanc, G., *Les Télécommunications françaises. Quelle statut pour quelle entreprise?* (Paris: La Documentation Française, 1985).

Booker, E., 'Putting Packet Technology into Overdrive', *Telephony*, 14.12.87, 48–9.

Brenac, E., Jobert, B., Mallein, P., Payen, P., and Toussaint, Y., 'L'Entreprise comme acteur politique: la DGT et la genèse du plan câble', *Sociologie du Travail*, 27(3) (1985), 304–15.

Brenac, E., and Payen, G., *Une politique en dérive. La DGT et le plan câble* (Grenoble: Université de Grenoble, 1988).

British Telecom, *Annual Report and Accounts* (London: BT, annual).

—— *Summary of Charges 1989* (London: BT, 1989).

Brock, G. W., *The Telecommunications Industry: The Dynamics of Market Structure* (Cambridge, Mass. and London: Harvard University Press, 1981).

—— *Telecommunications Policy for the Information Age: From Monopoly to Competition* (Cambridge, Mass.: Harvard University Press, 1994).

BZW, *Telephone Sector Network Review 1990* (London: BZW, 1990).

Cabinet Office, ITAP, *Cable Systems* (London: HMSO, 1982).

Cable Authority, *Annual Report and Accounts 1989–90* (London: Cable Authority, 1990).

Campbell, J. L., 'Institutional Analysis and the Role of Ideas in Political Economy', *Theory and Society*, 27(4) (1998), 377–409.

Canes, M., *Telephones—Public or Private?* (London: IEA, 1966).

Carsberg, B., Statement, 'Telephone Services and Prices' (London: Oftel, 1987).

—— 'Injecting Competition into Telecommunications', in C. Veljanovski (ed.), *Privatisation and Competition* (London: IEA, 1989).

—— 'Office of Telecommunications: Competition and the Duopoly Review', in C. Veljanovski (ed.), *Regulators and the Market* (London: IEA, 1991).

Carter Committee, *Report of the Post Office Review Committee*, Cmnd. 6850 (London: HMSO, 1978).

Cave, M, 'Competition in Telecommunications: Lessons from the British Experience', *Communications & Strategies*, 13 (1994), 61–78.

Cawson, A., 'Introduction. Varieties of Corporatism: The Importance of the Meso-Level of Interest Intermediation', in A. Cawson (ed.), *Organized Interests and the State: Studies in Meso-Corporatism* (Sage, 1985).

—— *Corporatism and Political Theory* (Oxford: Basil Blackwell, 1986).

—— Holmes, P., Webber, D., Morgan, K., and Stevens, A., *Hostile Brothers* (Oxford: Clarendon Press, 1990).

CEPT, *Statistiques annuelles* (Paris: PTT Ministry, annual).

Cerny, P., 'State Capitalism in France and Britain', in P. Cerny and M. Schain (eds.), *Socialism, the State and Public Policy in France* (New York and London: Methuen and Pinter, 1985).

Champseur, P., *Rapport du groupe d'expertise sur la loi de réglementation* (Paris: DGPT, March 1996).

Chatain, D., and de la Chapelle, J., 'Le Réseau interurbain à l'aube de l'an 2000', *Revue Française des Télécommunications*, 63 (1987), 24–33.

Chester, N., *The Nationalization of British Industry* (London: HMSO, 1970).

Chevallier, J., *L'Avenir de la Poste* (Paris: La Documentation française, 1984).

—— 'Quelle définition pour le service public?', *Le Communicateur*, 2 (1987), 147–9.

—— 'Les Enjeux juridiques: l'adaptation du service public des télécommunications', *Revue Française d'Administration Publique*, 52 (1989), 37–52.

—— La Mutation des postes et télécommunications, *Actualité Juridique—Droit Administratif*, October 1990, 667–87.

—— 'La Nouvelle réforme des télécommunications: ruptures et continuités', *Revue Française de Droit Administratif*, 12(5) (1996), 909–51.

Clark, J., McLoughlin, I., Rose, H., and King, R., *The Process of Technological Change* (Cambridge: Cambridge University Press, 1988).

Cohen, E., *Le Colbertisme 'high tech'* (Paris: Hachette, 1992).

Collins, R., and Murroni, C., *New Media, New Policies: media and communications strategies for the future* (Cambridge, MA: Blackwell, 1996).

Commission of the European Communities, *Recommendations on Telecommunications* (COM(80) 422, final, 1 September 1980).

—— *Communication from the Commission to the Council on telecommunications* (COM(84) 277, 18 May 1984).

—— *Towards a Dynamic European Economy—Green Paper on the development of the common market for telecommunications services and equipment* (COM(87) 290, 30 June 1987).

—— *Commission Directive of 16 May 1988 on competition in the markets in telecommunications terminal equipment* (88/301/EEC OJ L 131/73, 27.5.88).

—— *Commission Directive of 28 June 1990 on competition in the markets for telecommunications services* (90/388/EEC, OJ L 192/10, 24.7.90).

—— *Commission Directive of 13 October 1994 amending Directive 88/301/EEC and Directive 90/388/EEC in particular with regard to satellite communications* (94/46/EC, OJ L 268/15, 19.10.94).

—— *Commission Directive 95/51 of 18 October 1995 amending Directive 90/388/EEC with regard to the abolition of the restrictions on the use of cable television networks for the provision of already liberalized telecommunications services* (95/51/EC, OJ L 256/49, 26.10.95).

—— *Commission Directive of 16 January 1996 amending Directive 90/388/EEC with regard to mobile and personal communications* (96/2/EC, OJ L 20/59, 26.01.96).

—— *Commission Directive 96/19/EC of 28 February 1996 amending Directive 90/388/EEC regarding the implementation of full competition in telecommunications markets* (96/19/EC, OJ L 74/13, 22.03.96).

—— *The Single Market Review. Subseries II, vol. 6, Telecommunications: Liberalized Services* (Luxembourg: European Communities, 1998).

Conruyt, P., 'Reseaux à valeur ajoutée: une demande évolutive', *Revue Française des Télécommunications*, 65 (1988), 70–7.

Council of the European Communities, *Council Directive of 21 December 1976 coordinating procedures for the award of public supply contracts* (77/62/EEC, OJ L 13/1, 15.1.77).

—— *Council Directive of 28 June 1990 on the establishment of the internal market for telecommunications services through the implementation of open network provision* (90/387/EEC, OJ L 192/1, 24.07.90).

—— *Council Directive of 17 September 1990 on procurement procedures of entities operating in the water, energy, transport and telecommunications sectors* (90/531/EEC, OJ L 297/1, 21.10.90).

—— *Council Resolution of 22 July 1993 on the review of the situation in the telecommunications sector and the need for further development in that market* (OJ C 213/1, 06.08.93).

—— *Council Directive of 13 December 1995 on the application of open network provision (ONP) to voice telephony* (95/62/EC, OJ L 321/6, 30.12.95).

Cour des Comptes, *Rapport au président de la République* (Paris: Cour des comptes, 1989).

Crandall, R. W., *After the Breakup: U.S. Telecommunications in a More Competitive Era* (Washington: Brookings, 1991).

—— and Waverman, L., *Talk is Cheap: The Promise of Regulatory Reform in North American Telecommunications* (Washington: Brookings, 1995).

Crouch, C., and Streek, W. (eds.), *Political Economy of Modern Capitalism* (London: Sage, 1997).

CSO, *National Accounts* (London: HMSO, annual).

——*Business Monitors* PQ 81, PQ 363, PQ 3441 (London: HMSO, quarterly).

Curien, N., and de la Bonnetière, G., 'Les Transferts de revenus induits par la tarification téléphonique entre catégories d'abonnés et entre types de prestations', *Annals des Télécommunications*, 39(11–12) (1984), 469–89.

Dandelot, M., *Le Secteur des Télécommunications en France: Rapport au Ministre de l'Industrie, des Postes et Télécommunications et du Commerce Extérieur* (Paris: PTT Ministry, July 1993).

Dang Nguyen, G., 'Telecommunications: A Challenge to the Old Order', in M. Sharp (ed.), *Europe and the New Technologies* (London: Frances Pinter, 1985).

——'Telecommunications in France', in J. Foreman-Peck and J. Müller (eds.), *European Telecommunication Organization* (Baden-Baden: Nomos, 1988).

——*Analyzing the Competitive Process in a New Industry: Mobile Telephony* (Bretagne: ENST, 1990).

——and Arnold, E., 'Videotex: Much Ado about Nothing?', in M. Sharp (ed.), *Europe and the New Technologies* (London: Francis Pinter, 1985).

David, P. A., 'Clio and the Economics of QWERTY', *Economic History*, 75(2) (1985), 332–7.

Delion, A., and Durupty, M., 'La Réforme en suspens du statut de France Télécom', *Revue française d'administration publique*, 73 (1995), 177–81.

Department of Industry, *The Post Office*, Cmnd. 7292 (London: HMSO, 1978).

——*The Future of Telecommunications in Britain*, Cmnd. 8610 (London: HMSO, 1982).

——*General Licence under section 15(1) for Telecommunications Systems used in Providing Value Added Network Services* (London: Department of Industry, 1982).

Department of Trade and Industry, *Licence granted by the Secretary of State for Trade and Industry to British Telecommunications under Section 7 of the Telecommunications Act 1984* (London: HMSO, 1984).

——*Class Licence for the running of telecommunications systems providing value added and data services* (London: Department of Trade and Industry, 1987).

——*The Infrastructure for Tomorrow* (London: HMSO, 1988).

——*Class Licence for the running of branch telecommunications systems* (London: Department of Trade and Industry, 1989).

——*Competition and Choice: Telecommunications Policy for the 1990s* (London: HMSO, 1990).

——*Competition and Choice: Telecommunications Policy for the 1990s*, Cmnd. 1461 (London: HMSO, 1991).

——*Creating the Superhighways of the Future: Developing Broadband Communications in the UK*, Cmnd. 2734 (London: HMSO, 1994).

——*Telecommunications Liberalization in the U.K.* (London: Department of Trade and Industry, 1997).

Derthwick, M., and Quirk, P., *The Politics of Regulation* (Washington, DC: Brookings, 1985).

DGPT (Bruno Lasserre), *Quelle réglementation pour les télécommunications françaises?* (Paris: Ministère de l'Industrie, des Postes et des Télécommunications et du Commerce Extérieur, 1994).

——*Intervention de France Télécom dans le secteur concurrentiel* (Paris: DGPT, 1994).

DGT/FT, *Statistique Annuelle* (Paris: DGT/France Télécom, annual).

DiMaggio, P. J., and Powell, W. W., 'Introduction', in W. W. Powell and P. J. DiMaggio (eds.), *The New Institutionalism in Organizational Analysis* (Chicago and London: University of Chicago Press, 1991).

Dobbin, F., *Forging Industrial Policy: The United States, Britain, and France in the Railway Age* (Cambridge: Cambridge University Press, 1994).

Docquiert, H., *SOCOTEL: Expérience de coopération État–Industrie* (Paris: Socotel, 1987).

Dogan, M., and Pelassy, D., *How to Compare Nations: Strategies in Comparative Politics* (Chatham, NJ: Chatham House, 2nd. edn. 1990).

Duch, R., *Privatizing the Economy: Telecommunications Policy in Comparative Perspective* (Ann Arbor: University of Michigan Press, 1991).

Dunlavy, C. A., *Politics and Industrialization: Early Railroads in the United States and Prussia* (Princeton: Princeton University Press, 1993).

Dyson, K., *The State Tradition in Western Europe* (Oxford: Martin Robertson, 1980).

——'The Cultural, Ideological and Structural Context', in Dyson, K. and Wilks, S. (eds.), *Industrial Crisis* (Oxford: Martin Robertson, 1983).

——and Humphreys, P., 'Introduction: Politics, Markets, and Communications Policies', in K. Dyson and P. Humphreys (eds.), *The Political Economy of Telecommunications* (London and New York: Routledge, 1990).

Eckstein, H., 'Case Study and Theory in Political Theory', in F. Greenstein and N. W. Polsby (eds.), *Handbook of Political Science*, vii (Reading, Mass.: Adison-Wesley, 1975).

Elixmann, D., and Hermann, H., 'Strategic Alliances in the Telecommunications Service Sector: Challenges for Corporate Strategy', *Communications & Stratégies*, 24 (1996), 57–88.

Essig, F., 'La Pointe de vue des entreprises', in *Le Communicateur*, 2 (1987), 82–5.

European Parliament and Council, *Directive 97/13/EC of the European Parliament and of the Council of 10 April 1997 on a common framework for general authorizations and individual licences in the field of telecommunications services* (OJ L 117/15, 07.05.97).

——*Directive 97/33/EC of the European Parliament and of the Council on interconnection in telecommunications with regard to ensuring universal service and interoperability through application of the principles of open network provision (ONP)* (OJ L199/32, 29.10.97).

——*Directive 97/51/EC of the European Parliament and of the Council amending Council directives 90/387/EEC and 92/44/EEC for the purpose of adaptation to a competitive environment* (OJ L 295/23, 29.10.97).

Evans, P., Rueschemeyer, D., and Skocpol, T. (eds.), *Bringing the State Back In* (Cambridge: Cambridge University Press, 1985).

Feynerol, M., 'Télécommunications: un nouvel environnement', *Revue Française des Télécommunications*, 62 (1987), 17–23.

Fligstein, N., 'Fields, Power, and Social Skill: A Critical Analysis of The New Institutionalisms', in M. Miller (ed.), *Power and Organization* (London: Sage, 1999).

Foreman-Peck, J., and Müller, J. (eds.), *European Telecommunication Organization* (Baden-Baden: Nomos, 1988).

France Télécom, *Rapport d'activité/Rapport annuel* (Paris: France Télécom, annual from 1989).

——*France Télécom Tariffs* 1990 (Paris: France Télécom, 1990).

Gailhardis, P., 'Numéris: le réseau du futur simple', *Revue Française des Télécommunications*, 69 (1989), 30–49.

——Bacot, C., Beugin, M., and Brillaud, J.-P., 'Satellites "Télécom 1": bilan et perspectives', *Revue Française des Télécommunications*, 70 (1989), 44–61.

Gensollen, M., 'Les Réformes institutionelles et réglementaires des télécommunications en 1990', *Communications & Stratégies*, 3 (1991), 17–34.

Ghillebaert, B., 'Le Système cellulaire de télécommunication avec les mobiles', *Annals des Télécommunications*, 42(7–8) (1987), 44–9.

Gillies, D., and Marshall, R., *Telecommunications Law* (London: Butterworths, 1997).

Gist, P., 'The Role of Oftel', *Telecommunications Policy*, 14(1) (1990), 26–51.

Goldstein, J., and Keohane, R. O. (eds.), *Ideas and Foreign Policy. Beliefs, Institutions and Political Change* (Cornell: Cornell University Press, 1993).

Gouiffès, J.-Y., and Roulet, M., 'La Charte de gestion à moyen terme des Télécommunications', *Revue Française des Télécommunications*, 47 (1983), 14–18.

Graham, C., and Prosser, T., *Privatizing Public Enterprises* (Oxford: Clarendon, 1991).

Grendstad, G., and Selle, P., 'Cultural Theory and the New Institutionalism', *Journal of Theoretical Politics*, 7(1) (1995), 5–27.

Griset, P., 'Le Développement du téléphone depuis les années 1950', *Vingtième Siècle/Revue d'Histoire*, 24 (1989), 41–53.

Grosvenor Press International, *Developing World Communications* (Hong Kong: Grosvenor Press International, 1988).

Hall, C., Scott, C., and Hood, C., 'Regulatory Space and Institutional Reform: The Case of Telecommunications', *CRI Regulatory Review* 1997.

Hall, P. A., 'Policy Innovation and the Structure of the State: The Politics–Administration Nexus in France and Britain', *The Annals*, 466 (1983), 43–59.

——*Governing the Economy* (Cambridge: Polity Press, 1986).

——'Policy Paradigms, Social Learning and the State', *Comparative Politics*, 23 (1993), 275–96.

——'The Role of Interests, Institutions, and Ideas in the Comparative Political Economy of the Industrialized Nations', in M. I. Lichbach and A. S. Zuckerman (eds.), *Comparative Politics. Rationality, Culture and Structure* (Cambridge: Cambridge University Press, 1997).

Hall, P. A., 'The Political Economy of Europe in an Era of Interdependence', in H. Kitschelt, G. Marks, P. Lange, and J. Stephens (eds.), *Change and Continuity in Contemporary Capitalism* (Cambridge: Cambridge University Press, 1999).

—— and Taylor, R. C. R., 'Political Science and the Three New Institutionalisms', *Political Studies*, 44(4) (1996), 936–57.

Ham, C., and Hill, M., *The Policy Process in the Modern Capitalist State* (Hemel Hempstead: Wheatsheaf, 2nd edition 1993).

Hancher, L., and Moran, M. (eds.), *Capitalism, Culture, and Regulation* (Oxford: Oxford University Press, 1989).

Harper, J., *The Third Way* (Stevenage: IEE, 1990).

Hartley, N., and Culham, P., Telecommunications Prices under Monopoly and Competition', *Oxford Review of Economic Policy*, 4(2) (1988), 1–19.

Hattam, V. C., *Labor Visions and State Power: The Origins of Business Unionism in the United States* (Princeton: Princeton University Press, 1993).

Hausman, J., 'Réglementation et incitations aux alliances dans les télécommunications', in L. Benzoni and J. Hausman (eds.), *Concurrence, Innovation, Réglementation dans les Télécommunications* (Paris: CNET/ENST, 1991).

Hayward, J. E. S., *The State and the Market Economy* (Brighton: Wheatsheaf, 1986).

High-Level Group [chairman, M. Bangemann], *Europe and the Information Society: Recommendations to the European Council* (Brussels: Commission, 1994).

Hills, J., *Information Technology and Industrial Policy* (London and Canberra: Croom Helm, 1984).

—— *Deregulating Telecoms: Competition and Control in the United States, Japan and Britain* (London: Pinter, 1986).

Home Office, *Report of the Inquiry into Cable Expansion and Broadcasting Policy*, Cmnd. 8679 (London: HMSO, 1982).

—— *The Development of Cable Systems and Services*, Cmnd. 8866 (London: HMSO, 1983).

Horwitz, R. B., *The Irony of Regulatory Reform: The Deregulation of American Telecommunications* (New York and Oxford: Oxford University Press, 1989).

House of Commons, *Report of the Committee of Inquiry on the Post Office*, Cmnd. 4149 (London: HMSO, 1932).

—— Select Committee on Nationalized Industries, *The Post Office*, HC 340–341 (London: HMSO, 1967).

—— Trade and Industry Select Committee, *Optical Fibre Networks, Third Report, Session 1993–94* (London: HMSO, 1994).

Huber, P. W., Kellog, M. K., and Thorne, J., *The Telecommunications Act of 1996* (New York: Little Brown, 1996).

Humbert, M., 'Présentation: les nouvelles industries de l'information et de la communication', *Revue d'Economie Industrielle*, 39 (1987), 1–3.

Humphreys, P., 'France: A Case Study of "telematics" ', in K. Dyson and P. Humphreys (eds.), *The Political Economy of Telecommunications* (London: Routledge, 1990).

Immergut, E. M., *Health Politics: Interests and Institutions in Western Europe* (Cambridge: Cambridge University Press, 1992).

—— 'The Theoretical Core of the New Institutionalism', *Politics and Society*, 25(1) (1998), 5–34.

INSEE, *NAP 2911* (Paris: INSEE, annual).

Inspection général des finances, *Rapport d'enquête de MM Capron, d'Hinnin et Rubinowicz* (Paris: Cour des Comptes, 1987).

Institut Français des Sciences Politiques, *Les Déréglementations* (Paris: Economica, 1988).

ITU (International Telecommunications Union), *Annual Statistics* (Geneva: ITU, annual).

Jannès, H., *Le Dossier secret du Téléphone* (Paris: Flammarion, 1970).

Kato, J., 'Review Article: Institutions and Rationality in Politics—Three Varieties of Neo-Institutionalists', *British Journal of Political Science*, 26(4) (1996), 553–82.

Katzenstein, P. (ed.), *Between Power and Plenty* (Madison: University of Wisconsin Press, 1978).

Kay, J., 'The Privatization of BT', in D. Steel and D. Heald (eds.), *Privatizing Public Enterprises* (London: RIPA, 1984).

King, D. S. (1992), 'The Establishment of Work-Welfare Programmes in the United States and Britain: Politics, Ideas and Institutions', in S. Steinmo, K. Thelen, and F. Longstreth (eds.), *Structuring Politics. Historical Institutionalism in Comparative Analysis* (Cambridge: Cambridge University Press, 1992).

King, D. S., *Actively Seeking Work* (Chicago and London: University of Chicago Press, 1995).

—— and Rothstein, B., 'Government Legitimacy and the Labour Market: A Comparative Analysis of Employment Exchanges', *Public Administration*, 72(2) (1994), 291–308.

—— —— 'Institutional Choices and Labour Market Policy: A British–Swedish Comparison', *Comparative Political Studies*, 26(2) (1993), 147–77.

King, D. S., and Wood, S., 'The Political Economy of Neoliberalism: Britain and the United States in the 1980s', in H. Kitschelt, G. Marks, P. Lange, and J. Stephens (eds.), *Change and Continuity in Contemporary Capitalism* (Cambridge: Cambridge University Press, 1999).

Kitschelt, H., Marks, G., Lange, P., and Stephens, J. (eds.), *Change and Continuity in Contemporary Capitalism* (Cambridge: Cambridge University Press, 1999).

Klinger, R., *The New Information Industry: Regulatory Challenges and the First Amendment* (Washington: Brookings, 1997).

Koelble, T. A., 'The New Institutionalism in Political Science and Sociology', *Comparative Politics*, 27(2) (1995), 231–43.

Kolko, G., *The Triumph of Conservatism: A Reinterpretation of American History 1900–1916* (New York: Free Press, 1977).

Komiya, I., 'Intelsat and the debate about satellite competition', in K. Dyson and P. Humphreys (eds.), *The Political Economy of Telecommunications* (London and New York: Routledge, 1990).

Krasner, S. D., *Defending the National Interest: Raw Materials, Iinvestments and US Foreign Policy* (Princeton: Princeton University Press, 1978).

Krasner, S. D., 'Approaches to the State: Alternative Conceptions and Historical Dynamics', *Comparative Politics*, 16 (1984), 223–46.

—— 'Sovereignty: An Institutional Perspective', *Comparative Political Studies*, 21(1) 1988, 66–94.

Landreau, Y., 'Negotiating Structural and Technological Change in the Technological Services in France', in B. Bolton (ed.), *Telecommunications Services: Negotiating Structural and Technological Change* (Geneva: ILO, 1993).

Larcher, G., *L'Avenir du secteur des télécommunications*, rapport du Sénat no.129 (Paris: Sénat, 1993).

—— *L'Avenir de France Télécom: un défi national*, rapport du Sénat no.260 (Paris: Sénat, 1996).

Lasserre, B., 'Service public et télécommunications: une rencontre difficile', *Le Communicateur*, 2 (1987), 150–9.

—— 'L'Autorité de régulation des télécommunications (ART)', *l'Actualité Juridique Droit Administratif*, 3 (March 1997), 224–8.

Lawson, N., *The View from No.11* (London: Corgi edn., 1993).

Le Diberder, A., *La Modernisation des reseaux de télécommunications* (Paris: Economica, 1983).

Levi, M., *Of Rule and Revenue* (Berkeley, Calif.: University of California Press, 1988).

Libois, L.-J., *Genèse et croissance des télécommunications* (Paris: Masson, 1983).

Lijphart, A., 'Comparative Politics and the Comparative Method', *American Political Science Review*, 65 (1971), 682–93.

Likierman, A., *Public Expenditure* (Suffolk: Penguin, 1988).

Lintingre, J., *Droit des télécommunications et de la communication audiovisuelle* (Paris: ENST, 1990).

Littlechild, S., *Regulation of British Telecommunications Profitability* (London: Department of Industry, 1983).

Locksley, G., *The EEC Telecommunications Industry: Competition, Concentration and Competitiveness* (Brussels: Commission of the European Communities, 1982).

Long, C., *Telecommunications Law and Practice* (London: Sweet and Maxwell, 2nd edn., 1995).

Longuet, G., *Télécoms. La Conquête de nouveaux espaces* (Paris: Dunod, 1988).

Lukawaszewicz, J. P., 'Service public administratif ou entreprise commerciale', *Actualité Juridique—Droit Administratif*, February 1975, 52–71.

McDowell, M. E., *Oftel Working Paper no. 2, International Comparison of Telephone Charges* (London: Oftel 1987).

Maddox, B., *Beyond Babel* (London: Andre Deutsch, 1972).

Mailhan, J.-C., Huret, E., Tréheux, M., and Gheysen, A., 'Communication d'entreprise: la nouvelle donne', *Revue Française des Télécommunications*, 73 (1990), 38–63.

Mansell, R., 'Telecommunications Network-Based Services', *Telecommunications Policy*, 12(3) (1988), 243–56.

—— 'Network Governance: Designing New Regimes', in R. Mansell and R. Silverstone (eds.), *Communication by Design: The Politics of Information and Communication Technologies* (Oxford: Oxford University Press, 1996).

March, J., and Olsen, J., 'The New Institutionalism: Organizational Factors in Political Life', *American Political Science Review*, 78(2) (1984), 734–49.

——— *Rediscovering Institutions: The organizational basis of Politics* (New York: The Free Press, 1989).

——— 'Institutional Perspectives on Political Institutions', *Governance*, 9(3) (1996), 247–64.

Martin, J., *Future Developments in Telecommunications* (Englewood Cliffs, NJ: Prentice Hall Internation, 1971).

Maxwell, W. J., 'Regulation and Competition: French Telecommunications Licensing', *Communications et Stratégies*, 22 (1996), 145–60.

Melody, W. H. (ed.), *Telecom Reform: Principles, Policies and Regulatory Practices* (Lyngby: Technical University of Denmark, 1997).

Mitchell, B. M., 'The Cost of the Telephone Service', *Telecommunications Policy* 7(1) (1983), 53–63.

Monopolies and Mergers Commission, *The General Electric Company PLC and the Plessey Company PLC: Report on the Proposed Merger* (London: HMSO, 1986).

——— *Chatlines and Other Message Services* (London: HMSO, 1989).

——— *Telephone Number Portability* (London: Stationary Office, 1995).

Moon, J., Richardson, J. J., and Smart, P., 'The Privatisation of British Telecom: A Case Study of the Extended Process of Legislation', *European Journal of Political Research*, 14 (1986), 339–55.

Morgan, K., 'Telecoms in Britain and France: The Scope and Limits of Neo-Liberalism and Dirigisme', in M. Sharp and P. Holmes (eds.), *Strategies for New Technologies: Case Studies from Britain and France* (London: Philip Allen, 1989).

Mougenot, N., *State Intervention in the French Telecommunications Sector: Analysis of a Succes, Minitel, and Current Evolution* (Sandvica: Norwegian School of Management, 1998).

Mouline, A., 'Les Stratégies internationales des opérateurs de télécommunications, *Communications & Stratégies*, 21 (1996), 77–93.

Müller, J., *The Benefits of Completing the Internal Market for Telecommunications Equipment, Services, in the Community (Research on the "Cost of Non-Europe", Basic Findings,* (Brussels: Commission of the European Communities, 1988).

Musso, P., 'Les Débats autour du vote del la loi de 1923' in Bertho, C. (ed.), *L'Etat et les Télécommunications en France et à l'étranger* (Geneva: Droz, 1991).

Negrine, R., 'Cable TV in Great Britain', in R. Negrine (ed.), *Cable Television* (London and Sydney: Croom Helm, 1985).

——— (ed.), *Cable Television* (London and Sydney: Croom Helm, 1985).

Newman, K., *The Selling of BT* (London: Holt Rinehart and Winston, 1986).

Noam, E. M., 'International Telecommunications in Transition', in R. W. Crandall and K. Flamm (eds.), *Changing the Rules: Technological Change, International Competition and regulation in Telecommunications* (Washington: Brookings, 1989).

Noam, E. M., 'Network Tipping and the Tragedy of the Common Network: A Theory for the Formation and Breakdown of Public Telecommunications Systems', *Communications et Stratégies*, 1 (1991), 43–72.

Nora, S., and Minc, A., *L'Informatisation de la société* (Paris, La Documentation Française, 1978).

Nordlinger, E., *On the Autonomy of the Democratic State* (Cambridge: Harvard University Press, 1981).

—— Lowi, T., and Fabbrini, S., 'The Return to the State: Critiques', *American Political Science Review*, 82(3) (1988), 877–901.

North, D. C., *Institutions, Institutional Change and Economic Performance* (Cambridge: Cambridge University Press, 1990).

O'Brien, M., 'Will the Fax Boom Go Bust?', *Telephony*, 25.9.89, 41–6.

Octogan, *Guide to Electronic Messaging Services 1989* (London: Octogan, 1989).

OECD, *Principal Economic Indicators* (Paris: OECD, quarterly).

—— *Telecommunications. Pressures and Policies for Change* (Paris: OECD, 1983).

—— *The Telecommunications Industry* (Paris: OECD, 1988).

—— *Satellites and Fibre Optics* (Paris: OECD, 1988).

—— *Telecommunications Network Based Services* (OECD, Paris: 1989).

Oftel, *Annual Report* (London: HMSO, annual).

—— *Competition Bulletin* (London: Oftel, quarterly).

—— *The UK Telecommunications Industry: Market Information* (London: Oftel, annual).

—— *Determination of Terms and Conditions for the Purposes of an Agreement on the Interconnection of the BT System and the Mercury Communications Ltd System* (London: Oftel, 1985).

—— *British Telecom's Procurement of Digital Exchanges* (London: Oftel, 1985).

—— *British Telecom's Price Changes, November 1985* (London: Oftel, December 1985).

—— *The Quality Of Telecommunication Services* (London: Oftel, 1986).

—— *Prices of Access Lines and Private Circuits* (London: Oftel, 1986).

—— *Review of British Telecom's Tariff Changes* (London: Oftel, 1986).

—— *British Telecom's Quality of Service* (London: Oftel, 1987).

—— *The Regulation of British Telecom's Prices. A Consultative Document* (London: Oftel, 1988).

—— *Chatlines and Other Message Services* (London: Oftel, 1988).

—— *Statement on the Telecommunications Standards Review Committee* (London: Oftel, 1988).

—— *Representation on behalf of PanAmSat* (London: Oftel, 1988).

—— *Quality of Service on the Cellular Networks* (London: Oftel, 1989).

—— *The Control of the Quality and Prices of BT's Private Circuits* (London: Oftel, 1989).

—— *Advice. International Telephony: Simple Resale and Control of Prices* (London: Oftel, 1990).

—— *Licence Modification Proposals to Implement Duopoly Review Conclusions* (London: Oftel, 1991).

——*Modifications to the Conditions of the Licences of British Telecommunications plc and Mercury Communications Ltd* (London: Oftel, 1991).

——*The Regulation of BT's Prices. A Consultative Document* (London: Oftel, 1992).

——*Future Controls on British Telecom's Prices: A Statement by the Director General of Telecommunications* (London: Oftel, October 1992).

——*Interconnection and Accounting Separation* (London: Oftel, 1993).

——*Statement. Future Controls on BT's Private Circuit Prices* (London: Oftel, 1993).

——*Interconnection and Accounting Separation: The Next Steps* (London: Oftel, 1994).

——*A Framework for Effective Competition: Consultative Document* (London: Oftel, 1994).

——*Pricing of Telecommunications Services from 1997: Consultative Document* [first], (London: Oftel, 1995).

——*Effective Competition: Framework for Action* (London: Oftel, 1995).

——*Beyond the Telephone, the Television and the PC* (London: Oftel, 1995).

——*Pricing of Telecommunications Services from 1997: Consultative Document* [second], (London: Oftel, 1996).

——*Statement. Pricing of Telecommunications Services from 1997* (London: Oftel, 1996).

——*Statement. Oftel's Proposals for Price Control and Fair Trading* (London: Oftel, 1996).

——*The UK Telecommunications Industry: Market Information 1992/93 to 1996/97* (London: Oftel, 1997).

——*Submission by the Director General of Telecommunications to the Department of Trade and Industry Review of Utility Regulation* (London: Oftel, 1997).

——*Network Charges from 1997. Consultative Document* (London: Oftel, May 1997).

——*Universal Telecommunication Services: Proposed Arrangements* (London: Oftel, February 1997).

——*Universal Service. Statement* (London: Oftel, July 1997).

——*Network Charges from 1997* (London: Oftel, July 1997).

——*Guidelines on the Operation of Network Charges* (London: Oftel, October 1997).

OMYSC, *Telecommunications Statistics* (Paris: ENST, annual).

Palmer, M., and Tunstall, J., *Liberating Communications* (Oxford: Basil Blackwell, 1990).

Peacock, A., *Report of the Committee on Financing the BBC*, Cmnd. 9824 (London: HMSO, 1986).

Peltzman, S., 'Towards a More General Theory of Regulation', *Journal of Law and Economics*, 14 (1976), 109–48.

——'The Economic Theory of Regulation After A Decade of Deregulation', *Brookings Papers on Economic Activity* (Microeconomics), 1989, 1–41.

Peston, P., 'Cellular Radio—The Revolution Rolls On', in Grosvenor Press International, *Developing World Communications* (Hong Kong: Grosvenor Press International, 1988).

Peterson, J., and Sharp, M., *Technology Policy in the European Union* (Basingstoke: Macmillan, 1998).

Pierson, P., 'When Effect Becomes Cause: Policy Feedback and Political Change', *World Politics*, 45 (1993), 595–628.

Pierson, P., 'The Path to European Integration: A Historical Institutionalist Analysis', *Comparative Political Studies*, 29(2) (1996), 123–63.

—— 'Not Just What but When: Issues of Timing and Sequence in Comparative Politics' (Boston: APSA conference paper, 1998).

Pigeat, H., and Virol, L., *Du Téléphone à la Télématique* (Paris: Commissariat du Plan, 1980).

Pitt, D., *The Telecommunications Function in the Post Office: A Case Study in Bureaucratic Adaption* (Hampshire: Saxon House, 1980).

—— 'An Essentially Contestable Organisation: BT and the Privatisation Debate', in J. J. Richardson (ed.), *Privatisation and Deregulation in Canada and Britain* (Aldershot: Dartmouth, 1990).

Pontusson, J., 'From Comparative Public Policy to Political Economy: Putting Political Institutions in Their Place and Taking Interests Seriously', *Comparative Political Studies*, 28(1) (1995), 117–47.

Post Office, *Report and Accounts* (London: Post Office, annual).

Post Office/British Telecom, *British Telecommunications Statistics* (London: Post Office/British Telecom, annual).

Postmaster General, *The Inland Telephone Service in an Expanding Economy*, Cmnd. 2211 (London: HMSO, 1963).

—— *Reorganisation of the Post Office*, Cmnd. 3233 (London: HMSO, 1967).

Post Office Engineering Union, *The Telephone Ring: It's Time to Investigate* (London: POEU, 1962).

Prévot, H., *Rapport de synthèse* (Paris: PTE Ministry, 1989).

Prezeworski, A., and Teune, H., *The Logic of Comparative Inquiry* (New York: Wiley, 1970).

Prosser, T., *Nationalised Industries and Public Control* (Oxford: Basil Blackwell, 1986).

—— *Law and the Regulators* (Oxford: Clarendon, 1997).

PTT Ministry, *Les Télécommunications françaises* (Paris: PTT Ministry, 1982).

—— *Bulletin Officiel* (Paris: PTT Ministry, weekly).

Purton, P., 'Slow Progess of VANS', *Communications International*, 15(7) (July 1989), 27–32.

Quatrepoint, J. M., *Histoire secrète des dossiers noirs de la Gauche* (Paris: Moreau, 1986).

Quelin, B., 'L'Avenir de la réglementation du secteur des télécommunications', *Revue d'Economie Industrielle*, 76 (1996), 125–40.

Redwood, J., and Hatch, J., *Controlling Public Expenditure* (Oxford: Basil Blackwell, 1982).

Renaud, J.-L., 'The Role of the International Telecommunications Union: Conflict, Resolution and the Industrialized Countries', in K. Dyson and P. Humhpreys (eds.), *The Political Economy of Communications* (London and New York: Routledge, 1990).

Richardson, J. J. (ed.), *Policy Styles in Western Europe* (London: Allen and Unwin, 1982).

Richer, L., 'Note. Conseil d'Etat: Avis du 18 novembre 1993', *Actualité Juridique Droit Administratif*, 1993, 463.

Robertson, J. H., *The Story of the Telephone* (London: Isaac Pitman, 1947).

Robinson, H., *The British Post Office: A History* (Princeton: Princeton University Press, 1948).

Rofe, C., and Rowe, F., *Data Transmission Flows Assessment: Application to the French Economy*, ITU international conference paper, 1990.

Rogy, M., 'Price Cap Regulation in European Telecommunications', *Communications & Stratégies*, 15 (1994), 47–75.

Rose, R., *Do Parties Make A Difference?* (London: Macmillan, 1984).

——Inheritance before Choice in Public Policy', *Journal of Theoretical Policy*, 1(2) (1990), 263–91.

Rothstein, B., 'Labor-Market Institutions and Working-Class Strength', in S. Steinmo, K. Thelen, and F. Longstreth (eds.), *Structuring Politics: Historical Institutionalism in Comparative Analysis* (Cambridge: Cambridge University Press, 1992).

Roulet, M., *Rapport sur l'avenir du groupe France Télécom* (Paris: Ministère de l'Industrie, des Télécommunications et du Commerce extérieur, 1994).

Roussel, A.-M., 'French Telecom Opens Up to Competition (Slowly)', *Data Communications*, October 1993.

Rowe, F. (ed.), *Entreprises et Territoires en Réseaux* (Paris: Presses de l'Ecole Nationale des Ponts et Chaussées, 1991).

Rugès, J. F., *Le Téléphone pour tous?* (Paris: Seuil, 1970).

Sachs, P. M., 'State Structure and the Aysmmetrical Society', *Comparative Politics*, 12 (1980), 349–74.

Sandholtz, W., *High-Tech Europe* (Berkeley, Los Angeles, and Oxford: University of California Press, 1992).

Sauter, W., 'The System of Open Network Provision Legislation and the Future of European Telecommunications Regulation' in C. Scott and O. Audéoud (eds.), *The Future of EC Telecommunications Law* (Cologne: Bundesanzeiger, 1996).

Savage, J. G., *The Politics of International Telecommunications Regulation* (Boulder and London: Westview, 1989).

Schmidt, S., 'Sterile Debate and Dubious Generalisation: European Intergation Theory Tested by Telecommunications and Electricity', *Journal of Public Policy*, 16(3) (1996), 233–71.

——'Commission Activism: Subsuming Telecommunications and Electricity under European Competition Law', *Journal of European Public Policy*, 5(1) (1998), 169–84.

Schmidt, V. A., *From State to Market? The Transformation of French Business and Government* (Cambridge: Cambridge University Press, 1996).

Schmitter, P., and Lembruch, G. (eds.), *Trends toward Corporatist Intermediation* (Beverly Hills: Sage, 1979).

————(eds.), *Patterns of Corporatist Policy-Making* (Beverly Hills and London: Sage, 1982).

Schneider, V., and Werle, R., 'International Regime or Corporate Actor? The European Community in Telecommunications Policy', in K. Dyson and P. Humphreys (eds.), *The Political Economy of Telecommunications* (London and New York: Routledge, 1990).

Schulte-Braucks, R., 'European Telecommunications Law in the Light of the British Telecom Judgement', *Common Market Law Review*, 23 (1986), 39–59.

Scott, C., 'The Future of Telecommunications Regulation in the United Kingdom: Tinkering, Regulatory Reform or Deregulation?', *Utilities Law Review*, 6(2) (1995), 13–17.

—— 'The UK Information Superhighway', *Utilities Law Review*, 6(3) (1995), 70–2.

—— 'Changing Patterns of European Community Utilities Law and Policy: An Institutional Hypothesis', in J. Shaw and G. More (eds.), *New Legal Dynamics of European Union* (Oxford: Oxford University Press, 1996).

—— 'Current Issues in EC Telecommunications Law', in C. Scott and O. Audéoud (eds.), *The Future of EC Telecommunications Law* (Cologne: Bundesanzeiger, 1996).

—— 'Anti-Competitive Conduct, Licence Modification and Judicial Review in the Telecommunications Sector', *Utilities Law Review*, 8(4) (1997), 120–2.

Scott, W. R., 'The Adolescence of Institutional Theory', *Administrative Science Quarterly*, 32(4) (1987), 493–511.

Sénat, *Rapport sur l'avenir des télécommunications* (Paris: Sénat, no.250, 1987).

Sharp, M. (ed.), *Europe and the New Technologies* (London: Frances Pinter, 1985).

—— and Holmes, P. (eds.), *Strategies for New Technologies: Case Studies from Britain and France* (London: Philip Allen, 1989).

Shepherd, W. G., 'Alternatives for Public Expenditure', in R. E. Caves (ed.), *Britain's Economic Prospects* (Washington, DC, and London: Brookings Institute and Allen and Unwin, 1968).

Shonfield, A., *Modern Capitalism* (Oxford: Oxford University Press, 1969).

SI3T/SIT (Syndicat des Industrious de Télécommunication), *Rapports d'Activité* (Paris: SI3T, annual).

Skocpol, T., *States and Social Revolutions* (Cambridge: Cambridge University Press, 1979).

—— *Protecting Soldiers and Mothers: The Political Origins of Social Policy in the United States* (Cambridge, Mass.: Harvard University Press, 1992).

Smith, S. de, and Brazier, R. *Constitutional and Administrative Law* (Harmondsworth: Penguin, 7th edn., 1988).

Soskice, D., 'The Institutional Infrastructure for International Competitiveness: A Comparative Analysis of the UK and Germany', in A. B. Atkinson and R. Brunetta (eds.), *Economics for the New Europe* (Basingstoke: Macmillan, 1991).

—— *German Technology Policy, Innovation, and National Institutional Frameworks* (Berlin: Wissenschaftszentrum Berlin für Socialforschung, Discussion paper 96–319, 1996).

Stanley, K. B., 'International Settlements in a Changing Global Telecom Market' in W. H. Melody (ed.), *Telecom Reform: Principles, Policies and Regulatory Practices* (Lyngby: Technical University of Denmark, 1997).

Steel, D., and Heald, D. (eds.), *Privatising Public Enterprises* (London: RIPA, 1984).

Stehmann, O., *Network Competition for European Telecommunications* (Oxford: Oxford University Press, 1995).

Steinmo, S., *Taxation and Democracy* (New Haven and London: Yale University Press, 1993).

—— Thelen, K., and Longstreth, F. (eds.), *Structuring Politics: Historical Institutionalism in Comparative Analysis* (Cambridge: Cambridge University Press, 1992).

—— and Tolbert, C. J., 'Do Institutions Really Matter?', *Comparative Political Studies*, 31(2) (1998), 165–87.

Stigler, G. J., 'The Theory of Economic Regulation', *Bell Journal of Economics and Management Science*, 2(1) (1971), 1–21.

Stone, A., 'Le "néo-institutionnalisme" ', *Politix*, 20 (1992), 156–68.

Swenson, P., *Fair Shares: Unions, Pay and Politics in Sweden and West Germany* (London: Adamantine Press, 1989).

Tarifica, *European Telecommunications Services* (London: Tarifica, annual).

Teune, H., 'A Logic of Comparative Policy Analysis', in D. E. Ashford (ed.), *Comparing Public Policies: New Concepts and Methods* (Beverly Hills, Calif.: Sage, 1978).

Thatcher, M. (Baroness), *The Downing Street Years* (London: Harper Collins, 1993).

Thatcher, M., 'Regulatory Reform and Internationalization in Telecommunications', in J. E. S. Hayward (ed.), *Industrial Enterprise and European Integration* (Oxford: Oxford University Press, 1995).

—— 'The Development of European Regulatory Frameworks: The Expansion of European Community Policy Making in Telecommunications', in E. Stavridis, E. Mosialos, R. Morgan, and H. Machin (eds.), *New Challenges for the European Union* (Aldershot: Dartmouth, 1997).

—— 'Regulation, Institutions and Change: Independent Regulatory Agencies in the British Privatised Utilities', *West European Politics*, 21(1) (1998), 120–47.

Thelen, K. A., *Union of Parts* (Ithaca and London: Cornell University Press, 1991).

—— 'Historical Institutionalism in Comparative Politics', *The Annual Review of Political Science 1999* (Palo Alto: Annual Reviews, 1999).

—— and Steinmo, S., 'Historical Institutionalism in Comparative Politics', in S. Steinmo, K. Thelen, and F. Longstreth (eds.), *Structuring Politics: Historical Institutionalism in Comparative Analysis* (Cambridge: Cambridge University Press, 1992).

Théry, G., *Les Autoroutes de l'Information. Rapport au Premier Ministre* (Paris: La Documentation Française, 1994).

Tilly, C. (ed.), *The Formation of States in Western Europe* (Princeton: Princeton University Press, 1975).

Touret, B., 'Le Financement privé des télécommunications', *Actualité Juridique—Droit Administratif*, June 1974, 284–97.

Tuthill, L., 'The GATS and New Rules for Regulators', *Telecommunications Policy*, 21(9–10) (1997), 783–98.

Ungerer, H., and Costello, N., *Telecommunications in Europe* (Brussels: Commission of the European Communities, 1988).

Vedel, T., 'La Déréglementation des Télécommunications en France: politique et jeu politique', in Institut Français des Sciences Politiques, *Les Déréglementations*, (Paris: Economica, 1988).

Vedel, T., 'Information Superhighway Policy in France: The End of High Tech Colbertism?', in B. Kahin and E. J. Wilson III (eds.), *National Information Infrastructure Initiatives* (Cambridge, Mass., and London: MIT Press, 1997).

Veljanovski, C, *Privatisation and Competition* (London: IEA, 1989).

—— 'The Regulation Game', in C. Veljanovski (ed.), *Regulators and the Market* (London: IEA, 1991).

—— (ed.), *Regulators and the Market* (London: IEA, 1991).

Vickers, J., and Wright, V., 'The Politics of Privatisation in Western Europe: An Overview', in J. Vickers and V. Wright (eds.), *The Politics of Privatisation in Western Europe* (London: Frank Cass, 1989).

———— (eds.), *The Politics of Privatisation in Western Europe* (London: Frank Cass, 1989).

Vickers, J., and Yarrow, G., *Privatization: An Economic Analysis* (Cambridge, Mass.: MIT, 1988).

Virol, L., 'Du téléphone à la télématique', *Revue Française des Télécommunications* 38 (1981), 40–51.

Voge, J.-P., 'A Summary of French Regulatory policy', in M. Snow (ed.), *Marketplace for Telecommunications: Telecommunications Regulation and Deregulation in Industrialized Democracies* (New York: Longman, 1986).

Vogel, S. K., *Freer Markets, More Rules: Regulatory Reform in Advanced Industrial Countries* (Ithica and London: Cornell University Press, 1996).

Wade, W., and Forsyth, C., *Administrative Law* (Oxford: Clarendon Press, 6th edn., 1988).

Weaver, R. K., and Rockman, B. A. (eds.), *Do Institutions Matter?* (Washington, DC: Brookings, 1993).

Weir, M., *Politics and Jobs: The Boundaries of Employment Policy in the United States* (Princeton: Princeton University Press, 1992).

—— Orloff, A.S., and Skocpol, T., 'Introduction. Understanding American Social Politics', in M. Weir, A. S. Orloff, and T. Skocpol (eds.), *Understanding American Social Politics* (Princeton: Princeton University Press, 1988).

Wilks, S., and Wright, M. (eds.), *Comparative Government–Industry Relations* (Oxford: Clarendon Press, 1987).

Williamson, J., 'Can Packet Switching Survive ISDN', *Telephony*, 27 July 1987, 76.

Williamson, O., *Markets and Hierarchies* (New York: The Free Press, 1975).

—— *The Economic Institutions of Capitalism* (New York: The Free Press, 1985).

Willman, P., 'Negotiating Structural and Technological Change in the Telecommunications Services of the United Kingdom', in B. Bolton (ed.), *Telecommunications Services: Negotiating Structural and Technological Change* (Geneva: ILO, 1994).

Wolmer, Viscount, *Post Office Reform: Its Importance and Practicability* (London: Nicholson and Watson, 1932).

Woods, L., 'Regulation of Premium Rate and Similar Services: The Proposals', *Utilities Law Review*, 7(2) (1996), 44–7.

Wright, V., *The Government and Politics of France* (London: Unwin Hyman, 3rd. edn., 1989).

—— (ed.), *Privatization in Western Europe: Pressures, Problems and Paradoxes* (London and New York: Pinter, 1994).

Zimmerman, F., 'Data Flies Higher on a Bird', *Telephony*, 25 May 1987, 44–9.

Zysman, J., *Governments, Markets and Growth* (New York: Cornell University Press, 1983).

—— 'How Institutions Create Historically Rooted Trajectories of Growth', *Industrial and Corporate Change*, 3(1) (1994), 243–83.

Glossary of Terms

analogue form   signals in the form of a modulated electric current, so that the signal frequency varies continuously with variations in the pitch of the voice or other message being transmitted.

bandwidth   transmission capacity.

cellular radio   mobile communications systems whereby areas are divided into small 'cells'; radio transmitters serve only one cell, and as a user moves from one cell to another, the central computer automatically 'hands over' calls in progress to the radio frequency used for the new cell.

CPE   customer premises equipment—equipment attached to networks to obtain services, such as telephone sets, fax machines, data terminals.

digital form/binary form   signals in the form of 'off' and 'on'.

electro-mechanical switches/exchanges   switches which use mechanical parts to connect callers and to perform 'control' functions, such as maintaining a connections for the duration of calls and identifying callers; the main types were Strowger exchanges and Crossbar exchanges.

ISDN   integrated services digital network—a network in which transmission and switching are wholly digitalized.

leased lines/private circuits   transmission capacity on the PSTN set aside for the exclusive use of the lessee; often used as the transmission basis for VANS/VADS, and can be used as private networks if switched by a PABX.

managed data networks   specialized networks for data transmission, the most common being packet switched networks, in which data is broken up into 'packets' for more efficient transmission.

multiplexing   interleaving several communications so that they all share one telephone line.

network operation   transmission of signals on the PSTN and fixed link voice telephony.

PABX   private automated branch exchange—equipment which switches signals between leased lines to create a private network (for instance, within a building or organization), so that everyone within the network can call all others on it without having to use the PSTN.

public switches/exchanges   equipment in the PSTN linking calls from the caller to the person called.

PSTN   the public switched telephone network—the general fixed link telephone network.

space division switches/exchanges   switches in which the 'control' functions of public switching are performed by micro-electronics, although callers are still linked by a physical path in the exchange; signals are switched in analogue form.

time division switches/exchanges switches in which micro-electronics perform both 'control' functions and the linkage of callers by allocation of a time slot for each connection; signals are switched in digital form.

VANS/VADS value-added network services/value-added data services—services whose features offer added value to mere transmission of signals by altering signals, such as electronic mail, fax services, or videotex services.

videotex systems equipment which allows users to consult computer databases, receiving information on a terminal screen, and, if interactive, to send messages back to the computer database.

Index

access charges 298–9
access lines 233 n.
accounting rate system 78–9
Achille-Fould, Aymar 126 n.
actors 47, 249
  decision-making 9, 31, 68–70, 137, 322;
    Britain 113; France 188
  and national institutions 12–16, 18, 21, 25,
    131, 249
  private 206, 263, 322
ADCs (access deficit contributions) 209–10
administration PPT/DGT as 156, 257
  broad objectives 306, 309–10, 320
  during seventies: brake on reform 102–4,
    106, 109–10; policy making 126, 129,
    138–9
  during eighties 190–1, 200, 202–3
  during nineties 216, 220, 225–6
  historically 40, 44
advanced networks and services 5, 60–7, 264,
  321
  Britain 94, 99, 258
  convergence 298–9
  France 158, 241, 256
  policy making 228–59
  pressure for change 73, 76, 78, 81
  supply 52, 55, 285–97
  see also broadband networks; cellular
    networks; computing; CPE; leased lines;
    paging networks; satellites; specialized
    networks; value-added services
Advisory Committee on Telecommunications
  Systems Definitions 99
AEI (Associated Electrical Industries) 36,
  116
Agritel 137 n.
AIPT (*L'Association des ingénieurs des postes et
  télécommunications*) 108
airwave television channels 166, 243
AIT (*Association des ingénieurs des
  télécommunications*) 153
Alcatel 159, 182, 219–20, 308
  advanced services 251–2, 254
  nationalization 153
AMPS (Advanced Mobile Phone System)
  238 n.

analogue:
  cellular systems 62, 251, 294
  switching 48, 50–3, 56, 287–8, 295; to
    digital 63–4
answering machines 254, 296–7
answering services 236
AOIP 131 n., 134 n.
ART (*Autorité de régulation des
  télécommunications*) 164–70, 223, 225
Astra satellites 253
Atlas 221, 294
ATM (asynchronous transfer mode) 53
AT&T (American Telephone & Telegraph
  Co.) 57, 207
  break up 146, 315
  and BT 212 n., 213
  and CGE 196–7
  and France Télécom 221, 250, 322
  pressure for change 72–3, 76–7, 208
Attali, Jacques 191, 195, 198
ATT/Philips 182, 194
audiovisual broadcasting 50, 166
automatic switching equipment 34, 36, 40–1
  see also digital, switching; electro-
    mechanical exchanges
Automatic Telephone Engineering 36
autonomy 2, 14, 306–7, 309–10
  Britain 169, 173, 179, 203; lack of 114,
    120, 138
  France: during seventies 107–10, 126, 129,
    138–9; during eighties 153–4, 188–9,
    195, 200; during nineties: and
    competition 218, 224–5, 247, 257,
    institutional framework 156, 159, 161,
    164
  historical roots 40, 43–4, 46
AXE 10 (System Y) 182–3, 197

Baby Bells, *see* RBOCs
Baker, Kenneth 94, 181, 230
Balladur, Edouard 160–1, 197, 199, 223
bandwidths 48, 61–2, 287
Bangemann Report (1994) 83
banks 66, 137, 176
Barclays Merchant Bank 176
Barlow, Sir William 121

Barre, Raymond 190 n.
basket of services:
    comparisons 282–3
    tariffs for 178, 186
BBC (British Broadcasting Corporation) 37,
    231, 238
BEAB (British Electro-Technical Approvals
    Board) 240
Beesley, Professor Michael 175–6, 235
Beesley Report 145
Benn, Anthony Wedgewood 93, 100, 113 n.,
    121
BGSL (Branch Systems General Licence)
    236 n.
'Big Three' firms 113, 117–19, 124, 173,
    181–2
    see also GEC; Plessey; STC
binary switching, see digital, switching
Blair, Tony 232
Bon, Michel 162, 215 n., 218
borrowing 68–9, 310
    Britain 45–6, 96, 98; during seventies 110,
        113, 123–5, 139; during eighties 184–7,
        201–3
    France 45–6, 309, 316; during seventies
        103, 106–7, 127, 138–9
bottlenecks 37, 211
Boublil, Alain 194–5
Bourgeois case 105
Bouygues 217, 251–2
Bridgeman Committee of Inquiry (1932)
    37–8
Britain 2–5, 7, 22
    economic outcomes 263–5, 270, 287, 298,
        300
    historical roots 44–5
    institutional framework: seventies 92–101,
        109–11; eighties 143–52, 169–70;
        nineties 143, 152, 169–70
    national institutionalist analysis 305–15,
        317–21, 323
    network operators: during eighties
        172–87, 199–201, 204; during nineties
        205–15, 224–7
    policy making: advanced networks,
        services and CPE 228–40, 255–9; during
        seventies 112–25, 137–8
    pressures for change: international
        regulatory environment 71, 78, 85–6;
        technological and economic 47–8, 51,
        69–70
    see also British Telecom; equipment

manufacturing subsector; government;
    Post Office
British Government:
    Cabinet Economic Committee 181
British Telecom (BT)
    autonomy 310, 320–1
    Board 144, 146
    and competition 199, 236, 322; Mercury
        178, 207; monopolies ended 148–9, 229,
        232, 255, 308; during nineties 205–12,
        217, 220–2, 225
    costs 275, 298
    divergence 173, 175, 179–80, 198, 200–1
    economic outcomes 265–9, 277, 284–5,
        288–91, 299
    equipment suppliers 148–9, 181–4
    institutional framework 144–6, 160,
        169–70
    international regulatory environment 76,
        79, 85 n.
    investment and borrowing 125 n., 201–3,
        231, 272, 316
    licensing 174, 177, 209, 213; of equipment
        suppliers 144, 147–9
    privatization 148, 176, 306–7, 314, 318, and
        new regulatory regime 145–7
    regulation 145–7, 185, 210, 214
    revenue 268, 270, 274–6, 283; leased
        lines/private circuits 256, 287–9; profits
        and profitability 274, 300; regulation
        185, 210, 214
    services 318; advanced 230–2, 237–40,
        250, 255–8, 292–4; CPE 144, 230, 239
    unions 146, 176
    see also autonomy; government;
        monopoly; Oftel; Post Office;
        privatization; switching
British Telecommunications Act (1981) 144,
    176, 229, 235, 238, 258
British Telephone Development Committee
    36
broadband networks 54, 229, 242–5
    national 230–3, 257
broadcasting sector 253
    boundaries, sectoral 50, 66, 69, 152, 247
    and British Telecom 233
    cable networks 230, 256
    Cable Plan 242–3
    French policy framework 153–4, 189
    satellite networks 238, 243, 252–3
    technological advances 62, 148, 228
BSA (Bulk Supply Agreement) 36, 45, 116

BSI (British Standards Institute) 240
BT, *see* British Telecom
BTS (British Telecommunications Systems)
120
BTUC (British Telecom Union Committee)
146
budget (France):
    budget annexe 156, 203; historical legacy
    43, 45; institutional framework 104,
    106, 109; reform 129, 139
    general 104, 109, 308, 311
    Ministry 157, 191, 193, 219
Bulk Contracts Committee 36
Bulk Supply Agreements (BSA) 36, 45, 116
Bull 160 n., 219, 249
business users 11, 55, 68, 76, 283, 318
    Britain: large 99, 146, 179; small 151, 215;
    strategy towards 123, 187, 235; TMA
    (Telecommunications Managers
    Association) 150, 176
    France 127, 166, 190, 199, 246, 249, 257
    large 233, 271, 277
bypassing networks 57, 69, 198, 250, 322
    see also indirect competition

Cable and Broadcasting Act (1984) 148 n.,
    231
Cable and Wireless 176, 212, 251
    sale of 144–5
cable networks:
    equipment 33, 42, 54, 67, 105; provision
    58, 231, 245; *see also* coaxial cable;
    optical fibre cable
    France 198, 241–5, 252, 256, 258, 308
    television 62, 84, 217; Britain 95, 177, 206,
    208, 230–3, 256, licences 148 n.
Cable Plan (*Plan Câble*) 198, 241–5, 256, 258,
    308
Cable Television Authority 148 n.
Caducée 245
cahier des charges (licence conditions) 156,
    164, 167
Caisse Nationale des Télécommunications (CNT)
    106
call boxes 177–8, 180, 210
call charges, *see* tariffs
call termination services 211 n.
call-back services 57
capacity
    leased line 73, 81, 233
    network 52, 57, 64
    resale 81, 175, 179, 233, 236

transmission 52, 287
capital:
    expenditure 40–5, 69, 96, 107; combined
    with current 98, 110, 145
    investment and borrowing 114, 145
car phones 62
Carsberg, Sir Bryan 174, 178–9, 182–3, 186–
    7 n., 208, 213, 232–3, 236, 324
Carter, Sir Charles 100
Carter Committee 101, 119
'Carterfone decision' (1968) 72 n.
CBI (Confederation of British Industry) 100,
    122
CEGB (Central Electricity Generating Board)
    37
Cegetel 217
Cellnet 149, 238, 296
cellular networks 54, 208, 217–18, 238–9
    Britain 57, 61–3; competition 69, 74, 83–4,
    149, 177; and Oftel 238, 256
    economic outcomes 265, 286, 294–7 n.,
    299–300
    France 160, 241, 250–2, 255–7
    'handover' facility 61–2, 294
CEPT (Conference of European Postal and
    Telecommunications Administrations)
    288
CFDT (*Confédération française démocratique du
    travail*) 154, 156, 163
CGC (*Confédération des cadres*) 161
CGCT (*Compagnie générale de constructions
    téléphoniques*) 42, 131, 133–4 n., 153–4,
    193–7, 325
CGE group (*Compagnie générale d'électricité*)
    42–3, 131–2, 134, 153–4, 193–7, 217
CGT (*Confédération générale du travail*) 154,
    156, 160, 163
Champsaur committee 218
change, transnational pressures for 3–4,
    7–20, 23
    during seventies 91–4, 105–9, 112
    during eighties 172, 204
    historical roots 31–46
    international regulatory environment
    71–87
    and national institutionalism 305, 315–17,
    319, 322–3
    technological and economic developments
    47–70, 228
    see also reform
charge cap 211
    see also tariffs

Charte de gestion (1983) 198, 215
Chataway, Christopher 113 n., 121, 124, 324
Chevènement, Jean-Pierre 188, 194
Chirac, Jacques 109, 155, 189, 196–7
CIT-Alcatel 42–3, 70, 130–2, 139, 194–5, 197
City of London 147, 233, 318
civil service 33–4, 38–9, 44–5, 70, 305, 316–17
    Britain 92–5, 113–14, 146, 306
    France 306, 316; during seventies 102–3,
        106, 109, 169; during eighties 154, 200;
        during nineties 156–7, 159–61, 164–5,
        169, 219, 225
Clarke, Sir John 119 n., 324
closed user networks 167
CNCL (*Commission nationale de la
    communication et des libertés*) 154–5, 188,
    193
CNES (*Centre nationale d'études spatiales*) 192
CNET (*Centre nationale d'études des
    télécommunications*) 41–3, 105, 129–33,
    139, 325
CNT (*Caisse nationale des télécommunications*)
    136–7, 139, 325
coaxial cable 48, 54, 56, 231, 244
    see also cable networks
Codétel 137 n.
COGECOM 267 n.
Colt 207
Com-dev 217
Commissariat du Plan 104, 125
Commission supérieure du service public (Public
    Service Commission) 165–6
Communications Ministry (France) 190, 242
Communist Party (PCF—*Parti communiste
    français*) 107, 136–7, 160
Compagnie générale des eaux 217, 251
compagnie nationale du téléphone 107
competition 47, 49, 59, 202, 310, 322
    Britain 259, 320; during eighties 172–4,
        178–9, 183, 201, 203; during nineties
        207–9, 225, 232, 237
    direct and indirect 57, 319
    France 308; advanced networks and
        services 229, 233, 246, 256–8; during
        eighties 190–2, 198, 203; during nineties
        163, 165, 216–18, 220, 224–5
    network operation 205–27
    regulation 63–5, 68; DRG/DGPT 159,
        167–8, 241, 246, 252, 255–9; Oftel
        209–12, 230, 236–7, 239, 311, 320, and
        licensing 175–8

    in supply 73, 166–7, 295; competitive
        tendering 116, 134, 181, 219
Competition and Service (Utilities) Act (1992)
    152, 180 n.
Computer I Inquiry (United States, 1971)
    73
Computer II decision (United States, 1980)
    73
computer-aided design (CAD) 66
computing 22, 73, 99, 294–5
    driving force for change 47, 49–52, 58,
        60–1, 66–9
    France 128, 193, 228–9, 246–9, 256
concentration, pressures for 58, 70
Concert 76, 212 n.
congestion 123, 127–8, 273
connection 178, 230
    advanced services and networks 232, 289,
        291–2, 296
    tariffs 35, 123, 275–6, 278–9, 291
Conseil de la concurrence 166
Conseil d'État 105, 161, 166, 218
*Conseil supérieur des Postes et
    Télécommunications* 108
Consent Decree (United States, 1956) 73
Conservatives 38, 240, 316, 318
    during seventies 93–4, 99, 113 n., 124
    during eighties 144–7, 152, 170, 176, 185
contestable markets 73
Contrat de plan 220, 225, 241
    (1991–4) 215, 221–3
    (1995–8) 215, 222, 246
convergence 3–5, 21, 23, 27, 110, 143, 255
    and competition 205, 227
    despite international divergence 263–301
    national institutional theory 308, 310, 318,
        321
copper wire cable 56
    coaxial cable 48, 54, 56, 231, 244
    multipair 48
    twin-pair 54, 62, 287–8
Corpac 400, 251
Corps des ingénieurs des Postes et Télégraphes 40
Corps des ingénieurs des télécommunications
    103, 106, 128–30, 225
cost:
    based pricing 87, 273–8, 322
    Britain 123, 187, 233
    cost-plus basis 116, 131
    France 134, 154, 198, 223, 246, 254
    pressures for change 47, 52, 56–7

fixed, *see* capital, expenditure; investment; labour
CPE (customer premises equipment) 48–9, 63–6, 72–3, 76, 322
  and advanced services 80, 82, 239–40, 254–5
  Britain 144, 169, 240, 256
  economic outcomes 285–300
  institutional framework 95, 101–2, 149–51
  liberalization 83, 94, 258
cream-skimming 190, 198
Créditel 137 n.
Cresson, Edith 196, 220
crise du téléphone 106, 108
critical junctures 17, 19
Crossbar electro-mechanical exchange 34, 41–2, 48, 51–2, 56, 118, 132
cross-national comparison 12, 15, 19–25, 255, 317–19
  during seventies 91, 112
  during eighties 171, 173
  during nineties 205, 226
  economic outcomes 265, 274
cross-subsidization 277, 298, 319
  Britain 211, 230, 237, 239–40
  France: advanced services and networks 242, 246, 252, 258; during eighties 190, 198; during nineties 158, 168, 223
Cruickshank, Don 207, 209, 213–14, 324
CSA (*Conseil supérieur de l'audiovisuel*) 166, 188
CT2 (Telepoint) systems 62
Culture Ministry (France) 190, 242, 250
current and capital expenditure combined 98, 110, 145

D10 switch (SLE Citeral) 133
DAI [I] (*Direction des affaires industrielles [et internationales]*) 126, 129–30, 132
Dandelot, Marc 157–60 n., 161, 217 n., 221 n.
data, comparability of 95, 264–5, 281, 297, 326–8
data communications 73, 236
data processing 95, 235
data terminals 49
data transmission 63–6, 81, 236
  economic outcomes 286–7
  France 155, 245, 250, 257
databases 61, 286, 290

DATAR (*Délégation de l'aménagement du territoire et de l'action régionale*) 125, 135–6
DBS (direct broadcasting by satellite) 63, 238
de Gaulle, Charles 41, 106–7, 136
decision making process and overall policy pattern:
  during eighties: Britain 173–5
  decision-making strategies 25, 86, 112–15, 173–5, 206–7, 229–30
Délégation générale de la stratégie 193
demand growth 47, 112, 115, 306
Department of Industry, *see* DoI
Department of Justice (USA) 74
Department of Posts and Telecommunications 113
depreciation 121, 274–5, 299
deregulation 82, 153
Deutsche Telekom 85 n., 160, 162–3, 217 n., 220–1
Deutsches Bundepost 184
DGP (*Direction Générale de la Poste*), *see* La Poste
DGPT (*Direction générale des postes et télécommunications*) 283, 309
  and advanced services and networks 241–2, 246, 250, 252–9
  during nineties 159, 167–8, 216–20, 223–4, 226–7
DGT (*la Direction générale des télécommunications*) 205 n.
  advanced services and networks 241, 243–7, 250–5, 258
  calls for *société publique* (public enterprise) status 152–5, 169
  economic outcomes 265–75, 277, 283, 285–9, 293–4, 299
  equipment manufacturing subsector 130–4, 193–7
  functioning of 191–3
  funds extracted from by political executive 320
  historical roots 40, 42, 44–6
  institutional divergence 173, 188–9, 191–8, 200–4
  institutional framework 102–11
  internal organization 128–30
  international regulatory environment 76, 79
  investment 69–70
  monopoly 68, 243–4, 248–9, 256

DGT (*cont.*)
  policy and change 305, 307–11, 316, 318, 320–1
  policy making 125, 128–35, 137–40
  profits and tariffs 104, 135, 203
  see also administration; France Télécom; *service public*
digital:
  cellular systems 62, 251, 295
  switching 59, 242, 288, 308; during seventies 98, 115, 119, 126, 131; during eighties 179–80; exchanges 43, 50–3, 270, 295, private circuits 287, 295, 299, trunk network 56, 182; lines 233, 287; technological and economic pressure for change 49–54, 58, 60 n., 67–8
  television 63, 253
Director General:
  Fair Trading (DGFT) 150
  Telecommunications (France) 152, 169–70, 191; *see also* DGT
  Telecommunications (UK) 35, 147–51, 177–8, 207–10, 320–1
directory enquiries 177, 186, 213 n.
dishes, personal satellite 54
distance, *see* long-distance; transmission
divergence:
  away from monopoly 205
  institutional: change 172–204, 229; framework 92, 109–11, 143, 152, 169–70
  international 263–301
  and national institutionalism 3–5, 23–4, 27, 306–10, 317, 322
DOI (Department of Industry):
  advanced services and networks 230, 235, 238, 255
  institutional divergence 173–4, 176–7, 179, 181–2, 200–1
  institutional framework 101, 144–6
  policy making in during seventies 113–20, 137
Dondoux, Jacques 188, 191, 195–9, 248, 325
DRG (*Direction à la réglementation général*) 193, 309
  and advanced services and networks 241–2, 246, 250, 252–3, 255–9
  during nineties 159, 167–8, 216–17, 223–4, 226
DRT (*Directions régionales des télécommunications*) 129

DTI (Department of Trade and Industry) 324
  and advanced services and networks 229–30, 232, 236, 238, 240
  seventies 94, 118
  eighties 144 n., 173–4, 177, 180–4, 200–1, 255
  nineties 206, 208, 224
duopoly 178, 202, 207–9
Duopoly Review (1991) 207–8, 232

E10 exchange 53 n., 116, 131–2, 134
  E10S switch 195–6
E12 trunk exchange 133
earth stations 53, 63
École supérieure de télégraphie 40
economic outcomes 24–6, 263–301, 305, 311–12, 321, 323
economic performance 4–17, 21–6, 143, 265
  and national institutionalism 305, 313, 319–23
economic policy 9, 22, 308–10
  economic liberalism 154, 190
  fiscal policy 35, 152, 189–90, 215, 219, 279
  macro-economics 96, 123–4
Economics Ministry (France) 157
economies of scale:
  CPE 64, 81, 254
  digital switches 56, 59, 195
Eden, Sir John 113 n.
EDF (*éléctricité de France*) 107, 217
EFLs (external financing limits)
  seventies 98, 121, 139
  eighties 145, 185, 201, 203
EFTPOS (electronic funds transfer at point of sale) 66, 290
eighties (1980s), economic indicators 7, 264–5, 308
  advanced services 291–4, 296; cellular networks 294–6
  equipment manufacturing subsector 284–6, 290, 297, 300
  finances: costs 275; investment 267, 272; profitability 273–4, 277–8; revenue 266, 270, 275; tariffs 277, 279–83, 287–9
  labour 272, 284
  network size 268–9
  PSTN exchange types 271, 288, 299
Electricité de France 107, 217
electro-mechanical exchanges 48, 51, 118

French import 131–2
  phased out 56, 58, 70, 115–16, 270–1
electronic data interchange services 290
electronic payments 237
  see also EFTPOS
electronic telephone directories 247
electronics 69, 193, 242
Élysée 156, 218, 307
  advanced services and networks 242, 252
  institutional divergence 188, 191, 194–6,
    198, 200
  policy making during seventies 125–8, 133,
    135–6
e-mail 61–6, 236–7, 290, 292, 294, 299
emergency services 150 n., 213 n., 223
employment policy 9, 157, 189, 270–3, 284
engineers, Post Office 34–6, 38, 93, 180
enhanced basic services 60
enterprise à statut public 154
enterprise nationale (national company) 107,
  163, 189, 318
equipment manufacturing subsector:
  Britain: advanced services and CPE 243,
    247, 252, 321–2; no industrial policy
    173–4, 320; relationship with BT 146,
    148, 201, 212, 307; relationship with PO
    31, 36–7, 68–70, 112–13, 138–40, 306–8,
    allocation of orders 98–9, 116–19
  economic outcomes 284–6; advanced
    services and CPE 297–8, 300
  France: advanced services and CPE 243,
    247, 252, 321–2; industrial policy 153,
    188–9, 192, 200, 308, 320, to commercial
    linkages (France Télécom) 215, 219,
    225; relationship with DGT 42–5, 47,
    68, 129–30, 138–40, 193–7
Ericsson 42, 118, 133, 154, 182–3, 197
Ericsson Telephones 36
Esambert, Bernard 136
ESS5 public switch 196
Essig, F. 190 n.
Établissement public à Caractère commercial
  (EPIC) 108
établissement public administratif (public
  corporation) 153
Eunetcom 221
Europe:
  pressure for change 72, 75–7, 86
  PTOs 59, 77, 223, 239
  reforms 306, 311–12, 319
  semi-conductor production 67

VANS 291
European Community (EC) 22, 190, 212,
  282
  Commission 81, 83–7, 217 n., 221; DG IV
    (Directorate General for competition)
    83–4; DG XIII (Directorate General for
    Telecommunications, Information
    Industries, and Innovation) 80
  Council of Ministers 81–5
  Directives: on Leased Lines (1992) 246; on
    mutual recognition (1991) 254; Open
    Network Provision (1990) 246; on
    procurement procedures (1990) 81; on
    Satellites (1994) 254; on Services (1990)
    250
  regulation 5, 23, 315–16, 319, 322;
    legislation 143, 158–9, 205–7, 216–17,
    228, 252; and pressure for change 71,
    77, 80–7, 306
European Court of Justice 80, 83, 85, 87
European Economic Community (EEC) 155
European Parliament 83, 85
European Union (EU) 167
Eutelsat 78 n., 253–4
exchanges, see switching
exogenous factors:
  institutions as 21, 23, 306
  international regulatory environment 71,
    86
  technological and economic developments
    47, 67–8
  see also change
expansion 33, 39, 322
  France 126–8, 139, 308
  and modernization 115–16
exploitant public (public corporation) 156
exports 10, 59, 285, 296 n., 300
  Britain 99, 116, 119–20, 179
  France 132, 134, 194, 247

Fabius, Laurent 188, 191–2, 194–6
Fair Trading Act (1973) 150–1
fair trading licences 206 n., 211, 214, 225
fax machines 49, 60–5, 294–5, 297
FCC (Federal Communications Commission)
  72–3, 78, 160, 221
  'open sky' decision (1972) 74
filière électronique 192
Fillon, François 158 n.–159 n., 215 n.–217 n.,
  218, 223 n.
Filoud, Georges 242, 248

Finance Law (France, 1923) 43
Finance Ministry (France) 69–70
   competition in PTOs 215, 221, 223
   historical legacy 39–40, 43
   institutional divergence 188, 193, 197–9
   and institutional framework 104, 106–7,
      111
   and national institutionalism 45, 306–7
   policy making 125–8, 135–6
financial sector 22, 66, 68, 237
   economic outcomes 286, 290
financial targets, Post Office 138
Finextel 137 n.
firms, see business users
fiscal management 35, 152, 189–90, 279,
   309
   privatization 170–1, 215, 219
Flexible Access System 233
Force Ouvrière 154, 156, 161, 163
forwarding services 236
France 2–5, 7, 22
   advanced services and CPE 228–9, 241–56,
      258–9, 290–1, 293, 295–7
   competition in network operation 205–6,
      215–27
   economic outcomes 263–6, 298–301;
      equipment manufacturing and supply
      284, 287, 294; network operation 267–
      70, 273, 277, 280, 284
   equipment manufacturing subsector 53 n.,
      204, 284–6, 288, 297
   historical roots 31, 39–45
   institutional divergence 172–3, 188–201,
      203–4
   institutional framework 92, 102–11, 143,
      152–70
   international regulatory environment 71,
      79, 83, 85–7
   and national institutionalism 305–21, 323
   policy making 112, 125–39, 188–90, 215–
      16, 241–2
   PSTN 40, 271, 276
   reforms 75–7, 91, 224, 316
   tariffs 202, 278–80, 282–3, 289
   technological and economic developments
      47–8, 67–70
   see also DGT; France Télécom; political
      executive
France Télécom:
   advanced networks and services 241–6,
      249, 252–4, 259, 287–9, 292–4

Board 156, 164, 218–19
   competition 205–6, 215–17, 220, 223
   economic outcomes 265–9, 271–5, 279 n.,
      284–5, 290, 298
   institutional divergence 173, 188
   institutional framework 155–6, 163, 168–9,
      171
   international regulatory environment 76,
      79, 85 n.
   monopoly 157, 217, 250–1, 253, 318;
      ended 166, 225–7, 257
   and national institutionalism 306, 308–10,
      315, 318, 321–2
   privatization 220–2, 314
   PSTN 257, 275, 288, 291
   staffing 219, 299
   status 158–64, 169, 216–20, 226, 258
   statut 161, 300, 320
   tariffs 218, 270, 277, 283
   see also administration; DGT; political
      executive
Francetel 137 n.
free trade arrangements 78
freephone services 60, 292

Galley, Robert 106–7, 126 n., 127–8, 131
GATS (General Agreement on Trade in
   Services) 78–9
GATT (General Agreement on Tariffs and
   Trade) 78
Gaullist Party (RPR) 159, 191
GEC (General Electric Company) 36, 59, 70,
   146, 181–4
   and government policy 113, 116–18
General Agreement on Trade in Services
   (GATS) 78–9
general budget (France) 104, 109, 308, 311
general competition law 150
Germain, Hubert 108, 126 n.
Germany 45, 160, 197, 253, 311
   equipment manufacturing 33 n., 59
   see also Deutsche Telekom
Giscard d'Estaing, Valéry 44, 107–9, 128–9,
   133, 135–6, 191, 246–7
Global One 76, 221
global services 221
golden shares 152, 212–13
gold-plating 177
Gomez, Alain 193 n., 194
government:
   British 307, 309; during seventies 100–1,

114–15, 117–18, 120–5, 139; during
eighties 182; during nineties 212, 225,
235–6, 256; Home Office 230–1; *see also*
DoI; DTI; Information Technology
Minister; Parliament; Post and
Telecommunications Ministry; Treasury
French 138, 164–5, 254, 257; *see also*
budget, Ministry; Commerce Ministry;
Communications Ministry; Conseil des
ministres; Culture Ministry; Economics
Ministry; Finance Ministry; Industry
Ministry; National Assembly; PTE;
PTT
Government Advisory Council for Science
and Technology 231
GPT 184
grand projet strategy 126, 130, 138–9, 152–3,
222, 308
advanced networks and services 241, 244–
7, 252–4, 256–8
Greene, Harold 74
growth, economic 9–10, 31, 269, 300
France 138, 307
growth Plan (*Plan de relance*) 136
GSM (Groupe Spécial Mobile) 251–2
GTE (General Telephone and Electronics)
74
Guéna, Yves 41, 106–7, 126 n., 128, 136, 325

'handover' facility 61–2, 294
Henrot, François 161, 218
high definition television 54
see also digital, television
Hirel, Jean-Claude 153 n., 189 n., 192–3 n.
historical roots 15, 23, 31–46
Hunt, Lord 231
'Hush-a-Phone' case (1956) 72 n.

IBM 77, 236–7, 247, 249, 252–3
imports 131–2, 146, 286, 296 n.
incentive regulation 174
independent regulatory bodies:
Britain 145, 147–8, 224, 227
Federal Communications Commission
(FCC) 72–4, 78, 160, 221
France 154, 157, 169, 188, 203, 258;
lacking in 257, 259, 309–10, 315, 317–18
see also CNCL; CSA; Oftel
indirect competition 69
industrial action, *see* strikes; trade unions
industrial policy 2, 9, 22

Britain 45, 124–5, 139–40, 202, 257
France 308, 310–11; advanced networks
and services 241, 252, 257; historical
legacy: post-war years 41–3, 45, during
seventies 129–34, 138, 140, during
eighties 189, 192, 194, 202, during
nineties 215, 219, 225
Industry Ministry/Minister (France) 40, 125,
188–97, 215, 309
information industry 49–50
information superhighways 192, 222, 232,
242, 244
see also broadband networks
Information Technology Minister (Britain)
230
ingénieurs des télécommunications 41, 156,
218–19
institutional:
arrangements 94–9, 264–5, 311; under
Telecommunications Act (1984) 148–
52
divergence 172–204
frameworks 23, 39, 86, 309, 317–20;
during eighties and nineties 143–71;
during seventies 91–111
isomorphism 18–19, 315
reform 25; Britain 144–7, 173, 182, 200,
202–4, 257; economic outcomes 263,
298, 300–1; France 169, 229, 241, 255,
257–8, during eighties 152–4, 190, 199,
202, during nineties 215–17, 221, 223,
226; and national institutionalism
306–9, 311, 319–20
institutionalism, national 2–15, 20–2, 26–7,
263–4, 305–23
institutions 1–2, 5, 11
defined 25
and policy making: advanced services and
networks and CPE 228–59; competition
in network operation 205–27
Intelsat satellites 53–3 n., 77–8
interactive television 54
interconnection 165, 174 n., 178
arrangements 207–11
terms 218, 225–7, 242
interest groups 9, 12–13, 16, 22
interest/finance 275, 299
international:
alliances 77, 163, 308, 315
competition 195, 208; equipment 132,
233

international (*cont.*)
  networks: cables 54, 180; calls 123, 185–7,
    198–9, 265 n., 268, 276–8, *see also* long-
    distance; and services 79, 178–9, 211 n.,
    213, 236, 282
  organizations 77–9, 86
  regulatory environment 26, 91, 110, 112,
    204; advanced networks and services
    228, 238; differing paths from monopoly
    205, 227; and institutional frameworks
    143, 158, 171; and national
    institutionalism 312, 319, 323; pressures
    for change 71–87
International Telecommunications Union
  (ITU) 77
internationalization 162, 171, 203
  and competition 215, 219–21
  as pressure for change 58, 70, 76, 87
  see also globalization
internet 53, 57, 61, 249, 294, 299
  see also e-mail; information superhighway
inter-tandem conveyance 211 n.
inter-urban calls 277, 281–2
investment 14, 64
  and borrowing 56, 136–7, 316
  Britain: seventies: institutional framework
    95, 99, 101, policy making 112–13,
    121–5, 139; eighties: institutional
    divergence 173–5, 179, 184–7, 201–3;
    nineties: advanced networks and
    services 247, 252, 254, competition in
    network operation 212, 214–15
  economic outcomes of 264–5, 267, 270–3,
    298–9
  France 157; seventies: institutional
    framework 106, 108, policy making
    125, 127, 135–6, 138–9; eighties:
    institutional divergence 200, 203;
    nineties: advanced networks and
    services 231–2, 247, competition in
    network operation 221–3, 226; and
    national institutionalism 306, 309
  historical legacy 31, 33–5, 37–41, 43, 45
  and national institutionalism 306, 312, 317,
    321
  technological and economic pressure for
    change 47, 49, 67–8
ISDN (integrated services digital network)
  61, 158, 168, 233–4, 243
  economic success 288–90, 299
ITAP (Information Technology Advisory
  Panel) 231

itemised billing 60, 213 n.
ITT (International Telephone and Telegraph
  Company) 42, 116, 131, 133–4, 196–7
ITU (International Telecommunications
  Union) 78, 266–7 n., 270 n., 275–6 n.,
  290, 296–7
ITV (Independent Television, UK) 231

Japan:
  international telephony rates 266, 282–3
  investment 67, 267
Jefferson, Sir George 145, 179–81, 185
Jenkin, Lord Patrick 145–7, 176, 181, 238, 324
Joint Electric Research Committee 98
Joseph, Sir Keith 113 n., 144, 175–6, 235, 240
JOVE 237
Juppé, Alain 159, 162

Kingston upon Hull 32 n.
Kiosque system 248
Kohl, Helmut 221

labour:
  organization of, *see* trade unions
  productivity 267, 270–3, 300
Labour Party 38
  during seventies 93, 100, 113, 124
  during eighties 145, 147, 152
L'Agence nationale des fréquences 166
Lang, Jack 242, 248
Larcher, Gérard 159 n., 162 n.
Lasserre, Bruno 158 n., 159, 189 n., 216, 325
LATAs (local access and transport areas)
  74–5
law, French 39, 43–4, 102
  on Audiovisual Communication (1982)
    248
  loi des Finances 104, 107; (1926) 103; (1963)
    105; (1969) 106
  loi Léotard (1986) 154–5
  loi no. 96–559 163, 167–8
  loi no. 96–659 162, 166
  loi no. 96–660 162–3
  on public service and telecommunications
    (1984) 153, 156
Lawson, N. 146 n., 179 n.
Le 22 à Asnières 127
leased lines:
  advanced networks and services 61–4,
    233–4
  Britain 179, 256
  capacity 73, 81

France 107, 155, 157, 168, 218, 229, 245–6, 249
  international 221, 236
  tariffs 235, 246, 257; resale 81, 177
  volume of 286–90, 299–300
Left, political (France) 318
  during eighties 152–3, 155–7, 189
  during nineties 155–7, 159, 161–3, 171
Lelong, Pierre 109, 126 n.
Léotard, François 190
Liberal Party 37
liberalization 32, 318, 320
  advanced networks and services 229, 235–6, 238, 240, 249, 257–8
  during eighties 145, 154, 175, 179, 198
  during nineties 159, 161–2, 212, 225–6
  international regulatory environment 75, 77, 79, 81–3
Libois, Jean-Louis 129, 131
licensing 39, 43, 84
  Britain 306–7; during eighties 148–51, 169–70, 173–80, 186–7, 200–1, 203; during nineties 206–7, 224–6, and advanced networks and services 229, 237–9, 255, conditions 212, 230, modification 205–6, 214, 226–7
  France 157, 163–9, 227; advanced networks and services 241, 252, 255, 258
L'Information de la société (Nora & Minc) 247
Littlechild, Professor Stephan 177
LM-Ericsson 117, 131
LMT (La matériel téléphonique) 42, 130–1 n., 133–4
local:
  calls 177–8, 273, 284; tariffs 123, 185–7, 198–9, 222, 277–81, 298
  exchange networks 40, 179–80, 242, 270–1, 299; cabling 208
Logica 289 n.
long-distance:
  calls 273, 276; tariffs 56, 69, 135, 198, 222, 278, 287; traffic 57, 298; transmission 53, 56, 146
  services 76, 177, 206
Longuet, Gérard 154–5, 157, 161, 188–9 n., 190–1 n., 192–3, 197–9, 215 n., 217 n., 242 n., 244, 249 n., 251–2, 278 n.
low user schemes 187
LTT 133–4
Lunley Report (1950) 38 n.
La Lyonnaise des eaux 217

Maastricht Treaty (1993) 83, 160
MAC standard 253
MaCaw Cellular Communications 74
McKinseys 93
macro-economic policy 96, 123–4
Madelin, Alain 190, 197
managed data networks 237
manual switching 35, 39–41, 48, 130, 271
manufacturing, see equipment manufacturing subsector
marginal cost-based pricing 59, 187
Marples, Ernest 38 n.
Marzin, Pierre 129 n.
Matignon 128, 133, 136, 188, 215, 218, 307
Matra 154, 197, 251, 254
Mauroy, Pierre 191
MCI (Microwave Communications Inc.) 152, 160, 199, 212, 221
  and international regulatory environment 73–4, 77, 85 n.
Mercury:
  duopoly 176, 178, 203
  licence 147, 149, 207, 209, 237
  network 179, 182, 231–3, 269
mergers 59, 120, 174, 212
  of ring firms 182–4
Messmer, Pierre 127, 136
Mexandeau, Louis 153, 188–9 n., 191–6, 198–9, 242–4, 248, 251
microchip industry 49, 247
microelectronics 47, 49–51, 60, 67–8, 322
microwave radio 48, 57, 73
Minc, A. 247 n.
miniaturization 49, 53
Minitel 245–9, 257, 293–4, 300, 308
Mission à la réglementation 193, 249
Mitel 240
Mitterrand, François 156, 194–5, 199, 221
mixed public–private companies 42
MMC (Monopolies and Mergers Commission):
  advanced networks and services 234, 237, 240
  competition in network operation 206, 209, 212, 224
  institutional divergence 175, 180, 183–4, 186–7
  institutional framework 149–51
Mobile Communications Directive (1996) 84
mobile phone communications, see cellular networks
modems 63, 99

modernization 40–1, 321–2
  Britain 114, 119, 173, 179, 185, 230–1
  economic outcomes 264, 270–3, 299–300
  France 220, 307–8; divergence 155, 190,
    192, 200; policy making 126, 130–4,
    137–9
modification 21, 25, 27, 32
  institutional 18, 24, 91
  licence 205–6, 214, 226–7
  policy 16, 21, 255
Modified Final Judgement (US Department
  of Justice, 1984) 73
monopoly:
  Britain 95, 113, 228; British Telecom's
    ended 92, 148, 150, 201, 320; Post Office
    32–3; public 44, 46
  France 77, 102, 109, 112, 137, 153–4; DGT
    189–91, 198, 202, 258; France Télécom
    245–6; PTT Ministry 39, 168–9, 171;
    public 44, 46
  pressures for change 319; international
    regulatory environment 72–3, 76, 79,
    83, 85–6; natural monopoly 75, 99, 175,
    190, 228; technological and economic
    57, 64, 68–9
Motorola 251
MT switch 193
multiplexing 33 n., 50–1 n., 54, 61
Murdoch, Rupert 253

National Assembly (France) 159, 162, 165
national champion policy 130–3, 139–40, 316
National Consumers Council 180
National Economic Development Council
  116 n.
National Enterprise Board 120
national institutionalism and change 2–27,
  263–4, 305–23
National Plan (Britain, 1965) 35
national security 96, 165, 167
National Telephone Company 32
nationalization 43, 153, 193
NEC 133
NEDO (National Economic Development
  Office) 120
network operation 5, 309
  Britain 33, 236; finances 184–7, 213–15;
    and monopoly 94, 176, 212–13, 224–7,
    320; national institutions 109–12, 114,
    175, 202; policy making 113–15, 138;
    size 269–70

economic outcomes 264, 266–85, 298–
    9
  equipment, see equipment manufacturing
    subsector
  France 155, 206, 241, 269–70; finances
    197–9, 221–3; institutional framework
    102, 105, 109–12, 202
  pressures for change: international
    regulatory environment 79, 84;
    technological and economic
    developments 48, 50–8, 61, 65–6
new services and technology 56, 129, 150,
  228, 264, 270
nineties (1990s), economic indicators 7,
  264–5, 308
  advanced services 287–94, 296; cellular
    networks 295–6
  equipment manufacturing subsector
    284–6, 297, 300
  finances: costs 275; investment 267, 272;
    profitability 273–4, 277–8; revenue 270,
    275; tariffs 266, 279–83
  labour 272, 284
  network size 268–9
  PSTN exchange types 271, 288, 299
  tariffs 287–9
Nokia 251
non-discrimination 82
non-institutional factors 17, 19, 21–2, 38
non-interactive cable networks 154
Nora-Minc Report 247
Northern Telecom 182
number portability 206 n., 212
numéros vert (freephone) 292

OECD 53, 266, 293, 326, 329
office equipment 66, 69
Office of Fair Trading 150
off-peak calls 187, 278
Oftel:
  advanced networks and services 229,
    232–4, 236–40, 255–6, 258
  and competition 206–7, 209–14, 224–7
  institutional divergence 159, 173–5, 178–
    80, 182–7, 200–3
  and national institutionalism 306–7, 309–
    11, 320
  outcomes of regulation 273 n., 277–8,
    282–4, 287 n., 290 n.
Olivetti 249
One2One 295 n.

Open Network Provision (ONP) Directive
(1990) 82 n.
'open sky' decision (United States, 1972) 73
operator assistance 34, 186, 213 n.
optical fibre cable:
distance and costs 56–7
improved transmission 54–5, 62
national broadband network 270–1, 299;
Britain 179–80, 230–1; France 198, 220,
242, 244
see also cable networks
optical switching 58
opto-electronics business 243
Orange 295 n.
OSI (Open Systems Interconnection) 237,
250
overseas markets, see exports

PABX (private automated branch exchanges)
61, 63, 99, 184, 236 n., 239, 295
packet switched networks 53, 61, 64
growth of 265 n., 287–8, 291, 299; Britain
233, 256; France 155, 157, 168, 245
paging networks/services 62, 229, 238, 251,
296, 299–300
PanAmSat 77, 238–9
PAPs (Plans d'action prioritaires) 136
Parliament, French 39, 44, 104, 156, 162,
165–6
Parliament, Houses of 36 n., 97–8, 110, 113,
150–1, 169
Telecommunications Bill 147
Trade and Industry Select Committee 231
patent pooling 36, 42, 45, 99, 105, 117
path dependency 16, 318, 321
PCF (Parti Communiste Français) 156, 162, 196
PCM (pulse code modulation) 50
PCN (personal communications network) 238
Peacock, A. 231
Pébereau, Georges 193 n., 194–7
Peterson, J. 80 n.
Philips 117, 134, 194, 196
Phoenix 76, 221
Plans, French 41, 127–8, 136, 198
Plan Câble 270
Plan de rattrapage du téléphone 128, 247
plan de redressement 40
Plan télématique 198, 241, 247–8, 254
Plessey 324
during seventies 113, 116–18, 120
during eighties 181–4

PDF fax 297 n.
and privatization 59, 70
POEU (Post Office Engineering Union) 38,
93, 100, 144, 147, 180
Pointel 252
policy:
expertise 200–1
feedback 16–18
formation 5, 7, 9, 15
learning 17–18, 71
making process 4–16, 20, 22–7
during sixties 31, 38, 47
during seventies 59, 102, 112–40
during eighties 71, 143, 146, 172, 199–200
during nineties 205–6, 224, 259
and national institutionalism 305, 307,
309–11, 313–15, 319–23
political executive 9, 11–12, 26
Britain 121, 257, 309, 316
France 70, 170; advanced networks and
services 241, 252, 255, 257–8;
institutional divergence 188, 192–3,
197–8, 200, 202–3; introduced
competition 205, 218, 220–1, 225; and
national institutionalism 307–11, 316,
320; policy making during seventies
112, 126, 137–40
Pompidou, Georges 107–8, 127, 136–7
Posner, Michael 124
Post and Telecommunications Ministry
(Britain):
and institutional framework 94–9, 101,
105, 110
and policy making 113–14, 118, 122, 124,
137, 139
Post and Telegraph Office 43
Post Office 79
advanced networks and services 229,
234–5, 238, 240, 258, 287–9, 293
and equipment manufacturers 36–7, 51,
70, 116–19
finances 139, 273–5; investment 69, 93,
271–2; profits and profitability 121–3,
265–6, 269, 282 n., 285, revenue 268,
270, 275–6, 283, 287–9
institutional framework 44–6; Board 34,
94, 96, 100, 113, 120, 122; during
seventies 92, 94–6, 99, 101, 109; during
eighties 145, 169; monopoly 68, 99,
144; public corporation status 306, 318,
321

Post Office (*cont.*)
  and national institutionalism 305, 307–10,
    314, 318, 326
  policy making during seventies 113–15,
    117–19, 138
  service provision 32–5, 124, 273
  staffing 120–1, 299
  Trading Fund 35, 38, 45, 93
Post Office Act 123, 137
  (1961) 34, 38–9, 93
  (1969) 144, 229, 235, 309; institutional
    framework 92, 94–9, 110; and policy
    115, 118, 121, 138–9
Post Office Bill (1968) 93
*Post Office/British Telecom, Annual Reports and
  Accounts* 265
postal services:
  Britain 92–4, 316–17; separation 34,
    38, 44–6, 111, 305–6; *see also* Post
    Office
  France 40, 102, 129, 305, 316–17; links
    with telecommunications 43, 109, 189;
    separation 44–6, 169, labour opposition
    106, 108–9, 155
  see also La Poste; PTE; PTT
La Poste 102, 106, 108, 129, 153–7, 192
Postmasters General (PMG) 32–3, 37, 44–5,
    92–4
POUNC (Post Office Users National Council)
    97, 100–1, 113, 121–2
prélèvements (special levies) 160, 191–3,
    197–8, 200, 220
premium rate services 60, 237
Prestel 235, 247, 293, 300
Prévot, Hubert 155–6, 158 n., 325
price cap regulation:
  Britain 177, 186–7, 206 n., 213–14, 234
  France 222, 226–7
Price Code limits 123
Price Commission 121–3
price control agreements 177, 186, 210–11,
    214–15
private circuits 246, 285, 287–8, 299
  networks 39, 49, 63, 95, 148, 236; French
    154, 167, 244; licensing 43, 154; satellite
    systems 78–9
  rentals 234, 288–9
  see also leased lines; PABX
privatization 315–16
  Britain 202, 255, 309–10; and institutional
    framework 94, 99, 148, 169

France 157, 161, 197, 221–2, 226, 306–7;
    fiscal advantages 170–1; partial 162–4,
    169
profits and profitability 14
  Britain 114, 184–7, 277
  economic outcomes of privatization
    264–5, 273–8, 299
  France 221–3, 248–9
Programme de Provins 136
PS *(Parti Socialiste)*, *see* Socialists
PSBR (public sector borrowing requirement)
    98, 123–5, 145, 173, 185
  pressure for change 310, 316–17
  see also EFLs
PSS (Packet Switch Stream) 233, 289
PSTN (public switched telephone network)
    157
  economic outcomes of use 271, 275–7,
    295
  technological developments 48–9, 55, 57,
    61, 63–4, 322; advanced networks and
    services 208, 239, 248–50, 253,
    broadcasting 232, 256
PTE Ministry 157, 206, 215–18, 224, 241
PTOs (public telecommunications operators)
    110, 149, 151, 170, 208
  and EC 77, 80–1
  licensing 148, 208–9
  technological and economic developments
    76–9, 82, 84, 86–7
PTT (Posts and Telegraph Ministry):
  advanced networks and services 242, 249,
    253–5, 258–9
  institutional framework: during sixties
    39–46; during seventies 102–8, 110,
    125–31, 133–6, 138; during eighties
    153–5, 188, 190–3, 198; during nineties
    155–9, 164–5, 167, 169–70, 215 n.
  and national institutionalism 306–7,
    309–10, 325
  PTT Code 102, 105, 167, 251
PTT-SUD 160
Public Accounts Committee 36 n., 97
public call boxes 157, 168, 177, 213
public corporation status:
  British Telecom 144–5, 200, 203, 257, 316
  France Télécom 258
  Post Office 37–8, 93–4, 97–8, 110, 123, 138,
    144
  see also *enterprise nationale*
public enterprise 107, 163, 189, 318

public switching 130, 132, 181, 285, 322
  equipment 58–9, 183, 193, 243, 247, 300
Pye 117

quality of service 50, 180, 220, 234, 267,
  270–3, 279
quasi-vertical relationships 120
Quilès, Paul 155–6, 188–90, 215 n.

Racal 238
radio communications 62, 154, 166
Radiocom 251, 296
radiopaging 295
rate of return regulation 174 n., 177, 186–7,
  201, 215
Rausch, Jean-Marie 215 n.
RBOCs (regional Bell operating companies—
  Baby Bells) 73, 75–6, 195–6, 208
reform 2–5, 16, 18–21, 23–4, 318
  Britain 44–6, 169, 201; historical roots
    31–2, 34, 37–9, 313; during seventies 91,
    99–101, 111–12
  France 44–6, 201, 205–6, 227, 309; during
    seventies 91, 129–30; during eighties
    154, 190–1, 199; during nineties 156,
    161, 163–8, 170, 219, 223–4, 249;
    financial 110; historical roots 31–2, 40,
    43–4
  international regulatory environment 71,
    77–8, 86
regulation 14, 25, 306–7
  Britain 174–6, 201, 203, 308; competition
    206–8, 239; framework 169, 201;
    technological and economic
    developments 230, 232–3
  France: advanced networks 245, 258;
    competition 206, 216, 221, 225;
    divergence 193, 202; institutional
    framework 102, 158, 163, 166, 255
  international 73, 76–7, 84, 87
  technological and economic developments
    60, 64, 68–9
  see also Oftel
rental:
  advanced services 289, 292, 296
  tariffs 123, 135, 160, 177–8, 185, 222;
    economic outcomes 275–6, 278–80,
    291
Reorganization of the Post Office (White Paper,
  1967) 93
resale 78, 256

international capacity 208, 236
  leased line capacity 81, 175, 233, 236
  unrestricted 235–6
research and development 58, 80
  during seventies 131–2
  during eighties 150, 183, 194
  pre-seventies 41–3, 45
  see also investment
retail price regulation 207, 225
revolution, change as 9, 50, 306
'Ring' firms 36–7, 113, 117–19, 124, 173,
  181–2
  see also GEC; Plessey; STC
Rocard, Michel 155–6
Rossi, José 215 n., 242 n.
rotary switches 42
Roulet, Marcel 159 n.–160 n., 161, 188–9 n.,
  191, 218–20, 249 n., 325
Rozmaryn, Charles 220 n.
rural coverage 147, 150 n., 177
Ryland, Sir William 100, 117, 121, 124 n.

Satellite Directive (EC, 1994) 83
satellites 53–4, 243, 252–4, 256–7
  networks 56–7, 62–3, 73, 177, 217
  policy 77, 198, 252–4
  services 63, 208, 229, 238–9
Schweitzer, Louis 194–5
Secretary of State for Trade and Industry
  148, 151, 170, 184
sectoral:
  boundaries 47, 50, 65–6, 69–70
  regulation 172, 193
Securicor 238
Ségard, Norbert 126 n., 133
SEL 197
Select Committee on Nationalized Industries
  93, 97–8
selective deregulation 207
semi-electronic exchanges, see space division
separation of postal and telecommunications
  services 38, 317
  Britain 93, 99–101, 120, 144, 306, 316
  France 106–10, 129, 153–6
service public 43, 318
  during eighties 153–5, 189–92, 201
  during nineties 156–8, 163–8, 216, 223,
    226–7
service sectors 68
Services Directive (EC, 1990) 81, 83
SES 253–4

seventies (1970s), economic indicators 7, 264, 308
 advanced services 287–9, 293; cellular networks 294
 equipment manufacturing subsector 284–6, 297
 finances: costs 275; investment 267, 272; profitability 273–4, 277; revenue 266, 270, 275; tariffs 279–83, 287–9
 labour 272, 284
 network size 268–9
 PSTN exchange types 271, 288, 299
SFR *(La Société française du radiotéléphone)* 218, 251–2, 295 n.
SFT-Ericsson 42, 131, 133
Shepherd, Richard 146 n.
Siemens 59, 182, 184, 197
signal strength 50, 54
signals repeaters 33 n.
single European market 86
SIO *(service interurbain optionnel)* 199
SLE Citeral and D10 switch 133
SLECs *(Sociétés locales d'exploitation commerciale)* 243–4
SNA (Systems Network Architecture) 237
social objectives 9, 17, 19, 209, 223
Socialists *(Parti Socialiste)*:
 during seventies 107, 136–7
 during eighties 153, 155, 196, 199
 during nineties 160–2
société nationale 153
société publique 154
sociétés de financement du téléphone 106–8, 136–7, 139, 198
Socotel *(La Société mixte pour le développement de la commutation dans le domaine des télécommunications)* 42, 45, 105, 130, 138
software engineering 117, 119
Sotélec *(La Société mixte pour le développement de la technique des télécommunications par câbles)* 42, 45, 105, 134, 138
Souviron, Jean-Pierre 126, 128, 130, 132–4, 325
space division exchanges 33 n., 51–2, 56–8, 115–18, 132–4, 270–1
space industry 193
SPC (stored programme control) 51–2
specialized networks 73, 229, 233–4, 245–6, 286–90

SPL (self provision licence) 237
Sprint 74, 77, 160, 199, 221
stability, institutional 7–27, 32, 47, 71, 91
 and reform 313–16
staffing 95, 120–1, 180, 275, 299
standardization of equipment 36
Statistique Annuelle (DGT/FT) 265
statut 242, 307, 316
 institutional framework 102, 111, 153–6, 160–1, 171; divergence 191, 202
 and network competition 218–20, 224, 226
STC (Standard Telephones and Cables) 36, 99 n., 113, 116–18, 120, 181–2
Sterling, Sir Jeffrey 147 n., 181
stock exchanges 66, 68
Stonehouse, John 113 n., 122, 124
stop–go policies 93
strategic sectors 22–3, 26, 66–7, 69
strategies, firms' 71, 126
Strauss-Kahn, Dominique 162
strikes 147, 161, 163, 180, 219
 see also trade unions
Strowger switch 35, 48, 51–2, 56
structural change 72, 75, 176
SUD-PTT 163
switching 75, 183, 270, 298, 322
 equipment suppliers 105, 114, 116, 194, 285
 historical roots 33–7, 42–3, 45, 115, 130
 modernization 48–51, 56, 67–8, 242, 245
 see also electro-mechanical exchanges; space division exchanges; time division exchange
Syncordia 212 n.
System 12, 196
System X 115–17, 119–20, 179–84, 233
System Y (AXE 10) 182–3, 197
Systems Business (BT) 230

TACS (Total Access Cellular System) 238 n.
take-overs, *see* mergers
target rates of return 121–3, 137, 139, 185
tariffs 45, 104, 138, 157, 187, 234
 economic outcomes 264, 268, 275–84, 287, 295, 298–300
 policy: divergence 172, 184–7, 200, 203; pressures for change 64, 68–9, 72–3, 78, 82, 84; rebalancing 76, 160, 175, 178, 202, advanced services 233–4, 252, and competition 209, 215, 217, 222–3, 226,

economic outcomes of 278, 298, 300,
    and national institutionalism 308–9, 322
Tarifica 293 n., 296
TAT satellites 54
TDF (Télédiffusion de France) 251, 253
Tebbit, Norman 182
technological & economic pressures for
    change 33, 47–70, 112, 228, 263
  competition in network operation 205,
    227
  defined 4–5, 9, 18, 23, 26
  and institutional framework 91, 110, 143,
    158, 171, 204
  international 71, 81, 87
  and national institutionalism 306, 311, 316,
    319, 322
Telecommunications Act (Britain, 1984)
    147–52, 174, 183, 202, 309, 320
  and competition 207, 224
  economic outcomes 238, 255
Telecommunications Act (United States,
    1996) 75
Telecommunications Board 120–1
Telecommunications Modernization
    Commission (France) 41
telegraph 32
Telegraph Act (1868 & 1869) 32
Telematics Plan (Plan télématique) 198, 241,
    247–8, 254
telephone density 33, 35, 39–41, 127–8
Telephone Development Committee 37
telephone engineers 34–6, 38, 93, 180
Telephone Users' Association 240
Telepoint service 62, 238, 251
Télétel service 245–9, 257, 293–4, 300, 308
television broadcasting 73, 208, 253
telex services 81, 155, 157, 236, 294
terminal equipment 67, 235, 285
  see also CPE
Terminals Directive (EC, 1988) 81, 83
Thatcher, Margaret 146 n., 176
Théry, Gérard 109, 126, 128–30, 132–4, 188,
    191, 222, 242, 244, 325
Thomson 132–4, 160 n., 192, 194, 219, 250
  Corpac 400 251
  MT switch 134, 193, 195
  nationalization 153, 193
Thorn 118, 182–3
Thorn-Ericsson 182–3
time division exchange 270–1

development 52, 56, 58, 70
policy making: seventies 115–17, 119–20,
    131–4; eighties 180–2, 184, 194, 196–8
TMA (Telecommunications Managers
    Association) 113, 146, 150, 176
trade unions 12, 313, 316, 318
  Britain: seventies 93, 99–101, 113, 117, 122,
    124; eighties 144, 146, 182
  France 307; seventies 107–9, 111, 125,
    130, 136–7; eighties 152, 154–6, 191;
    nineties 158, 160–1, 163, 170–1, 218–19,
    223
  historical legacy 38, 43, 46
transmission 35, 73, 115, 146, 285
  equipment suppliers 48, 67–8, 134, 184,
    300
  improvements 40–1, 50–5, 287, 298
transmitters 62
Transpac network 245, 248, 289–90, 294
Treasury 306, 309–10
  historical legacy 33–5, 37–8, 45
  institutional framework: during seventies
    93–4, 96–7, 110, policy making 113–14,
    121, 123; during eighties 145, 149;
    divergence 173, 184–5, 200–1, 203
  technological and economic pressures for
    change 69–70
Treaty of Rome 81–3, 85, 209
Trésor 103–4, 160
Tribunal des conflits 103, 105
TRT 134
trunk:
  calls 34, 123, 178, 185, 199; economic
    outcomes 268, 273, 277–8, 281–2, 284
  networks 35, 40, 56, 179, 271; cable
    companies 32, 73, 208; coaxial cable 54
  digital 115, 179–80
  optical fibre cable 180, 242, 299
Trunk Task Force (TTF) 115
TSL (telecommunications services licence)
    236–7
TUA (Telecommunications Users
    Association) 113
Tuthill, L. 79 n.
two-wire analogue/telephone circuits 287–
    8
TXE4 exchanges 117–19, 181

Unisat consortium 238
Unisource 76

United States 5, 45, 101, 112, 312, 322
  and British Telecom 152, 187, 198–9, 208,
    212–13
  investment 67, 267
  pressure for change 72–7, 87, 195–6, 221,
    238–9
  reform 71–8, 86, 91, 306
  liberalization 175–7, 228, 315, 318–19;
    competition 57, 145–6, 160, 197–8
  switch prices 52 n.–53 n., 59 n.
  tariffs to 187, 266, 282–3
  telephone density 33, 39, 41
universal service 168, 189, 209–10, 213,
  223
UPW (Union of Postal Workers) 93, 100–1,
  144
Ursot case 103, 105
Uruguay Round (GATT) 78
usage tariffs 135, 289, 292, 296
users 47, 97–9, 103–5, 109, 113, 173
  large 155, 187–8, 192, 198, 214
  protection 206, 213, 240
  residential 166, 187, 198, 203, 222, 228–9
  vulnerable (disabled and pensioners) 147,
    150–2, 177, 180, 210, 213
  see also business users

Vallance, Iain 180, 208 n.
value-added services 60–1, 73, 190
  VADS (value added and data services) 167,
    236–7
  VANS (value-added network services) 81;
    Britain 175, 229–30, 233–7,
    liberalization 235–6, licensing 290 n.;
    economic outcomes 286–7, 290–4, 299;
    France 220–1, 246–50, 256, 258,

liberalization 154, 249, licensing 256,
    258, 290 n.
Varley, Eric 113 n., 124
VAT, French (TVA) 199, 279, 326, 328
vertical integration 64–5, 69, 72, 75
  advanced networks and services 230, 238,
    240, 256
videoconferencing 62–3
videotex networks 229, 234–6, 242–4, 247,
    254–7
  economic indicators 290–3, 295, 300
  and reform 61, 63, 65
visiophone 243
visual services 62–3, 95
Vodafone 149, 295 n., 296
voice telephony 157, 250, 258, 286
Voice Telephony Directive (1995) 84
VSAT (very small aperture terminals)
    networks 253
waiting lists 35, 41
  Britain 45, 99, 115, 123, 179
  France 45, 127–8, 251, 271–3
Weinstock, Lord Arnold 117, 119 n., 146–7,
    181, 183
Western Electric 72–3
wireless telegraphy 95
Wireless Telegraphy Act (1949) 95, 148
Wolmer, Viscount 33 n., 36 n.–37 n.
World Partners 76
Worldcom 57
WTO 78–9, 212

X400 standard 294

Young, Lord David 179, 184, 239, 324

Zuccarelli, Émile 215 n.